STRATEGIC MARKETING CASES
FOR 21ST CENTURY ASIA

John A. Quelch
Swee Hoon Ang
Siew Meng Leong
Chin Tiong Tan

Prentice
Hall

Singapore London New York Toronto Sydney Tokyo Madrid
Mexico City Munich Paris Capetown Hong Kong Montreal

Published in 2000 by
Prentice Hall
Pearson Education Asia Pte Ltd
317 Alexandra Road
#04-01 IKEA Building
Singapore 159965

Pearson Education offices in Asia: *Bangkok, Beijing,
Hong Kong, Jakarta, Kuala Lumpur, Manila, New Delhi,
Seoul, Singapore, Taipei, Tokyo*

Printed in Singapore

5   4   3   2   1
04   03   02   01   00

ISBN 0-13-027601-4

Contents

John A. Quelch is Dean of London Business School and a Professor of Marketing at London University. He was previously the Sebastian S. Kresge Professor of Marketing at Harvard Business School. He has authored 13 books and over 100 articles in *Harvard Business Review*, *Sloan Management Review*, *McKinsey Quarterly*, and other journals. Dr Quelch has conducted management seminars in more than 50 countries and is also a non-executive director of WPP Group plc.

Swee Hoon Ang is Associate Professor at the Faculty of Business Administration, National University of Singapore. She received her Ph.D. from the University of British Columbia. She was a Visiting Professor at the Helsinki School of Economics and Business Administration. She is a co-author of *Cases in Marketing Management and Strategy: An Asia-Pacific Perspective* and *Marketing Insights for the Asia Pacific*. In addition, she has written articles for journals and conferences, including *Journal of Advertising*, *Journal of Consumer Marketing*, *Psychology & Marketing*, and *International Business Review*. Her research and teaching interests are in advertising and consumer behavior, with an Asian perspective. Dr Ang has consulted and taught for Singaporean and multinational companies including Citibank, Glaxo-Wellcome Pharmaceuticals, and Johnson & Johnson Medical.

Siew Meng Leong is Professor at the Faculty of Business Administration, National University of Singapore. He received his MBA and Ph.D. from the University of Wisconsin, Madison. He is a co-author of *Cases in Marketing Management and Strategy: An Asia-Pacific Perspective* and *Marketing Insights for the Asia Pacific*. He has published in *Journal of Consumer Research*, *Journal of Marketing*, *Journal of Marketing Research*, *Journal of International Business Studies*, *Decision Sciences*, and other international journals and conference proceedings. His research focuses on consumer behavior, sales management, and marketing research. Dr Leong is editor of the *Asian Journal of Marketing* and serves on the editorial boards of *Journal of Marketing Communications* and *Marketing Education Review*. He has consulted and gave seminars for such clients as American International Assurance, DBSLand, Du Pont, Economic Development Board of Singapore, and Philips.

Chin Tiong Tan is Provost at the Singapore Management University. He received his Ph.D. from Pennsylvania State University. He has taught at the

Helsinki School of Economics and Business Administration and the University of Witwatersrand, and was a Visiting Scholar at the Stanford Business School. He is a co-author of *Cases in Marketing Management and Strategy: An Asia-Pacific Perspective, Marketing Insights for the Asia Pacific*, and *New Asian Emperors*. He has published in *Journal of Consumer Research, Journal of International Business Studies, International Marketing Review, European Journal of Marketing*, and other international journals and conference proceedings. Dr Tan sits on the boards of several companies and committees of government agencies. He is the academic advisor to Singapore Airlines' Management Development Center, and has consulted for companies like Acer Computer, Altron Group, Inchcape, and Singapore Telecom.

Preface

In *Cases in Marketing Management and Strategy* by John A. Quelch, Siew Meng Leong, Swee Hoon Ang, and Chin Tiong Tan, marketing in the Asia Pacific was described as exciting, challenging, and different. These qualities are even more evident today. Toward the end of the 20th century, the region experienced one of its most tumultuous economic and social periods. During the Asian crisis, currencies depreciated, long-established businesses folded up, foreign investors divested, stock markets plummeted, and governments were toppled—making it even more exciting, challenging, and different for marketers and marketing in the region. As regional economies recover, businesses are restructuring and refocusing themselves, and are adopting a more market-oriented perspective in attempting to regain their competitiveness.

With a set of 19 new cases, this book incorporates these developments and much more. The cases span nine countries—China, Hong Kong, India, Indonesia, Japan, South Korea, Malaysia, Singapore, and Vietnam. Several cases provide pan-regional coverage. The cases cover a wide range of products from consumer goods such as newspapers, coffee, and clothing to industrial products such as car navigation systems, hospital management, and water purifiers. As most of the cases center on companies that people can readily identify with—Amway, Cathay Pacific, Creative Technology, Daewoo, De Beers, Gillette, and Starbucks—they will stimulate much interest and discussion among readers. For balance, we have also included cases on several smaller businesses to provide a unique, local flavor. Annalakshmi Restaurant, a popular Indian vegetarian restaurant in Singapore, is one such example. Attesting to its quality, six of this book's cases are from Harvard and two from INSEAD.

This case book is founded on four principles. First, its structure follows that of *Marketing Management: An Asian Perspective* (2nd edition) by Philip Kotler, Swee Hoon Ang, Siew Meng Leong, and Chin Tiong Tan. This will enable instructors to assign relevant case materials corresponding to the five major sections of that text: Understanding Marketing Management, Analyzing Marketing Opportunities, Developing Marketing Strategies, Planning Marketing Programs, and Managing the Marketing Effort. This will also facilitate better student understanding and application of marketing theories, tools, and techniques to the solution of marketing management and strategy problems.

The cases follow the Harvard case writing style, giving them the rigor, depth, and length for comprehensive, in-depth analyses. They provide suitable materials for senior marketing undergraduates, MBA students, and participants of executive programs. For practitioners, the cases are useful as they give added insights into company operations and market responses.

Third, all the companies and the information given in the cases are real. We use actual companies and the cases report actual or secondary research in real company settings. This allows the possibility of supplementing the cases with additional information from external sources such as the library or field observation.

Fourth, all the cases deal with contemporary marketing management and strategy problems. All feature problems and issues from the mid-1990s.

Many individuals have assisted in the preparation and publication of this case book. We are grateful to the contributors of our cases who are acknowledged on the opening page of each case. The encouragement of our respective Business Schools—London Business School, National University of Singapore, and Singapore Management University—is also sincerely appreciated. We want to thank our colleagues and former students who repeatedly prodded us for more Asian case materials. We are also grateful to the staff at Pearson Education Singapore, namely Lee Ming Ang, Yew Kee Chiang, and Christine Chua, for creating the physical product before you.

Finally, we are indebted to our respective families, whose support over the years has proven constant and inviolate.

John A. Quelch
Swee Hoon Ang
Siew Meng Leong
Chin Tiong Tan

July 2000

Giordano: Making a Value-for-money, High-volume, and High-quality Service Strategy Work

"... we are committed to provide our customers with value-for-money merchandise, professional customer service, and comfortable shopping experience at convenient locations."

—Giordano's corporate mission

Giordano is a retailer of casual apparel in East Asia, Southeast Asia, and the Middle East. In 1999, it operated outlets in China, Dubai, Hong Kong, Macao, the Philippines, Saudi Arabia, Singapore, South Korea, and Taiwan. Giordano's sales grew from HK$712 million (US$91.9 million)[1] in 1989 to HK$2,600 million (US$335.6 million) in

Jochen Wirtz and Swee Hoon Ang prepared this case as the basis for class discussion rather than to illustrate either effective or ineffective handling of an administrative situation.

Jochen Wirtz and Swee Hoon Ang are Associate Professors at the National University of Singapore.

The authors greatly acknowledge the generous support in terms of time, information, and feedback on earlier drafts of this case provided by Charles Fung, Chief Operating Officer and Executive Director of Giordano (Southeast Asia). The authors would also like to acknowledge the research assistance of Cindy Kai Lin Koh and Jerome Sze Wee Kho, who gathered much of the data and assisted with the writing of the case.

Copyright © 2000 by John Wiley & Sons (Asia) Ltd. The final version of this case was published in Asian Case Research Journal, Vol. 4.

[1] The exchange rate at the time the case was written (end-1999) was US$1 = HK$7.75.

1998 (Tables 1–1 and 1–2). This case describes the success factors that allowed Giordano to grow rapidly in some Asian countries. Further, the case looks at three imminent issues that Giordano faced in maintaining its success in existing markets and in new markets that it planned to enter in Asia and beyond. The first concerns Giordano's positioning. In what ways, if at all, should Giordano change its current positioning? The second concerns the critical factors that contributed to Giordano's success. Would these factors remain critical over the coming years? Finally, as Giordano sought to enter new markets, the third issue of whether its competitive strengths can be transferred to other markets needs to be examined.

Table 1–1   Consolidated profit and loss account (in HK$ million)

	HY 1999*	1998	1997	1996
Turnover	1,429.2	2,609.2	3,014.4	3,522.0
Operating profit	130.8	66.9	55.9	293.5
Profit before taxation	161.3	88.3	82.0	315.4
Profit after taxation	132.5	76.2	62.7	261.2

* The 1999 figures are for the first six months of Giordano's 1999 financial year, ended June 30, 1999.

COMPANY BACKGROUND

Giordano was founded by Jimmy Lai[2] in 1980. Lai thought that an Italian name would evoke sophistication, and thus borrowed the name of a New York pizza restaurant for his retail chain. In 1981, Giordano started by selling in Hong Kong casual apparel manufactured predominantly for the U.S. market by a Hong Kong-based manufacturer, the Comitex Group. Initially, Giordano focused on wholesale trade of high-margin merchandise under the Giordano brand in Hong Kong. In 1983, it scaled back on its wholesale operation and started to set up its own retail shops in Hong Kong. It also began to expand its market by distributing Giordano merchandise in Taiwan through a joint venture. In 1985, it opened its first retail outlet in Singapore.

However, in 1987, sales were low and the business became unprofitable. Lai realized that the pricey retail chain concept was not the way to go. Under

---

[2] Jimmy Lai left the management of Giordano in 1991 and has not been directly involved in the running of Giordano since then; he is now managing his new venture, a Hong Kong publication called *Next Magazine*.

Table 1-2 Financial highlights (amounts expressed in HK$ million)

(Consolidated)	FY 1999*	1998	1997	1996	1995	1994	1993
Turnover	1,429.2	2,609.2	3,014.4	3,522.0	3,482.0	2,863.7	2,334.1
Turnover increase (%)	12.6	(13.4)	(14.4)	1.2	21.6	22.7	40.5
Profit after tax and minority interests	132.5	76.1	68.0	261.2	250.2	195.3	137.6
Profit after tax and minority interests increase (%)	535.6	11.9	(74.0)	4.4	28.1	41.9	19.6
Shareholders' fund	n.a.	n.a.	1,068.9	1,138.3	911.7	544.5	454.7
Working capital	n.a.	n.a.	654.2	670.3	496.0	362.0	297.4
Total debt to equity ratio	n.a.	n.a.	0.3	0.4	0.7	0.9	0.8
Bank borrowings to equity ratio	n.a.	n.a.	0	0	0	0.1	0.1
Inventory turnover on sales (days)	32	45	48	58	55	53	59
Return on total assets (%)	n.a.	n.a.	4.8	16.5	16.4	18.8	16.7
Return on average equity (%)	n.a.	n.a.	6.2	25.5	34.4	39.1	33.7
Return on sales (%)	n.a.	n.a.	2.3	7.4	7.2	6.8	5.9
Earning per share (cents)	18.9	10.8	9.6	36.9	38.8	30.9	22.0
Cash dividend per share (cents)	6.5	5.0	4.5	16.0	13.5	11.0	9.0

Notes:
* The 1999 figures are for the first six months of Giordano's 1999 financial year, ended June 30, 1999. Percentages for 1999 were calculated over the figures for the same period in the previous year.

"n.a." indicates that data were not available at time of print.

a new management team, Giordano changed its strategy. Until 1987, Giordano sold exclusively casual apparel for men. When it realized that female customers were increasingly attracted to its stores, Giordano changed its positioning and started selling unisex casual apparel. It repositioned itself as a discounter of casual unisex apparel with the goal to maximize unit sales instead of margins, and sold value-for-money merchandise. Its shift in strategy was successful. Since then, its sales had almost quadrupled, from HK$712 million (US$91.9 million) in 1989 to HK$2,600 million (US$335.6 million) in 1998 (Table 1–2).

MANAGEMENT VALUES AND STYLE

Learning Through Trial and Error

Lai believed in flexibility and learning through trial and error. In Giordano, making mistakes was considered part of the learning process and not a stumbling block. Believing that mistakes are unavoidable as business dynamics are ever changing, Lai was quoted as saying "… we can only learn through trial and error because the market is changing too fast these days … Information, technology, and innovation … stimulate the consumer much more than ever before …"

Mistakes were therefore viewed in Giordano as an indicator of what is not possible at the moment, leaving them the possibility of trying what is right. Lai always made Giordano's employees feel comfortable with making mistakes by role-modelling it. "… Like in a meeting, I say, 'look, I have made this mistake. I'm sorry for that. I hope everybody learns from this. If I can make mistakes, who do you think you are that you can't make mistakes?'" Lai also strongly believed in empowerment, for if everyone was allowed to contribute and participate, mistakes would be minimized.

Managing Employees As an Asset

Besides the willingness to accept employees' mistakes, another factor that contributed to the success of Giordano was that it had a dedicated, trained, and ever-smiling sales force. It considered front-line workers to be its customer service heroes. Charles Fung, Giordano's Chief Operation Officer/Executive Director (Southeast Asia) said, "Even the most sophisticated training program won't guarantee the best customer service. People are the key. They make exceptional service possible. Training is merely a skeleton of a customer service program. It's the people who deliver that gives it form and meaning."

Giordano had stringent selection procedures to make sure that only those candidates who matched the profile of what Giordano looked for in its employees were selected. Selection even continued into its training workshops. Fung called the workshops "attitude training" in which the service orientation and character of a new employee were tested. These situations, he added, were an appropriate screening tool for "identifying those made of grit and mettle."

Giordano's philosophy of quality service could be observed in its overseas outlets as well. In Singapore, it was awarded the ISO 9002 certification for its service documentation. Its obsession with providing excellent customer service was best described by Fung: "The only way to keep abreast with stiff competition in the retail market is to know the customers' needs and serve them well. Customers pay our pay checks; they are our bosses ... Giordano considers service to be a very important element (in trying to draw customers) ... service is in the blood of every member of our staff."

According to Fung, everyone who joined Giordano, even office employees, worked in a store for at least one week as part of their training. "They must understand and appreciate every detail of the operations. How can they offer proper customer assistance—internal and external—if they don't know what goes on in operations?"

In Singapore, for instance, Giordano invested heavily in training its employees. In 1998, it spent 3.9% of its overall payroll on training, with each employee receiving an average of 224 hours of training per year. It had a training room complete with one-way mirrors, video cameras, and other electronic paraphernalia. A training consultant and seven full-time line trainers conducted training sessions for every new sales staff, and existing staff were required to take refresher courses. Its commitment to training and developing its staff was recognized when it was awarded the People Developer Award in 1998.

However, providing training programs was not as important as ensuring the transfer of learning from the workshops and seminars to the store. As Fung explained, "Training is important. Every organization is providing its employees training. However, what is more important is the transfer of learning to the store. When there is a transfer of learning, each dollar invested in training yields a high return. We try to encourage this (transfer of learning) by cultivating a culture and by providing positive reinforcement, rewarding those who practice what they learnt."

For Giordano, investment in service meant investment in people. Giordano paid high wages to attract and keep its staff. Giordano offered what Fung said was "one of the most attractive packages in an industry where employee turnover is high. We generally pay more than what the market pays." With higher wages, there was a lower staff turnover rate. Together, the higher wages and its emphasis on training had resulted in a corps of eager-to-please sales force.

Managing its vital human resources (HR) became a challenge to Giordano when it decided to expand into global markets. To replicate its high-service quality positioning, Giordano needed to consider the HR issues involved when setting up retail outlets on unfamiliar ground. For example, the recruitment, selection, and training of local employees might require modifications to its formula for success in its current markets due to differences in culture, education, and technology of the new countries. Labor regulations would also affect HR policies such as compensation and providing welfare. Finally, expatriate policies and management practices needed to be considered.

Simplicity and Speed

Giordano maintained a flat organizational structure. Fung believed that "this gives us the intensity to react to market changes on a day-to-day basis." Overall, the management style was easygoing, with little display of office perks to senior executives. Working closely with lower line staff, managers, and even the CEO, worked in cubicles separated only by shoulder-high partition panels. This facilitated communication, quick responses, and decision making, which were important in a world of fast-changing consumer tastes and fashion trends. Speed allowed Giordano to keep its product development cycle short. Similar demands in quickness were also expected of its suppliers.

KEY COMPETITIVE STRENGTHS

Home base Hong Kong was flooded with retailers, both big and small. To beat the dog-eat-dog competition prevalent in Asia, especially Hong Kong, Lai felt that Giordano must have a distinctive competitive advantage. Although many retail outlets in Hong Kong competed almost exclusively on price, Lai felt differently about Giordano. Noting successful Western retailers, Lai astutely observed that there were other key factors for success. He began benchmarking Giordano against certain successful practices—computerization (from The Limited), a tightly-controlled menu (from McDonald's), frugality (from Wal-Mart), and value pricing (from Marks & Spencer).

Such emphasis on service and value-for-money concept proved to be successful. Lai said, "As a retailer, the product is half of what we sell. The other half is service. Our volume is so high we have to have customers come back, and good service is the best way to get them to return. We are not just a shirt retailer, we are not just an apparel retailer. We are also a service retailer because we sell feeling. Let's make the guy feel good about coming into here (our stores)."

Service

Giordano's commitment to excellent service was reflected in the list of service-related awards it received. It was ranked No. 1 by *Far Eastern Economic Review* for being innovative in responding to customer needs for three consecutive years—1994, 1995, and 1996. And when it came to winning service awards, Giordano's name kept cropping up. In Singapore, it had won numerous service awards over the years. It was given the Excellent Service Award for three consecutive years: 1996, 1997, and 1998. It also received three Tourism awards: "Store of the Year" in 1991, "Retailer of the Month" in 1993, and "Best Shopping Experience—Retailer Outlet" in 1996. The awards mentioned are just some of the awards won by Giordano. The list goes on (Table 1–3).

How did Giordano achieve such recognition for its commitment to providing excellent customer service? It began with the Customer Service Campaign in 1989. In that campaign, yellow badges bearing the words "Giordano Means Service" were worn by every Giordano employee. The "Giordano Means Service" philosophy had three tenets: We welcome unlimited try-ons; we exchange—no questions asked; and we serve with a smile. The yellow badges reminded employees that they were there to deliver excellent customer service.

Since its inception, several creative, customer-focused campaigns and promotions had been launched to extend its service orientation. For instance, in Singapore, Giordano asked its customers what they thought would be the fairest price to charge for a pair of jeans. Customers responded and decided on the final price. This resulted in 3,000 pairs of jeans sold each day over the month-long campaign. Other service-related campaigns included asking customers to criticize any aspect of Giordano's service in exchange for a free T-shirt. In that campaign, some 10,000 T-shirts were given away. This campaign was not just another "building awareness" campaign. Giordano acted on customer feedback by changing aspects of its merchandise, such as doing away with the Giordano logo, which was disliked by some customers who liked the quality but not the "value-for-money" image of the Giordano brand.

Against advice that it would be abused, Lai also introduced a no-questions-asked and no-time-limit exchange policy, which made Giordano one of the few retailers in Asia outside Japan with such a generous exchange policy. Giordano claimed that returns were less than 0.1% of sales.

Table 1-3 Recent Giordano Originals (S) Pte Ltd company awards*

Award	Awarding Organization	Category	Year(s)
Excellent Service Award[a]	Singapore Productivity and Standards Board	—	1996, 1997, 1998
Tourism Award	Singapore Tourism Promotion Board	Best Shopping Experience	1996
American Service Excellence Award	American Express	Fashion/Apparel	1995
ISO 9002[b]	Singapore Institute of Standards and Industrial Research	—	1994
People Developer Award	Singapore Productivity and Standards Board	—	1998
Ear Award	Radio Corporation of Singapore	Listeners' Choice (English Commercial)	1996
Ear Award	Radio Corporation of Singapore	Creative Merits (English Jingles)	1996
Top Advertiser Award[c]	Radio Corporation of Singapore	—	1991 to 1994

Notes:

* These are awards given to Giordano Originals Singapore.

[a] To be nominated for the Excellent Service Award, a company must have had, among other things, significant training and other programs in place that ensured quality service. These included systems for recognizing employees and getting customer feedback.

[b] ISO 9002 refers to the guidelines from the Geneva-based International Organization for Standardization for companies that produce and install products.

[c] The Top Advertiser Award is given to companies in different categories that spend the most on advertising during a year. When Giordano received the award, an advertising and promotions budget of S$3 million was considered to be a lot. However, by 1999, the market was more competitive and many big players were spending more than S$8 million on advertising and promotions.

To ensure that every store and individual employee provided excellent customer service, performance evaluations were conducted frequently at the store level, as well as for individual employees. The service standard of each store was evaluated twice every month, while individual employees were evaluated once every two months. Internal competitions were designed to motivate employees and store teams to do their best in serving customers. Every month, Giordano awarded the "Service Star" to individual employees based on nominations made by shoppers. Further, every Giordano store was evaluated every month by mystery shoppers. Based on the combined results of these evaluations, the "Best Service Shop" award was given to the top store.

Value for Money

Lai explained the rationale for Giordano's "value-for-money" policy: "Consumers are learning a lot better about what value is. Out of ignorance, people choose the brand. But the label does not matter, so the business has become value-driven, because when people recognize value, that is the only game in town. So we always ask ourselves how we can sell it cheaper, make it more convenient for the consumer to buy, and deliver faster today than yesterday. That is all value, because convenience is value for the consumer. Time is value for the customer."

Giordano was able to consistently sell value-for-money merchandise through careful selection of suppliers, strict cost control, and resisting the temptation to increase retail prices unnecessarily (Table 1–4). For instance, to provide greater shopping convenience to customers, Giordano in Singapore broke away from traditional downtown retail areas and opened retail outlets in densely populated housing estates.

Inventory Control

In markets with expensive retail space, retailers try to maximize every square foot of the store for sales opportunities. Giordano was no different. Its strategy involved not having a back storeroom in each store. Instead, a central distribution center replaced the function of a back storeroom. With information technology (IT), Giordano was able to skillfully manage its inventory and forecast demand. When an item was sold, the barcode information identifying size, color, style, and price, was recorded by the point-of-sale cash register and transmitted to the company's main computer. At the end of each day, the information was compiled at the store level and sent to the Sales Department and the distribution center. The compiled sales information became the store's order for the following day. Orders were filled during the night and were ready

Table 1–4 Operation highlights for retail and distribution division (figures as at year end unless specified)

	1997	1996	1995	1994	1993
Number of retail outlets					
• directly managed by the Group	324	294	280	283	257
• franchised	316	221	171	77	481
Total number of retail outlets	640	515	451	360	738
Retail floor area directly managed by the Group (sq. ft)	313,800	295,500	286,200	282,700	209,500
Sales per square foot (HK$)	8,000	9,900	10,500	10,600	12,600
Number of employees	8,175	10,004	10,348	6,863	2,330
Comparable store sales increase (%)	(11)	(6)	8	(9)	15
Number of sales associates	1,929	1,958	2,069	1,928	1,502

for delivery by early morning, ensuring that before a Giordano store opened for business, new inventory was already on the shelves.

Another advantage of its IT system was that the information was disseminated to production facilities in real time. By identifying purchase patterns, production was fine-tuned so that working capital would not be tied up in slow-moving inventories. "If there is a slow-selling item, we will decide immediately how to sell it as quickly as possible. When the sales of an item hit a minimum momentum, we pull it out, instead of thinking of how to revitalize its sales." Giordano stores were therefore well stocked with fast-moving items and customers were happy as there were seldom stockouts.

The use of technology also afforded more efficient inventory holding. Giordano's inventory turnover on sales was reduced from 58 days in 1996 to 48 days in 1997, allowing it to thrive on lower gross margins (Table 1–5). Savings were passed to customers, thus reinforcing its value-for-money philosophy. All in, despite the lower margins, Giordano was still able to post healthy profits. Such efficiency became a crucial factor when periodic price wars were encountered. Giordano was able to carve out ever greater slices of the market because it was easy money competing against companies that were used to relying on high-gross margins to make up for slow inventory turnover.

Table 1–5 Regional highlights, 1997

	Hong Kong	China	Korea	Singapore	Taiwan
Net sales (HK$ million)	762.1	565.2	337.0	284.4	753.2
Sales per sq. ft (HK$ million)	16,300	20,600	8,360	10,300	4,500
Comparable store sales increase (%)	(18)	(1)	27	(15)	(9)
Retail floor area (sq. ft)	51,400	29,200	46,000	28,700	168,500
Number of sales associates	427	344	255	235	787
Number of outlets					
• directly managed	53	10	77	33	191
• franchised	0	160	0	0	0

Besides the use of information technology and real time information generated from the information system, Giordano's successful inventory control was achieved through the close integration of the purchasing and selling functions. As Fung elaborated, "There are two very common scenarios that many retailers encounter: slow-selling items stuck in the warehouse and fast-selling popular items that are out of stock. Giordano tries to minimize the probability of occurrence of these two scenarios, which require close integration between the purchasing and selling departments."

But more than technology and inventory control, Giordano had another competitive edge over its competitors. As Fung explained, "In the 1980s and early 1990s, when few retailers would use IT to manage their inventory, the use of IT gave Giordano a leading edge. However, today, when many retailers are using such technology, it (IT) is no longer our real distinctive competitive strength. In a time when there is information overload, it is the organizational culture in Giordano to intelligently use the information that sets us apart from the rest." And this was further explained by Lai, "None of this is novel. Marks & Spencer in Britain, The Gap and Wal-Mart in America, and Seven-Eleven in Japan have used similar systems for years. Nowadays, information flows so fast that anybody can acquire or imitate ideas. What matters is how well the ideas are executed." Indeed, with rapid development in Internet and Intranet technologies, packaged solutions (e.g., MS Office, point-of-sale [POS], and enterprise resource planning [ERP] software), and supporting tele-communications services (e.g., Broadband Internet Access), acquiring integrated IT and logistics technology has become more widely accessible and cost-effective than ever before. Hence, a competitive advantage based on technology and its implementation is likely to become smaller and more difficult to maintain in the medium to long-term future.

Product Positioning

When a business becomes successful, there is always a temptation to expand into more products and services to meet the customer's every need. However, Giordano recognized the importance of limiting its expansion and focusing on one specific area. Fung said, "Focus makes the business more manageable: positioning in the market, keeping the store simple, and better inventory management. And we can get the best out of limited resources." Simplicity and focus were reflected in the way Giordano merchandised its goods. "You'll see no more than 100 items in a Giordano store. We have 17 core items; other retailers have 200 to 300 items. Merchandising a wide range of products causes retailers to take a longer time to react to market changes." (See Figure 1–1 for a Giordano store.)

Figure 1–1   Giordano's range of clothes

Giordano learnt from its mid-1996 decision to stray from its core business and venture into mid-priced women's fashion and decided to "stick to its knitting." With its "Giordano Ladies" line of smart blouses, dress pants, and short skirts, the company was hoping to attract young, stylish women and benefit from the fatter profit margins enjoyed in more upscale niches of women's clothing—about 50% to 60% compared with 40% for casual wear. Giordano, however, wandered into a market crowded with seasoned players. While there were no complaints about the look or quality of the line, it had to vie with more than a dozen established brands already on the racks, including Theme and Esprit. It also failed to differentiate its new clothing line, and tried to sell both through the same outlets. Value appeared to be the wrong image to project in women's fashion. The clothing line not only failed to draw new customers, it also confused the company's regulars. To protect its image and competitive position, Giordano decided to gradually discontinue this line by the end of 1999, and refocus on its men's and women's casual wear positioning. Nevertheless, Giordano was far from admitting defeat—it would continue to experiment with ideas of reaching the slightly trendier, upscale segment. Currently, Giordano Ladies focuses on a select segment, with 15 high-profile stores in Hong Kong and Taiwan offering personalized service (e.g., staff are trained to memorize names of regular customers and recall past purchases).

More recently, Giordano in Hong Kong began to reposition itself, by emphasizing sensible but stylish clothes, and broadening Giordano's appeal by overhauling the stores and apparel. This indicated a move to re-examine its image and positioning in line with its globalization strategy and changing consumer needs. Giordano's relatively low-end positioning worked well when inexpensive but contemporary looking outfits appealed to Asia's penny-pinching customers, especially during the Asian economic crisis. However, over time, this image did not help in building Giordano's brand equity. Said one of Giordano's top executives, "The feeling went from 'this is nice and good value' to 'this is cheap.' When you try to live off selling 100-Hong Kong-dollar shirts, it catches up with you."

Aggressive Advertising and Promotion

Fung said, "Giordano spends a large proportion of its turnover on advertising and promotions. No retailer of our size spends as much as us." For the past five years, Giordano in Singapore had been spending about S$1.5 million (US$0.894 million)[3] to S$2 million (US$1.19 million) annually on its

---

[3] The exchange rate at the time the case was written (end-1999) was US$1 = S$1.68.

advertising and promotional activities. It won the Top Advertiser Award from 1991 to 1994 (Table 1–3). In addition to its big budget, Giordano's advertising and promotion campaigns were creative and appealing. One such campaign was the Round the Clock Madness Shopping with Singapore radio station FM93.3 on May 1, 1994. Starting from midnight, different items were put on sale with a 10% to 60% discount. From midnight to 1 a.m., polo T-shirts were offered at a 20% discount. Jeans, pants, and bermudas were sold at a 30% discount, followed by accessories, which were sold at a 40% discount from 2 a.m. to 3 a.m. To keep listeners awake and excited, sales items were revealed only at the specified hour. Nobody knew which items would be offered next. Listeners to the radio station were cajoled into going to Giordano stores throughout the night. In 1996, Giordano won the Singapore Ear Award. Its English radio commercial was voted by listeners to be one of the best, with the most creative English jingle.

A recent success was its "Simply Khakis" promotion launched in April 1999, which emphasized basic, street-culture style that "mixed and matched" and thus fitted all occasions. In Singapore, within days of its launch, the new line sold out and had to be re-launched two weeks later. By October 1999, over a million pairs of khaki trousers and shorts were sold. This success could be attributed partly to its clearly defined communications objectives, as Garrett Bennett, Giordano's executive director in charge of merchandising and operations, said, "We want to be the key provider of the basics: khakis, jeans, and the white shirt." Elsewhere in the region, sales were booming for Giordano despite only a moderate recovery experienced in the retail industry. Giordano's strength in executing innovative and effective promotional strategies helped the retailer to reduce the impact of the Asian crisis on its sales, and to take advantage of the slight recovery seen in early 1999.

THE ASIAN RETAIL INDUSTRY

Severely hit by the Asian crisis from 1997 to 1999, the Asian retail industry went through dramatic restructuring and consolidation. Many retailers reduced the number of shops in their chains or closed down completely. Almost everyone in the industry implemented cost-cutting measures while at the same time cajoled reluctant customers with promotional strategies. Yet, there was a silver lining as the more competitive firms were able to take advantage of lower rentals and the departure of weaker companies. Some firms, including Giordano, worked toward strengthening their positioning and brand image to better compete in the long haul. Some retailers also explored opportunities or accelerated their presence in markets that were less affected by the Asian crisis, i.e., in markets mostly outside Asia.

During the crisis and in the immediate future until a full recovery set in, industry analysts predicted that opportunities would continue to be driven by value. Thus, Giordano's value proposition appeared appropriate during these times. It was not surprising, then, that in spite of its problems, Giordano was ranked the 14th most competitive company overall in Asia by *Asia Inc.*, a regional business magazine (Table 1–6). Giordano's ranking must be credited to its management's swift cost control strategies, and the immediate implementation of stringent inventory controls. The economic downturn had indeed tested the management's flexibility and responsiveness in making decisive moves.

The retailing environment was becoming more dynamic than before, a change that was perhaps led by growing sophistication of tastes, and rapid advancements in the media, communications, and logistics environment. Giordano's response to these trends would be the key to its ability to compete in the future, especially as they seem to "commoditize" Giordano's current competitive edge in IT, stock control, and logistics.

COMPETITION

Until recently, Giordano's main competitors for low-priced apparel were Hang Ten, Bossini, and Benetton. However, its shift in positioning, and also the squeeze of the retailing sector caused by the crisis, pushed formerly more upmarket firms such as Esprit and Theme to compete for Giordano's value-for-money segment. Table 1–7 provides a list of their websites for more information regarding their product lines and operations. Table 1–8 shows the relative positioning of Giordano and its competitors, Figure 1–2 shows its sales turnover and profits, and Figure 1–3 shows a possible relative positioning map. Table 1–9 shows the geographical areas these firms operate in.

U.S.-based Hang Ten, Italy-based Benetton, and Bossini, belonged to international firms and were generally positioned as low-price retailers offering reasonable quality and service. The clothes emphasized versatility and simplicity. But while Hang Ten was more popular among teenagers and young adults, Benetton and Bossini had a more general appeal. Their distribution strategies were somewhat similar. For instance, the Benetton Group distributed its low-priced casual wear line through 7,000 retail outlets in 120 countries, under brands like United Colors of Benetton, Sisley, and 012. However, Benetton sold a wider range of clothing and accessories, and was traditionally known for its strong position in corporate social responsibility, promoting its brand with thought-provoking images related to a broad spectrum of social issues.

Table 1–6 Asia's most competitive companies

Rank	Company	Country	Industry
1	Sony Corp.	Japan	Electronics
2	Acer Inc.	Taiwan	Computers
3	Honda Motor Co.	Japan	Automobiles
4	Toyota Motor Corp.	Japan	Automobiles
5	Canon Inc.	Japan	Electronics
6	Taiwan Semiconductor Mfg. Co.	Taiwan	Semiconductors
7	Suzuki Motor Corp.	Japan	Automobiles
8	Hyundai Motor Corp.	Korea	Automobiles
9	Reliance Industries Ltd.	India	Petrochemicals/ textiles
10	Rohm Co.	Japan	Electronic components
11	Ranbaxy Laboratories Ltd.	India	Pharmaceuticals
12	Shangri-La Asia Ltd.	Hong Kong	Hotels
13	Singapore Airlines Ltd.	Singapore	Aviation
14	**Giordano International Ltd.**	**Hong Kong**	**Retail clothing**
15	Jollibee Foods Corp.	Philippines	Food
16	Sundram Fasteners Ltd.	India	Auto parts
17	Venture Mfg. (Singapore) Ltd.	Singapore	Contract manufacturing
18	United Microelectronics Corp.	Taiwan	Semiconductors
19	Arvind Mills Ltd.	India	Textiles
20	Bajaj Auto Ltd.	India	Automobiles
21	Mosei Vitelic Inc.	Taiwan	Semiconductors
22	Ayala Land Inc.	Philippines	Real estate
23	Television Broadcasts Ltd.	Hong Kong	Media
24	Nintendo Co.	Japan	Electronic games
25	Samsung Electronics	Korea	Electronics

Note: The ranking was based on a survey and financial analysis of 4,500 companies across Asia, measuring their competitiveness along eight key factors using Porter's framework from his book *Competitive Strategy*. These factors were: (1) cost leadership—ability to control costs and prices; (2) differentiation—ability to distinguish itself from competitors; (3) entry barriers—ability to prevent competitors from entering their markets; (4) strategic focus—ability to focus on a well-defined business strategy; (5) competitive environment—ability to thrive in a highly competitive industry; (6) economies of scale—efficiency gained from high-volume operations; (7) marketing skills—ability to attract and keep profitable customers; and (8) technology leadership—ability to develop, acquire, and exploit leading-edge technology. For a full explanation of the methodology used refer to Asia Inc. Online site at: www.asia-inc.com.
Source: Adapted from "Aiming High: Asia's 50 Most Competitive Companies", *Asia Inc.*, 1997, pp. 34–7.

Table 1-7 Websites of some of the casual apparel retailers

Firms	Website addresses
Benetton	www.benetton.com
Bossini	www.plateadas.com/bossini
Esprit	www.esprit-intl.com
The Gap	www.gap.com
Giordano	www.giordano.com.hk
Hang Ten	www.hangten.com
Theme	www.theme.com.hk

Table 1-8 Competitive positioning

Firms	Positioning	Target market
Giordano/ The Gap	Value for money Style for all occasions	Unisex casual wear, teens, and young adults
Hang Ten	Value for money Sporty lifestyle	Casual wear and sportswear, teens, and young adults
Bossini	Low price (comparable to Giordano)	Unisex apparel, both young and old (above 30s)
Benetton	Reasonably priced fashion Vibrant lifestyle	Unisex appeal, older adults (above 30s)
Esprit	More upmarket than Giordano Stylish, trendy	Ladies casual, but also other specialized lines for children, etc.
Theme	Upmarket, stylish	Ladies smart fashion, ladies businesswear

Esprit is an international fashion lifestyle brand, principally engaged in the image and product design, sourcing, manufacturing, and retail and wholesale distribution of a wide range of women's, men's, and children's apparel, footwear, accessories, and other products under the Esprit brand name. The Esprit name was promoted as a "lifestyle" image and products were strategically positioned as good quality and value for money—a position that Giordano was occupying. As of 1998, Esprit had a distribution network of over 6,500 stores and outlets in 40 countries in Europe, Asia, Canada, and Australia. The main markets were in Europe, which accounted for approximately 62% of the 1998 sales, and in Asia, vertically integrated corporate structure and advanced management system. However, its ambitious expansion proved to be costly in view of the crisis with interest soaring on high levels of debt. In 1999, the company announced a HK$106.1 million net loss for the six months to September 30, 1998, and it closed 23 retail outlets in Hong Kong, which traded under its subsidiary The Shop Clothing. Recently, Theme International had been targeted for an acquisition by Giordano as well as by a few of Giordano's competitors, including Hang Ten.

In general, although these firms had slightly different positioning strategies and targeted dissimilar but overlapping segments, they all competed in a number of similar areas. For example, all firms emphasized heavily the use of advertising and sales promotion to sell rather than design and fashion trends at attractive prices. Almost all stores were also primarily situated in good ground-floor locations, drawing from high-volume traffic and facilitating shopping, browsing, and impulse buying. However, Giordano clearly distinguished itself from its competitors with its high-quality service and cost leadership that together provided great customer value that none of its competitors had been able to match.

According to a study by Interbrand on top Asian marquees, Giordano was Asia's highest-ranking general apparel retailer. It was ranked No. 20. The clothing names next in line were Australia's Quicksilver at No. 45, and Country Road at 47. However, Giordano as a world label was still far off. As a spokesperson on consumer insights for advertising agency McCann-Erickson said, "It is a good brand, but not a great one. Compared to other international brands, it doesn't shape opinion."

A threat from U.S.-based The Gap was also looming. Giordano was also aware of the American retailer that was invading Asia. The Gap was already in Japan. After 2005, when garment quotas are planned to be abolished, imports into the region would become more cost-effective. Hence, Giordano had to examine whether its intention to shift toward a higher position from its current value-for-money position was viable.

GIORDANO'S GROWTH STRATEGY

As early as the 1980s, Giordano realized that it was difficult to achieve substantial growth and economies of scale if it operated only in Hong Kong. The key lay in regional expansion. By 1997, Giordano had opened 640 stores, out of which Giordano (Table 1–4) directly managed 324 stores. For the past years, five markets had dominated its retail and distribution operations—Hong Kong, Taiwan, China, Korea, and Singapore (Table 1–5).

Giordano cast its sight on markets beyond Asia, partially driven by its desire for growth, and partially trying to reduce its dependence on Asia which was shown only all too clearly during the crisis. Giordano announced in 1999 that it would spend US$10 million opening its first outlet in Melbourne, Australia, while adding 15 to 20 outlets by the year 2000. It planned also to set up three to five franchises in Brazil, Colombia, the Dominican Republic, and Panama. Setting up stores in Britain and South Africa was also under consideration.

While the crisis made Giordano rethink its regional strategy, it was still determined to enter and further penetrate new Asian markets. For instance, in China, after a period of deadlock with the government, some progress was made, as three of its shops in Shanghai were re-opened in April 1999. There were also plans to open two outlets by end of 1999 in Jakarta, and to enter Japan and Vietnam.

Giordano's success in these markets would depend on its understanding of the markets, and consumer tastes and preferences for fabrics, colors, and ad appeals. In the past, Giordano relied on a consistent strategy across different countries, and elements of this successful strategy included its positioning and service strategies, information systems and logistics, and human resource policies. However, tactical implementation (e.g., promotional campaigns) was mostly left to local managers in their respective countries. A country's performance (e.g., sales, contribution, service levels, and customer feedback) was monitored by the regional headquarters (e.g., Singapore for Southeast Asia) and the head office in Hong Kong. Weekly performance reports were made accessible to all managers. In recent years, it appeared that as the organization expanded beyond Asia, different strategies had to be developed for different regions or countries. Even within Asia, there were some variations between countries. For instance, while the Hong Kong head office proceeded with plans to pursue a more upmarket segment with plans to acquire Theme International, the regional headquarters in Singapore appeared to maintain its positioning at the lower, value-for-money end. However, major strategic decisions, such as which markets to enter, were still made exclusively in the Hong Kong head office.

THE FUTURE

Giordano was confronted with some important issues as it prepared itself for the new millennium. Although Giordano had been extremely successful, as its revenue, profits, and the many awards it received clearly showed, the question arose on how Giordano could maintain this success in the new millennium. First, how, if at all, should Giordano reposition itself against its competitors in

Creative Technology

Only seven months after announcing Creative's new personal digital entertainment strategy, Mr Wong Hoo Sim, Chairman and CEO of Creative Technology, was at work again. This time, he surprised the market by articulating Creative's intent to turn "dot.com," a new Internet vision.

The personal digital entertainment strategy was not well received by market analysts. Creative's stock price in fact slid 18% right after its announcement. Critics were not convinced that Creative could compete with the big consumer brand names like Sony and Panasonic in the personal digital entertainment industry.

Reception to Creative's new Internet strategy, which Sim called the Creative.Com strategy was mixed. Many critics were of the view that Creative could have entered the Internet race earlier, and at this point, it might have to play a catch up game. However, the critics were also aware that Creative had no other option but to go Internet, although some expressed concerns that Creative's capability was in the hardware business and not e-business.

Although Creative had dominated the sound card business for the last two decades, it was struggling with a lack of new hit products. Its much publicized foray into the CD-ROM drive business in the 1990s that resulted eventually in a huge write-off and several years of losses was still fresh in the minds of many. Over the years, Creative had moved into several new product areas like graphics cards, DVD players, high-end speakers, etc. But none came close to repeating the

---

This case was prepared by Professor Chin Tiong Tan as the basis for class discussion rather than to illustrate either effective or ineffective handling of an administrative situation. Some of the data have been disguised.

All denominations are in Singapore dollars unless otherwise stated.

success of the Sound Blaster. The personal digital entertainment and Internet strategies were bold attempts, and at a press meeting in August 1999, Sim confidently said, "After this transition, the painful times should be over."

THE MAN BEHIND CREATIVE[1]

The Dream

One starry night, more than 20 years ago, a young man walked out of a big Japanese factory in Jurong. He had moonlighted on a long and weary project for several months and was relieved at its completion. As he walked to his motorcycle in the large and empty car park, he happened to look back and before his eyes was this huge and dark monolith factory. Something struck him. He said to himself, "Someday, I will have a building of this size and it will come with a big car park!"

The Kampong (Village) Boy

A Bukit Panjang kampong boy with no real toys, all Wong Hoo Sim had was a dream. He was an ordinary child, obedient and hardworking. When the other boys were flying kites, he was never able to bring a kite to the sky. When they were catching spiders to fight, Sim could not differentiate the male from the female spiders, so sometimes the spiders mated instead. Maybe he did not even care.

Apart from doing household chores, he always spent his time creating his own toys. He invented his own board games a-la Monopoly because he could not afford one. But nobody would play with him. He created his own art style, but none of his art teachers appreciated it. Maybe he did not even show it to them. Still, none of these really bothered him. All he knew was that he liked to create. Though he received no encouragement, he persevered.

Today, the 44-year-old Sim heads Creative Technology Ltd, a US$1.2 billion giant he founded in 1981, whose flagship product, the Sound Blaster, set the world standard for PC audio today. Creative is the undoubted technological market leader in the global multimedia market.

Sim had certainly come a long way. Born of a lower income family, he studied at two kampong schools in Bukit Panjang. Before the afternoon school session, he would sit shyly at an obscure corner in the market each morning trying to sell his basket of eggs. Barely making one cent an egg, he seldom sold more than 20 eggs. He was careful not to let the eggs get confiscated though.

---

[1] Creative Corporate Document: "The Uncharted Journal," published in *The Straits Times*, February 2, 1999, pp. 14–15.

First Love

Sim's sister gave him a harmonica when he was about 11 years old. The harmonica became his constant companion. Every now and then, in between household chores, he would pull it out from his pocket and play it. The harmonica was definitely his first love. It was a natural attraction because it was cheap and convenient. It released the creative energies in him.

In 1972, his life changed when he joined the Ngee Ann Harmonica Troupe as a shy first-year Electrical and Electronics Engineering student at the Ngee Ann Polytechnic. In the second year, he was asked to arrange harmonica pieces for the troupe, something they traditionally did on their own. This stirred up a lot of passion. Finally, he could create something that people could appreciate.

The Two Seeds of Creative

"If I had not joined the harmonica troupe, there would be no Sound Blaster," reminisced Sim. This was not an overstatement. The harmonica was an instrument for the masses, and so was the original Sound Blaster. The kampong environment was the fertile ground and it was the harmonica that planted the first seed of creativity in him. In his second year, as the deputy troupe leader, he needed to provide accompaniments to the popular sing-along sessions. The limitations of the harmonica spurred him to join Practice Theater School, run by the famous drama director, Kuo Pao Kun, to learn to play the accordion.

"It was there that I saw creativity at the highest level of appreciation," he said. Bold new concepts were introduced regularly at the school. But what bowled him over was that accordion students were allowed to compose their own songs. Practice Theater School planted the second seed of creativity in Sim. Three months into the course, Sim was accompanying the troupe during their impromptu sing-along sessions with the accordion, albeit with some struggle.

The Prelude

The long journey began sometime in 1977 when Sim dreamed of having his own building. It was just a dream then, and he did not tell anybody about it. Early in 1978, he used up his leave to work in a local electronics company. He joined the company as a "do-it-all" assistant electronics engineer. To him, his bosses did not look extraordinary. If they could start up companies, there was no reason why he could not do it too. Sim left after a year and was immediately asked to be a relief teacher in a kampong school. Without an "O" level credit in English, he was not qualified for the job but the principal had very little choice. Who would come all the way to a remote kampong school in Chua Chu Kang, walk 20 minutes from the nearest bus stop, to teach a bunch of rowdy kids for $15 a day?

While most people would have shunned this job, Sim actually loved it. The Chinese stream students were struggling with the transition to English textbooks. To help them, Sim conducted the Mathematics and Science classes in Chinese and even gave free tuition to the weaker ones at their homes. This short three-month stint prepared him for the bigger challenges ahead. He got the job of a computer engineer in a small seismic firm even though he had no computer background. There, he developed two computer-controlled seismic instruments which according to his proud boss, were the most advanced in the world.

"Very Enterprising"

In 1979, he organized a reunion for his Secondary 4 classmates whom he had not seen for eight years. He had set himself the goal of locating every single classmate. This was the kampong class of 1971. At that time, few had telephones and many had relocated. Armed with a never-give-up attitude and his motorcycle, he went tracking his classmates down with the addresses from the old school registers. He even managed to borrow the school premises for the reunion. Sim located everyone. For many, the reunion night was emotionally overwhelming. The programs brought back sweet memories. A souvenir magazine was also produced and someone commented in it: "Very enterprising."

The Journey Begins

It was midnight, January 1, 1981. Sim was on an oil-rig. After completing two projects, he had decided to move on. Although his was the dream R&D job that an engineer like him would kill for, he had no love for the seismic line he was in. Under the open starry sky of the South China Sea, Sim contemplated his life, mulling over the phrase "very enterprising." He realized that what people considered "very enterprising" actually came very naturally to him. From arranging harmonica pieces and accordion accompaniments, to organizing outings and mountain climbing trips, he just kept doing these "enterprising" things for free without needing people's appreciation or attention.

"But, what if from now onward, I do all these things consciously, and direct them to a very clear goal," he thought, "then, maybe I can achieve something really great." He knew that clear quantifiable goals worked very well for him and he was not afraid of setting high goals for himself. He had no vision, no

thousand per month, compared to about a couple of hundred PCs per month. CMS was heaven. And best of all, CMS required zero support.

But then Sim noticed a worrying trend. There were no re-orders. To get people to buy without deliberation would require the sound card to become a de facto world standard. "To set a world standard, I must go to the U.S.," Sim told his colleagues. On August 9, 1988, Sim left alone for the U.S. with one clear goal—to sell 20,000 CMS or he would not return.

Uncharted Lands

When Sim arrived in the U.S., he set up his company quickly in his two-bedroom apartment, using the living room as the office and the garage as the warehouse. He realized that the U.S. market was much tougher and more treacherous than one could imagine. He faced "one thousand and one problems of every kind in the year, averaging about three per day." If he could not solve any of these problems, he had to pack and return home. Sim realized that the U.S. market was more game-centric. For tactical reasons, CMS was renamed "Game Blaster." He went round providing free developer support to any PC game developer interested in putting sound in their games. He faced an uphill battle to get people's attention. Finally, through his tenacity and reliable support, he won their respect and people started to talk to him about their wish-list for a "killer" sound card.

In mid-1987, Tandy Corporation, a consumer electronics retailer, wanted to buy 20,000 Game Blasters for their 8,000 RadioShack stores. Short of time, but eager to clinch the deal, Creative went ahead to order all the components without a purchase order from Tandy. Then the worst nightmare came. Tandy withdrew their order at the eleventh hour. This would certainly kill Creative. Sim knew that he could not fail. There was no retreat. He kept going back with all kinds of sweeteners. Sim's perseverance was rewarded. While it was a money losing deal, it was one of his proudest moments when the huge RadioShack truck pulled into his factory to load the products. He could go home! He got most of his money back, so he could use it to launch the new "killer card."

The De Facto Audio Standard

In November 1989, Creative had a 300-square-foot booth in Comdex Trade Show in Las Vegas under the Singapore Trade Development Board's pavilion. Despite its size, it was the noisest booth in this huge computer exhibition. The Sound Blaster was born.

Sound Blaster took the world by storm. Creative's booth was packed. Throughout the five-day show, there was a non-stop queue to order the product. An amazing 600 orders were taken—four minutes per order. Michael Jackson who happened to visit Comdex that year dropped by the booth unannounced and was so captivated that he stayed for almost 30 minutes. The Sound Blaster gave Creative the break it needed. Perfect timing, people would have thought. But little did they know that Creative had survived on a shoestring budget for over eight years for this "perfect" timing. And when it came, Creative seized it.

When competitors started to clone the Sound Blaster in 1991, Sim knew that it had become the de facto standard for PC. Between 1990 to 1995, Creative grew at a furious rate of almost three times every year compounded. Revenue grew from US$7.5 million in 1990 to US$1.2 billion in 1995. On August 10, 1992, Creative became the first company in Singapore to be listed on the U.S. NASDAQ stock market. Because of the huge complexity, it was called the "IPO from hell." NASDAQ gave it the visibility it needed in the U.S. market. In 1994, Creative came back to Singapore and was also listed on the Stock Exchange of Singapore. After the IPO, there was even more pressure from the investing communities to grow revenue. Creative went into all kinds of products in the loosely defined multimedia market, including the highly competitive CD-ROM drive market. Creative started to defocus.

The $500 Million Lesson

In 1995, Creative was this huge bulky engine running at a maddening pace with too many heads wanting to go in their own directions. In early 1996, CD-ROM drives became oversupplied and prices crashed. A brand new CD-ROM drive that cost US$80 to build was selling at an insane price of US$18. The whole industry lost billions of dollars. The largest player in the market probably lost over US$250 million. Sim estimated that Creative lost about US$100 million on the CD-ROM drives. In the fiscal year of 1996, Creative lost US$38 million net. This indicated that the Sound Blaster was still making good money.

The stock of Creative dropped to a historic low of S$5.05 in the middle of 1996 and the public thought this was the end of a home-grown company. In a span of less than two years, Sim's net worth fell by about $500 million. Sim felt that it was a good $500 million lesson for him. The entire company was mobilized, starting from the senior managers. There was no slash and burn. Instead he started by fixing the culture of Creative. The newly formalized culture, based on many good traits that Creative had, became known as the

6Fs Culture: Family, Friendliness, Fortitude, Failure tolerance, Fast-paced, and Fun!

Creative went back to the basics and refocused on its strength, which was audio. Sim also went on a global road tour to meet and motivate Creative employees. Following that were seven consecutive record quarters. In recognition of Sim's efforts in this dramatic turnaround, he was given the Businessman of the Year award for the second time by *The Business Times*. The first was in 1993.

The Future

Going into the next century, Creative's new strategy was to center on audio and expand into the personal digital entertainment market. This was a hugely expanded market that used the personal computer as the center of entertainment. It included all the "best-of-the-breed" components Creative was supplying for PCs and external PDEs or personal digital entertainment devices such as keyboards, speakers, digital amplifiers, portable digital audio players, etc. All PDEs are devices that have the element of audio and can be linked to the PC.

Its Sound Blaster Live! was a revolutionary product that gave a whole new meaning to audio—environmental audio—very realistic surround audio that gives you the living experience. Environmental audio would be extended to cover all these PDE devices. In the future, Creative wants to build a personal digital entertainment center in the home based on the PC. Having gone through all these challenges, Creative had grown to be a company that was "built to last." When asked what drives him, Sim answered:

> "Creative is a CAUSE—to change the world for the better by creating "creative" products. Creative is an IDEAL—to build a family where people can work happily together like brothers and sisters. Creative is a DREAM—to fulfill the boldest dream!
> Take away these and I will quit!"

PERSONAL DIGITAL ENTERTAINMENT STRATEGY

In 1998, Creative launched Sound Blaster Live! This marked Creative's entry into the personal digital entertainment industry. With speakers providing a theater-like sensurround environment, Sound Blaster Live! allowed users to feel the "boom" as a bomb exploded and the "woosh" as jets flew across the PC screen. Sim said, "I am preparing myself to move into the consumer electronics entertainment industry. Creative's aim has been to make the PC fun to use and to improve a user's multimedia experience. We want to focus on enhancing a family experience with their personal digital entertainment center in the living room."

When Sound Blaster Live! was launched at the Comdex 98 Trade Show in Las Vegas, reviews were most positive. The strategy to enter the personal digital entertainment business would pitch Creative against the likes of giant players such as Sony and Philips. Sim was confident that Creative's best of breed product range would give him an edge over its competitors. His intention was to leverage on Creative's flexibility and ability to move quickly to outsmart the larger players that often got caught up with issues like what standards to follow.

Creative launched its Blaster PC in 1998. It was packed with all of Creative's powerful award-winning components. Users could experience awesome audio, cinema-quality DVD movies, impressive arcade quality 3D games, etc. Figure 2–1 shows a Blaster PC advertisement in Singapore featuring a heavy bundle of Creative's best components like Sound Blaster Live!, Graphics Blaster RIVA, Creative's PC-DVD player, and its Cambridge 4-point surround speakers and system. To allow for maximum effect in the multimedia experience on Internet, Creative integrated the ADSL modem and ATM card with its Blaster PC for 2,500 kbps high speed Internet access with Singtel Magix (a ADSL Internet service provider). The total package of "best of Creative" PC sold at a price only marginally higher than a regular PC.

The critics, however, were not convinced that the personal entertainment center strategy could provide Creative with its much needed new lift. Many still could not forget the CD-ROM fiasco.

The CD-ROM venture was an expensive lesson for Creative. Not only was the setback a huge financial one that dragged Creative into the red for several years, its stock price also dipped to an all time low of S$5.05 in 1996. The episode taught Creative a valuable lesson that experience gained in the sound card business would not work in the CD-ROM business. Creative was caught flat-footed with a huge inventory position like many other players, which finally led to the decision to exit CD-ROM manufacturing and to refocus on audio technology in 1997.

Countering critics of his personal digital entertainment center strategy, Sim had this to say, "Creative in 1999 is in its best shape ever to take on new challenges, this is like deja-vu 1989. Creative in 1989 was a US$1 million company facing consumer audio giants like Yamaha and Roland, 1,000 times our size and yet we prevailed. Today, Creative is a US$1 billion company and we are still up against consumer electronic giants 50 times our size. Which

Figure 2–1 A Blaster PC advertisement

Creative do you think is in a better position?"[2]

On the general concern that Creative's core audio business was going down the tubes, and that it would be crushed by consumer electronics giants in selling the new range of audio gadgets, Sim stated that his audio margins were at 50% and rising, the latest flagship card Sound Blaster Live! was at even higher margins than previous products. Creative market share for the sound card had jumped 50% year on year during the last quarter of 1998 while lower margin audio chips for original equipment manufacturers (OEMs) also soared tenfold. The new Sound Blaster Live! sold one million units in the four months since its launch.

However, Sim cautioned that upside growth for audio margin would flatten and competition would come in. He noted that Creative had established a strong business fighting the electronics giants as it had leapt to No. 2 in retail and No. 3 in distribution for graphics in a market which in 1995 no one thought Creative could win. It also gained market share for speakers from entrenched competitors like Philips and Altec, capturing the No. 1 position in distribution and No. 2 in retail within a year of entering the market.

Addressing concerns that Creative lacked mainstream consumer distribution channels for new PC products like home theaters and pianos, Sim said the company had always had access to these channels through its Cambridge chain of speakers stores and its subsidiaries E-Mu and EnSoniq. He stressed that while giants may come out to play and would move quickly, Creative had learned to be street smart from its ill-fated foray into making CD-ROM drives.

Creative's personal digital entertainment strategy would continue to center on audio, which was required in all forms of entertainment, be it movies, music, or games. The company would continue to be vertically integrated in all audio functions, from chips to speakers, ensuring control over margins. Other add-ons like graphics cards and DVD-ROM drives were produced with partners. In the same vein, new personal digital entertainment devices would be built by Creative with its partners. The strategy would gradually result in a complete PC-related entertainment system, built around audio. Each product would be driven by a "killer" software application produced either by Creative or its partners.

Sim articulated his intent that rather than generating only a couple of hundred U.S. dollars in sales for each PC in existence, every PC could in a few years generate US$2,999 in personal digital entertainment spending—a big

---

[2] *The Business Times*, February 18, 1999.

potential cash cow. Whether consumers would jump in quickly to buy up these high-end gadgets was unclear to market analysts.

Creative planned to introduce its full range of products over time. A digital audio player, based on the MP3 standard, but with enhancements, was launched in late 1999. The strategy would result in Creative restructuring its audio division, U.S.-based E-Mu systems, to combine with lower end sound card maker Ensoniq to produce digital pianos and other products. This, Sim felt, was timely since the professional electronics audio market was stagnant, given the recent return to acoustics instruments by professional musicians.

Sim had a major restructuring of Creative in mind. He said, "I am throwing everything into the pool again and then they will all divide. Instead of having fixed product groups, the new structure could have fluid teams, with engineers mixed up for individual projects."

CREATIVE.COM

On August 6, 1999, Sim announced at a press conference that he did not want to be known as the sound card maker anymore. Instead, he wanted to be known as the man who harnessed the Internet successfully to build on the company's hardware capabilities. Creative was to create five separate companies; each with the potential to become bigger than its parent. The restructuring of Creative with the new dot.com parts was to push Creative strongly into e-business. The announcement took the market by surprise.

INVENTORY WOES

History would have repeated itself if Creative did not take drastic actions to avoid a recurrence of its earlier CD-ROM write-off. Confronted with an inventory problem for its graphics cards, Creative could have a difficult half year into 1999. This time, Sim was quick in responding by flushing out inventory of low-end graphics cards and de-emphasizing the retail distribution channels. Creative had to take a US$11 million charge for its low-end graphics products during the last three months and announced its plan to move out of the retail distribution channel for such products and refocus on selling them via the Internet.

The graphics cards hit a snag earlier in the year when its chip supplier S.J. Inc. was acquired by rival Diamond Multimedia Systems. Craig McHugh, president of Creative's U.S. arm Creative Labs, described the tie-up between S.J. and Diamond as a great disappointment and said the group had been having quality problems with the S.J. stock, making it one of the biggest problematic products that Creative had in a long time. It had to take a drastic price cut to flush out all the stock. To ensure that such inventory overhang problems were not repeated, the low-margin products were to be shifted to a direct electronic commerce model, thereby reducing expenses and inventory exposure.

Addressing such issues opened up avenues on the Internet as a new strategic direction for Creative. The immediate task for the graphics cards business was to allow Creative to turn what had been bad business into good business. Overall, Creative reported sales of US$1.3 billion for the year compared to US$1.23 billion in the previous year, and net income dropped to US$115 million from US$134 million a year ago.

CREATIVE'S INTERNET STRATEGY

Sim wanted to position Creative in the new entertainment-centric Internet future to "unleash" its shareholder value. He said, "We have been undervalued by the market for a long time. We are restructuring to show the real value of our business. People should look at us not just as a hardware company. We are so many things."[3]

The vision of his Internet strategy was the Creative.Com concept, a new plan to create a structure of Internet-related business around Creative's core competency—audio technology. Sim saw Creative having a strong chance in becoming a leader in the upcoming broadband wave of the Internet, which would enable powerful home entertainment possibilities. He insisted, "A year ago, we had no personal digital entertainment product, our modems were losing money, we were fighting for a share in speakers, and we had no strength in graphics … But, Creative is now a leader in almost all segments."

The Creative.Com concept could be seen as a holding company as well as a main website acting as a portal to five separate business units. Creative Technology Ltd, the group's traditional hardware business, would continue to provide high-margin technologies and products, and an installed base of loyal users. Creative Labs, its U.S. subsidiary and the driver of its powerful U.S. retail operations, would act as a worldwide sales and marketing unit, maintaining three channels: traditional retail, business to business e-commerce, and business to consumer e-commerce. The latter would take the form of SI Direct, a website dedicated to system integrators who bought Creative's low-margin products in large volumes and installed them in large corporate projects. The intention was to shift its low-end graphics cards and offer low-margin products to SI Direct.

---

[3] *The Business Times*, August 7, 1999.

The third wing of Creative.Com is hifi.com, an advanced business to consumer website devoted to "all things home entertainment." Formerly the website of Creative's Cambridge Sound Works speaker unit, hifi.com was made an independent Creative subsidiary and would re-launch its full service website soon. The site would also sell rival products like Marantz sound systems. Although hifi.com's sales were around US$10 million, Sim expects sales to jump to several hundred millions in a few years.

The fourth wing is a group of "inside.coms" from inside Creative. An example is Lava.com, which caters to Internet music enthusiasts. These "inside.coms" can help draw in new users, sell hardware, and when ready, be spun off.

The last is Venture Capital Group. A US$50 million venture fund was set up for investing in Internet-related companies. About half of this has been invested in eight companies, three of which are Singapore companies. Examples are emusic.com and Centillon, a broadband chip maker. Figure 2–2 shows the new Creative.Com structure.

Sim is confident that each of these new parts of Creative may someday be bigger than Creative today. Thus far, it had been serious investment to put in place the necessary systems. In mid-1999, Creative spent US$3 million on marketing and hiring staff for the initiatives. In mid-1999, it spent another US$10 million and another US$15 million is in the pipeline. All these are investing in staff and logistics infrastructure for e-commerce to ensure Creative's new future.

GETTING IT RIGHT THIS TIME

While the critics were quick to point out that Creative's Internet strategy was nothing new, others were confident that while Creative was late in the Internet game, it had a good chance of advancing Creative's dominance of sound related business on the Internet.

It was probably the first time that Creative had been able to put together a vision that looked coherent. Various pieces of Creative's businesses were now put on a strategic platform that might just take off to new heights. The new organic integration had significant synergy. The mother site—Creative.Com— had one of the best known brand names in the business, linking up with other web businesses that were synergistic. Each of the five business entities should be able to leverage on the other.

As with all Internet ventures, the possibilities are limited only by the imagination. What could go awry? In a word, execution. While the new business model looks ready, getting it into operation may take a while. One key

Figure 2–2 The new Creative.Com structure

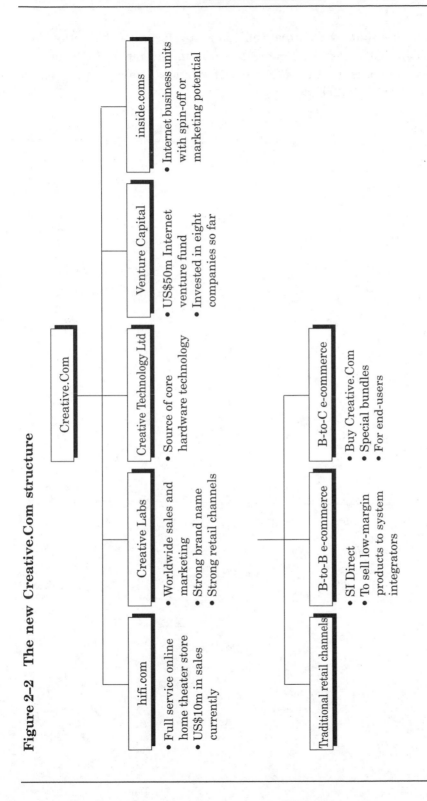

consideration is how quickly Creative can come to grips with the notion that its experience in the bricks and mortar world might mean little on the Internet. A new way of doing things to support the new strategy may suggest a re-inventing of Creative Technology.

HMI Holdings

On a bright sunny afternoon in late 1998, Yeo Hwee Tiong, Chief Executive Officer of HMI Holdings Ltd, was leading a senior management meeting in formulating a new strategic thrust for HMI Balestier Hospital, a small hospital in Singapore that recently won a management contract and acquired a stake in Mahkota Medical Center in Malacca, Malaysia.

The spirit in the boardroom was high, full of excitement, and brimming with hope for HMI. The upbeat atmosphere contrasted sharply with the general gloomy economic condition in Singapore and the rest of the region. The 1997 Asian economic crisis had badly hit the once vibrant corporate scene of Asia. Several published economic forecasts were not optimistic about a fast recovery and corporate executives were very cautious about any expansion plan into the region.

In contrast, the big event in HMI's boardroom was an opportunity to transform HMI from a small little known hospital to a major hospital management group in the region. The road ahead was clearly not going to be a smooth one. In fact, Yeo and his team expected many challenges and obstacles in their quest to grow in the region. They were, however, determined to work out a new strategic direction in anticipation of the next boom in Asia.

HMI BALESTIER HOSPITAL

HMI Balestier Hospital began operations in September 1991 as the Balestier Medical Center (BMC), providing a range of primary and

---

This case was prepared by Professor Chin Tiong Tan as the basis for class discussion rather than to illustrate either effective or ineffective handling of an administrative situation. Some of the data have been disguised.

Copyright © 1999 by Singapore Management University.

secondary healthcare services and facilities including operating theaters, inpatient wards, 24-hour outpatient consultations, specialist clinics, a health screening center, a clinical laboratory, diagnostic X-ray, ultrasound imaging, and physiotherapy. From the hospital's inception, a Diabetes Center was established with a mission to promote awareness of the disease and seek its early detection through health education and lifestyle management. A key feature of the hospital is its Health Screening Center. Health screening programs are part of the preventive medicine that focuses on the early detection of diseases. HMI Balestier Hospital believes that prevention is the key to maintenance of good health and its Health Screening Center seeks to detect early signs of disease through clinical examination and investigative/diagnostic procedures.

The range of specialities offered at the hospital increased as more specialists from different disciplines became accredited to it. The hospital has also identified certain niches where it believes that it will be able to offer competitive medical services. For example, in 1996, HMI Balestier Hospital established its Excimer Laser Center in a joint venture with a group of 12 eye specialists. This center focuses mainly on the correction of short-sightedness and astigmatism. The hospital has also expanded its Day Surgery and Health Screening Centers.

Having laid its foundation through its experience in BMC and perceiving the opportunities available in the region, the Group expanded its activities to include the provision of healthcare and healthcare-related project management and consulting services to the region. Internationally, the Group developed its affiliations through the signing of a Memorandum of Understanding for Strategic Partnership with the Massachusetts General Hospital in Boston, U.S. To reflect this wider range of activities, BMC changed its name in 1995 to HMI Balestier Hospital, the abbreviation HMI standing for Health Management International.

The Hospital

HMI Balestier Hospital is a 62-bed hospital providing a range of medical, surgical, therapeutic, diagnostic, and preventive healthcare services. Its mission is to provide high-quality, cost-effective hospital services in a personalized, comfortable, and caring environment. The hospital provides four main classes of services:

- *Inpatient services*
  Inpatients are patients who spend at least one night in the hospital.

These patients comprise acute and chronic illness cases, accident and emergency cases, and surgical cases and are cared for by a team of resident doctors and nurses providing 24-hour coverage. The hospital has an endoscopy room and four operating theaters, which can handle a range of operations, including minimally invasive surgery. The inpatient wards are divided into single, double, three and four-bedded rooms. All rooms are air-conditioned with attached bathrooms and furnished with electrically operated beds, personal telephones, and television sets. The hospital also has an Intensive Care Unit with two beds.

- *Outpatient services*
  HMI Balestier Hospital operates a 24-hour walk-in and Accident and Emergency clinic for the treatment of common medical ailments. A procedure room for minor surgery and the treatment of accident cases forms part of this clinic.

  There are also specialist clinics for many speciality disciplines, including cardiology, neurology, ophthalmology, endocrinology, and orthopaedics. These clinics are operated on a time-sharing basis, by various specialists who are not employed by, but are accredited to, the hospital. Apart from using the hospital's facilities and services, these specialists are provided with a consultation room to attend to their patients. The hospital charges the specialists a fee for the use of the consultation room, the facilities, and services.

- *Day surgery*
  At the Day Surgery Center, patients undergo surgery or procedures that do not require overnight hospitalization.

- *Health screening*
  A range of health screening programs is available to assess patients' overall well-being and to detect early signs of disease. A program may include some or all of the following: physical examination, laboratory tests, X-ray, computerized spirometry, audiogram, tonometry, retinogram, treadmill (cardiac stress) test, electrocardiogram, pap smear, mammogram, and ultrasound of the abdomen and pelvic organs.

Supporting these services are facilities for diagnostic imaging and physiotherapy as well as a pharmacy and a clinical laboratory.

In 1996, an Excimer Laser Center was set up within the hospital. As its name implies, the center uses an excimer laser to correct short-sightedness and astigmatism. The center has also acquired the equipment to perform LASIK (laser in situ keratomileusis), which is suitable for individuals with a high degree of short-sightedness. The surgery conducted at the center does not require hospitalization and patients may be discharged within hours of the surgery. To more closely tie the eye specialists' interest with that of the hospital, the Excimer Laser Center has been set up as a joint venture between the hospital and a group of 12 ophthalmologists, or eye specialists. It operates as a distinct division within the hospital with HMI Balestier Hospital holding 52.9% of the joint venture and the eye specialists the remaining 47.1%.

Marketing

HMI Balestier Hospital's advertising activities are conducted so as to comply with the relevant laws and regulations, and guidelines issued by the Ministry of Health. It therefore relies on recommendations of patients and referrals from general practitioners and specialists.

The hospital also receives referrals from Integrated Health Plans' (IHP) network of approximately 182 GP clinics and 112 specialists. IHP has developed a managed healthcare plan, called HealthPlus, that provides members of the plan with access to a range of healthcare services at more favorable rates than would be available to them otherwise. IHP had already negotiated with these GPs and specialists for preferred rates for members. HealthPlus currently has a membership of about 44,500 members from about 395 companies.

IHP's clients are companies which have signed agreements with IHP for their staff to become members of HealthPlus. IHP then provides these clients with the following main services: centralized consolidated billing each month for all clinics and specialists within the IHP network; detailed records of employee utilization of medical services including medical leave records; and health education programs for employees. Basically, IHP manages the administration of staff healthcare benefits for these employers, in effect becoming the healthcare coordinator of these companies' human resources departments. These companies also benefit from lower healthcare costs as a result of the preferred rates negotiated by IHP. For its efforts, IHP imposes an administrative payment on the fees charged by the GPs and specialists.

The management looks at IHP as a synergistic relationship with the Group through referrals from IHP's network of GP clinics and specialists to HMI Balestier Hospital. IHP's business can also be considered as part of the Group's core business of healthcare management. It is further believed that this "managed healthcare" concept can be exported to other countries within the region by leveraging on IHP's experience in Singapore.

As Balestier Hospital is the preferred hospital in IHP's network, it benefits from referrals from other members of this network. Although these GPs and specialists are not obligated to refer their patients to the hospital, HealthPlus members would not be able to enjoy the preferred rates negotiated by IHP at other hospitals.

Competition

HMI Balestier Hospital competes with other hospitals, both private and public, for patients for its day surgery and inpatient departments and it competes with these hospitals and general practitioner clinics for patients for its outpatient services. However, it should be noted that different private hospitals target different segments of the population and some hospitals specialize in one or more fields of medicine like obstetrics and gynecology.

HMI Balestier Hospital competes on the basis of price and believes that it provides quality healthcare at affordable prices. These prices have not been achieved by sacrificing either service or facilities and HMI believes that its service is comparable to other hospitals in Singapore.

HMI nonetheless acknowledges that the healthcare industry in Singapore is very competitive with many healthcare service providers, both private and public. It intends to focus most of its future efforts in Malaysia where the healthcare industry is undergoing a restructuring and where there are more opportunities compared to Singapore. In 1997, the total number of private hospital beds in Singapore was 2,185. In that same year, the total number of patients admitted to public sector hospitals in Singapore was 275,339 and the number admitted to private hospitals was 94,117. There are no readily available statistics to show HMI's share of the other segments of its medical services business such as health screening.

Sales Performance, 1994–98

Sales growth for HMI had been steady since it started operations in 1991. Despite the highly competitive market in Singapore, with big private hospitals like Gleneagles Hospital and Mount Elizabeth Hospital and the resource rich public "restructured" hospitals like Singapore General Hospital, National University Hospital, Tan Tock Seng Hospital, etc., the company recorded a healthy sales trend over years.

Profitability of HMI was, however, less satisfactory. Like all new startup ventures, it incurred losses for many years (see Table 3–1). The turnaround only came in 1997. In that year, HMI recorded a profit of slightly more than $1 million. Since 1997, HMI had been lucrative.

Table 3–1   HMI's financial results (S$'000)

	1995	1996	1997	1998
Turnover	13,635	17,728	18,570	17,987
Profit (loss) before taxation	(2,118)	(496)	1,142	796
	Breakdown of HMI's turnover			
	1995	1996	1997	1998
Income generated from hospital operations	12,392	16,496	17,332	16,587
Project management	1,243	1,232	1,238	1,400
	13,635	17,728	18,570	17,987

Prospects

In the short term, HMI believes that the current economic and financial environment could dampen its prospects in Singapore. The demand for private healthcare is expected to decline as patients seek cheaper services at public hospitals. Aesthetic surgery and procedures are likely to be postponed, reducing the revenue for HMI Balestier Hospital. However, because of these difficult times, many patients from Indonesia, Malaysia, and Brunei are looking at alternative lower cost suppliers of quality healthcare, in particular private hospitals in Malaysia.

Thus there are opportunities for HMI to expand as regional hospitals seek new funds and management expertise. An example is the Mahkota Medical Center in Malaysia.

In the longer term, the regional economies will recover and HMI expects demand for private healthcare services to resume its growth, encouraged by governments. It is believed that the demand for healthcare services is greater than the facilities available. HMI is therefore committed to developing its healthcare business in the region starting in Malaysia. In subsequent years, as the regional economies recover and its experience and resources increase, it intends to expand into other Asian markets.

Malaysia is attractive to HMI because the Malaysian government is privatizing and corporatizing its government hospitals and letting market forces keep costs down. This is also likely to give rise to opportunities for HMI as hospitals that are unable to compete look for new managers and new investments. There will also be increased demand for healthcare training which is an activity that HMI is also developing.

It is an accepted fact that the regional healthcare market has significantly greater growth potential. For example, Malaysia targets to increase the number of doctors and nurses such that there will be one doctor for every 1,500 people and one nurse for every 448 people in the year 2000. By comparison, Singapore already has one doctor in active practice for every 661 people and one nurse or midwife in active practice for every 255 people in 1997. HMI intends to leverage its experience in managing hospitals in Singapore to participate in this growth in the healthcare sector.

A NEW REGIONAL OPPORTUNITY

The Asian economic crisis had put many corporations in the most badly hit countries such as Thailand, Malaysia, and Indonesia insolvent. Many "star" corporate groups of Asia were forced to restructure their operations and businesses. Unprofitable and non-core businesses were sold at prices below their net tangible book values. Opportunities were abundant for investors and companies looking for new growth paths into Asia. The Mahkota Medical Center (MMC) was one such example.

The hospital, a wholly-owned company of the diversified Lion Group of Companies of Malaysia, was a financial burden to its parent. It was losing money and poorly managed. The Lion Group was keen to sell it off and/or to bring in professional management to turn it around. In November 1998, HMI bought a stake in MMC and took on a management contract to restructure and manage the hospital's operation.

The Mahkota Medical Center

Completed in October 1994, the Mahkota Medical Center (MMC) is a 288-bed tertiary hospital located in Malacca, Malaysia. Its abiding philosophy is the provision of accessible quality medical services at affordable prices. Housed in its 11-story building are 12 operating theaters, a coronary/critical/intensive care ward with 18 beds, three floors of specialist medical suites, an Accident and Emergency department as well as supporting facilities such as a clinical laboratory and a diagnostic imaging laboratory. To provide quality healthcare to its patients, MMC has assembled a team of medical personnel with diverse training, experience, and backgrounds.

It offers a wide range of specialities, including thoracic and cardiovascular surgery, oncology and radiotherapy, neurosurgery, urological surgery, and in-vitro fertilization, that are usually only found in larger and better equipped hospitals. To facilitate these major disciplines, MMC has acquired high-tech medical equipment including a lithotripter and a linear accelerator. The lithotripter allows non-invasive "blasting" of kidney stones while the linear accelerator is used in MMC's cancer treatment center for radiotherapy treatment of cancers in combination with chemotherapy.

MMC is particularly proud of its cancer treatment center and its linear accelerator which it believes to be among the very few linear accelerators in Malaysia south of Kuala Lumpur. The linear accelerator allows the center's specialists to provide painless and safe radiotherapy treatment of many types of cancer. MMC's heart center has the personnel and equipment to perform angiograms as an alternative to cardiovascular surgery. The heart center, cancer treatment center, and neurosurgery department are the top three revenue generators for the medical center.

Another feature of MMC is its operating theaters for neurosurgery and cardiac surgery. These enable MMC to provide emergency and trauma response not commonly or readily available in many other private hospitals in Malaysia. This level of specialization sets the platform for potential collaboration with major teaching and research hospitals like the Massachusetts General Hospital through technical and medical exchanges. In addition, the medical center also has an operating theater for urology, which is an indication of the number of such procedures performed at MMC.

Although MMC currently has 288 beds, it has sufficient room to expand to 400 beds should demand for its services increase. MMC's market extends from Malacca to parts of the southern Malay peninsula and even into Sumatra, Indonesia, and Brunei. It estimates that only about 35% of its revenue is attributable to Malacca residents with another 35% attributable to Johor residents and the remainder to patients from Indonesia and Brunei. In fact, the medical center is only a 45-minute direct flight or a two-hour ferry ride from Sumatra or a two-hour drive from Johor Bahru.

MMC also operates a nursing college which offers a diploma course in nursing and post basic nursing training. The diploma course qualifies successful candidates to practice in Malaysia and other Commonwealth countries. At the moment, 160 nurses are in various stages of the three-year training program. The nursing college is a vital source of qualified nurses for MMC and will allow it to ensure that its nurses are properly trained before joining the hospital. With Malaysia currently experiencing a shortage of qualified nursing and paramedical staff, the college ensures that MMC will continue to be able to recruit nurses who are able to provide medical care of the standard required by MMC.

With its seafront location, Malacca can be directly accessed in four hours by daily fast ferry from Dumai and by direct flight from Pekan Baru,

Indonesia. Since the economic downturn, the number of Indonesian patients visiting MMC for medical care has increased dramatically. Interviews with Indonesian patients indicated that preference for medical care has shifted significantly from Singapore to Malaysia because of the high foreign exchange differential between the Indonesian rupiah and the Singapore dollar. Even on a par dollar to dollar basis, the cost of seeking medical care in Malaysia is generally lower if not at par with Singapore, thus adding further incentive for Indonesians to opt for Malaysia over Singapore.

Attesting to this growth, in 1998 alone, the number of Indonesian patients to MMC increased on average 2.2 times between January and December of that year. On a larger scale, the number of Indonesian patients also doubled from 1997's 3,086 patients to 1998's 6,187 patients (refer to Figure 3–1). The growing popularity of MMC in the Indonesian market is encouraging and HMI is confident that MMC will pose a serious challenge to Singapore and even Kuala Lumpur as the medical center and hospital of choice in the region.

Figure 3–1   Annual total of Indonesian patients

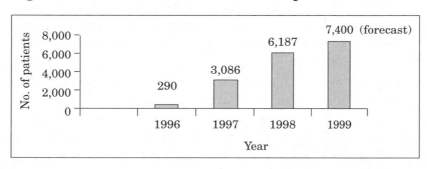

While MMC has been quite successful in capturing its target markets in Indonesia and certain states in Malaysia, it has not been able to substantially penetrate the local Malacca market itself. The management attributes this inequity to the lack of local support in terms of referrals from general practitioners at the primary care level. Another attributing factor is due to Ayer Keroh Medical Center, a competitor in the local private healthcare market, which has the bulk of the older resident specialists whereas MMC's mix consists of younger specialists from other states in Malaysia. The management, however, expects this trend to change as MMC and its team of specialist doctors become more established and more involved in servicing the local market. Table 3–2 shows MMC's financial performance in 1998.

Table 3–2 Financial results of MMC (RM'000)

	1998
Total revenues	58,515
Total cost of sales	33,620
Gross profit	24,805
Profit before tax	266

Hospital Management Concept

MMC adopted a hospital management concept similar to those practiced in Taiwan. Various hospital practices like long hospital stays and strong insurance backed managed healthcare system were adopted. From September 1994 to October 1998, MMC was managed like a Taiwan hospital, unfortunately, it failed to make significant impact despite its modern infrastructure and competitive advantage. HMI is however convinced of MMC's immense potential to be a leading tertiary care hospital in the region. HMI also identified a few key issues which, if managed and addressed properly, could quickly enhance the profitability of its operations.

The most crucial of these issues was to create an identity for the 32 specialists currently operating from within small consultation rooms on the ground and first floors. These consultation rooms are provided rent free by the hospital, thus depriving the hospital, of an alternative income source.

Originally built and equipped for 630 beds, MMC is operating below capacity (averaging 150 beds at any one time). HMI has gazetted three of its floors within the hospital for medical suites, adopting in similar fashion the current practices of private hospitals in Singapore and Kuala Lumpur to be sold or leased out to existing specialists. The move is aimed at generating income from sale or lease of the units to doctors, defraying the maintenance cost for these floors, and freeing the prime ground floor for other purposes such as sale or lease of space for gift and flower shops, retail pharmacy (currently lacking in MMC), cafeteria, banks, and other retail outlets. The introduction of sale or lease of medical suites on the upper floors was initially received with mixed reaction, as this concept was new to the medical industry in Malacca. A number of specialists visited Singapore at HMI's invitation to view similar medical suite setups in Mount Elizabeth Medical Center and Gleneagles Medical Center. Feedback from these doctors was encouraging, as the visits had given them an opportunity to appreciate the benefits of this arrangement.

HMI is now opening up the units for sale to the doctors and will eventually release the units up for lease after those electing to purchase have selected their units.

Apart from the above, HMI has also identified management systems, which could be made more efficient in providing services, information, and education to the public as well as management information systems for decision-making processes. Also in line for change is human resource management through training and re-deployment to minimize overtime and enhance workflow efficiency. Space planning by department to increase sharing of medical equipment and human resources, will be carried out in the later phases of the restructuring of MMC.

Nursing College

Another competitive advantage of significant importance to MMC is its in-house nursing college, which offers recognized nursing qualifications from basic diploma to post-basic specialities. The nursing college provides three major advantages to MMC:

1. With an acute shortage of qualified nurses in the market, nurses bonded with MMC through its college programs ensure MMC of a ready supply of a well-trained and experienced nursing team. The nursing college ensures that MMC will not be pressured by market shortages into compromising its standards in its service delivery.

2. With its pool of nursing students of various training and experience, MMC is currently supplying graduate nurses to other medical facilities for a fee. Income generated is modest but, over time, the management foresees this to be a lucrative spin-off as private hospitals, with their more exacting demands, would prefer to seek nurses trained from other established private hospitals such as MMC.

3. Student nurses are required to undergo on-the-job training which in turn allows for a reduction in the number of permanent staff required to man MMC. The cost savings in the long term are expected to be substantial.

Marketing

Pursuing diligently the Indonesian market, HMI has directed and even made trips to Indonesia's Pekan Baru and Dumai to establish local agencies to promote awareness of MMC and its services. Databases of Indonesian clients have been collated and MMC, under HMI's directions, will be constantly updating these groups through newsletters, which HMI plans to reinstate as a marketing tool.

Concurrent to marketing its services to Indonesia, MMC has another team actively pursuing health education and talks in the states of Negri Sembilan, Malacca, and Johor to create medical awareness and to promote its range of facilities and services to the public. Augmenting its efforts, HMI plans to introduce its highly successful PPO (Preferred Provider Organization) Healthcare Management System to Malaysia through MMC or a related company as a base for corporate referrals to MMC. HMI's PPO which is managed under IHP Pte Ltd currently holds the largest market share in Singapore for managed healthcare with over 45,000 members at the last count.

Future Strategy

HMI management looks at Malaysia as an ideal place for investing in medical centers and hospitals. Already in its expansion pipeline are the following projects:

1. Ipoh Medical Center—This was a stalled hospital project by the Lion Group because of its lack of expertise in hospital management to run it. HMI was invited to review the project objectives, prepare a business plan, and to reactivate the project. Already, a number of specialists have taken positions with the medical center as the hospital is located on prime land in the town center and adjacent to Lion's successful shopping complex, Ipoh Parade. The hospital will be ready and fully commissioned by the third and last quarter of the year 2000.

2. J.B. Medical Center—The center was expected to be completed by end of 1999 or January 2000. It has the support of 18 specialists from various disciplines. The center aims to be a secondary healthcare provider and, in the future, the management has plans to expand the services of the medical center to cater to the rapidly growing Johor Bahru market. Planned for the mid to longer term is a facility designed and constructed to meet the forecast patient load and scope of services to be rendered.

Over the longer haul, the management is targeting markets like Sungei Petani in Kedah, Kuantan in Pahang, and Sabah in East Malaysia to set up secondary care hospitals. The management's objective in investing in operating medical centers and hospitals is to gain leverage from economies of scale and to create a comprehensive referral network for tertiary medical care. Some areas where the management has identified economies of scale are:

1. Operations, accounting, MIS, etc. Cost of duplicating, setting up, and managing systems will be lower.
2. Pharmaceuticals, consumables, laboratory reagents, etc. Collective and central purchasing will be made to extract the best bulk purchasing discounts.

Of immediate concern to HMI's management, however, is the extent its capabilities can be successfully transferred to MMC and its expansion into the region. While it has to continue with its development of a market presence in Singapore, it has to also ensure that it can leverage its know-how and expertise to Malaysia which has very different market characteristics.

Starbucks Coffee:
Expansion in Asia

HISTORY

Starbucks Coffee Company was founded in 1971 by three coffee aficionados. Starbucks, named after the coffee-loving first mate in *Moby Dick*, opened its first store in Seattle's Pike Place Public Market. During this time, most coffee was purchased in a can directly from supermarket shelves. Starbucks' concept of selling freshly roasted whole beans in a specialty store was a revolutionary idea.

In 1987, Howard Schultz, a former Starbucks employee, acquired the company. When Schultz first joined Starbucks in the early 1980s as director of retail operations, Starbucks was a local, highly respected roaster and retailer of whole bean and ground coffees. A business trip to Milan's famous coffee shops in 1983 opened Schultz's eyes to the rich tradition of the espresso beverage. Schultz recalls, "What I saw was the unique relationship that the Italian people had with the ubiquitous coffee bars around Italy. People used the local coffee bar as the third place from home and work. What I wanted to try and do was re-create that in North America." Inspired by the Italian espresso bars, Schultz convinced executives to have Starbucks' stores serve coffee by the cup. And the rest is history!

This case was prepared by Valerie Darguste, Ana Su, Ai-Lin Tu, and Peggy Wei of New York University's Stern School of Business under the supervision of Masaaki Kotabe of The University of Texas, Austin, for class discussion rather than to illustrate either effective or ineffective handling of an administrative situation.

This case was adopted from Masaaki Kotabe and Kristiaan Nelson, *Global Marketing Management*, New York: John Wiley & Sons, Inc Ltd., 1998.

Starbucks went public in 1993 and has done extremely well in turning an everyday beverage into a premium product. The green and white mermaid logo is widely recognized; the brand is defined by not only its products, but also by attitude. It is all about the Starbucks experience, the atmosphere, and the place that is a refuge for most people to get away from everyday stresses. The average customer visits a Starbucks 18 times in a month and about 10% of all customers visit twice a day. Starbucks has created an affinity with customers that is almost cult-like. Today, Starbucks is the leading roaster and retailer of specialty coffee in North America with more than 1,000 retail stores in 32 markets.

MISSION STATEMENT

Starbucks' corporate mission statement is as follows: "Establish Starbucks as the premier purveyor of the finest coffee in the world, while maintaining our uncompromising principles as we grow. The following guiding principles will help us measure the appropriateness of our decisions:

1. Provide a great work environment and treat each other with respect and dignity.
2. Apply the highest standards of excellence to the purchasing, roasting, and fresh delivery of our coffee.
3. Develop enthusiastically satisfied customers all of the time.
4. Contribute positively to our communities and our environment.
5. Recognize that profitability is essential to our future success."

Starbucks' corporate objective is to become the most recognized and respected brand of coffee in the world. To achieve this goal, Starbucks plans to continue to expand its retail operations rapidly in two ways. First, to increase its market share in existing markets and secondly, to open stores in new markets. Starbucks' retail objective is to become a leading retailer and coffee brand in each of its target markets by selling the finest quality coffees and related products. In addition, Starbucks provides a superior level of customer service, thereby building a high degree of customer loyalty.

SALES AND PROFITS

Starbucks' net earnings in 1996 were US$42.1 million, which is a significant increase from the previous year's US$26.1 million earnings (see Figure 4–1). Furthermore, its revenues grew by 575% from US$103.2 million in 1992 to US$696.5 million in 1996 (see Figure 4–2). The increase in revenues and sales was a direct result of the numerous new stores that were opened. During this

Figure 4–1   Net earnings (US$ million)

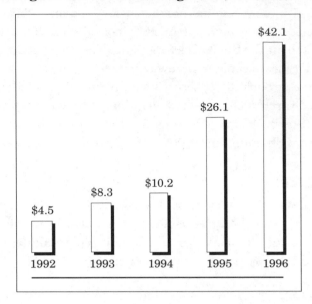

Figure 4–2   Net revenues (US$ million)

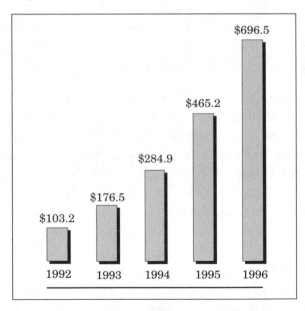

period, Starbucks stores grew 508% from 165 stores to 1,006 stores. But Starbucks has not stopped yet; it plans on opening 325 more stores in 1997.

COMMITMENT TO COFFEE

Starbucks is committed to selling only the finest whole bean coffees and coffee beverages. Starbucks roasts more than 30 varieties of the world's finest Arabica coffee beans, therefore the company goes to extreme lengths to buy the finest Arabica coffee beans available on the world market, regardless of price. Arabica beans have a very refined flavor and contain about 1% caffeine by weight. These beans account for 75% of world production, and are sought by specialty roasters.

To ensure compliance with its rigorous standards, Starbucks is vertically integrated, controlling its coffee sourcing, roasting, and distribution through its company-operated retail stores. It purchases green coffee beans for its many blends and varieties from coffee-producing regions throughout the world and custom roasts them to its exacting standards. Currently, there are three roasting plants in the U.S. Roasts that do not meet the company's rigorous specifications, or beans that remain in bins more than a week, are all donated to charity. Starbucks sells the fresh beans, along with richly brewed coffees and Italian-style espresso beverages, primarily through its company-operated and licensed stores.

COMMITMENT TO THE COMMUNITY

Despite becoming extremely profitable, Starbucks has not lost sight of being socially responsible. Starbucks has contributed to CARE, a non-profit charity organization for the needy in coffee-growing countries, since 1991. As North America's leading corporate sponsor, Starbucks has helped establish health and literacy programs in Guatemala, Indonesia, Kenya, and Ethiopia. This long-term charity program has helped improve living conditions in the coffee-producing countries that Starbucks buys from. It is the company's way of providing assistance to those developing nations which it does business. In addition, in 1996, Starbucks established a Code of Conduct policy, which is the first step in a long-term commitment to improving social conditions in the world's coffee-growing nations.

CURRENT SITUATION

Coffee consumption in the U.S. has climbed to its highest level in nearly a decade. In 1989, there were only 200 specialty coffee stores in the U.S. Today, there are more than 5,000; the Specialty Coffee Association projects 10,000 stores by 1999. The entire coffee market is estimated to be a US$30 billion industry.

In keeping with its corporate mission, Starbucks is expanding its retail outlets at an incredible rate. Most recently, Starbucks has entered several new markets including Toronto, Rhode Island, North Carolina, and Tokyo. In 1997, Starbucks is looking forward to entering Phoenix, Miami, Hawaii, and Singapore, and by the year 2000, Starbucks plans to have 2,000 locations throughout North America. Today, three million people a week visit Starbucks.

In addition to retail operations expansion, the company plans to selectively pursue other opportunities to leverage and grow the Starbucks brand through the introduction of new products and the development of new distribution channels (see Table 4–1). Joint ventures with companies like Dreyer's Grand Ice Cream, Inc., Pepsi-Cola, and Capitol Records have enabled Starbucks to introduce new product lines into the market. In 1994, the company entered into a joint-venture agreement with Pepsi-Cola to develop ready-to-drink coffee products. By the spring of 1996, the company launched a new bottled coffee drink called Frappuccino^{TM}, a low-fat, creamy blend of Starbucks brewed coffee and milk. On October 31, 1995, a long-term joint venture with Dreyer's Grand Ice Cream was announced. The joint venture yielded a premium line of coffee ice creams distributed to leading grocery stores in the U.S. This line has become the number one selling super-premium coffee-flavored ice cream in the nation. Finally, joint ventures with record companies such as Capitol Records have enabled Starbucks to sell customized music CDs in its stores.

Starbucks specialty sales and marketing team has continued to develop new channels of distribution as the company is growing. Its plan to become a nationally known brand is being pushed forward by its 1995 deal with United Airlines, which gives Starbucks exclusive access to 75 million domestic and international travelers. However, the company's goal of expansion does not stop at airports. For two years, Starbucks has been the only coffee brand served in ITT Sheraton Corporate Hotels. In 1996, it also became the coffee of choice in Westin Hotels & Resorts. More recently it formed an alliance with U.S. Office Products to sell Starbucks coffee to offices throughout the U.S. This alliance is a tremendous opportunity for Starbucks to serve the workplace environment, and overall strengthen its customers' relationship with the Starbucks brand. Finally, Starbucks' direct response group launched a new America Online Caffe Starbucks store to sell its products via Internet.

Though profits for Starbucks have increased significantly over the years, there is still cause for the company to be worried. Overall sales are still growing quickly, but the rate of growth is slowing at existing stores. Annual sales growth at stores has slid from 19% in 1993 to 7% in 1996. The biggest cause of sluggish sales growth is attributed to store cannibalization. Starbucks

Table 4-1   Starbucks' business ventures

March 1995	Released *Blue Note Blend* coffee and CD jointly with Capitol Records.
September 1995	First Starbucks retail store opened within an existing and newly opened state-of-the-art Star Markets.
October 1995	Signed an agreement with Sazaby Inc., a Japanese retailer and restauranteur, to form a joint-venture partnership to develop Starbucks retail stores in Japan. The joint venture was called Starbucks Coffee Japan, Ltd. The first store opened in Tokyo in the summer of 1996 and marked Starbucks' first retail expansion outside of North America.
October 1995	A long-term joint venture with Dreyer's Grand Ice Cream was formed to market a premium line of coffee ice creams. Nationwide distribution to leading grocery stores occurred in the spring of 1996.
November 1995	Formed a strategic alliance with United Airlines to become the exclusive coffee supplier on every United flight.
January 1996	The North American Coffee Partnership was formed between Pepsi-Cola and Starbucks New Venture Company, a wholly-owned subsidiary of Starbucks. The partnership announced its plan to market a bottled version of Starbucks' Frappuccino™ beverage.
February 1996	Formed an agreement with Aramark Corp. to put licensed operations at various locations marked by Aramark. The first licensed location opened at the end of 1996.
September 1996	Introduced Double Black Stout™, a new dark roasted malt beer with the aromatic and flavorful addition of coffee with Redhook Ale Brewery.
October 1996	Formed an agreement with U.S. Office Products Company, a nationwide office products supplier to corporate, commercial, and industrial customers. The alliance allowed Starbucks to distribute its freshly roasted coffee and related products to the workplace through U.S. Office Products' extensive North American channels.
1996	Formed a joint venture with Intel Corp. The venture would help push Starbucks into the market of cybercafes.

has been known to open stores within one block of each other in hopes of saturating the market. In addition, growth has also been hurt by poor merchandising efforts that have left many products—like mugs and coffee makers—on display for years.

INTERNATIONAL EXPANSION

With a stable business in North America, Starbucks plans on extensively expanding abroad. Starbucks' international strategy is to utilize two expansion strategies—licensing and joint-venture partnerships. The success of expanding into foreign markets is dependent on Starbucks' ability to find the right local partners to negotiate local regulations and other country-specific issues.

Currently, Starbucks exists in only two foreign countries—Japan and Singapore. The company feels that Asia offers more potential than Europe. According to one executive, "The region is full of emerging markets. Consumers' disposable income is increasing as their countries' economies grow, and most of all, people are open to Western lifestyles." Finally, coffee consumption growth rates in Southeast Asia are estimated to increase between 20% to 30% a year. With this in mind, Starbucks has plans to invest US$10 million in developing its Asian operations and up to US$20 million with its joint-venture partners in Asia. The countries Starbucks is currently looking at include: Taiwan, South Korea, Hong Kong, Malaysia, and Indonesia.

Starbucks does not have a roasting plant in Asia as yet. Instead, one shipment of coffee beans arrives in Asia every other week to supply the company's shops in Singapore and Japan.

JAPAN

On October 25, 1995, Starbucks Coffee International signed a joint-venture agreement with Sazaby Inc., a Japanese retailer and restauranteur, to develop Starbucks retail stores in Japan. The joint-venture partnership is called Starbucks Coffee Japan, Ltd. This alliance proves to be a strong one because it combines two major lifestyle companies that provide the Japanese consumer a new and unique specialty coffee experience. Under this partnership, Starbucks opened its flagship Tokyo store in the upscale Ginza shopping district, its first retail store expansion outside of North America.

Japan is an essential part of Starbucks' international expansion plan because the nation is the third largest coffee consuming country in the world, behind the U.S. and Germany. Japan is also an ideal country because it has the largest economy in the Pacific Rim.

Starbucks currently has 3 stores in Tokyo and is expecting to open 10 to 12 more stores by next September. The stores offer the same menu as the U.S. ones, although portions are smaller. The names of items, such as "tall" and "grande", are also the same as the ones used in the U.S. All of the stores also feature the company's trademark decor and logo. In addition, Japanese customers are able to purchase Starbucks' coffee beans, packaged food, coffee-making equipment as well as fresh pastries and sandwiches.

Currently, Starbucks' Japanese sales are 25% above the originally expected sales figures. On opening day, the Japanese crowded into Starbucks and as many as 200 customers formed lines around the block to get a taste of Starbucks' high-quality coffee. Starbucks hopes to cultivate the same kind of coffee craze in Japan as the one it had created in North America. However, profits from the Japanese venture will not happen for several years. Operating costs, like rent and labor, in Japan are extremely high, and Starbucks will also have to pay for coffee shipment from its roasting facility in Kent to Japan. Retail space rent in downtown Tokyo is also more than double that of Seattle's.

Starbucks plans to eventually open a roasting plant in Japan to help keep costs down. However, this is contingent if the stores in Japan prove to be a success.

SINGAPORE

Economic Background

According to the U.S. Department of State, Singapore, otherwise known as the Lion City, has an annual growth rate (1998—in real terms) of 11%. The country's per-capita income is US$8,782, which is the third highest in Asia after Japan and Brunei. However, Singapore is a country that relies heavily on industry with the industrial sector (including food and beverages) making up about 17% of Singapore's real GDP. It imports about US$44 billion in crude oil, machinery, manufactured goods, and foodstuff from the U.S., European Community, Malaysia, and Japan. In addition, Singapore is constantly looking for new products and new markets to drive its export-led economy. It is attempting to become a complete business center, offering multinationals a manufacturing base, a developed financial infrastructure, and excellent communications to service regional and world markets.

However, 1996 was not a very good year for Singapore. The economy grew by only 7%, which was down from the 8.8% in 1995. The main sector that was hurt by this slow growth was the manufacturing industry, which grew by 3.4%, down from 10% in 1995. In addition, the commerce sector grew by 6% down from 9% in 1995. Analysts claimed that weak economic growth, global competition, and a very slow tourist season made Singapore's retail industry very sluggish. The restaurants and hotels also recorded weak growths.

Despite slow economic growth, domestic demand grew by 12.5% compared to 7.2% in 1995. Total consumption expenditures grew by 10%, compared with 6% in 1995.

Living in Singapore

Singapore has one of the best living conditions in Asia. In 1995, its per-capita GNP was US$15,308.45. Furthermore, Singapore is known for its diversity. There are 3.01 million Singaporeans: ethnic Chinese, Malays, and Indians make up 77%, 14%, and 7% of the population, respectively. The most practiced religions are Buddhism/Taoism (53.9%), Islam (14.9%), Christianity (12.9%), and Hinduism (3.3%). The main languages are Malay, Chinese (Mandarin), Tamil, and English. English is the language of administration, while Malay is the national language.

With a moderately high cost of living, Singaporeans are able to indulge in luxury goods. Much of Singapore's entertainment is influenced by Western culture. For instance, many theaters show Broadway musicals such as *Les Miserables* and pop concerts like Michael Jackson. Television programs are in English, Chinese, Malay, and Tamil. In 1992, pay TV channels such as CNN, Movievision, HBO, and Chinese Variety were introduced.

Singaporeans are known to indulge themselves with food. So discriminating have Singaporeans become on the subject of quality and price that eating has become a national obsession. Singapore has an array of restaurants, coffeehouses, fast-food outlets, and food centers that are easily accessible and offer a variety of foods at affordable prices. Most of these food places are not air-conditioned except for those located in shopping complexes. However, eating in an air-conditioned restaurant, regardless of income level, is an affordable luxury. The average lunch or high tea buffet spread offering a wide variety of dishes is available at many hotel coffeehouses and restaurants, and it costs about $15 (Singaporean currency) or more per person. Most restaurants and coffeehouses impose a 10% service charge, but tipping is not encouraged.

Singapore's Love Affair with Coffee

According to Singaporean social commentator Francis Yim, "Coffeehouses are a sign that Singaporeans have achieved the status of a developed nation and we are breaking new ground in the area of becoming a cultured society." In the past, during the construction of Singapore, Singaporeans did not have the time to enjoy their cup of Java. Regardless of their religion and beliefs, Singaporeans went to coffeehouses in the evenings for their meals and drank coffee in order to keep themselves awake. Now coffee is viewed as a beverage instead of a drink. People want to take the time to savor their coffee. It is not just a drink, but a personality altogether. The various flavors that coffeehouses offer reflect the different moods as well as tastes.

The first Starbucks coffee outlet in Singapore opened on December 14, 1996, in Liat Towers, with the help of BonStar Pte. Ltd., a subsidiary of Bonvests Holding Ltd., a Singaporean company with food services and real estate interests. The store in Liat Towers is located in Singapore's main shopping district in Orchard Road, which is a very trendy shopping area where Planet Hollywood resides. There are plans to open 10 to 12 more Starbucks in Singapore within the next year. The licensing agreement with Starbucks currently only covers Singapore, but Bonvests hopes to expand the franchises into other Asian markets. Starbucks' expansion into Singapore is its first into Southeast Asia. Bonvests Holdings anticipates that the Starbucks retail stores will generate at least US$40 million in sales over the next five to six years.

Bonvests is an ideal partner for several reasons. Bonvests has acquired expertise in running food businesses, like the local Burger King chain. It also knows and understands the local consumer market, government regulations, and the local real estate market.

Starbucks chose Singapore for its entry into the Southeast Asian market because of the highly "Westernized" ideas and lifestyles it had adopted. Some have described Starbucks as being another American icon, like McDonald's. Some even say that Starbucks has created an American coffee cult. Slowly, but surely, gourmet coffee bars have been penetrating into the food scene in Singapore. It is estimated that Singaporeans drink more than 10,000 gourmet cups a day. In addition, the market in Singapore has tremendous growth potential. According to Bruce Rolph, head of research at Saloman Brothers Singapore Pte. Ltd., "People should increasingly focus on Singapore not as a mature market with low earnings and growth potential, but as a uniquely positioned beachhead to get leverage over what's happening in Asia." Finally, the Singaporean market still has no clear leader in the specialty coffee industry. This means that Starbucks still has a good chance to become one of the top contenders in this market.

Despite the opportunities that exist for Starbucks in Singapore, there are still obstacles that Starbucks must overcome to be successful in Singapore. Competition is fierce with 14 players and 38 stores between them (see Table 4–2). With Starbucks' entry into the Asian market, bigger retail stores, like Suntec Dome Holdings, are already gearing up for a coffee battle. However, smaller companies like Burke's Café and Spinelli are welcoming Starbucks' entry. Their strategy is to open an outlet right next to Starbucks to attract the customers that overflow from Starbucks.

One of Starbucks' biggest competitors, Suntec Dome Holdings, has already established itself in Singapore. Suntec Dome Holdings already has a good

Table 4–2 Competitor profiles

Spinelli

Spinelli Coffee Company, long regarded by many as San Francisco's best coffee retailer, has been licensed by Equinox for expansion into Southeast Asia. Equinox is a joint venture between Golden Harvest, a Hong Kong film company, and Singapore Technologies Industrial Corp., a Singapore conglomerate. Seven outlets are expected to be opened in Singapore's central business district by fall of 1997, with up to 40 locations targeted for the region by the year 2000. In addition, Spinelli is also in the process of setting up roasting factories to supply the Asian market. Spinelli brings to Asia years of experience in sourcing, producing, and selling premium coffee drinks and whole bean coffee.

Suntec Dome Holdings

Dome Café is a cafe modeled on European lines and was discovered by a Singaporean lawyer. It is best known for its distinctive sidewalk and atrium cafes, where the food menu is longer than the coffee list. It serves light snacks and full meals all day, from sandwiches made with foccacia (a flat, Italian bread) to exotic entrees like duck and pumpkin risotto. Suntec Dome Holdings was formed in 1996 when Suntec Investment, an investment vehicle for a group of Hong Kong tycoons, bought a 51% stake in the Dome chain. Ronald Lee and Sebastian Ong, founders of Dome, imported the European-styled Dome concept from Australia. They are expecting to increase the number of outlets from 7 to 17 within three years, an estimated US$7 million is expected to be allocated for the expansion of outlets. Plans to build more roasting plants to distribute Dome's coffee in Asia are to follow, though roasting factories in Singapore and Australia exist already. Their growth strategy is to expand into several Asian countries, with 6 outlets within two years in Malaysia. Plans for further expansion into Indonesia, Thailand, Hong Kong, and China are in the development stage.

Coffee Club

Established coffee trading company Hiang Kie, now 60 years old, sniffed out the gourmet coffee trend and whipped up its first outlet in Holland Village in 1991. There are 37 variations, from the humble Kopi Baba to the spicy, vintage tones of Aged Kalossi Coffee. The best attraction is the Iced Mocha Vanilla—Macciato coffee and milk topped with vanilla ice cream and a drizzle of chocolate syrup. In addition, it serves light meals of cakes, salads, sandwiches, and home-made ice cream.

Coffee Connection

Coffee Connection is the latest, trendier incarnation of Suzuki Coffee House, started in the 1980s by Sarika Coffee to showcase its Suzuki Coffee Powder. So far it is the mothership of coffee bars, with 69 different drinks ranging from cool coffee jelly to Bleu Mountain Chaser. The best attraction is the Cappuccino Italiano—espresso infused with hot milk, topped with a frothy milk cap, and dusted lightly with chocolate powder. It also serves ice cream, pasta, pizza, and foccacia sandwiches.

Burke's Coffee

The origins of Burke's Coffee started with four Singaporean students who studied in Seattle, liked the espresso bars, and brought back the concept. Burke's Coffee is a Seattle-styled cafe, bringing the lifestyle of the Pacific Northwest to Singapore. Burke's has made a name for itself as a friendly and inviting place in the midst of the hustle and bustle of downtown Singapore. The store has established a loyal customer base of young professionals who visit the store frequently. Burke's serves sandwiches, soups, and desserts. There are seven basic coffee drinks, plus 12 Italian syrups that you can add on request. The best attractions are the Mocha Freeze and Hazelnut Latte.

name recognition with Suntec Walk, Suntec City, Dome Cafe, and so on. Suntec is distinctive from the other retail coffee stores in that it is seen more as a restaurant than a coffee chain. It targets a broader market segment with a lower budget range. It is also backed by major supporters with the capital to counter Starbucks' expansion strategy. In addition to Singapore, Suntec Dome Holdings has plans to expand to other markets such as Malaysia, Indonesia, Thailand, Hong Kong, and China. Spinelli, a smaller competitor, also plans to expand into the region. With these plans of expansion to be completed by the year 2000, Spinelli will be potentially a major threat to Starbucks.

More well-known coffee spots to Singaporeans are Coffee Connection and Coffee Club, which are also direct competitors of Starbucks. The customers that go to Coffee Connection and Coffee Club like the atmosphere and the service they receive there. As reflected here, Singapore has seen a proliferation of gourmet coffee outlets in the past few years, therefore, the market is slowly becoming overcrowded.

Starbucks will need to turn some heads and create the brand equity they need to stay in competition. However, they do have an advantage entering this market. Starbucks packages a coffee-drinking experience that the Singaporeans want, both trendy and American. As mentioned earlier, Singaporeans love American products and, hopefully, that will translate into major dollars for Starbucks in Singapore.

Starbucks faces a challenge in Singapore amid a prolonged and still-deepening crisis in the retail industry. Major retailers, like Kmart and France's Galeries Lafayette, have recently left Singapore after much failure.

De Beers: Diamonds are for Asia

Diane arrived in Hong Kong from London on a July morning to stay with her friend, Emily Chan, for a few days. She had never been out of Europe, but she had got to know the Chinese girl pretty well during the three years they worked together in a fashionable retail store in London. Now Emily works for a Hong Kong property developer. Diane was looking forward to meeting Emily's husband, C.Y. Apparently he came from the same comfortable middle-class Hong Kong Chinese background as Emily.

Diane and Emily sat down to watch the video of the latter's wedding, which had taken place earlier that year, in February 1998. It looked an elegant affair, and Emily was wearing a fantastic diamond ring which she had already described in letters to Diane. "But why aren't you wearing your ring now?" asked Diane. "Oh, I certainly wouldn't wear it every day, it's far too valuable for that. I wore it for the first time on my wedding day of course, but only on one or two special occasions since then," replied Emily.

Diane was puzzled: "But I wear my engagement ring every day, and I'll go on wearing it every day after Mark and I get married. It's a token of his love for me and that's why I wear it all the time." Emily laughed, "Things aren't quite like that here, you know. We don't go around talking about love all the time, like you Westerners do! I can show you the ring later if you'd like, but first see what you think about this."

This case was prepared by Jocelyn Probert and Hellmut Schütte as the basis for class discussion rather than to illustrate either effective or ineffective handling of an administrative situation.

Jocelyn Probert is Research Analyst and Hellmut Schütte is Professor of International Management at INSEAD Europe-Asia Center.

"This" was a smart looking solitaire diamond pendant peeping through the neck of Emily's blouse. "That's gorgeous!" cried Diane, "Was it a birthday present from C.Y.?" "No, of course not! I bought it for myself. I've worked really hard this past year, the bonuses were good, and I thought I deserved a present from myself. C.Y. didn't mind at all when I showed it to him, he thought it was a great idea. A couple of girls in the office bought themselves diamonds too."

"Well," reflected Diane, "people certainly do behave differently around here. I can't imagine buying a diamond for myself. That's up to Mark to give me a surprise one day." She could not imagine walking into a jewelry shop and choosing something like that by herself. Anyway, she would not know how to recognize a good diamond.

THE DE BEERS STORY

The brilliance and beauty of diamonds have tantalized and excited the rich and powerful for centuries. No two diamonds are alike, which adds to the aura and mystique that surround them. They are the ultimate luxury product. Even Nicky Oppenheimer, chairman of De Beers, has said, "Unique among major raw materials, the gem diamond has no material use to man."[1]

Only 20% of the diamonds mined each year are of gem quality, i.e., with a minimum weight of 0.2 carats. Near-gems, accounting for 30% of annual diamond production, are smaller, lower quality stones weighing less than 0.2 carats. The rest are industrial-grade diamonds, which are widely used in precision cutting and grinding machinery.

Gem diamonds are valued on the basis of four criteria, known as the 4Cs—carat, clarity, color, and cut. Although carat is the best known, all four criteria have a bearing on the value of an individual diamond. Assuming cut, clarity, and color are equally good, the price of a one-carat diamond will be more than twice that of a half-carat stone because fewer than 0.5% of all gem diamonds weigh one carat (200 milligrams) or more. Valuing a diamond is a highly skilled task, which partly explains why diamonds are not traded on world commodity markets in the same way as precious metals such as gold, platinum, or silver.

The "Diamond Pipeline"

The De Beers name is intimately linked with the development of the diamond industry through its involvement in all stages of the "diamond pipeline"

---

[1] Quoted in Bristol Lan Voss's "The Diamond Business Gets Rough," *Journal of Business Strategy*, July/August 1998.

(Figure 5–1). It is the largest diamond mining organization in the world, producing about half of the world's gem diamonds. Its Central Selling Organization (CSO) sells rough diamonds but De Beers does not cut or polish the stones itself, nor does it make or sell diamond jewelry. Its Consumer Marketing Division (CMD) promotes diamond jewelry for the industry as a whole, as a means of stimulating demand for rough diamonds.

Figure 5–1   The diamond pipeline

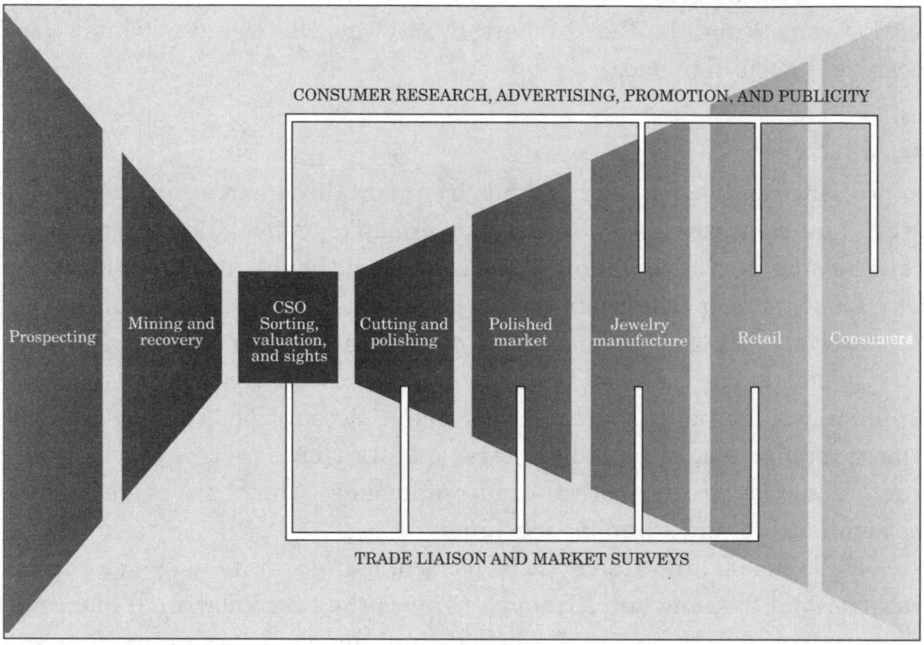

Source: De Beers.

De Beers established CSO in 1934 to manage the supply of rough diamonds to world markets, eliminate price fluctuations, and maintain public confidence in the value of diamonds as a luxury product. For over 60 years CSO has bought rough diamonds from producing nations and in the open market as well as handled De Beers' own mining output. At the CSO offices in London the rough diamonds are sorted into 14,000 categories based on the 4Cs described earlier. Approximately 160 "sightholders"—leading diamond cutters and polishers or dealers from all over the world—gather in London ten times a year to attend "sights," at which they buy rough diamonds which will eventually be cut and traded, and then turned into jewelry.

In 1997, the CSO's "single channel marketing" system accounted for 65%–70% of world diamond production. It cannot influence the flow to the market of diamonds mined by non-users of CSO, such as Argyle in Australia which is the world's largest source of near-gems.[2] In times of recession, when demand for diamonds and diamond jewelry falls, De Beers continues to buy rough diamonds but reduces the volume that reaches the world's trading centers by holding back supplies at the "sights." In response to the Asian crisis which began in July 1997, CSO reduced sales of rough diamonds by nearly half during the first six months of 1998.

The final contribution of De Beers to the "diamond pipeline" is the promotion of diamond jewelry for the industry, through advertising campaigns developed from extensive market research, trade promotion activities, and jewelry design competitions. CMD spends approximately US$200 million per year on this activity. By 1998, advertising campaigns were being conducted in 34 countries across the world and in 21 different languages.

In 1995, worldwide sales of polished diamonds were US$9 billion. In jewelry form they were worth US$45 billion. According to De Beers, the global retail market for diamond jewelry rose by 40% more than the rate of inflation between 1980 and 1997. CSO has raised rough diamond prices by 50% between 1986 and 1998. Retail prices of gem diamonds remained stable despite the financial crisis in Asia, whereas near-gem prices fell 20% in the wake of substantial over-supply from Russia and Australia.[3]

A Diamond Is Forever

The global message to consumers from De Beers is that a diamond is a gift of love. In one of the most enduring advertising campaigns in the world, it has used since 1938 the slogan "A Diamond is Forever," a phrase which not only echoes the durability of a diamond but also appeals to the emotional attachment of the owner to the stone. According to Charles Stanley, London-based marketing director for Japan, "The traditions and cultural imperatives that exist in all countries are opportunities for De Beers to propose a gift of

---

[2] The discovery of the Argyle mine led to the development in the 1980s of the much less expensive near-gem diamond jewelry market. Argyle sold its rough diamonds through CSO until 1996, when it decided to handle its own marketing. De Beers has promoted only larger gem diamonds in its advertising since 1996.

[3] The Russian government signed a new contract with De Beers at the end of 1997, after a year of operating outside CSO. De Beers has handled Russia's diamonds for over 40 years. The Argyle mine remains outside CSO.

love." The gift of a diamond engagement ring before marriage is a custom thoroughly embedded in the U.S. and Europe.

The "gift of love" emotion, according to the worldwide director of CMD, Stephen Lussier, "Is a powerful cultural position that separates diamonds from the herd of luxury goods.... There are commonalities in diamond perceptions more than there are differences. Elements of the cocktail vary, necessitating different marketing approaches, but the fundamental dream is the same. So we take a global approach as our starting point but we are culturally sensitive to opportunity in each market."

That global market positioning of love and the diamond engagement ring is crucial for CMD to fulfill its business objective of maximizing the profit of CSO. The diamond content and value of an engagement ring are normally much higher than for other pieces of diamond jewelry because the stone will be a solitaire rather than one or several smaller diamonds in multi-stone pieces such as eternity rings. Once the diamond engagement ring custom is culturally embedded, De Beers extends its "gift of love" positioning to other events or rites of passage, such as a youngster's coming of age, or a couple's 25th wedding anniversary. By the 1990s, 80% of all diamond jewelry sold in the West was given as a present. Very few Western women bought their own diamonds.

DE BEERS ENTERS ASIA

In the mid-1960s, De Beers considered that the rise in personal incomes in Japan was sufficiently rapid, and attitudes to Western ideas sufficiently open, for it to promote diamond jewelry. It entered the Japanese market with the same "gift of love" positioning that it had used in the West.

The growth in demand for diamond jewelry was such that, by the late 1980s when De Beers was considering entering other Asian markets, Japan was taken as the development model. It had become the second largest market in the world for diamond jewelry, behind the U.S. Ownership rates were very high. Moreover, the average price of every piece sold was more than twice that of the U.S. or Europe because the size and quality of the diamonds used were so much greater.

Developing Demand for Diamond Jewelry in Japan

The diamond engagement ring. Because the "gift of love" positioning is so central to the De Beers global strategy, the first promotional focus in Japan was on diamond engagement rings. Advertising campaigns communicated the emotional qualities of a diamond and established clear motivational factors for purchase with such phrases as the "ultimate precious stone," "a beauty unmatched by other gemstones," and "contemporary and modern." All these descriptions were highly relevant to the institution of marriage.

De Beers' strategy was to endow diamonds with a symbolism that fitted into an existing social custom. In Japan, the ideal entry point was the *yuino*, or traditional engagement ceremony, which proved to be an enduring institution despite the decline of arranged marriages. In 1991, even though only 10% of couples went through an arranged marriage, more than three-quarters had a *yuino* ceremony. Traditionally the gifts exchanged during the *yuino* did not include a ring of any kind, but the custom had entered from the West during the postwar years. De Beers' challenge was to make new brides expect a diamond ring rather than one with a pearl or other gemstones.

The first cinema advertisement De Beers aired in Japan showed a Hollywood scene that did not in any way reflect the reality of life for young people in Japan in the 1960s. Nevertheless, it appealed to the Japanese fascination with all Western things at that time. The proportion of women receiving a diamond engagement ring at the *yuino* grew from zero to a peak of 76% in 1994 (Figure 5–2), even more than in the U.S. (Figure 5–3), as

Figure 5–2 The percentage of Japanese brides receiving diamond engagement rings

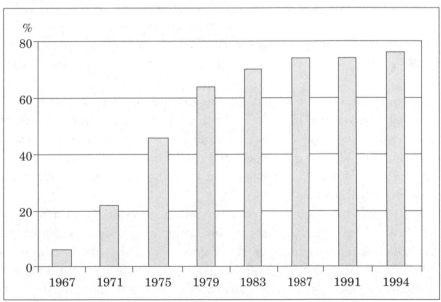

Source: De Beers.

Figure 5–3 The percentage of brides acquiring diamond engagement rings or jewelry, 1991

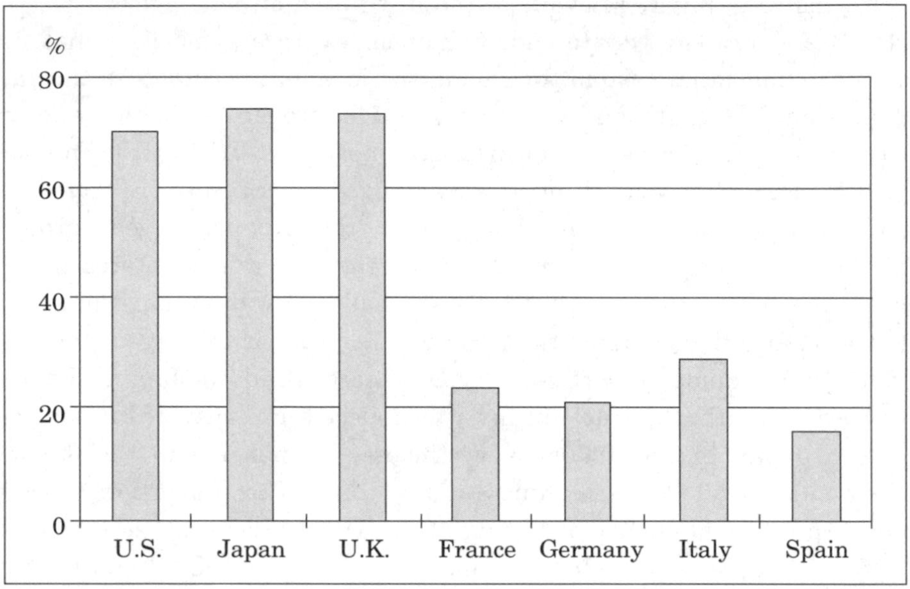

Source: De Beers.

families realized the status value such a ring endowed. A family that gave a diamond to the bride was obviously well-to-do. However, unlike in the West, Japanese women only wore their diamond engagement rings on a few special occasions after the wedding day, partly because of the impracticality of the most popular design, the *tatezume* (commonly known in the West as the Tiffany setting).

The economic downturn that Japan entered in 1991 demonstrated the recession-proof nature of De Beers' "gift of love" positioning. Discretionary purchases could be postponed, but the diamond engagement ring market held steady as soon-to-be-married couples and their families adhered to custom and the expectations of society. De Beers had seen the same thing happen during economic downturns in the U.S.

Several years later, with the economy still in recession, a number of social changes were beginning to emerge, including a reaction by young people against the formal traditions of the *yuino*, which in turn began to affect attitudes toward diamond engagement rings. By 1996, diamond engagement ring acquisition rates had plunged to only 64% among couples getting married. Encouraged by declarations in the media from several celebrities, more and more couples were rejecting the formality of the *yuino* and its implied social conformity in favor of *jimi-kon*, a plainer, less elaborate way of getting married. *Jimi-kon* weddings did not include diamond engagement rings.

This raised the fundamental question whether people in Japan had ever accepted diamonds as a "gift of love." Perhaps they had only bought diamond engagement rings because this was what conformity to the tradition of the *yuino* had demanded. De Beers' consumer surveys had shown for a long time that only around 40% of women approaching engagement thought of diamonds as a "symbol of love," a far lower percentage than in the U.S. When the key societal pressure of conformity weakened, the Japanese people did not reject the idea of diamonds *per se*; they simply wanted to save on the expense of an engagement ring, which De Beers had been telling them for a decade should cost three months of the bridegroom's salary.[4]

The salary guideline had worked well in the booming 1980s, but the mood in the 1990s was quite different. De Beers had to revise its approach, to make the woman feel that a diamond was "a meaningful symbol of his true, everlasting feelings for her" rather than a symbol of social conformity. How could it arrest the decline in diamond wedding ring acquisition rates as well as a noticeable fall in both diamond size and average price paid?

Other diamond jewelry in Japan. The engagement ring segment accounted for only 20% of diamond jewelry sales in Japan at the end of the 1980s. Women's diamond jewelry covered many different categories and age ranges, from 20-year-olds upward. One issue De Beers faced in Japan after the boom years of the 1980s was the "democratization" of the diamond, since acquisition rates were rather high. Many married women bought diamonds for themselves with the agreement of their husbands, as they were in charge of the family finances and knew what the household could afford. Young working women, still living at home before getting married, also bought themselves diamonds.

For De Beers, the 35 to 54 age range was the core target group among married women. This group bought more expensive pieces than the younger ones, and the population of Japan was aging rapidly. Younger women bought jewelry more for adornment. The average diamond jewelry prices paid by the under-35 group were relatively low (around US$860), and half the pieces cost

---

[4] The concept of setting salary guidelines to tell people how much to spend on a particular item was established decades ago in Japan. When De Beers adopted the practice, it proved so successful in raising the value of diamond engagement rings purchased that the idea was also introduced in its U.S. and European advertising, with a similar result.

less than US$350. De Beers hoped to find suitable triggers to motivate these young women to buy a special piece, at a higher price, as a reward for a particular achievement.

There was definitely such a thing in Japan as a diamond that was "too big." Perfection, rather than size or ostentation, was the key criterion. Stones of more than 0.5 carats were perceived as less wearable. Compared with the U.S., dressing habits remained rather formal. De Beers wanted women to feel that diamonds were appropriate to wear for the office. It launched a new positioning called "Simple Diamond" which sought to give women an extra justification for buying diamonds: they could be worn every day.

Discretionary purchases of diamond jewelry in Japan were badly hit in the somber economic environment of the 1990s. Nevertheless, in 1998, Japan was still the world's second largest diamond market with 22%–23% of diamond sales worldwide. Average prices paid were still over US$1,300. The question for De Beers was, how could it recover the crucial link with love that distinguished diamonds from other luxury goods, and re-establish the diamond engagement ring tradition, but in a less formal way?

Expanding into East and Southeast Asia

In the mid-1980s, De Beers began to devote considerable advertising resources to East Asia to capitalize on several trends: rapid economic growth; a youthful population, attitudinally different from their parents, who would be the diamond buyers of the future; an expanding group of newly wealthy people ("new" money was more readily spent to demonstrate success than "old" money); urbanization, which encouraged the spread of modern ideas; openness to change, compared with ingrained attitudes in Western countries; and the presence of jewelry retailers operating on narrow margins and high inventory turns, in contrast to Western jewelers' high margins and low turns.

De Beers' managers at first handled Asia from the consumer marketing division's offices in London. Account executives based in the Asian offices of J. Walter Thompson, the advertising agency De Beers used worldwide, commissioned surveys in each country on social trends, gift-giving occasions, attitudes toward diamonds, motivations for purchase, and acquisition rates, from which they developed advertising campaigns. Finally, in 1994, a De Beers regional office was opened in Hong Kong, the only location outside London for the consumer marketing division, in order to put its managers more closely in touch with regional trends. At the same time, May Wong was hired as the Asia-Pacific regional marketing director in London to be the "Asian voice" and "query how the questions are asked," as she expressed it. Previous surveys into diamond-buying motivations had shown some cultural bias in the way that questions were phrased.

Understanding the markets. A key issue for De Beers was that "Asia" was not a homogenous region, and there was no such person as an "Asian consumer." The more De Beers learned about the different markets through its survey and market research activities, the more it became apparent that pan-regional campaigns would not work. Purchasing motivations were driven by different historical and cultural influences. There were sufficient similarities across cultures on which to build regional brand strategies, but equally there were many local nuances to take into account for individual country advertising. Chinese-language commercials, for example, had to be in several forms, to cater to Mandarin or Cantonese speakers, and to readers of complex or simplified Chinese characters.[5]

In general, the role of jewelry had always been important in Asia. Often a gift of jewelry marked a rite of passage, such as when a girl entered womanhood, got married, or came of age. It was an important part of the inheritance traditionally passed from mother to daughter, and older women would often buy jewelry specifically for this reason. Spare family resources tended to be invested in jewelry in case of emergency or for inheritance purposes. In Asia, the jewelry a woman owned was crucial if she were to be widowed or divorced, as she would get nothing from her husband's family. Jewelry was therefore a store of wealth. However, this was more true of gold, which was readily tradable and valued by weight, than of diamonds, where the value lay in the quality of the stone. For women, jewelry was an expression of self-enhancement, a symbol of femininity. Throughout the region, large, "showy" gemstone jewelry was an important means of demonstrating the status of the wearer and the family.

Jewelry traditions varied across Asia, however. In Korea, Taiwan, Hong Kong, China, and Singapore, people primarily viewed jewelry as a store of wealth. Very little jewelry was worn with traditional Chinese clothing. Korean jewelry traditions centered on the wedding, for which the mother-in-law would buy the *haam*, several sets of jewelry comprising necklace, bracelet, earrings, and ring (and whose designs modern brides generally disliked). In the

---

[5] In Hong Kong, people spoke Cantonese and read complex Chinese characters; in Taiwan, Mandarin was spoken and complex characters written; in Singapore, Mandarin was spoken and simplified characters used, and the Chinese in Malaysia spoke Mandarin and wrote complex characters. In China, Mandarin was spoken, along with 72 dialects, and simplified characters were used.

Southeast Asian countries of Thailand, the Philippines, Malaysia, and Indonesia the desire for adornment influenced jewelry wearing habits, to the extent that "they don't feel dressed without it," according to Fiona Hindmarsh, regional strategic planning director for De Beers at JWT in Hong Kong. In the Philippines, where Spanish and American influences coupled with Christian beliefs were strong, people bought a lot of small, low-quality stones and wanted matching sets of rings and earrings. In predominantly Muslim countries like Malaysia, on the other hand, because the *zakat*, or Islamic wealth tax, did not apply to jewelry people bought expensive pieces. Jewelry designs in Thailand were beautiful and delicate, and used locally mined rubies, emeralds, and sapphires.

Psychological differentiation showed that although people in Hong Kong appeared to have very modern attitudes, inwardly they were highly traditional with strong adherence to such Chinese values as filial piety and respect for elders. Singaporeans tended to be less "showy" in their wealth and demonstrations of status than other Chinese-based cultures; they liked to think of themselves as cosmopolitan, and were very much influenced by international events. The distinguishing feature of Taiwan was the financial emancipation of women, who increasingly sought "modern" marriages to match their own self-confidence.

De Beers' research revealed clearly the distinction between "modern" and "traditional" women throughout the region (Table 5–1). At first, De Beers distinguished these two groups by age (above or below 35), but later realized that the significant factor was their outlook on life, not how old they were. Women could be "modern" even though they were married and over the age of 35, while some "traditionals" were unmarried and in their 20s. Age no longer determined behavior as much in Asia as it used to, although both men and women still felt pressured to marry at a suitable age. The purchasing motivations of the "traditional" and the "modern" women were completely different. The "modern" women was far more likely to buy diamond jewelry for herself. Her "traditional" counterpart was more likely to buy gold or jade.

Attitudes toward love, romance, and marriage in Asia were also rather different. There was some difficulty in talking about love ("I don't say 'I love you' a lot. It depends on the occasion, but she likes to hear it. It's a hassle," responded one unmarried Hong Kong man during a survey). As for romance, in some languages (Chinese, Thai, Malay, and Korean) the word did not exist, suggesting that it was a Western concept new to these cultures. People thought of romance as the outward expression of love and did not expect it to last after marriage, when they had responsibilities.

Table 5–1   Target audiences in Asia: "Traditional" and "modern" women

Traditional singles	Modern singles
<ul><li>Family piety and authority are very strong.</li><li>She lives at home and will be happy to move to her parents-in-law's home once she is married.</li><li>She works to fill time between school and becoming a wife.</li><li>She enjoys spending her money on fun and fashionable things, but is very careful not to be seen as wasteful or wanton.</li><li>She is careful to be sure she is always seen in a good light for a potential husband.</li></ul>	<ul><li>She is a loyal daughter who (usually) lives at home, but she can be outspoken and headstrong in her views and desires. At heart, her family values remain strong, but she tempers them with her need for independence.</li><li>Work is an important part of achieving independence. She wants a career so she can prove this to herself, her family, and friends.</li><li>She enjoys spending money as it is part of the manifestation of her independence and confidence. She buys items that can be seen by her friends and colleagues.</li><li>She wants to get married, but the right man will have to prove himself of being worthy (including having prospects and money).</li></ul>
Traditional married women	Modern married women
<ul><li>She sees herself as an extension of her husband and family, she is a devoted and caring wife, mother, and daughter.</li><li>If she works, her priority is her family. Work gives her a social context and is economically-driven.</li><li>Her self-worth and validation are based on her husband and family doing well. She takes great pride in seeing them succeed.</li><li>She feels guilty spending money on herself, unless it is approved of by her husband and money is spent primarily to give her husband/family face (status).</li></ul>	<ul><li>She sees herself as a woman who has two responsibilities:<ul><li>to her husband and family (her priority) *and*</li><li>to herself.</li></ul></li><li>She validates herself on her personal success and the success of her husband and family.</li><li>She has confidence in knowing her own self-worth.</li><li>She does not feel guilty spending money (her money) on herself. It is important for her to feel good and look good.</li><li>She is a caring, loving, and devoted wife, mother, and daughter.</li></ul>

Source: J. Walter Thompson, "Asia Pacific Diamond Consumers," Hong Kong, June 1998.

In Asia, relationships with the extended family tended to be close, even in outwardly modern places like Hong Kong: "I really couldn't adjust to it in the beginning. I only wanted to stay in the world of the two of us but he goes home to see his mother every day," was the way one young married woman expressed it. May Wong commented, "There is a perception in the West that if you are a traditional you spend time with your family. But in Hong Kong people always spend time with their family on Sundays, even if they have a high-powered job every other day. Core beliefs don't change as fast or in the way that Westerners think."

Market positioning. Through interviews with many women across Asia De Beers sought to discover the motivations underlying diamond purchases and the benefits these women anticipated from wearing diamonds.

Based on these findings, De Beers adopted a two-pronged brand positioning. The "love" positioning focused on diamond wedding rings, which better fit local traditions than the idea of an engagement ring in Japan. In parallel—and after much internal debate—it created the "women's desire" campaign to appeal specifically to the Asian self-purchase market.[6] This segment represented a major difference between markets across Asia and those in the West and had major implications for De Beers' strategy. Research showed that women in Asia appreciated getting gifts, but did not want to wait to own a diamond. Clearly, if De Beers were to project only a "gift of love" message that suggested women should not buy diamonds for themselves, it risked alienating a large part of its potential market.

The key to all diamond communication messages was to find the right balance between aspiration and relevance. Diamonds were perceived as glamorous, but to portray them being worn with ballgowns made them irrelevant to Asian women's lifestyles. On the other hand, diamonds should keep their special aura, the "diamond dream." "People feel beautiful and special because of the physical attributes of the diamond: its beauty, which confers beauty on the wearer (and distracts from the wrinkles, some say!), and its sparkle. Other gems, or jade, or gold, don't sparkle, so other people will notice if you're wearing one," explained Fiona Hindmarsh. "It's not so much about feeling loved, it's about your status within your peer group. If you're a 'modern' woman you feel confident and successful; if you're a 'traditional', you feel valued and proud" (Figure 5–4).

---

[6] A third, much more limited campaign was "diamonds for men," for which there was clearly a market in Taiwan, China, Indonesia, the Philippines, and Thailand. De Beers wanted to embed the idea of diamonds for men in these countries before the "feminization" of diamonds took over as it had in Western countries.

Figure 5–4 The diamond dream

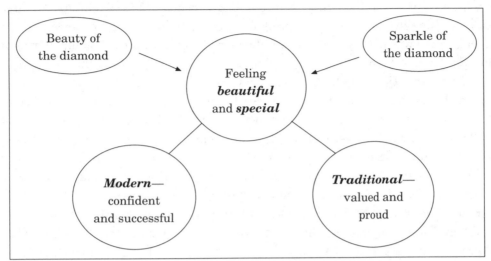

Source: J. Walter Thompson, "Asia Pacific Diamond Consumers," Hong Kong, June 1998.

Sparkle—and size, which reflected status—counted, even for diamond wedding rings. Surveys showed that people in Asia could repeat De Beers' "gift of love" message, but only because they knew it from the advertisements. In the U.S. women had an emotional attachment to their diamond rings which Asian women lacked, and this was in spite of the fact that American men gave their brides smaller stones of lower quality than their Asian counterparts. Few women in Asia expressed an emotional motivation for wanting a diamond wedding ring, instead they were driven by peer recognition and status ("All my friends got a diamond when their boyfriends proposed to them. They will admire me if I have a big stone.").

The "love" positioning was nevertheless the basis of all De Beers' Asian wedding ring advertisements. It was played out in the social context of marriage because of the importance of the extended family. Test commercials showing only the relationship between the bride and groom—which was the normal presentation in Western markets—had not been well accepted anywhere in Asia. One of De Beers' most successful advertisements for the diamond wedding ring was called Rainshower, which was based on a Korean folk-tale. It showed a little boy and girl playing happily together until forced to separate, only to meet again years later and marry. The advertisement worked very well throughout the region except for China, where it was thought to be too romantic.[7] There was no attempt to establish a salary guideline for spending on a wedding ring. Far too many people worked outside regular salaried employment, as entrepreneurs, for it to have any meaning. Even people on low monthly salaries would buy a high-quality diamond: it was a family-driven purchase.

The execution of De Beers' "women's desire" message differentiated between "modern" and "traditional" attitudes. A highly popular and effective television commercial shown across the region (in different languages) until 1996 was called Sparks. Aimed at young "moderns," it showed three young women enjoying themselves in a coffee shop, teasing a young man at another table by letting the light catch on their diamond ring or pendant, with the voiceover saying, "For me, for now, for ever." A newer version, aimed at the "traditionals" again featured a coffee shop and a group of women of unidentifiable age, one of whom was wearing a diamond ring. This time, the voiceover stated, "Only a little more, but they said I have so much more."

De Beers found that once a woman owned one diamond it lowered the barriers for future purchase. A critical issue, therefore, was to lower the barriers for first-time purchasers. This involved not only providing justifications for purchase ("I deserve it") but encouraging jewelry retailers to be more customer-friendly, for example, by showing prices in the shop windows, making security guards less obtrusive, and having available plenty of literature explaining the 4Cs.

Results in East and Southeast Asia. In terms of volume, women's self-purchase diamond jewelry accounted for up to 60% of total sales in every Asian country except Korea. There, because of the importance of the *haam* wedding set market, 80% of diamonds bought were for weddings. By the late 1990s, more than half of Korean brides were receiving diamonds in their *haam*.

Overall penetration rates by 1998 were still not high except in Singapore, where 54% of the target population (women over the age of 18) owned a diamond. In Taiwan, only 34% of the women targeted had a diamond. In the U.S., Europe, and Japan, ownership rates were in the 70%–80% range, largely because of the engagement ring tradition. Many "moderns" in Asia were still non-owners.

Reflecting the low ownership rates, the total diamond jewelry retail value of Asian countries was relatively small except in Korea, which ranked fourth

---

[7] Rainshower was shown in Korean cinemas, targeting young couples; a separate print campaign was directed at the groom's mother, who actually chose and bought the wedding jewelry.

in 1996 behind the U.S., Japan, and Italy. However, in terms of average prices, number of carats per piece of jewelry, and diamond value per carat, countries like Korea, Taiwan, Hong Kong, and Singapore were much bigger than any Western country. This was partly because the size of the stone was so important as a status symbol. People wanted the biggest stone they could afford. A second critical factor was that jewelry manufacturers in Asia were often also the retailers, and margins were therefore much lower. Purchasers of jewelry could get much more for their money in Asia than anywhere else in the world.

Entering China

De Beers started investigating China in 1986, with awareness-raising seminars for the trade and television documentaries for consumers while building relationships with people in the government. "We took a politically conscious approach, stressing our long-term vision—we talked about the year 2010—and our wish to be good corporate citizens. We asked them, "What can we do for you?"" explained Jonathon Pudney, the marketing director formerly in charge of China. In the early 1990s it started working closely with Beijing on measures to help the jewelry industry develop, and on diamond certification standards (since counterfeiting was a problem). "Our corporate governance programme paid off," remarked Pudney. "We had been concerned that the government would brand us as anti-social." National gem standards were introduced in 1996, requiring all diamonds to be certified by an authorized gem center.

Consumer knowledge about diamonds in the early 1990s was limited to scientific facts. In line with the tradition of buying gold as a store of value, gold jewelry dominated jewelers' sales. Any demand for diamonds was restricted to the government and business elite. De Beers' advertising campaigns aimed to change this, broadening demand to the top 20%–30% of the population.

Geographically, the focus in 1993–94 was on the relatively rich cities of Guangdong, Fujian, and Shanghai. Later, Beijing, Tianjin, Chengdu, and other regional cities were added. De Beers found that the diamond acquisition threshold in China was a household income of Rmb2000 (US$250) per month. Around half the population in Shanghai had such an income, 60% of the people in Guangdong, and 25% in Chengdu. By 1998, De Beers was advertising in 17 of China's more than 800 cities, yet reaching 50% of the value of the diamond market. The dilemma was how to target long- and short-term opportunities in Shanghai without forgetting the 50% of sales that took place outside the targeted cities.

In line with the regional strategy, the diamond wedding ring was the key to entering the market: China was expecting to celebrate over two million marriages in 1994. "We have to establish the diamond wedding ring first. Unless we give diamonds a love positioning, they are just another status symbol," commented Seth Grossman, account planner for De Beers in JWT's Shanghai office. A second marketing campaign targeted married women who had not received a diamond wedding ring.

Positioning the diamond wedding ring. The question De Beers had to face was, what did "love" mean in the China context?

Research revealed that attitudes to love and marriage in China were considerably more materialistic than elsewhere in the region. A survey of the X-Generation (18 to 28-year-olds) jointly commissioned in 1996 by De Beers and a number of other Western firms showed that this generation used wealth as the key criterion for judging success, even to the extent of choosing their friends based on perceptions of the status of others' families. Peer admiration was essential. It was not clear to these young people whether power or wealth came first, but the trappings of wealth included major foreign brands, a large house, and diamonds. Success was important because it led to self-recognition and the recognition of others (Figure 5–5). Marriage was a partnership toward achieving future success. Motivations in China were driven more by status than emotions, to an extent much greater than anywhere else in the world (Figure 5–6).

It was not surprising therefore that, according to the surveys, Chinese women selected husbands on the basis of their financial status and prospects, rather than love ("If you're planning to get married, then the most practical question is whether you have enough cash or not in order to live better after you get married ..."—unmarried Shanghai woman.). Love, in China, was a luxury. Men, meanwhile, accepted that they needed to prove their worth if they were to find a suitable wife but resented the financial expectations placed upon them. Money (or lack thereof) therefore played a pivotal role for both.

Both men and women in China described marriage as "the graveyard of love." Views on ideal love were similarly bleak (Table 5–2). Expectations of roles within marriage were highly traditional, even among the X-Generation: the man should be the provider and protector, while the woman should be virtuous, do the cooking, and be a good mother (but at the same time she wanted more equality even if he was the provider, and he would tolerate his wife having a career as long as it did not interfere with his home comforts). The woman focused heavily on the importance of the career of her husband or future husband.

Figure 5–5 The X-Generation: Why success is so important

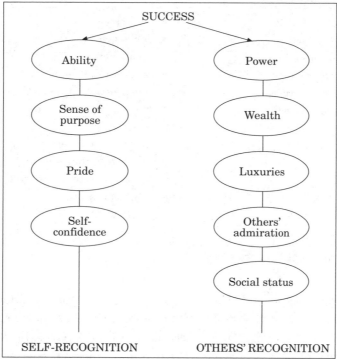

Source: "China: The X-Generation—Conclusions," J. Walter Thompson, Shanghai, August 1996.

Figure 5–6 Love versus status around the world

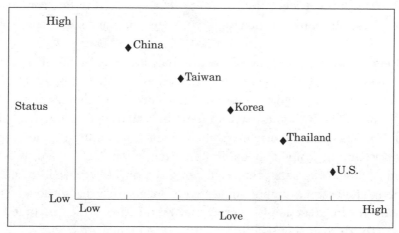

Source: De Beers.

Table 5–2   Ideal love: Perceptions in China

Ideal husband	Ideal wife
• has reliable career • earns a good salary—rich • can afford to buy a house • will not cheat on me • likes to give me surprises • understands my moods • is handsome • is healthy	• is pretty • can leave her at home and not worry about her • is like a doll—does not know too much about the outside world • will not figure out that I have a mistress • has a tender personality • keeps the house clean • knows how to dress well • is graceful, quiet • is virtuous • manages household finances well

Source: DWR Regional Research Debrief.

Against this background, De Beers faced the dilemma that diamond rings had never been part of the wedding ceremony in China. It therefore had to "establish cultural imperatives," according to Seth Grossman. "Wedding tradition is ingrained. It is not just an individual choice but one for the families of you and your partner. We have to try to introduce the idea of a diamond wedding ring into a country with a 5,000-year history. We have to make it represent more than a beautiful sparkling stone." Young Chinese people were looking for material success and emotional stability, and they were much better educated and wealthier than their parents. They seemed to feel comfortable in linking their aspirations for marriage with the diamond's sparkle, cost, and image.

De Beers tested a number of positioning statements (Table 5–3) for its diamond wedding rings. People broadly rejected the idea of a diamond symbolizing love—any object could do that. They also dismissed the idea of purity in love: the Rainshower commercial which had proved so popular elsewhere in Asia did not motivate Chinese women to want a diamond wedding ring. Aspirationally, most people identified with the "need to express perfection" while at the same time criticizing the phrase for its immodesty and ostentation. The best statement suggested a "bright future," although this was hard to capture in advertising terms. Showing a future which included a child suggested too much responsibility to the young men.

Table 5–3 Diamond wedding ring positioning statements in China— and typical reactions to them

Diamond. Symbolizes unmatched purity of love.
Reactions—insincere and not practical.

Diamond. Gift of love.
Reactions—anything can symbolize love; why a diamond?; not realistic; old-fashioned.

Diamond. The symbol of our ultimate commitment.
Reactions—smacks of insincerity, as if caught doing something they shouldn't; "commitment" is an empty word; too absolute.

Diamond. The symbol of our bright future.
Reactions—describes a perfect married life; future is everlasting—good feeling, good future.

Diamond. Symbolizing we are a couple. Made by heaven.
Reactions—too superstitious; old-fashioned; nothing to aspire to.

Diamond. Our need to express perfection.
Reactions—vulgar, materialistic; ostentatious desire; too direct and straight but the implication is good; this sort of thing should not be mentioned out loud.

The positioning was finally expressed as "The symbol of our enduring commitment, to build a future of harmony, brightness, success, and happiness," summed up in the Chinese phrase, *mei man*. A *mei man* marriage was a contented, solid relationship filled with love, trust, care, and support, and it could withstand adversity; the couple had the relaxed feeling of best friends as well as lovers; and the home life was materially prosperous and successful.

Women's diamond jewelry: The *xing fu* woman. The second major strand of advertising was aimed at married women in the 25–44 age range who had not received a diamond wedding ring. Over 80% of diamond purchasers were married women. A typical married woman, as the manager of the household finances, decided which diamond she wanted and brought her husband along for the purchase although he was in no way involved in the process. Because the market was less developed, De Beers did not segment its message further by age or attitude as it did in other parts of Asia. Although commercials did not express it explicitly, the underlying motivation for purchases of diamonds by these women was status demonstration.

Xing fu, meaning fortunate, encapsulated the idea of the "complete woman." As a wife, mother, lover, friend, and attractive woman, she had reached the ultimate state of life. A woman who could demonstrate all these attributes by wearing a diamond—itself an expression of beauty and rarity—had the status of a *xing fu* woman. This concept was first implied in the Best Friends commercial, which ran very successfully between 1993 and 1997, and then stated more explicitly in the Complete Woman advertisement which followed it (Table 5–4). Using phrases such as "Only a little more, but they said I have so much more" (Figure 5–7) and "My most admired friend," these advertisements conveyed a sense of specialness and uniqueness about the women wearing the diamonds.

The results. Wedding rings accounted for 22% of diamond jewelry retail sales in China in 1997, compared with 56% for women's non-wedding diamond jewelry. The remaining 22% was taken by diamonds for men—China was one of the few markets worldwide where men wanted diamonds: they were the

Table 5–4 Women's diamond jewelry advertising in China (English translation)

Best friend

Male voiceover (MVO):	Diamonds.
	Rare, precious.
Female voiceover (FVO) 1:	My closest friends.
MVO:	Diamonds.
	Every diamond is unique.
FVO 2:	My most admired friend.
MVO:	Diamonds.
	The treasures from nature.
FVO 3:	My friend forever.
MVO:	To own a diamond is not a dream.
	Diamond is forever.

Complete woman

MVO:	It is confidence shining through …
	It is beauty radiating brilliantly …
	It is *xing fu* sparkling brightly …
	It is time to let your brilliance shine even brighter through the sparkle of a diamond.
VO:	De Beers.
	A diamond is forever.

Source: J. Walter Thompson.

Figure 5–7 Women's diamond jewelry: Print advertisement for China

Headline: "Only a little more, but they said I have so much more."

Body copy: Precious, rare, brilliant ...

Because of this sparkle of the diamond, nothing else needs to be said.

(The advertisement goes on to explain the 4Cs and gives a size guideline.)

You will find a diamond is more affordable than you could imagine. Starting from Rmb3,500 you can select your own favorite diamond which lets your beauty shine more brilliantly.

perfect status symbol in a country where owning a Ferrari or a second home was not an option.

By 1998, only five years after De Beers' full promotion effort began, one-third of brides in Shanghai and half of the brides in the Rmb2,000 and above monthly income bracket were receiving a diamond ring on their wedding day. It had taken Taiwan ten years to reach the same acquisition rate. In Guangzhou the rate was only 13%.

A study of the elite population segment in Beijing, Shanghai, and Guangzhou—the top 5%, with monthly household incomes of Rmb20,000—indicated 88% ownership among women, which was higher than in the U.S. The acquisition rate per year in the target group was exceptionally high at 12%, and many were multiple owners (the average was 1.56 diamonds per person). Attitudes to diamonds were very positive compared with other gemstones.

Elsewhere in the country, ownership was minimal. De Beers hesitated to extrapolate from some of the data it collected because of the small sample sizes. The ownership rate in Shanghai, its biggest and most valuable market, was 7%. Was it more important for De Beers to increase ownership rates there, or to develop new markets in regional cities like Qingdao, for example?

Ultimately, would people in China buy diamonds because they believed in them as a symbol of love, or because diamonds were the best status symbol around? Could De Beers create the same unique positioning for diamonds in China that it had done in the West, which would distinguish it from the rest of the luxury goods market?

CRISIS IN ASIA

The financial crisis which swept Asia from July 1997 onward was a test of De Beers' skills at embedding diamond-buying practices into local cultures. Discretionary purchases motivated by status considerations—the "women's desire" brand—fell sharply across the region with the exception of Taiwan.

Even in Hong Kong, which did not feel the weight of the economic crisis until the summer of 1998, women were no longer buying so much jewelry. For the middle income earners (the target group in Hong Kong was people earning over US$2,000 per month—secretaries earned around US$2,300) it was out of the question to buy a diamond pendant or ring and show it off in the office the next day—which would have been one of the reasons for purchasing it. Among the elite segment of the population it was not so much that conspicuous consumption was inappropriate, rather that no one knew how long the economic downturn might last. Since diamonds were not bought as a store of value, they could not be traded in the same way that gold jewelry routinely was.

In Korea, which had been an important market for diamonds, all sales except for the wedding jewelry segment dried up. Sales in Thailand and Indonesia completely disappeared. Some people were sufficiently desperate to sell their diamonds—and were getting more for them than they had paid because of the depreciation of the local currency against the U.S. dollar.

In Japan, De Beers continued its efforts to make women really want a diamond engagement ring, but as Stephen Lussier recognized, "It's hard for them to justify spending US$5,000 on it if they only wear it on a few occasions. We have to make them want to wear their rings more by encouraging jewelers to create more practical designs which won't frighten off the traditionalists."

In China, other factors were at play. Between 1993 and 1996 the market had grown at around 20% per annum, slowing to 10% in 1997 and would probably be below that in 1998. De Beers' main market was Shanghai, and that was still growing. However, the middle class was not yet well established in China, which could give rise to problems if the economic crisis were to hit. Market reforms were introducing alternative ways of spending money. People were for the first time starting to buy their own homes. Consumer products such as air-conditioners competed for their share of discretionary spending against luxury goods like diamonds. Nevertheless, because De Beers believed that diamond-buying habits could approach those of the overseas Chinese as long as it got the market positioning right, it was prepared to continue to devote more of the annual advertising budget to China than current results warranted.

For the rest of Asia, the marketing budget was curtailed to reflect reduced opportunities. "The American market is booming. Women in Asia have closed their purses to this type of spending. Although we have several commercials, we don't have the media money now to air more than one of them in Asia so we are concentrating on the diamond wedding ring," explained Fiona Hindmarsh.

LOOKING TO THE FUTURE

De Beers' move into Asia had been an interesting experience. It learned that its "gift of love" message did not mean the same thing to everyone. And it discovered that there was a whole new category of diamond purchasers that it had never addressed before: women buying diamonds for themselves, for the joy of wearing them. Was this something that they should think about for the Western markets? Had they been alienating Western women who felt the same way that so many Asian women clearly did? Perhaps there was room for a "joy of wearing" message in the West that did not stress so strongly the "how to get your diamond" idea.

De Beers faced several challenges. In Japan, it was vulnerable to the rejection of the "symbol of love" message it had always projected. It needed to re-establish the position of diamonds as a "love" purchase outside the trappings of social conformity, and to show Japanese women that diamonds were jewels that were relevant to their everyday lives. Otherwise, the slow trend toward casualization of dress would isolate diamonds firmly in the niche "dress" sector.

East and Southeast Asian markets were badly hit by the crisis and would take time to recover. In China, market development was at a very early stage and remained vulnerable to economic downturns. The emphasis among young people on the pragmatism and materialism of marriage was slightly shocking to De Beers' traditionalists. Was "love" a relevant message to portray? But if it was not, how could diamonds be distinguished from other status symbols?

To Serve with Love: The Case of Annalakshmi Restaurant

Annalakshmi, a vegetarian restaurant in Singapore, is unique in that it is not only a not-for-profit restaurant that supports the fine arts and charitable activities, but it is also run by volunteers. As a placard (Figure 6–1) on the table says, "Your waiter or waitress could be your lawyer or teacher." The restaurant has been in operation from 1986. By 1998, the restaurant had not only seen an overall steady growth in customers and revenue (Table 6–1), but also opened another branch at one of Singapore's Changi airport terminals.

However, by mid-1998, Annalakshmi experienced a drop in its sales. This was not surprising as it is an upmarket restaurant and even Singapore was experiencing the effects of Southeast Asia's economic crisis. The restaurant was considering various means of bringing in a steady stream of customers and income without compromising its mission.

This case was prepared by Saroja Subrahmanyan as the basis for class discussion rather than to illustrate either effective or ineffective handling of an administrative situation. All data pertaining to Annalakshmi are based on factual information provided by the manager, Mr. Govindarajan. The author thanks Mr. Govindarajan for providing the information. She also thanks the reviewers for their helpful comments.

Please address all correspondence to: Dr. Saroja Subrahmanyan, Assistant Professor, Department of Marketing, Faculty of Business Administration, National University of Singapore, FBA2 Building, 17 Law Link, Singapore 117591, e-mail: fbasubra@nus.edu.sg

Reprinted from Asian Case Research Journal, Vol. 3, 195–214. Copyright © 1999 by John Wiley & Sons (Asia) Ltd.

Figure 6–1   Placard kept on the tables at Annalakshmi

What's going on here?

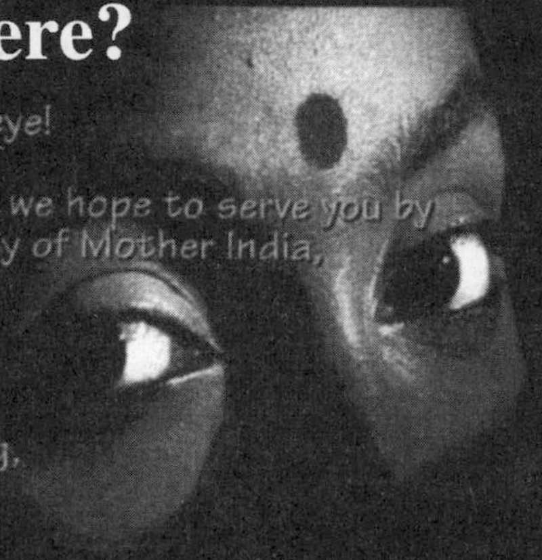

There's more to it than meets the eye!

We are not a business venture, but we hope to serve you by bringing you the splendorous beauty of Mother India, lovingly known as Barath Mata.

The visual arts and
The performing arts, and
especially through mother's cooking,
The culinary arts.

Take a closer look around you...

The people who serve you are not waitresses or waiters! They are our volunteers. They come together in a spirit of self-help and service. Your hostess could be your child's English Teacher, or your company's Lawyer, or your best friend's mother!! In the end enabling us to put in practise and bring to you the breadth and depth of Indian Culture through our many activities.

The decor you see around you that awakens your senses and charges your spirit, is the creative expression of the myriad of volunteers who grace our place.

The beautiful artefacts that you see are the enchanting expressions of artists, craftsmen, and sculptors through whose inspired fingers and hands flow the glorious beauty of Barath Mata. Most items are price tagged and are available for sale. You may also ask at, Lavanya Arts, our handicraft and boutique centre for more details.

Part of the activities on this floor include supporting an affordable medical clinic, Sivananda Medical Centre (SMC for short). Here the spirit of service takes on a new dimension. Helping heal body, mind and spirit. Do drop by for your health's sake!

Kala Mandhir (The Temple of Fine Arts) is probably one of the most innovative schools for Indian dance & music in this region. Aside from being the largest privately run school for the Indian arts in Singapore, it has to its credit many unique dance dramas, such as *Swan Lake, The Legend of the White Snake, Ramayana, Johnathan Livingston Seagull, Taj Mahal* and *A Midsummer Night's Dream*, as well as innovative Orchestral Ensembles. If you would like to know a bit more about Kala Mandhir please drop by our school's office, or ask any one of our many volunteers.

Annalakshmi, has recently extended her graceful self, and opened a restaurant to greet the weary traveller at the Changi Airport. It is located in Terminal 2, on the 3rd level near the waving gallery. Next time you have to greet a friend off, or welcome one here to Singapore, why not relax with us at our home away from home.

Table 6–1 Sales

Year	Sales (S$)	Year	Sales (S$)
1990	1,080,442	1994	3,249,683*
1991	1,749,326	1995	2,820,325*
1992	2,511,968*	1996	1,800,000
1993	2,880,420*	1997	1,850,000

* These figures included inflight meals to Singapore Airlines. The contract lasted for three years, from 1992–95.

Source: Annalakshmi.

BACKGROUND

A group of about 20 families in Singapore met every week for religious and cultural functions. These people who were of Indian origin were proud of their rich cultural heritage and wanted to share and impart Indian cultural values including art, music, and dance not only to the younger generation but also to anyone interested in learning them. With this aim they set up a non-profit organization called Kalamandir, which in Sanskrit means a "Temple of Fine Arts," in 1982. Since they did not want to put a price on learning or appreciating the fine arts, classes were offered at nominal prices. For example, a music course which comprised about five lessons a month cost as little as S$30 a month, compared to S$100 for similar classes offered at community centers. Famous musicians, dancers, and artistes from India were also invited to give public shows. For such shows, donations were sought from large corporations, but rarely were door tickets charged. The whole idea was to make enjoyment of the fine arts affordable to the general public. In addition to these, in-house productions of musicals, dramas, and so on were also put up. Most shows were very well attended. It was not uncommon to find about 4,000 people attending the shows over a three-day period. In addition to the performing arts, Kalamandir also supported a charitable medical clinic called Sivananda Medical Center, which was staffed by volunteer doctors and others from the medical profession.

However, they found that the system was not working too well monetarily as all the founders had regular salaried jobs outside of Kalamandir. They had no "godfather" as one of the founder members explained. To make the whole idea self-sustaining, they decided to start a restaurant on a not-for-profit basis as they discovered that they had a talent for making excellent food for large numbers of people. With this idea they set up Kalamandir Trading Private Limited (KTPL) in 1985 which now comprises three subsidiaries:

Annalakshmi, Lavanya Arts, and Hansa Designs. Lavanya Arts sells handcrafted artifacts and ethnic Indian apparel from India while Hansa Designs provides hotel and home designing, designs posters, banners, and other graphics for companies. Lavanya Arts and Hansa Designs were started when talented people in the organization volunteered their services to Kalamandir. The idea of offering such services to outside companies as a business venture was conceived. Thus, the various business ventures grew around Kalamandir in an organic manner so that they could support the arts and other charitable ventures.

KTPL has 20 shareholders. All these shareholders (except for two outside shareholders) are also "employees" or more accurately volunteers of Kalamandir and KTPL. None of them are paid monetarily for their services. No dividends are declared and profits are used to support Kalamandir or ploughed back into the business. Typically, 5% of their sales revenues go toward supporting Kalamandir. The support includes food and other services for visiting artistes, funding for public performances, rentals for conducting classes in the fine arts, donations to the Sivananda Medical Center, and scholarships to deserving students for higher studies in the performing arts or any field relevant to Kalamandir.

Since the aim of the organization is to inform the public about Indian culture, which includes food, starting a restaurant seemed to be a logical move. The members also felt that at that time (the early 1980s) there was no Indian vegetarian restaurant at which one could properly entertain guests. Vegetarian restaurants in Serangoon Road, a veritable mini-India with Hindu-styled temples, shops, and eating places selling Indian food, were mostly budget-styled ones which operated on a volume basis where diners had to eat quickly and clear the table as soon as possible. Sharing tables with total strangers was not uncommon. Annalakshmi was to be unique in that it would not only be a not-for-profit restaurant but would also provide high-quality food in a unique, artistic, and leisurely environment. The target market sought was business executives, families, and business visitors from India.

The founding members regard Swami Shantanand, a disciple of one of India's greatest yoga teachers, Swami Shivananda of Rishikesh, as their spiritual leader. He provided the inspiration to start the restaurant. They are thus committed to the philosophy of eating and serving vegetarian food.

OPERATING PHILOSOPHY

The restaurant is run totally on a volunteer basis. While most of the volunteers are also the founder members, students and parents of Kalamandir who like its philosophy also volunteer from time to time. According to the manager, this helps in keeping costs down, as manpower alone accounts for 30%–40% of the operating costs for a restaurant.[1] There are two paid cooks, one each at the two locations, to help out with mass cooking and the making of Indian breads. The women members do all other cooking. Many of the full-time volunteers are retired people who have no other major commitments but are physically and mentally agile. Volunteers may get their transportation costs reimbursed and do get to eat at the restaurant. The members appoint someone among themselves as a manager to coordinate all the day-to-day operations. At the time of writing this case, the manager happened to be a trained Certified Public Accountant. Roles are thus not rigid and anyone can double as a waiter, cook, cashier, or cleaner. A rough organizational structure of the restaurant based on the functions performed is given in Figure 6–2.

Figure 6–2   Organization chart

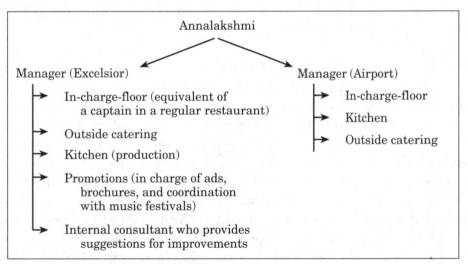

According to the manager, if the restaurant were not run on a volunteer basis, the minimum structure and remuneration for employees would have been as shown in Table 6–2.

None of the volunteers had any formal training or experience in the restaurant business when they started. However, they were a group of people

---

[1] According to the Economic Survey Series on Hotels & Catering by the Singapore Department of Statistics, the percentage of remuneration to operating expenditure for restaurants was 29.6% in 1997.

Table 6–2 Minimum manpower requirements and costs for the operation of a restaurant

	Number required	Cost (S$) per month based on minimum market value	
Floor Manager	2 (1 for each shift)	6,000	(2 × 3,000)
Food & Beverage Manager	1	2,500	
Cooks	3	6,600	(3 × 2,200)
Assistant Cooks	2	2,500	(2 × 1,250)
Captains	2	3,600	(2 × 1,800)
Waiters	6	7,800	(6 × 1,300)
Cleaners	3	4,500	(3 × 1,500)
Total cost		33,500	

Note: These figures were given by Annalakshmi's manager and indicate the approximate manpower costs that a regular commercial restaurant of Annalakshmi's size would have incurred.

who were not only committed to the cause but had a wide variety of skills in various disciplines. Each would thus contribute his energy and skill to helping the restaurant and also Kalamandir. For example, their computer system was set up by someone who had a background in that area and set it up in his free time. The philosophy on which the place is run also allows a free hand to any member with a creative vision. For example, the initial decor and layout were visualized by a volunteer who had absolutely no formal training in interior decoration and in fact was a technician. The decor won rave reviews from many people and the designer was subsequently invited to decorate several homes and hotels. The designer had since started his own design shop. Since the restaurant began, the decor had been changed about seven times, each time being designed by a different person who had a new idea. Everybody thus contributes his talent and time. The current manager quipped that the only time they go to an outside consultant is for audit.

Recently, the non-volunteer or paid cooks had to undergo an apprenticeship at a similar restaurant in India so that they understand the philosophy of the place. The volunteers believe that a proper attitude while cooking passes on the right "energy" to the food. Also, in the spirit of service, they offer cleaning and other odd jobs to ex-drug addicts and others from the Singapore Corporation of Rehabilitative Enterprises who need a place to work at while on parole. As required by government regulations, they also have an outside contractor to do the heavy duty cleaning of the kitchen. In 1998, the kitchen was awarded grade A for hygiene by the Ministry of Environment. This system of grading all eating establishments and requiring them to display the grade was started in May 1998 with grade A implying excellence in cleanliness and food hygiene.

Since much of the cooking is still done by the women members, many facilities in the kitchen were modified so that the women could cook much like at home. For example, the stoves, pots, and pans are smaller than in commercial kitchens. Food is also cooked in small batches so that typically it is made for about 30 to 40 people depending on the demand expected. Thus, wastage of food is reduced and direct costs kept under control. Guests also find that the food is very fresh. The downside is of course slower service when the restaurant is crowded.

Quality checks are done by the women who cook and serve the food. They ask themselves if they could offer the food cooked for their own special guests at home. This, they believe, keeps the quality of food quite high.

POTENTIAL MARKET

Singapore has a resident population of 3.1 million of which 76.4% are of ethnic Chinese origin, 14% Malays, and 7.4% Indians.[2] The variety of cuisines available here reflects the rich multicultural heritage of its residents. Cuisines from most other parts of Asia and the world are also available. In fact, Singaporeans consider shopping and eating out as their favorite pastimes. Food promotions are held often including the annual Singapore Food Festival in July.

There are over 3,000 eating establishments that are registered with the Registry of Companies and Businesses.[3] These include restaurants, fast-food outlets, coffeehouses, snack bars, and food caterers. In addition, there are hundreds of hawker stalls all over the island. A recent study[4] found that close to 90% of Singaporeans eat out at least once a week. While most eat at hawker stalls, food courts, canteens, and fast-food outlets, only 10% eat at restaurants during the same period.

---

[2] *Yearbook of Statistics*, Department of Statistics, Singapore, 1997.

[3] Hotels & Catering 1997, Economic Survey Series, Department of Statistics, Singapore, 1999.

[4] Kau, Ah Keng, Tan, Soo Jiuan, and Wirtz, Jochen. *Seven Faces of Singaporeans: Their Values, Aspirations and Lifestyles*, Prentice Hall, Singapore, 1998.

Tourists are an important segment of customers for the prepared foods market. In 1997 alone, about 7.3 million people visited the country. The largest group of tourists was from the neighboring ASEAN countries, and visitors from India formed the ninth largest group based on country of residence in 1997. (See Table 6–3 for information on visitor arrivals.) According to a Singapore Tourist Promotion Board survey,[5] Indians are the third largest spenders after visitors from ASEAN and Japan. However, only 10% of their expenditure is spent on food and beverages with the bulk being on electronic items. The survey also found that Serangoon Road is the third most visited tourist site among tourist attractions that do not require entry fees in Singapore.

Table 6–3   Tourist arrivals by country of residence, 1995–98

Residence	1995	1996	1997	1998 (Jan–May)
Americas	5.97	6.3	6.4	7.18
Asia	73.3	72.94	72.26	67.21
ASEAN	30.68	30.94	32.56	30.97
Japan	16.52	16.07	15.20	12.63
India	2.64	2.80	3.15	3.82
Others	23.46	23.13	21.35	19.79
Europe	13.53	13.75	13.72	16.52
Oceania	5.98	5.91	6.43	7.71
Africa	1.22	1.09	0.98	1.20
Total (%)	100	100	100	100
Total	7,137,255	7,292,521	7,197,963	2,566,252

Note: In 1997, in-transit visitors comprised 9.08% of all visitors. Also 75% of visitors arrived by air.

Sources: *Singapore Annual Report on Tourism Statistics*, 1996 and http://www.cybrary.com.sg for 1997 and 1998 arrivals.

Singapore's ethnic Indian population is not traditionally vegetarian and do not form Annalakshmi's target market. Also, the average income of this group

---

[5] *Survey of Overseas Visitors to Singapore, 1996*. Singapore Tourist Promotion Board, 1997.

is lower than that of the ethnic Chinese.[6] The Indians who frequent the restaurant are either more recent citizens or expatriates from India and other places. According to the manager, Chinese Singaporeans make up 30% of the clientele, Indians 15% while tourists and others form the rest. Many tourists visit the place as it has favorable reviews in tourist guides.

Although Buddhism and Hinduism advocate a vegetarian diet, many Singaporean followers[7] of these two religions are not traditionally vegetarian except on special days. For example, many Chinese Buddhists are vegetarian only on the 1st and 15th days of the lunar month while Hindus avoid eating meat on Tuesdays and Fridays. Vegetarianism, however, is on the increase in Singapore mainly for health reasons and vegetarian restaurants have seen a healthy growth.[8] Recently, outlets selling organically grown pesticide-free vegetables and foods have sprung up in Singapore. Many items in these stores are imported from the U.S. or Australia where such stores have gained popularity in the last two decades. These stores promote vegetarianism as part of a healthy lifestyle and some have sit down cafés attached to the store. There are also varying degrees of vegetarianism. For example, some consider themselves vegetarian if they avoid red meat. Others avoid all types of meat, but eat dairy products including eggs. Most Indian vegetarians are lacto-vegetarians who consume milk-based dairy products, but do not eat eggs. Annalakshmi offers this type of meals. Many Buddhist vegetarians do not consume any type of dairy product and may even avoid onions and garlic as they are supposed to agitate the mind.

VEGETARIAN RESTAURANTS

Annalakshmi does not consider itself to be in competition with anyone. However, for a customer who wishes to eat at a vegetarian restaurant, Singapore has 20 Chinese restaurants, 15 Indian restaurants, and 1 Western-styled vegetarian restaurant.[9]

---

[6] The average monthly household income for ethnic Indians is S$2,859 compared to S$3,213 for Chinese and S$2,246 for Malays. *Report on Labor Force Survey of Singapore*, Research and Statistics Department, Ministry of Labor, Singapore, 1997.

[7] Buddhism is practiced by 31.1% of the population, Taoism and traditional Chinese beliefs by 22.4%, Islam by 15.4%, Christianity by 12.5%, Hinduism by 3.7%, other religions by 0.6%, and no religion by 14.3%. *Singapore Census of Population 1990: Religion, Childcare and Leisure Activities*. Department of Statistics, Singapore.

[8] Lum, Magdalene, "Healthy $20-m business," *The Sunday Times*, May 10, 1998.

[9] Ibid.

Serangoon Road has most of the Indian vegetarian restaurants which serve popular and inexpensive meals and snacks. Apart from the locals, many tourists who visit Little India frequent some of the restaurants there as they are written up in tourist guides and give a flavor of unpretentious Indian food.

Unlike Indian vegetarian food which has a long tradition, Chinese vegetarian food is more recent and features mock meats and fish which are based on soyabean derivatives such as *tofu*. Mock meats are a favorite with those who want to eat a vegetarian meal but crave for the look and taste of meat and fish-based dishes. The Western vegetarian restaurant which opened in 1997 serves mostly Italian and Mediterranean type food and is very popular with expatriates from the U.S. and Europe. Prices here are considerably higher with a dish costing as much as S$20 on average. This restaurant also serves alcoholic drinks such as wine, which is uncommon among most vegetarian restaurants.

Among the 15 Indian vegetarian restaurants, only 3 are considered upmarket and are outside of the Serangoon Road area. One of them is run by Komala Vilas, which has its main restaurant in Serangoon Road and has been in existence for over 50 years. As it is featured in most tourist guides, tourists visiting Little India generally dine there. In 1996, Komala Vilas started Komala's Fine Dining, in a nearby location, which caters to an upmarket clientele. For example, in contrast to a meal for S$5 at their original restaurant, the fine dining restaurant has buffets for over S$10. Komala's also started a fast-food outlet, modeled after a typical McDonald's restaurant, next to its Fine Dining to draw in younger customers and those needing well-packaged takeaways. They have thus tried to target the various market segments.

Both the fast-food and fine dining concepts have become quite popular even with the Malays and Chinese. In early 1998, Komala's opened another fast-food outlet as well as a Fine Dining restaurant (renamed Gangezs) at Peninsula Plaza shopping center, which is on the same street as Annalakshmi. Annalakshmi's manager stated that Komala's Fine Dining has not affected its sales and has probably helped it. The main feature here is a lunch and dinner buffet that costs S$9.90. The Gangezs seats about 55 people. It also offers snack items that are not available at the adjacent fast-food outlet during teatime, i.e., from 3:30 p.m. to 6:00 p.m. It is open on Sundays.

Bombay Woodlands is located in Orchard Road, Singapore's prime shopping district. The restaurant takes its name after a famous outlet in India. The restaurant, being on street level, is visible to passers-by. Many tourists and expatriates living in that area frequent it apart from Indians. It is also open seven days a week and is open from 9:30 a.m. to 10 p.m. and prices are comparable to that of Annalakshmi's.

Both Komala's Fine Dining and Bombay Woodlands can seat about 55 people at one time. However, the tables are set rather close to each other and they do not have the spacious feel or ambience that Annalakshmi has.

MARKETING OF ANNALAKSHMI

Location

The restaurant is spacious, occupying about 360 sq. m. and can seat between 80 and 120 people at one time. It is located on the second floor of the Excelsior Hotel complex. The hotel which has 271 guestrooms is located in the heart of downtown Singapore which is also known as the Central Business District (CBD). Commercial rent is paid to the owners. This area was chosen so that people could easily access it as it is well served by public transport. Also, a year after its startup, the operations of Kalamandir were also shifted to premises on the same floor as Annalakshmi thus making it easier for working people to take classes in the fine arts after their office hours. Kalamandir and all businesses associated with it, including Annalakshmi, occupy an area of 900 sq. m. A rough floor plan of the second floor is given in Figure 6–3. Having Annalakshmi close to Kalamandir enables the volunteers to help out in the restaurant business easily and keeps the number working there flexible.

The first four floors of the Excelsior Hotel complex form the shopping area of the hotel. Facilities such as conference rooms and guestrooms start from the fifth floor onward. The first or street level has a café. The third floor has health and beauty related outlets such as a spa and beauty salons while the fourth floor is occupied by a Japanese restaurant as well as a Japanese karaoke lounge.

Next to the hotel is Funan Center, which is a popular place for buying computer hardware, software, and related peripherals. Two other shopping centers, the Peninsula Shopping Complex and Peninsula Plaza are also located on the same street (Figure 6–4).

Product/Service

The owners view their restaurant as offering a cultural experience and not just food. Apart from beautifully arranged artifacts, huge brass oil lamps are lit up which one rarely sees outside a traditional Hindu home. A guest remarked that "... the place has a spiritual accent." The people who wait at the tables do not wear uniforms. Women volunteers typically wear ethnic outfits such as silk

Figure 6–3 Floor plan of Kalamandir's premises at Excelsior Hotel complex

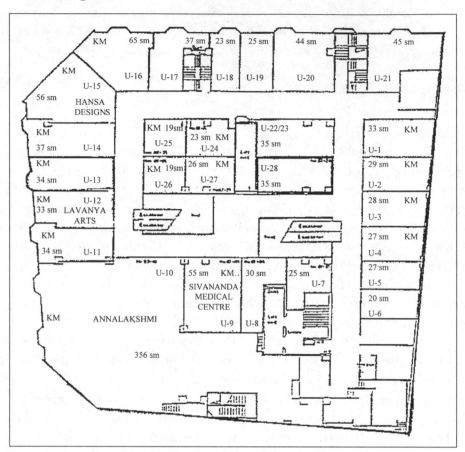

Note: Rooms occupied by Kalamandir are denoted by a KM. One square foot = approximately 0.09 square meters.

saris. This has indirectly helped in promoting sales of such products at Lavanya Arts.

The restaurant provides Indian vegetarian food at both lunch (11:30 a.m. to 3:00 p.m.) and dinner (6:00 p.m. to 9:30 p.m.) time. It is closed on Sundays. Both à la carte and buffet meals are offered at lunch time.

A typical Indian vegetarian meal consists of rice, Indian breads, lentils, vegetables, and yogurt-based dishes followed by fruit or Indian sweets. Traditionally, Indians sit cross-legged on the floor and eat off a banana leaf with their right hand instead of using spoons and forks. The type of food that Annalakshmi offers is based on this format, although the cuisine is more

Figure 6–4 Annalakshmi's location

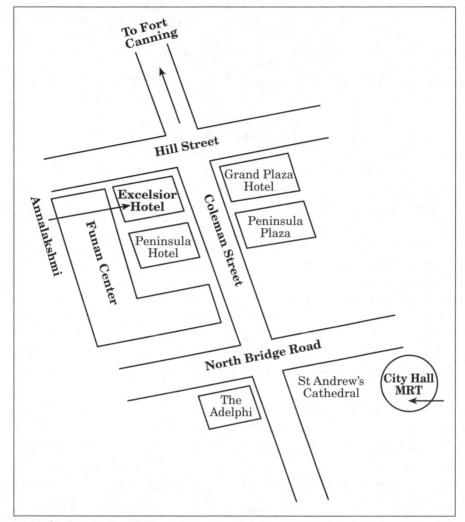

Note: This map is not drawn to scale. It is intended to show the neighboring buildings and location of Annalakshmi. MRT or MAss Rapid Transit is the rail network.

typical of Southern Indian vegetarian food. Guests sit at a table and food is served on elaborate silver lookalike plates and cutlery although a banana leaf is kept on the plate. The main categories of food that are offered and their price ranges are given in Table 6–4. Buffet is a lavish spread including three or four varieties of desserts.

Table 6–4 Main categories of food offered by Annalakshmi and their price ranges

	Price range (S$)
Breads	
• Unleavened flat breads (*poori*, *chapathi*, *naan*, and *bathura*)	1.50–5.00
If ordered with a vegetable as a complete meal, the prices are toward the higher side of the range.	
• Pancake-styled breads made from fermented dough of rice and lentils	4.00–6.50
They may have vegetable stuffing. The general types are called *dosais* and *oothapam*. These may be had by themselves as a light meal.	
Vegetable curries	
These may be made in several styles and are generally spicy.	5.00–6.00
Indian vegetarian snacks	
These include popular items called *samosas*, *vadas*, *idlis*, and *uppuma*.	3.00–5.00
Side dishes	
Include varieties of soups and yogurt-based dishes.	2.00–4.50
Indian desserts	
Include home-made ice-cream and milk-based sweets.	2.50
Hot beverages	
Tea/coffee including spicy versions of tea.	3.00–4.00
Other beverages	
Include fresh fruit juices, milk shakes, and yogurt-based drinks called *lassis*.	4.50–7.00
Set meals	10.00–25.00
These typically include rice, lentils, and vegetables and form a complete meal. There are several versions of these, with the most expensive called *sampoorna*. This version includes appetizers, soups, beverages, and desserts in addition to rice, vegetables, and breads. Also, many of the items are served in unlimited quantities.	

The volunteers feel that their unique selling proposition is food cooked just like an Indian mother would. In fact many comments in their guest book echo this. Says an Indian from India, "The only place which could be a threat to mother's cooking." Many also feel that the dedication of the volunteers and the joy with which they serve make the whole affair something one cannot experience at a regular commercial restaurant. A Chef de Cuisine, Steve Hunt, from Australia commented that, "I have eaten and experienced something which I cannot put into words. I have traveled to many places and have been to the best restaurants, but none have found the secret of cooking with their hearts. I feel humble but so happy. Thank you all for making my day."

In addition to regular meals in the restaurant, Annalakshmi also caters to parties of about 30 to over 1,000 people. Many customers also host birthday, engagement, or office parties for smaller groups within the restaurant itself.

Apart from eating at the restaurant, diners can also buy the handcrafted artifacts that are exhibited. According to the manager, everything from spoons and tables to artifacts can be bought except the name Annalakshmi! In fact the artifacts displayed at the Excelsior location had to be changed seven times since it started as all items had been sold out. The whole place thus works as a gallery for art pieces sold by Lavanya Arts. Annalakshmi also sells Indian sweets and savories airflown from India during Indian cultural festivals such as Deepavali. An initial venture to sell Indian spices, sweets, and savories was not successful.

Promotion

The main way customers come to know about Annalakshmi is through word-of-mouth. In the year of its inception, Kalamandir got a lot of publicity by setting up a float for the National Day Marine Parade Exhibition. This event was attended by over 40,000 people over a three-day period.

Annalakshmi naturally gets featured in all the cultural shows put up by Kalamandir. In addition, informal music concerts are arranged within the restaurant's premises. Often, the performers are well-known artistes visiting Singapore. At such times, the restaurant is closed.

Direct media advertising is rarely done. An exception is a print advertisement in *BE* magazine. This is a free publication that caters to New Age products and services. Even for this, payment to *BE* magazine is in the form of food vouchers.

One of its important markets is business executives from India. Annalakshmi was featured on one of India's most important current affairs programs "Surabhi." According to Annalakshmi's manager, many Indian executives to Singapore generally eat at Annalakshmi. A tour operator has featured a stop at Annalakshmi as part of the itinerary and this brings in regular customers.

Annalakshmi also has special menus on Valentine's Day and Mother's Day. The restaurant gets booked well in advance for such events that people have to be turned away. The Valentine's Day idea was suggested by younger volunteers who thought this would be in keeping with the times and also make good business sense.

Occupancy of the restaurant varies from about 30% to 80% for most days. However, there have been instances when a sudden influx of unexpected customers makes it necessary to turn away customers or keep them waiting for tables. Service tends to be slow when the restaurant is full. The practice of going vegetarian even among traditional non-vegetarians brings in regular customers on Tuesdays, Thursdays, and Fridays. Tuesdays and Fridays are considered holy by the Hindus, whereas on Thursdays, Chinese Buddhists and also followers of various gurus such as Sai Baba have vegetarian food. Vesak Day which is considered to be Buddha's birthday is another occasion when the restaurant gets fully booked. On Saturdays, the restaurant tends to be crowded at lunch time with families with young children.

Recently, Annalakshmi has revived a program to bring in schoolchildren so that they get educated on what Indian vegetarian food is all about and also how it is cooked. Schools such as the Singapore American School, the Japanese School, and other private schools bring in their students as part of their extracurricular activities. This is done during off-peak hours and brings in a nominal additional income. More importantly though, it indirectly helps in promoting the restaurant as the children go home and talk about it.

Another way Annalakshmi gets indirect advertising is offering its premises as a studio for television programs. Several television programs incorporate the restaurant setting for drama serials or as a background to conduct their current affairs program. Placards placed at the tables also provide information to customers about the restaurant's philosophy and any upcoming events.

Pricing

The pricing strategy was originally based on working backward to see if it would bring in enough revenues to cover overhead and other expected variable costs. The main components of cost as a percentage of sales at the two locations—main branch and airport—are given in Table 6–5.

However, before actually setting the price, customer reaction was also obtained through feedback from patrons. In the beginning, the prices were set

Table 6–5 Cost components as a percentage of sales

	Excelsior	Airport
Sales	100	100
Total costs	77	95
Direct cost (materials, utilities)	35	35
Rent	25	35
Transport	8	12
Advertising	1	5
Administration	8	8

Note: Cost of employing the two cooks is included under Administration. These figures were provided by Annalakshmi's manager.

much higher. For example, a typical buffet cost about S\$19 at lunch time and S\$25 at dinner time. Annalakshmi's most expensive feature, *sampoorna*, which is similar to a buffet but served in unlimited quantities at the table, was S\$35. Business executives who entertained guests did not mind this price. However, many others, especially Indians, felt that this was expensive even though the ambience and quality of food were considered good. Based on feedback from many customers, Annalakshmi decided to maintain the quality of food, but make it more affordable.

In April 1997, Annalakshmi slashed its prices by more than 50% by introducing a S\$10 buffet and removing some of the items which were earlier offered as part of the buffet. In addition, all à la carte items were removed from the lunch menu. Although the number of customers increased, revenue declined. Some customers were not happy that snack items were no longer offered as part of the lunch menu as they did not want a buffet meal. After a year of the S\$10 promotion, it reintroduced some items to the buffet and increased the price to S\$13. This, however, does not cover beverages, which were earlier offered at the S\$19 price. The current strategy increased revenue without reducing the number of customers. Snack items were also reintroduced as part of the à la carte lunch menu.

Annalakshmi's Branch at Changi Airport

Annalakshmi opened a branch at Terminal 2 at Changi airport in November 1995. The idea for starting a restaurant serving air travelers came about after they had completed a three-year contract with Singapore Airlines to provide inflight meals. They felt there existed a niche for serving vegetarian food at the airport. Also, several customers wrote to them saying that en route to the U.S.

and Australia from India they were unable to get vegetarian food. In addition, the airport staff were thought to be a potential market. No formal market survey was done.

The restaurant there occupies about 270 sq. m. and seats about 50–55 people. Although the restaurant has a more open walk-in concept, it too has an artistic decor and features handicrafts and art pieces from India. Unlike the main restaurant, it is open seven days a week. It features both à la carte snacks and meals as well as buffet-styled meals. Approximately 30% of Annalakshmi's sales are from the airport branch.

The prices for both meals and snacks are on average lower than at the main restaurant. Buffets are priced at S$10 at both lunch and dinner times. For almost an entire year after it started, customers who opted for the buffet were asked to pay whatever they thought the meal was worth. Many customers were rather skeptical at this novel idea. However, the average price that customers paid was about S$10 and this is the current price set. In fact, three times a year, both at the airport and at the main restaurant, customers pay what they feel the meal is worth. Interestingly, customers overpay by and large at both locations.

Most of the customers are travelers and others who visit it on Sundays when the main restaurant is closed. Families with children even travel all the way from the West Coast to eat there and watch planes take off and land from the viewing mall which is situated close by.

However, there has not been enough demand at this restaurant as few airport staff patronize it. Annalakshmi also realized that air travelers who visit Singapore prefer to go home or to their hotels soon after arrival. Those who are departing prefer to eat elsewhere before going to the airport. To stem losses, some of the outside catering services were transferred from the main restaurant to the branch. Recently, some people who work in offices in the vicinity of the airport have started patronizing the restaurant for lunch. Annalakshmi is looking into tapping the office market and is making plans to serve lunch packets to the offices directly provided there is sufficient demand.

FUTURE DIRECTIONS

As part of their strategic plan, the members and volunteers of Annalakshmi are trying to promote the idea of a one-stop Indian experience at the Excelsior location: a place where one can attend classes in fine arts, buy Indian artifacts, view art pieces, and have Indian food. They are trying to work with Singapore Tourist Promotion Board to offer an alternative Indian experience to the typical Serangoon Road one. The members feel that since they have limited resources, a long-term plan such as this will bring in synergistic returns for all areas related to Kalamandir.

At the airport, they are trying to work out how to attract the transit passenger and also identify other potential target markets. At a much later point in time, Annalakshmi would like to serve low-priced nutritious vegetarian meals that someone from the lower income strata can afford. This way they feel they can serve people from all income segments. However, they currently lack the resources to do so.

Annalakshmi has had offers from many business people who wished to enter into a joint venture. However, having a profit-seeking partner is against the philosophy of its members and they are resisting such a move. The members also feel that the organization has many part-time volunteers, from the younger generation, who will contribute more time after they retire from jobs outside of Annalakshmi.

AT&T USADirect In-language Service: India

In July 1994, Antoine George, worldwide manager of AT&T's USADirect in-language service was in his New Jersey office reviewing plans to launch a Hindi language service in India. This service would enable Indians calling relatives or friends in the U.S. to dial an AT&T access code and be connected with Hindi-speaking operators through whom collect calls could be made.

Origins and Nature of the Service

A call placer in a foreign country had several options when calling a friend or relative in the U.S. First, s/he could direct dial the U.S. number from a home telephone, if s/he had one. Second, s/he could call the operator of the local telephone company (PTT) and ask for a collect call to be placed.[1] This might be done from the caller's home, the home of a friend, a privately-run neighborhood calling center (PCO), or a telephone in a post office. Third, s/he could dial an access code for USADirect or for one of its competitors (such as MCI WorldPhone or Sprint Press) and have an in-language operator arrange the call.

This case was prepared by Professor John A. Quelch as the basis for class discussion rather than to illustrate either effective or ineffective handling of an administrative situation.

[1] In most countries, post, telephone, and telegraph (PTT) services were provided by state-owned monopolies.

Fourth, s/he could prearrange via mail for the friend or relative in the U.S. to call a certain telephone number at a particular time where s/he would wait to receive the call.

AT&T's USADirect service, launched in 1982, provided telephone service to the U.S. from abroad. Through a directly dialed access number, the call originator—often an American traveling overseas—could reach an AT&T operator located in the U.S. The service allowed both collect calling (whereby the call receiver accepted the phone charge) and card calling (whereby the call was billed to an AT&T calling card).

The USADirect in-language service was launched in 1986 to assist Spanish-speaking consumers in Latin America in calling friends and relatives in the U.S. Callers could reach AT&T operators in the U.S. who spoke Spanish. Early efforts to use English-speaking operators trained in basic Spanish failed; bilingual operators, often immigrants to the U.S., were hired to perform the service. By the end of 1993, the in-language service employed more than 200 operators based in the U.S. speaking either Spanish, Chinese (Mandarin), Filipino (Tagalog), Polish, or Hungarian.

REVENUE GENERATION AND COMPETITION

The revenue which AT&T received on calls from a foreign country to the U.S. varied according to how the call was made. AT&T obtained a settlement payment on calls placed to the U.S. through a foreign PTT but these calls were typically allocated among AT&T, MCI, Sprint, and other providers in proportion to each company's share of inbound calls from the U.S. to the other country. In India in 1993, AT&T's share was 70% and the settlement payment was US$0.90 per call minute. On calls to a foreign country placed by AT&T customers in the U.S., AT&T billed each U.S. customer and with part of the proceeds (US$0.90 per call minute), paid access and transmission fees to that country's PTT. Each quarter, the inbound and outbound accounts were reconciled. In most developing countries, outbound calls usually exceeded inbound calls; in such cases AT&T paid each foreign PTT a net sum each quarter.

AT&T aimed to persuade overseas call placers to use USADirect rather than the PTT. AT&T received all revenues on USADirect calls rather than a proportional share. Surcharges paid to the PTT for handling calls were lower (5% of the billed amount) because AT&T rather than PTT operators arranged the call. Although AT&T incurred the fixed costs of employing in-language operators and of marketing the service, the per minute contribution to AT&T on USADirect in-language service calls was almost always higher than if the local PTT were used—despite the fact that the USADirect cost per minute to the end consumer was invariably lower than the cost of an operator-handled call placed through the PTT.

The owners of PCOs, hotels, and other establishments could decide whether to encourage their customers to use the PTT, AT&T, or a competitor when placing calls to the U.S. Marketing managers for AT&T and its competitors offered these intermediaries both up-front payments and cooperative advertising (mentioning PCO locations in AT&T advertisements) to persuade them to sign exclusive contracts.

By 1993, MCI and Sprint had, like AT&T, established separate operating units within their organizations to pursue collect call business originating abroad. MCI's strategy appeared to be to target those countries with the highest volumes of collect call traffic and to try to switch call placers and calling centers to MCI WorldPhone on the basis of nominally lower call rates and promotional offers. MCI WorldPhone often used similar advertising to AT&T USADirect with just the access code changed in order both to secure speedy regulatory approval of the advertising and to benefit from consumer confusion. In addition, MCI focused on collect call receivers in the U.S., suggesting in direct mail pieces that they ask their friends and relatives overseas to switch to MCI WorldPhone and offering points-based reward programs as incentives. As George stated:

> In most overseas markets, USADirect currently has over 80% market share compared to MCI WorldPhone, Sprint Express, and the others. Over time, there'll be a tendency for these inbound market shares to mirror the providers' shares of outbound calls from the U.S. However, it's our objective to maintain market share at 80%.

The communications challenge for AT&T in any new overseas market was, first, to make potential callers to the U.S. aware of AT&T, USADirect, and (where applicable) the specific local brand name of AT&T's in-language service and, second, to educate them regarding the benefits of the service. Emphasis was placed on ease of use, convenience, speed, and reliability as well as on the efficiency, friendliness, and in-language speaking capability of the operator. These same benefits, along with competitive price, also had to be communicated to potential call recipients in the U.S. Transmission quality was not marketed as a point of differentiation since the same lines were used, whether a call from the foreign country to the U.S. was placed with the PTT or AT&T.

IN-LANGUAGE SERVICE PLANS: 1994–95

Preliminary plans called for AT&T's in-language service to generate 106 million minutes of calls worldwide in 1995, up from 95 million in 1994. Of this, the Asia-Pacific region was expected to contribute 12.8 million minutes, up from an estimated 7.6 million in 1994. In the Asia-Pacific region, USADirect in-language service was expected to be available in four countries. China and the Philippines had come on stream in 1992. India and Vietnam were slated to launch in late 1994. Comparative data on the four markets are presented in Table 7–1. Based on a fourth quarter introduction, demand in India was projected at only 99,000 minutes in 1994, rising to 1.25 million minutes in 1995. Averaged across all four countries, each minute represented about US$2.50 in gross revenues.

Table 7–1   Comparative data on four Asia-Pacific markets

	India	China	Philippines	Vietnam
Population (mil.)	890	1,100	66	65
U.S. immigrants ('000)	570	1,505	1,451	615
U.S. immigrants per year ('000)	36	27	64	78
Telephones per 100 persons ('000)	0.45	1.1	1.0	0.2
Literacy rate (%)	62	75	90	90
Collect placer market size ('000)[a]	125	370	750	220
Collect receiver market size ('000)[b]	80	122	500	110
Collect receiver USAD penetration ('000)[c]	5	30	128	n.a.
Average collect call length (min.)	6	8	8	n.a.
USAD 1994 minutes ('000)[d]	88	1,413	5,946	147
USAD 1994 revenues (US$'000)[d]	383	3,966	12,582	402

Notes:

[a] Estimated number of private telephones from which overseas collect calls to the U.S. were placed (July 1993–June 1994).

[b] Estimated number of private telephones in the U.S. accepting collect calls from each country (July 1993–June 1994).

[c] Estimated number of private telephones in the U.S. to which USADirect collect calls were billed (July 1993–June 1994).

[d] Estimates for calendar year 1994. Indian revenues assume price of US$15 for a five-minute call.

Worldwide, AT&T planned to spend US$13 million marketing its in-language services in 1995. AT&T's marketing investment in in-language services was typically around 10% of the revenue value of the incremental minutes they were expected to generate.

When AT&T launched its in-language service in a new market, the emphasis was on acquisition of new consumers, either directly or through the PCOs which AT&T tried to persuade to become its partners. In more developed USADirect markets, communications budgets were divided among consumer retention (30% of budget) and usage stimulation (28%) programs as well as consumer acquisition programs (41%). In these more developed markets, around 10% of the marketing budget was targeted in bill stuffers and direct mail offers at collect call receivers in the U.S. in the hope that they would persuade those who placed calls to them to use USADirect.

EXPLORING THE INDIAN MARKET

Telephone density in India was low, at one line per 200 people. In a country of 890 million people, there were 4.7 million telephones with one million households awaiting connections. The waiting period between application and connection averaged three years. As a result, many consumers had to rely on PCOs or friends and neighbors with telephones in order to make calls. Not all of the telephones were capable of generating direct-dial long distance calls; in these cases, consumers had to rely on local operators.

To make a long distance call, many Indian consumers therefore had to dial 186 to access a local Indian operator. The operator would note the name and telephone number of the consumer as well as the telephone number of the consumer to be contacted in the U.S. The Indian consumer would then be placed in a line and could hang up the phone. Meanwhile, the Indian operator would contact an AT&T operator who would call the party in the U.S., at which time the Indian operator would call back the Indian consumer and a connection would be made.

Almost all Indian PTT operators were required to know English and Hindi (each was spoken by 30% of the people) as well as one regional language. There are 16 official languages in India; usage of each is typically concentrated in a particular state.

In 1992, there were 57,000 Indians or persons of Indian ethnic origin in the U.S. Sixty percent were concentrated in five states (California, New York, Illinois, New Jersey, and Texas). During the early 1990s, around 36,000 Indians were immigrating to the U.S. each year and with the number growing by 5% annually. The area of Queens, New York, alone generated 10.8% of U.S. outbound calls to India and received 6% of inbound collect calls in 1993.

George and his staff decided to examine existing consumer call traffic between India and the U.S. before determining whether to launch an in-language service in that country. First, they found that AT&T billings to U.S. consumers for calls placed to India between August 1991 and July 1992 were US$89 million. AT&T revenues from operator-handled inbound calls and USADirect inbound calls were US$1.6 million and US$770,000, respectively. Of the USADirect revenues, 60% were billed direct to a calling card (presumably by Americans traveling in India or by a friend or relative in India who had been given a U.S. cardholder's telephone and personal identification numbers) and 40% were billed on a collect basis. Research indicated considerable overlap between outbound callers and recipients of inbound calls; almost half of those who accepted collect calls from India also made calls to India.

The top metropolitan areas receiving AT&T outbound calls from the U.S. to India were New Delhi (30%), Bombay (30%), Bangalore (18%), and Madras (14%). On the other hand, the top metropolitan areas originating AT&T collect calls from India were Madras (25%), Orissa (19%), Bombay (18%), and Kanpur (11%). Broadly speaking, AT&T telephone traffic volumes to and from particular cities were correlated with the number of immigrants from those cities living in the U.S.

The percentages of the population able to speak various languages in the cities listed above were as follows:

- Bombay: Marathi 60%, Hindi 40%, Gujarati 40%, English 50%
- New Delhi: Hindi 80%, Punjabi 30%, English 40%
- Madras: Tamil 85%, Telugu 20%, English 60%
- Bangalore: Kannada 60%, Tamil 40%, English 60%
- Kanpur: Hindi 90%, English 30%
- Orissa: Oriya 70%, Hindi 40%, English 30%

George's staff next set out to estimate the number of call minutes that might be generated in a year through a USADirect in-language service for each of the 16 languages in India. The market size (in minutes) for each language in each city was computed using the following model:

$$M_l^c = R^c \alpha_l^c (1 - \beta_e^c) \left[\frac{P_{coll}}{P_{USAD}} \right] + k \left[\frac{S^c}{\gamma} \right] \alpha_l^c (1 - \beta_e^c) \left[\frac{P_{sp}}{P_{USAD}} \right]$$

where

M_l^c = Total market size for language l in city c (minutes)

R^c = AT&T received collect minutes from city c

S^c = AT&T sent paid minutes to city c

α_l^c = Fraction of people speaking language l in city c

β_e^c = Fraction of people speaking English in city c

γ = AT&T sent paid market share for India (assumed to be 75%)

P_{coll} = Price for a collect call in India (based on average call duration of 8.2 minutes)

P_{sp} = Price for a direct-dial call from the U.S. to India (based on average call duration of 8.2 minutes)

P_{USAD} = Price of a USADirect call from India (based on average call duration of 8.2 minutes using the cheapest carrier, Sprint, at US\$1.23 per minute)

k = Fraction of direct-dial market that would consider migrating to USADirect in-language service (assumed to be 10%)

The total market size of language l could be computed as:

$$\overline{M}_l = \sum_{c \in C} M_l^c \text{ for all } l \in L$$

where C is the set of cities and L is the set of languages.

Summing across cities, Table 7–2 shows the estimated annual minutes of demand for various in-language services with and without discounting for the fraction of speakers of each language who also spoke English.

Table 7–2 Projected demand for USADirect in-language service, November 1992

Rank	Language	Estimated annual minutes	
		With English	Without English
1	Hindi	767,176	459,942
2	Tamil	506,646	202,658
3	Marathi	364,643	182,322
4	Gujarati	197,231	98,626
5	Oriya	134,426	94,098
6	Kannada	215,835	86,334
7	Punjabi	141,107	84,664
8	Telugu	85,354	34,142

The analysts who developed the model pointed out that the forecasts were conservative. First, they noted that γ (at 0.75) and k (at 0.1) were set low. Second, the analysts used the price of a collect call for USADirect, rather than the lower price of a card call. If the latter had been used in the computation, the demand estimates would have been higher.

Actual demand would also be a function of USADirect's pricing relative to competition, not only to the end consumer but also to the thousands of phone centers or other third parties that acted as gatekeepers. In addition, the effectiveness of communications programs targeting prospective call placers in India (which would require PTT approval) and call receivers in the U.S. would also impact the results.

DEVELOPING A MARKETING PROGRAM

Based on the forecasts and the fact that Hindi was the fourth most widely used language in the world (after English, Spanish, and Mandarin) George decided to investigate further the implementation of an in-language service for India. He commissioned additional consumer research; the principal results are summarized in Tables 7–3 and 7–4. He also determined that AT&T could find sufficient in-language operators in New York who could speak English, Hindi, Tamil, and even Marathi.[2] In January 1994, USADirect launched a Hindi in-language service.

AT&T's Indian advertising agency was asked to develop a communications program to launch USADirect Namaskar Seva service in the fourth quarter of 1993. The agency proposed a US$300,000 multimedia campaign including 70 insertions in a combination of nine newspapers and six magazines (33% of budget), to be followed by radio spots in nine cities (7%), television advertising (35%), and billboard advertisements. The balance of the budget would be spent on signing bonuses, incentives, and collateral materials (such as posters) for 3,600 PCOs whom AT&T hoped would agree to exclusively provide USADirect service to their customers.[3] Sample television and radio commercial scripts are presented in Tables 7–5 and 7–6. A proposed magazine advertisement is presented in Figure 7–1.

---

[2] Operators could be hired on a part-time basis at a fully loaded cost of US$25 per hour. At least two operators would have to be on duty around the clock.

[3] PCOs typically received 1% commission on the revenues generated by calls placed through AT&T's USADirect.

Table 7–3 India research findings on callers (N = 200)

a.	Reasons for calling the U.S.	%
	Inquire about health and welfare	38
	Special occasions (birthday, etc.)	36
	Business reasons	21
b.	**Reasons for not calling more often**	**%**
	Too expensive	53
	No need to call	21
	Write letters instead	6
c.	**Type of telephone used to call the U.S.**	**%**
	Home telephone	57
	Calling center telephone	55
	Family/friend's telephone	8
	Work telephone	7
	Post office telephone	1
d.	**How calls to the U.S. are paid for**	**%**
	Caller pays him/herself	90
	Call collect	8
	Sometimes pay/sometimes call collect	2
e.	**Problems when calling the U.S. (base = 12% of callers)**	**%**
	Hard to get connection/not enough lines/always busy	42
	Poor quality sound/hard to communicate	27
	Too expensive	8

Source: Adapted from *Research International* report for AT&T, July 1993.

The message strategy appealed to family values with the claim that USADirect "links you to your loved ones at the lowest cost." Research indicated that 80% of Indians' private overseas calls were to keep in touch with family and friends. Initial advertising also emphasized the USADirect access code, the service's association with AT&T, and its ease of use. The proposed billboard advertisements simply stated "AT&T's USADirect Namaskar Seva. Just dial 000-116 and call the U.S. collect."

All the proposed advertisements would require PTT regulatory approval before they could be placed. AT&T managers expected that their competitors would be tipped off and would also enter the Indian market within a year. Based on past experience, MCI would probably undercut the USADirect price.

Table 7–4 India consumer research findings

	Total callers (200) %	Heavy callers (105) %	Light callers (95) %	Non-callers (100) %
Age 35 years or more	51	48	55	62
High socio-economic status	57	66	46	46
Own a telephone	78	80	76	83
Have visited the U.S.	32	39	24	14
Have received incoming calls from the U.S. in the last 12 months	82	81	83	51
Mean number of incoming calls from the U.S. in the last 12 months	11.1	16.1	6.2	6.9
Mean number of outgoing calls to the U.S. in the last 12 months	9.1	15.6	3.2	n.a.
Caller pays for his/her outgoing calls	90	89	91	n.a.
Have encountered problems calling the U.S.	12	14	11	n.a.
Unaided awareness of the PTT (MTNL)	73	76	71	39
Unaided awareness of AT&T	20	25	15	9
Rate MTNL excellent or very good	8	6	10	7
Rate AT&T excellent or very good	42	48	32	36
Ever made a call from a calling center	75	79	72	64
Ever made a call to the U.S. from a calling center	56	63	50	n.a.
Rate last calling center experience excellent or very good	30	28	32	36
Aware of USADirect without description	15	22	9	8
Aware of USADirect with/without description	18	27	11	9

Note: The sample of callers included both collect callers and direct-dial callers.

Source: Adapted from *Research International* report for AT&T, July 1993.

Table 7–5 Proposed television commercial for AT&T USADirect in-language India campaign (English translation)

Video	Audio
Opens with a shot of father and mother sitting, holding an album.	Song (backs translation)
The camera zooms in above the father's shoulders to focus on a photograph (in the album) of the son on his graduation day.	Heart is out of the country
The photograph fills the frame and dissolves to show the son jumping over the sitting room sofa with a letter in his hand.	Love yearns in the country
Father seated, is reading the paper. He then hugs son while mother looks on joyfully.	Many oceans across
Dissolve to an airport scene. A tight shot of the parents. The son is straightening up after touching their feet. In the background, typical airport bustle.	He who understands the pain of the heart
Father dialing and speaking into the phone with mother next to him, misty-eyed. Next to the phone is a family portrait of father, mother, and the son hugging both of them.	Is the one that can join the strings of the heart
The number 000-116 appears one digit at a time as a super on the screen.	
Female AT&T operator with logo in background speaking. Super 000-116 remains in frame.	AT&T USADirect Namaskar Seva
Father speaks into the receiver.	I want to make a collect call to my son Deepak in California
Cut to telephone being picked up in an apartment that looks foreign. The person who picks it up is the son. His mouth forms the word papa.	Hi Dad! (In a happy mood)
Cut back to the Indian frame. Father hands over receiver to the mother who starts speaking. Happy expressions on their faces.	Song continues: When one hears the voice, love starts flowing from the eyes
Dissolve to son relaxing on sofa with phone.	
Dissolve to mother fighting back the tears, but happy.	
Cut to AT&T USADirect Namaskar Seva logo and 000-116.	AT&T USADirect Namaskar Seva (voiceover)
Cut to AT&T logo.	Joins the strings from heart to heart (voiceover)

Table 7–6 Proposed radio commercial for AT&T USADirect in-language India campaign (English translation)

Character	Audio
Mother	0-0-0-1-1-6
Sound effect	(Dialing tone)
Sound effect	(Beep, beep, beep)
Operator	AT&T USADirect Namaskar Seva.
Mother	Mrs. Sanyal here. I want to speak to my son Deepak in the U.S. The number is ...
Operator	Please hold.
Sound effect	(Ringing tone)
Operator (to Deepak)	There's a collect call from Mrs. Sanyal for Deepak Sanyal. Will you accept the call?
Deepak	Yes, of course.
Mother	Deepu, it's me!
Deepak	Mom! How are you?
Mother	I'm fine. How about you?
Deepak	I am alright, Mom. So, tell me, what's going on?
Mother (in an emotionally charged tone)	Nothing. Just wanted to hear your voice. I can't believe I can now talk to you so easily and quickly.
Male voiceover	AT&T USADirect Namaskar Seva, the best way to reach your loved ones in America. Call 000-116 now and through this "call collect" service, talk to your heart's content. For "call collect" means the call will be paid by the call receiver. All you have to pay is the cost of a local call. AT&T USADirect Namaskar Seva (000-116) links you to your loved ones.

In July 1994, a ten-minute direct-dial call from India to the U.S. cost US$24.75 while a ten-minute operator-handled collect call cost US$31.62. In the Philippines, AT&T had launched USADirect in-language service in 1993 at a price roughly midway between these two points. However, within six months, Sprint Express and MCI WorldPhone had entered the market at much lower rates, thereby reducing the credibility of AT&T's initial claims of cost competitiveness. AT&T had responded with price promotions and loyalty reward programs.

This experience led some AT&T managers in India to question whether rates should be mentioned in the launch advertising. Some managers argued

Figure 7–1 Proposed print advertisement for AT&T USADirect in-language India campaign (with English translation)

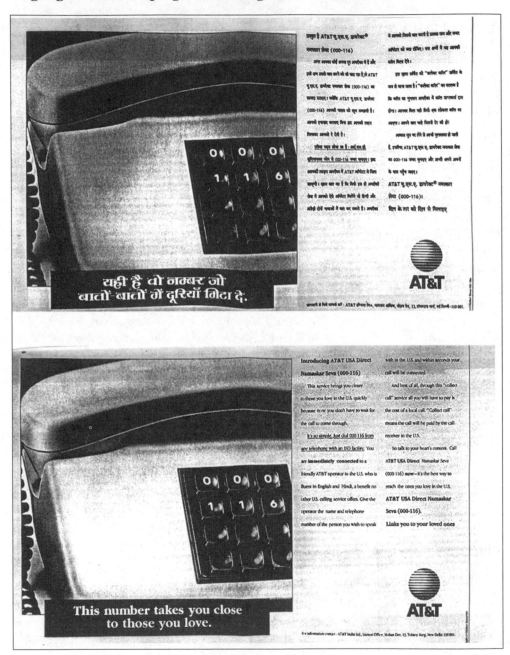

for a lower, "penetration" level launch price of under US$10 for a five-minute call versus the US$15 that had been proposed. A further issue was whether a USADirect in-language service call should cost more than a standard automatic USADirect call with no operator assistance and, if so, what the price premium should be.

CONCLUSION

As George contemplated launching a USADirect in-language service in India, he recalled how similar services had boosted significantly USADirect revenues in China and the Philippines within the year following their introductions. As he reviewed the comparative country data presented in Table 7–1, he wondered whether launching a Hindi in-language service would likewise boost AT&T's revenues and profits in India.

Sony Corporation: Car Navigation Systems

In April 1996, Masao Morita, president of Sony Personal & Mobile Communications Company, a division of Sony Corporation, pondered how to recover Sony's initial leadership in car navigation systems in Japan. As the first company to launch a reasonably priced (around US$2,000) after-market model in 1993, Sony could claim to have created the world's largest car navigation systems market in Japan. In the late 1980s, Sony had led a group of 40 companies in establishing an industry standard (called NaviKen) which enabled consumers to benefit from mutually compatible digital map software while manufacturers reduced their risk by sharing development costs. Sony's efforts saw the Japanese market grow from 58,000 units in 1992 to 160,000 in 1993. Sony held a 60% market share in 1993. Table 8–1 reports unit sales of car navigation systems in Japan through 1995 and forecasts from 1996 through 2005.

Market growth fueled intense competition in Japan, leading to many new product launches and lower prices. The average retail price per unit decreased from US$4,000 in 1990 to US$2,500 in 1995.[1]

This case was prepared by doctoral candidate Yoshinori Fujikawa under the supervision of Professor John A. Quelch as the basis for class discussion rather than to illustrate either effective or ineffective handling of an administrative situation.

[1] The average retail price per unit inclusive of a monitor is US$2,500. A system retailed at around US$1,500 in 1995 if a monitor was sold separately as shown in Table 8–1.

Table 8–1 Market development and forecasts in Japan

	Actual						Forecast (estimate)					
	1990	1991	1992	1993	1994	1995	1996	1997	1998	1999	2000	2005
Entire market												
(1) Unit sales	16,400	27,800	57,800	160,400	343,500	578,500	850,000	1,200,000	1,500,000	1,800,000	2,000,000	2,800,000
Growth rate year-on-year (%)		168	209	278	214	168	147	141	125	120	111	107
(2) Retail sales (¥ million)	6,430	10,290	15,470	25,020	51,530	83,880	114,080	150,000	170,000	190,000	200,000	230,000
Growth rate year-on-year (%)		160	150	162	206	163	136	131	113	112	105	103
(3) Retail price/unit (¥)	392,073	372,826	267,647	155,985	150,015	144,996	134,212	125,000	113,333	105,556	100,000	82,143
(4) % penetration of new cars	0.27	0.46	0.96	2.67	5.73	9.64	14.17	20.00	25.00	30.00	33.33	46.67
(5) Cumulative number of car navigation systems installed	16,400	44,000	101,800	262,200	605,700	1,167,800	1,990,200	3,132,400	4,472,000	5,928,500	7,350,000	12,385,000
(6) % penetration of all cars	0.03	0.07	0.17	0.44	1.01	1.95	3.32	5.22	7.45	9.88	12.25	20.64
After-market												
(7) Unit sales			39,000	139,016	297,900	462,500	550,000	700,000	800,000	850,000	900,000	1,100,000
Growth rate year-on-year (%)				356	214	155	119	127	114	106	106	104
% of entire market			67	87	87	80	65	58	53	47	45	39
OEM market												
(8) Unit sales			18,800	21,350	45,600	116,000	300,000	500,000	700,000	950,000	1,100,000	1,700,000
Growth rate year-on-year (%)				114	214	254	259	167	140	136	116	109
% of entire market			33	13	13	20	35	42	47	53	55	61

Notes:
(1) Manufacturer unit sales.
(2) Retail sales do not include monitors, adapters, and software. These are sold separately from the navigation systems.
(3) = (2)/(1)
(4) Assuming that annual new car sales in Japan were approximately 6 million (i.e., (4) = (1)/6 million).
(5) Assuming that the car navigation system will be renewed every five years (i.e., 1992 figure = 1990–92 total, 1997 figure = 1993–97 total, etc.).
(6) Assuming that there were approximately 60 million cars in Japan (i.e., (6) = (5)/60 million).
Sources: 1990–95 figures are actuals drawn from Yano Keizai Kankyusho, *1996 Car Navigation Systems: Market Forecast and Corporate Strategy* (Tokyo, Japan). 1996–2005 figures are forecasts of the case writer, based on research interviews.

Ironically, competitors not in the NaviKen group were able to introduce new and improved products more often and more rapidly by developing or acquiring proprietary digital map technologies. Increasingly sophisticated consumers sought out differentiated products with the latest features. In contrast, NaviKen member companies, including Sony, lost time while trying to agree on standard software upgrades. Sony's unit sales grew but at a slower rate than the market: Sony's market share fell from 60% in 1993 to 23% in 1994 and 17% in 1995, and was estimated to drop to 15% in 1996. Table 8–2 summarizes the major competitors' market shares. Table 8–3 compares sales performance of NaviKen and non-NaviKen companies.

In Europe and the U.S., Sony was also the first to launch car navigation systems in the automobile after-market. Fewer than 1,000 units had been sold in test markets to gather information in each region by the summer of 1996. In Europe, local manufacturers such as Philips and Bosch started to market competing products aggressively. Other Japanese competitors such as Alpine, Matsushita, and Pioneer were expected to enter Europe and the U.S. by 1997. Table 8–4 and Figures 8–1A and 8–1B summarize the market forecasts for car navigation systems by geographic region.

SONY CORPORATION: COMPANY BACKGROUND

Sony Corporation was founded in 1946 in the remains of a bombed out department store as the Tokyo Tsushin Kogyo (Tokyo Telecom-munications Engineering) by Akio Morita (Masao's father) and Masaru Ibuka. As a young company, Sony did not have a *keiretsu* of affiliated companies and lacked the strong domestic sales base and distribution networks that supported other companies.

With only US$500 in capital, the founders realized they would have to differentiate themselves from their larger competitors by developing more innovative products. And from the failure of their first new product—a tape recorder that customers deemed expensive and flimsy—they learned the importance of paying close attention to consumer needs. Throughout its history, Sony pursued the innovation of commercially appealing products, maintaining a large research organization and vesting unusual decision-making authority in its engineers. The company's first breakthrough occurred after Ibuka acquired a patent license for transistors. Morita and Ibuka began mass production of transistor radios in 1954, and dubbed their new product Sony, after *sonus*, the Latin word for sound. Soon thereafter, the pair renamed the company.

Table 8–2 Major competitors' unit sales and market shares in Japan, 1994–96

Company/Brand	Unit sales, total market (market share)						1996 unit sales (market share estimate)				1996 unit sales (sales composition estimate)	
	1995		1996 (estimate)		Three years		After-market		OEM		After-market	OEM
Pioneer	#####	(24%)	157,000	(19%)	351,000	(20%)	(21%)	17,000	(9%)	89%	11%
Sony	98,000	(23%)	124,000	(17%)	302,000	(17%)	(19%)	3,000	(2%)	98%	2%
Matsushita	90,000	(15%)	149,000	(16%)	289,000	(16%)	(18%)	30,000	(16%)	80%	20%
Alpine	87,000	(10%)	127,000	(15%)	250,000	(14%)	(11%)	57,000	(30%)	55%	45%
Mitsubishi	30,000	(1%)	41,000	(5%)	75,600	(4%)	(4%)	16,000	(8%)	61%	39%
Kenwood	27,000	(6%)	38,000	(5%)	84,000	(5%)	(6%)	—	(0%)	100%	0%
Zanavi	24,000	(0%)	45,000	(4%)	69,000	(4%)	(1%)	36,000	(19%)	20%	80%
Clarion	24,000	(5%)	39,000	(4%)	80,000	(5%)	(5%)	7,000	(4%)	82%	18%
Fujitsu Ten	20,000	(5%)	37,000	(3%)	75,000	(4%)	(6%)	—	(0%)	100%	0%
Nippon Denso	15,000	(2%)	26,000	(3%)	47,500	(3%)	(1%)	22,000	(12%)	15%	85%
Sharp	11,000	(2%)	13,000	(2%)	31,000	(2%)	(2%)	—	(0%)	100%	0%
Casio	10,500	(1%)	11,000	(2%)	26,500	(1%)	(2%)	—	(0%)	100%	0%
Sumitomo Denko	7,800	(3%)	10,000	(1%)	29,700	(2%)	(1%)	3,000	(2%)	70%	30%
Toshiba	6,000	(1%)	8,000	(1%)	17,500	(1%)	(1%)	—	(0%)	100%	0%
Citizen	6,000	(0%)	8,000	(1%)	14,000	(1%)	(1%)	—	(0%)	100%	0%
Calsonic	2,800	(0%)	4,000	(0%)	7,300	(0%)	(1%)	—	(0%)	100%	0%
NEC	2,000	(0%)	3,000	(0%)	6,500	(0%)	(0%)	—	(0%)	100%	0%
Chuo Jidosha	2,000	(0%)	2,000	(0%)	4,000	(0%)	(0%)	—	(0%)	100%	0%
Maspro	1,500	(0%)	1,000	(0%)	3,200	(0%)	(0%)	—	(0%)	100%	0%
Sanyo	1,200	(0%)	2,000	(0%)	3,500	(0%)	(0%)	—	(0%)	100%	0%
Nakamichi	700	(0%)	—	(0%)	700	(0%)	(0%)	—	(0%)	—	—
Total	####	(100%)	####	(100%)	####	(100%)	(100%)	####	(100%)	77%	23%

Source: Adapted from Yano Keizai Kankyusho, op cit.

Table 8–3   Sales comparison: NaviKen group versus non-NaviKen groups, 1994–96

Companies	NaviKen format group	Proprietary format (can read NaviKen)*	Proprietary format (cannot read NaviKen)*
	Sony	Matsushita	Pioneer
	Mitsubishi	Alpine	Clarion
	Zanavi	Kenwood	Nippon Denso
	Sharp	Fujitsu	Sumitomo Denko
	Casio		Nakamichi
	Toshiba		
	Citizen		
	Calsonic		
	NEC		
	Chuo Jidosha		
	Maspro		
	Sanyo		
Group Unit sales (% share)	**NaviKen format group**	**Proprietary format (can read NaviKen)***	**Proprietary format (cannot read NaviKen)***
1994	103,100 (30%)	123,000 (36%)	117,400 (34%)
1995	200,000 (35%)	216,000 (37%)	162,500 (28%)
1996 (estimate)	262,000 (31%)	361,000 (43%)	222,000 (26%)
1996 (estimate) group Unit sales (% composition)	**NaviKen format group**	**Proprietary format (can read NaviKen)***	**Proprietary format (cannot read NaviKen)***
After-market	246,000 (78%)	225,000 (73%)	173,000 (78%)
OEM	70,000 (22%)	82,000 (27%)	49,000 (22%)

* The second group's car navigation systems can read both proprietary and NaviKen software, while the first group's systems can only read NaviKen CD-ROMs. The third group's systems can only read their respective original software.

Source: Calculation of the case writer, based on the figures in Table 8–2.

Table 8–4 Market forecasts for car navigation systems by geographic region

	1996	1997	1998	1999	2000	2005
			Forecast (estimate)			
Japan						
(1) After-market (unit)	550,000	700,000	800,000	850,000	900,000	1,100,000
(2) OEM market (unit)	300,000	500,000	700,000	950,000	1,100,000	1,700,000
(3) Entire market (unit)	850,000	1,200,000	1,500,000	1,800,000	2,000,000	2,800,000
(4) Entire market (retail ¥ million)	114,080	150,000	170,000	190,000	200,000	230,000
(5) Entire market (retail US$ million)	1,141	1,500	1,700	1,900	2,000	2,300
(6) Retail price/unit (US$)	1,342	1,250	1,133	1,056	1,000	821
(7) % penetration of new cars	14.17	20.00	25.00	30.00	33.33	46.67
(8) Cumulative number of installed units	1,990,200	3,132,400	4,472,000	5,928,500	7,350,000	12,385,000
(9) % penetration of all cars	3.32	5.22	7.45	9.88	12.25	20.64
Europe*						
(1) After-market (unit)	10,000	50,000	100,000	200,000	400,000	900,000
(2) OEM market (unit)	20,000	50,000	100,000	150,000	200,000	900,000
(3) Entire market (unit)	30,000	100,000	200,000	350,000	600,000	1,800,000
(4) Entire market (retail ¥ million)	—	—	—	—	—	—
(5) Entire market (retail US$ million)	60	170	300	455	600	1,440
(6) Retail price/unit (US$)	2,000	1,700	1,500	1,300	1,000	800
(7) % penetration of new cars	0.33	1.11	2.22	3.89	6.67	20.00
(8) Cumulative number of installed units	30,000	130,000	330,000	680,000	1,280,000	3,752,000
(9) % penetration of all cars	0.02	0.10	0.25	0.52	0.98	2.89

Table 8–4 (cont'd)

		Forecast (estimate)				
	1996	1997	1998	1999	2000	2005
U.S.						
(1) After-market (unit)	10,000	50,000	100,000	250,000	400,000	1,000,000
(2) OEM market (unit)	10,000	50,000	100,000	300,000	500,000	1,400,000
(3) Entire market (unit)	20,000	100,000	200,000	550,000	900,000	2,400,000
(4) Entire market (retail ¥ million)	—	—	—	—	—	—
(5) Entire market (retail US$ million)	34	150	260	550	720	1,200
(6) Retail price/unit (US$)	1,700	1,500	1,300	1,000	800	500
(7) % penetration of new cars	01.3	0.67	1.33	3.67	6.00	16.00
(8) Cumulative number of installed units	20,000	20,000	320,000	870,000	1,770,000	4,720,000
(9) % penetration of all cars	0.01	0.06	0.16	0.44	0.89	2.36
Total (Japan, Europe, U.S.)						
(1) After-market (unit)	570,000	800,000	1,000,000	1,300,000	1,700,000	3,000,000
(2) OEM market (unit)	330,000	600,000	900,000	1,400,000	1,800,000	4,000,000
(3) Entire market (unit)	900,000	1,400,000	1,900,000	2,700,000	3,500,000	7,000,000
(4) Entire market (retail ¥ million)	—	—	—	—	—	—
(5) Entire market (retail US$ million)	1,235	1,820	2,260	2,905	3,320	4,940
(6) Retail price/unit (US$)	1,372	1,300	1,189	1,076	949	706

Notes:
* Europe figures include France, Germany, Italy, and U.K.
(1), (2), (3) manufacturer unit sales.
(3) = (1) + (2)
(4) The figures are for the value of retail sales.
(5) Assuming ¥100/US$1 from 1996 through the year 2005.
(6) = (5)/(3)
(7) Assuming that annual new car sales in Japan, Europe, and the U.S. were approximately 6 million, 9 million, and 15 million, respectively (i.e., (7) = (3)/6 million).
(8) Assuming that the car navigation system will be renewed every five years (i.e., 1992 figure = 1990–92 total, 2000 figure = 1996–2000 total, etc.).
(9) Assuming that there were approximately 60 million cars in Japan, 130 million in Europe, and 200 million in the U.S. (i.e., (9) = (8)/60 million).
Source: Forecast of the case writer, based on research interviews.

Figure 8–1A   Forecast global car navigation systems market (units)

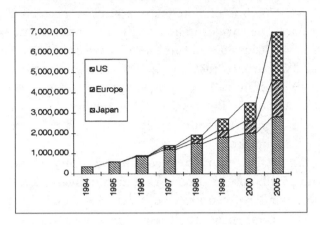

Figure 8–1B   Forecast global car navigation systems market (retail US$ million)

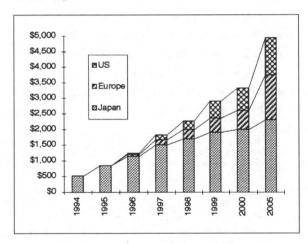

Internationally as well as in Japan, Sony was often first to market with technological innovations that set industry standards. In 1968, Sony's sophisticated Trinitron technology expanded the color television market. In 1979, it launched the legendary Walkman, a lightweight portable tape player with headphones. In the mid-1980s, Sony developed a compact size camcorder video camera. Such innovations turned Sony into a leader in consumer electronics with worldwide sales of over US$43 billion in the fiscal year 1995.

Sony's only significant failure came in the early 1980s, when its Betamax format video cassette recorder (VCR) lost out to VHS. Sony had developed the VCR as early as 1975, but motion picture studios protested that the new machine would encourage widespread copyright infringement of movies and television programs. Discussions of this matter gave Sony's competitors such as Matsushita and JVC time to develop a different VCR format, VHS, which permitted an additional three hours of playing time and was incompatible with Sony's Betamax. Although Betamax was generally considered technically superior, VHS soon became the industry standard, and Sony lost its early lead in the lucrative VCR market.

The Betamax VCR experience convinced Sony that technological innovation alone could not ensure market dominance, and that the match between hardware and software was critical. Subsequently, Sony began to cooperate more with competitors to develop industry standards. In the 1980s, for example, Sony joined Dutch electronic firm Philips to pioneer compact disc (CD) technology.

In the mid-1990s, Sony Corporation reorganized to keep the company market-driven and to increase autonomy. Sony organized its businesses into ten divisions, including Display, Home AV, Information Technology, Personal AV, Personal & Mobile Communications, Broadcast Products, Image & Sound Communication, Semiconductors, Components & Computer Peripherals, and Recording Media & Energy. To develop future top managers, Sony appointed promising young executives as presidents of each company with substantial autonomy. Masao Morita was appointed president of Sony Personal & Mobile Communications Company.

CAR NAVIGATION SYSTEMS

Evolving Products

A car navigation system plotted a driver's current location on a dashboard-mounted LCD monitor by calculating signals received from satellites and/or utilizing a dead-reckoning system fed by speed and gyro sensors. The system also showed the driver the best way to his or her destination by employing a digital map database stored on either a CD-ROM, a computer hard disk, or an IC card. Unlike VCRs and personal computers, car navigation system hardware and software were not standardized as of 1995, but a typical model consisted of hardware such as a satellite signal receiver, a CD-ROM player, an LCD monitor mounted on/in a car dashboard, and digital map software in the form of a CD-ROM. See Figure 8–2 for a picture of a typical car navigation system. Table 8–5 summarizes the cost and margin structure of the system.

Figure 8–2 Typical car navigation system model (Sony NVX-F160)

Source: Company materials.

Table 8–5 Typical cost and margin structure for car navigation systems

a. Typical cost and margin structure for car navigation systems

Retail price	100%
less dealer margin	35%
Manufacturer selling price	65%
less manufacturer margin	5%
Manufacturer total costs	60%
Indirect cost (SGA)	10%
Direct cost	50%
LCD monitor	30%
CD-ROM player	8%
CPU	7%
GPS receiver	3%
Other components	2%

b. Japanese model (e.g., Sony NVX-F16)

	US$
Retail selling price	2,000
less dealer margin[a]	700
Manufacturer selling price	1,300
less manufacturer total costs	1,200
Manufacturer margin	100

c. Overseas model (e.g., Sony NVX-F160)

	US$
Overseas retail selling price	3,000
less overseas dealer margin[a]	1,000
Manufacturer selling price	2,000
less manufacturer total costs[b]	1,800
Manufacturer margin	200

Notes:
[a] Dealers charged separate fee for product installation. Japanese dealers charged around US$200. U.S. and European dealers charged around US$30.
[b] Manufacturer total costs of overseas model included applicable transportation costs and import duties.
Source: Estimation of the case writer, based on research interviews.

In the late 1980s, the earliest car navigation systems could only report where a driver was, his/her desired destination, and whether or not the car was headed in the right direction. By the mid-1990s, however, the systems had become more intelligent. Recent models could inform a driver of his/her current location at all times and deduce the best route to a destination automatically by taking into account current traffic conditions. Some systems could even communicate verbally with the driver and provide turn-by-turn instructions on the LCD map or through voice.

Enabling Hardware

Car navigation systems were facilitated by the Global Positioning Satellite (GPS) system, a constellation of 24 satellites operated by the U.S. Department of Defense. GPS was originally developed at a cost of US$10 billion for military applications during the Cold War, but became available for civilian use at no charge in the late 1980s.

The central concept behind GPS was triangulation. If a car's exact distance from a satellite was known, the car's location had to lie somewhere on the sphere defined by that radius. If the driver's distance from a second satellite was also known, the car's position had to lie along the circumference of the circle where the two spheres intersected. Knowing the distance from a third satellite would result in two points where all three spheres intersected. GPS in fact used four signals from four different satellites to locate the position of the antenna.

Triangulation on GPS could result in accuracy as close as 30 meters. Worrying that GPS could be used by an enemy to guide missiles or smart bombs, the Department of Defense engineers intentionally built errors into the system for civilian use. The civilian signal could deliver 95% accuracy within 100 meters of the actual location. The GPS signal could also be blocked by tall buildings, trees, or overpasses, a common problem in large cities.

In order to improve the precision in identifying the car's location, the car navigation systems were equipped with a few supporting technologies. When GPS did not function accurately, a back-up dead-reckoning system of speed and gyro sensors typically installed in the car trunk could take over seamlessly and relay the car's speed and direction to the navigation system. Aided by the dead-reckoning system, map matching technologies enabled the car navigation system to pinpoint the car's position on the digital map.

In car navigation hardware, there was no dominant product standard. Some products utilized both GPS signals and dead-reckoning systems, but others employed only one of the two. Product interfaces were also diverse.

Some displayed a colorful digital map on an LCD monitor. On a typical LCD screen, a small red circle sign, representing the car, moved along a highlighted street leading the driver to his/her desired destination. Some other models' monitors showed only right or left arrow signs and the street name to signal the next appropriate turn. Others did not have display devices but provided directions verbally.

Diverse Software Formats

The software database technology used in car navigation systems was the offspring of GIS, or Geographic Information Systems. GIS was originally developed by the U.S. Department of Defense for guiding missiles. In essence, GIS software turned a conventional map into a digital database.

For accurate navigation, a digital map had to contain correct details of every street. Every sign, every painted line, every relevant piece of information along the road had to be included. For example, the database had to note whether there was a concrete divider along a highway, whether two streets intersect or one was on an overpass, and so forth. Consequently, each street corner required three to four dozen items of data.

As many data layers as desired could be added to the digitized map. Postal zip codes and phone numbers could be stored in the database so that a driver could find a destination by entering an address and/or phone number. Information on "points of interest," such as banks, restaurants, and gas stations, could also be digitized on the map. One could analyze these data in hundreds of different ways and, in conjunction with a GPS receiver, could interact with the data on a real-time basis. In real life, for instance, a stranger was not likely to know the automatic teller machine (ATM) closest to any given spot. However, with a points-of-interest database, a car navigation system could sort through ATMs by distance, find the nearest one operated by the driver's preferred bank, and provide route guidance to this ATM.

Collecting and digitizing all the road related information and the points-of-interest data were labor intensive. Government geological surveys and commercially published maps were often old and inaccurate. Hence, digital map companies had to send out research teams to take aerial and ground photos to fill in gaps and update the old information. Collecting and digitizing the necessary information on the city of Boston, for example, required 20 engineers to work for one year. Given continuous change due to road construction and store openings and closings, digital map companies had to retain local staff to update the data.

The cost of digitizing the cartography of the U.S. was estimated at US$1 billion with an additional US$100 million a year for updating. A single company starting this task in 1995 could not achieve payback before 2005. There were two major digital map companies in the U.S. competing independently. As of early 1996, Etak, a Silicon Valley division of Rupert Murdoch's News Corporation, had covered cities representing 80% of the U.S. population. NavTech, another Silicon Valley startup, had covered 90% of the U.S. population.

There were three digital map companies working in Europe. Etak had focused its European operation on the U.K. and had so far covered cities accounting for 80% of the population. EGT, NavTech's European subsidiary, had covered 80% of Germany and 70% of France. A third company, TeleAtlas, was digitizing Italian maps. These companies had developed independently non-compatible digital map software.

In Japan, 40 companies, including car companies, electronic firms, and digital map developers, had formed the Japan Navigation Research Association, known as NaviKen, in the early 1980s, and completed 100% digitization of the entire country by 1988. The NaviKen format was consistently applied in the navigation systems produced by the NaviKen member companies such as Sony and Mitsubishi. However, other incompatible formats had been developed independently by Pioneer and Matsushita, respectively, which did not join NaviKen. Table 8–6 compares the number of CD-ROMs available for different competitors' car navigation systems.

The data storage media also varied. Some devices used the digital map stored on a CD-ROM, while others on computer hard disk or IC card. CD-ROM-based navigation systems were popular in Japan and Europe, but hard disk and IC card were believed equally acceptable in the U.S., especially for low-end products.

Distribution Channels

Car navigation systems could be sold either on an original equipment manufacturer (OEM) basis or through after-market retail channels. Figure 8–3 summarizes the distribution alternatives.

In the OEM channel, car navigation systems producers contracted with car assemblers to supply car navigation systems to the automaker's specifications. The systems were either preinstalled by the car manufacturers or installed later by dealers as a purchase option on new cars.

After-market models were usually designed and marketed by car navigation system makers and distributed through wholesalers to auto parts retailers and

Table 8–6 Number of CD-ROMs by car navigation system producers, 1995

Software format	Sony NaviKen	Alpine Proprietary + NaviKen*		Matsushita Proprietary + NaviKen*		Pioneer Proprietary
General road maps	5	7	(2)	6	(1)	2
Sports (golf, ski, camping, etc.)	6	6	(0)	6	(0)	3
Travel (hotels, parks, etc.)	4	4	(0)	4	(0)	1
Shops/restaurants	1	1	(0)	1	(0)	1
Radar detection	0	0	(0)	0	(0)	1
Games/quizzes	4	4	(0)	4	(0)	6
Karaoke	0	0	(0)	0	(0)	56
Total	20	22	(2)	21	(1)	70

* Numbers include both original and NaviKen CD-ROMs, since Alpine and Matsushita's systems can read NaviKen software. Numbers in parentheses are proprietary CD-ROMs developed by Alpine and Matsushita.
Source: Adapted from various product catalogs.

Figure 8–3 Channels for car navigation systems

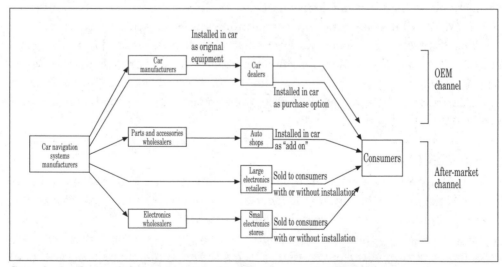

Source: Analysis of the case writer, based on research interviews.

electronics outlets. Sales to end consumers were either made on a cash and carry basis or involved dealer installation and other after-sales services.

All components of OEM models including LCD monitors were neatly installed together with audio equipment such as radio, cassette, and CD players in the car dashboard. In contrast, after-market systems usually had to be installed as "add ons" to the dashboard. Figure 8–4 shows OEM and after-market car navigation systems. Volume contracts with the car manufacturers meant that Japanese OEM products were technically one to two years behind and more expensive than after-market models.

Figure 8–4   OEM and after-market car navigation systems

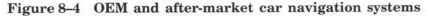

In the Japanese market, 80% of the systems were sold through after-market channels while 20% were sold on an OEM basis. However, as the technological innovation diffused and products became more standardized, the percentages were forecast to be even by 2000 and to be reversed by 2005. The fledgling European markets mainly involved OEM sales in 1995, but the proportion of after-market sales was expected to increase. The U.S. market was still undeveloped, but OEM models were expected to exceed after-market sales, especially if the price decreased substantially.

In Japan, major auto parts chains, such as AUTOBACS and Yellow Hat, accounted for 60% of after-market unit sales. Hybrid models based on both GPS and dead-reckoning sensors were distributed through these auto parts retailers since they required professional installation and maintenance. These auto parts retailers carried at most five brands on their shelves. GPS-based systems which did not require complicated installation were channeled mainly through large electronics discount chains and more subject to price competition.

MULTINATIONAL MARKETS

Advanced Japanese Market

The Japanese market for car navigation systems was the world's largest in 1995 with sales of 580,000 units and US$840 million.[2] Car navigation systems were installed in 10% of new Japanese cars in 1995. The penetration rate for all cars registered in Japan was 2%. With competition among 30 companies, the average retail price per unit decreased dramatically from US$4,000 in 1990 to US$2,500 in 1995. As competitors vied to introduce new models with the latest technological features, market shares fluctuated wildly.

The popularity of car navigation systems reflected the uniqueness of the Japanese car driving environment. First, the Japanese road system was more complicated than its European and U.S. counterparts. Since not all the streets had names and road signs were few and far between, people relied heavily on maps and landmarks for finding their way. Caught on narrow roads without the benefit of a highly developed highway system, drivers were always looking for a way to bypass heavily congested arteries, especially in major metropolitan areas.

Given serious traffic jams and well-developed train systems, most Japanese used their cars for weekend joy-riding rather than daily commuting.[3] Many therefore welcomed car navigation systems as a means of finding their way around in unfamiliar cities and towns.

Japanese car drivers, especially young people, were willing to spend heavily on cars and electronic accessories. Many drivers would readily invest

---

[2] The concept of the car navigation system had been around in Japan since the early 1980s. Honda claimed to be the first company to put a navigation system on the road. However, the dead-reckoning system, which required a driver to replace a slide-like map at each town boundary, did not attract consumers. The Japanese market remained small during the 1980s although electronic car component producers such as Alpine and Nippon Denso supplied car navigation systems on an OEM basis to the automobile assemblers. They offered the navigation systems as optional accessories on a limited number of their luxury models, such as the Honda Legend and the Toyota Crown. The navigation systems at that time were priced at around US$6,000.

[3] If all the cars registered in Japan were to be on the road at the same time, the distance between each would be only four feet.

over US$2,000; few U.S. drivers would invest more than US$1,000. Outside Japan, higher auto theft rates discouraged heavy investment in expensive electronic options. Table 8–7 summarizes the results of Japanese consumer and dealer surveys.

The Japanese car navigation market was boosted further by Japanese government investment in improving the efficiency of the Japanese road system. A real-time traffic information system called VICS (Vehicle Information and Communication System), was launched in Tokyo and Osaka in 1996.[4] With VICS information, the next generation of navigation systems would be able to incorporate real-time traffic and weather alerts so that drivers could avoid gridlock, accidents, or washed out roads.

Emerging European Market

The European market lagged behind Japan by some five years. However, once major electronics manufacturers such as Bosch and Philips introduced products in Germany, the market began to develop. The market was expected to grow from annual sales of 30,000 units and US$60 million in 1995 to 600,000 units and US$600 million by 2000 (see Table 8–4 and Figures 8–1A and 8–1B).

European road systems were complex, especially in historic inner cities. However, most streets had names and road signage was good. As a result, opinions differed on whether a car navigation system needed to show a digital map on an LCD monitor or if right/left arrow signs and voice guidance were sufficient.

European drivers frequently drove across borders. Car navigation systems therefore needed to provide multilingual guidance. Digital map software also had to correspond to different traffic rules and road regulations from country to country.

European governments collaborated on efforts to improve the highway system. For example, the European Union's DRIVE program analyzed how the car should relate to the road infrastructure, while the Prometheus project involving all major European manufacturers examined how cars could communicate with each other. The technologies developed through these projects contributed to Philips' and Bosch's development of navigation technologies such as route calculation and guidance.[5]

---

[4] The ATIS (Advanced Traffic Information System) was launched in 1995. The system allowed a driver to retrieve real-time traffic information by using a car cellular phone.

[5] "Smart Cars," *TelecomWorld*, August 1992, pp. 44–5.

Table 8–7   Results of Japanese consumer and dealer surveys, 1992–95

1992 consumer survey[a]

- Forty-five percent expressed their interest in buying a car navigation system in one or two years; two percent had already purchased one.
- Those who would buy a system were willing to spend US$500–US$1,000 (50%), US$1,000–US$2,000 (40%), and US$2,000+ (10%).
- Seventy-five percent of those who would buy a system rated "accuracy of road map" as an important factor for their purchase decision followed by "detailed traffic information" (56%), "number of CD-ROMs" (52%), and "up-to-date points-of-interest information" (43%).
- Benefits mentioned in order of frequency: can enjoy weekend drive better (90%); can drive in unfamiliar areas (80%); and can use landmarks for finding a route (75%).

1994 dealer survey[b]

- Eighty percent of respondents stated that the price of car navigation systems was too high. Among these, 80% believed US$1,500 was appropriate and 20% said US$1,000.
- The most frequently asked question by customers to retailers was: "Can I use NaviKen format CD-ROMs?"
- Ninety-two percent of dealer salespeople preferred selling systems with NaviKen compatible software.

1995 customer survey[c]

- Customer demographics were as follows:
  - 20–24 years (15%), 25–29 years (30%), 30–39 years (40%), and 40 years and older (15%);
  - married (44%) and not married (56%);
  - male (95%) and female (5%).
  - 75% owned new cars and 25% used cars
  - Average price of their cars was US$33,000.
- Respondents used car navigation systems: when driving in unfamiliar areas (95%); when enjoying weekend drives (85%); not during regular commute (70%); and all the time (15%).
- Ninety percent stated that a map display was essential for route guidance while 10% said arrow signs and voice guidance were sufficient.
- Important factors influencing the purchase decision in order of frequency of mention: accuracy of map and map-matching; automatic route calculation; easy-to-set-up destination; and speed of route calculation.
- Respondents wished to have the following information: "real-time traffic jam" (100%), "one-ways" (85%), "real-time parking space" (80%), "alternative bypass route" (80%), "expected arrival time to the destination" (75%).

Sources: Compiled from the following surveys conducted by one of the car navigation systems producers:

[a] Survey of 550 high potential purchasers, sampled from car audio magazine readers in October 1992.

[b] Survey of dealer salespeople in 20 largest auto parts chain stores, conducted in May 1994.

[c] Survey of 600 owners of car navigation systems, sampled from car audio magazine readers in October 1995.

Untapped U.S. Market

The U.S. market lagged behind both Europe and Japan. Car navigation systems were not widely known. However, one forecast expected the U.S. market to surpass the European market by 2000, with annual sales of 900,000 units and US$720 million, and approach the size of the Japanese market by 2005, with sales of 2.4 million units valued at US$1.2 billion a year (see Table 8–4 and Figures 8–1A and 8–1B).

The U.S. was well organized with street names, traffic signs, and highly developed highway systems. The value of car navigation systems which pinpointed a car's current location was not so obvious to the U.S. driver. For car navigation systems to be attractive, they had to provide turn-by-turn route guidance and other more sophisticated functions.

As of 1995, few U.S. consumers were familiar with car navigation systems. A manager at one digital map maker explained:

> If it were described to you before you experienced it, you might not understand. But after testing the system, most drivers come around. All it takes, after all, is the admission that a map database knows more about the road than you do.[6]

Consumer research studies indicated rising interest among U.S. consumers. One study reported that 58% of car owners had heard about vehicle navigation systems, primarily through television (37%) or published material (36%). Among those aware, most could recall the system's purpose and basic features, but relatively few understood what GPS meant, knew about voice prompts, or about systems being available in rental cars.

The same research reported that 70% of respondents were interested in purchasing a car navigation system. Among those, 26% were interested in buying an OEM, preinstalled, in-dash model with display, 57% voted for an after-market, on-dash model with a monitor, while 17% indicated preference for a lower-end, voice-navigation model with no display. Respondents were willing to pay US$700 to US$1,000 for a preinstalled OEM model, US$600 to US$700 for the second type, and US$500 to US$600 for the third type. Table 8–8 summarizes the research results.

Another survey conducted by J.D. Power and Associates focused on potential purchasers. The study involved 170 consumers taking two-day test drives of navigation system-equipped automobiles, and completing three

---

[6] *Wired*, Winter 1995.

Table 8–8   Survey of California car renters, January 1996

- Drivers were willing to pay, on average, US$5 more per day to rent a car with a navigation system.

- Drivers who would purchase or lease a car with a navigation system (70% of the sample) were willing to spend, on average, an extra US$550. Eleven drivers were willing to spend over US$1,000.

- Drivers who would buy navigation systems and install them in their current cars (35% of the sample) were willing to spend, on average, US$1,100.

- Twenty percent said they would buy the navigation system if it cost US$1,200.

- Twenty percent stated they used the system "all the time." Another 30% used it "a lot."

- Benefits mentioned in order of frequency: prevents you from getting lost in a new city; helps you find your destination; eliminates the need for maps; increases driving safety; you don't have to stop and ask directions; takes you via best route; gives feeling of confidence when driving.

- Problems mentioned in order of frequency: takes time to figure how to use it; destination not in computer; not able to calibrate alternate route; out of range error; directions unclear and/or hard to hear; monitor hard to read.

- Sixty percent found the navigation system worked better than they expected.

- Sixty percent used the system for guidance in getting to a destination. Twenty percent used it for finding points of interest, for experimenting with different routes and for determining current location.

- Two-thirds of respondents stated the device was easier to use when the car was parked. Forty percent believed it was distracting to use while driving.

Source: Compiled from a survey of 53 frequent Avis car renters in California, conducted by Center for Strategy Research, January 1996.

questionnaires: prior to driving the system-equipped cars (to assess awareness and image of the navigation systems); following a ten-minute test drive (to simulate consumer impressions after a dealership test drive); and after driving the car for two days (to simulate impressions following an experience driving a system-equipped rental car). Table 8–9 summarizes the research results.

The survey revealed that both the ten-minute and the two-day test drives enhanced respondents' understanding of the system's features, benefits, and ease of use. After the initial test drive, participants noted several key advantages including convenience, the ability to save time and money, the ability to replace maps, and less of a need to ask for directions. The extended two-day test drive led to lower stress and improved driving confidence. The

Table 8–9 Results of J.D. Power consumer survey, August 1995

- Using a ten-point scale for satisfaction, where ten is "extremely satisfied," 80% of respondents rated their overall satisfaction as a "nine" or "ten," resulting in a mean of 8.43.

- Sixty percent were "very likely" to recommend the system to family and friends after the ten-minute test drive. The percentage increased to 70% after the two-day test drive.

- Respondents preferred an in-dash OEM system to an on-dash after-market model by a margin of four to one due to perceived better quality and system reliability resulting from more professional installation and better integration with the vehicle's electrical system.

- Those who would buy an after-market system mentioned perceived transferability/portability and lower price as reasons for their preference. The average expected price for an after-market model was US$900, versus US$1,000 for an OEM system.

- Those preferring an after-market model expected to purchase it at "specialty store" (41%), "electronic store" (17%), "discount store" (13%), and "department store" (6%). "Specialty store" included outlets specializing in selling and installing alarms, audio systems, and vehicle cellular phones.

- Over 80% said that availability of a car navigation system would be an important factor in deciding which vehicle to purchase next time.

- Regarding the value of different points-of-interest information, "emergency assistance/hospital/police" was rated highest (9.03), followed by "auto care/gas" (8.23), "travel points" (8.13), "entertainment/tourist attractions" (8.04), "business facilities" (7.50), and "ATMs/banks" (7.39).

- Focus group discussions revealed high interest in points-of-interest listings of new and different entertainment and dining options, particularly in unfamiliar areas. Said one New York participant:

  "We went to Connecticut to visit relatives and arrived early and decided to get something to eat. We just looked through points-of-interest listings and selected a restaurant."

  A participant from Los Angeles noted:

  "The system opens up your world; it lists theaters, restaurants, and places you haven't heard of."

Note: This is a survey of 170 high potential purchasers by J.D. Power and Associates in July and August 1995. Respondents participated in a two-day test drive of a vehicle equipped with an Avis car navigation system. They were screened for the following criteria:
- Household income of at least US$50,000,
- Cellular phone ownership and monthly cellular phone bill of US$50 or more,
- Average of two or more hours per day in vehicle on business travel (excluding normal commute),
- Ages 25 to 59.

Source: Adapted from J.D. Power and Associates, *The Power Report*, November 1995.

longer test drive increased the likelihood of respondents recommending the system to family and friends.

In 1992, five years after Japan, the federal U.S. government began a six-year program of investing in smart highway technologies, including sensors, television cameras, and radars to monitor city traffic and relay traffic conditions to central computers. From workstations at command headquarters, technicians would be able to alter freeway signals and stoplights to reroute traffic, and relay advisories to cars equipped with more sophisticated navigation systems. On the other hand, safety regulations in 13 major states including California and New York prohibited any in-car visual devices, except for security purposes.

SONY IN INTERNATIONAL COMPETITION

Competition in Japan

In November 1990, the first GPS-based after-market car navigation system was introduced by Pioneer Electronic Corporation, a Japanese leader in car stereo and laser disc players. Since the GPS signal was not yet available around the clock and was easily interrupted by high-rise buildings in Tokyo, Pioneer defined the product as a "Satellite Cruising System," emphasizing the innovative and entertainment aspects of the product rather than its practical capabilities as a navigation device.[7] Pioneer had developed its own digital map software and stressed the variety of points-of-interest information its system could provide, ranging from hotels to restaurants. In addition, to distract drivers from Japan's endless traffic jams, Pioneer included entertainment software containing games, quizzes, horoscopes, and karaoke. Pioneer distributed the products through the same channels used for conventional car stereos, principally auto parts shops, since the product required professional installation. Despite a high retail price over US$5,000, Pioneer sold 20,000 units annually in the early 1990s.

The market changed dramatically in June 1993, when Sony entered the after-market segment with the NVX-F10 including a four-inch LCD monitor at a low price of US$2,000. Six months later, Sony introduced NVX-15 with a larger five-inch display at US$2,500. Unlike Pioneer, Sony emphasized the product's practical benefits and named it "Digital Map Car Navigation System." Sony advertised the product as a problem-solving device for drivers

---

[7] With only 12 satellites until 1992, GPS did not provide the signals necessary for 24-hour coverage. The system became complete with 24 satellites in 1993.

who did not want to face traffic jams, get lost in unfamiliar towns, or be late for appointments. These GPS-based products showed the driver's current position on the digital map screen, but did not provide route guidance toward the destination. However, sharply lower prices attracted many consumers. Aiming at rapid market expansion, Sony distributed almost 50% of its units through consumer electronics channels. Sony sold some 10,000 units monthly through 1993, achieving a 60% market share.

To develop the market further, Sony set out to establish an industry standard for digital map software. Sony was the most active member of the Navigation Research Association to set the NaviKen format for CD-ROM-based digital maps. The standard setting effort lowered entry barriers, resulting in ten new entrants in 1994 and another five in 1995. Competition fueled market growth from 160,000 units in 1993, to 340,000 units in 1994, and to 580,000 units in 1995.

Market growth encouraged intense competition and faster new product development. Table 8–10 reports the timing of product introductions by different competitors. Once every six months during 1994 and 1995, competitors introduced progressively more advanced products. In April 1994, Matsushita, which had not joined NaviKen, was the first to develop a hybrid system employing both GPS and the dead-reckoning sensor. The Matsushita model was also the first to be able to calculate and communicate the best route to a destination. In October 1994, Alpine, which was originally a NaviKen member but later became an independent developer, introduced the first hybrid model that could provide turn-by-turn route guidance. In early 1995, Pioneer introduced a new hybrid model with a flash memory chip in its central processing unit (CPU); this enabled the entire system to be upgraded by just installing a new CD-ROM. As shown in Figure 8–5, these more sophisticated hybrid models began to outsell the simpler GPS-based products by 1995.

NaviKen member companies, including Sony, did not respond quickly enough. It took the 40 NaviKen members more than a year to agree on a standardized software upgrade. In addition, NaviKen members saw little room to differentiate their products from each other. As shown in Table 8–11, Sony introduced new products almost every six months, but all were modified versions of the original GPS-based product, which did not provide automatic route calculation or turn-by-turn route guidance. In May 1994, Sony introduced NVX-F16, an extended version of the NVX-F15, but sold only 15,000 units by April 1996. In October 1994, Sony introduced NVX-B50 which employed a CD-ROM changer in which a driver could place six different CD-ROMs. The product sold only 9,000 units by April 1996. Sony had perhaps

Table 8–10 Number and timing of new product introductions in Japan: After-market models

Company/Brand	1990	1991	1992	1993	1994	1995	Total	1995 product line*
Pioneer	2	0	1	4	4	3	14	7
Sony	0	0	1	3	5	5	14	8
Matsushita	0	0	0	1	3	3	7	4
Alpine	0	0	0	3	2	2	7	2
Mitsubishi	0	0	1	1	3	4	9	6
Kenwood	0	0	1	0	3	2	6	3
Zanavi	0	0	0	0	0	4	4	4
Clarion	0	0	0	2	1	2	5	3
Fujitsu Ten	0	0	0	0	1	3	4	3
Nippon Denso	0	0	0	0	0	2	2	2
Sharp	0	0	0	0	3	0	3	2
Casio	0	0	0	0	1	1	2	2
Sumitomo Denko	0	0	0	1	3	1	5	3
Toshiba	0	0	0	2	2	3	7	5
Citizen	0	0	0	0	0	3	3	3
Calsonic	0	0	0	0	2	3	5	4
NEC	0	0	0	0	1	1	2	1
Chuo Jidosha	0	0	0	0	1	1	2	1
Maspro	0	0	1	0	1	1	3	2
Sanyo	0	0	0	1	0	3	4	3
Nakamichi	0	0	0	0	1	0	1	1
TOTAL	2	0	5	18	37	47	109	69

* After adjusting for discontinued products.

Source: Analysis of the case writer, based on research interviews.

introduced the product too early because the average navigation system owner had only 1.5 CD-ROMs as of 1995.

In July 1995, Sony finally introduced NVX-S1, a hybrid system with a route guidance function. However, the market did not respond well to this late entry. According to a trade magazine, NVX-S1, which still employed the NaviKen standard in its digital map database, calculated a route too slowly and provided turn-by-turn guidance too infrequently, compared to competitive products. See Table 8–12 for a summary of the magazine's product comparisons.

Figure 8–5   Unit market shares of advanced models in Japan, 1993–95

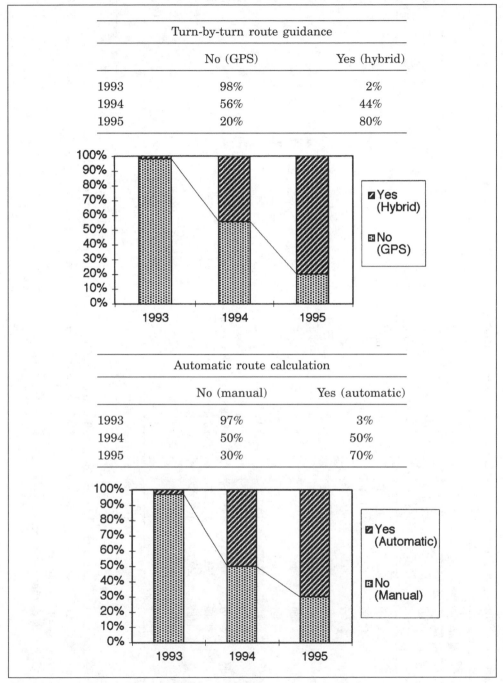

	Turn-by-turn route guidance	
	No (GPS)	Yes (hybrid)
1993	98%	2%
1994	56%	44%
1995	20%	80%

	Automatic route calculation	
	No (manual)	Yes (automatic)
1993	97%	3%
1994	50%	50%
1995	30%	70%

Source: Analysis of the case writer, based on research interviews.

Table 8–11 Sony product introduction chronology, 1992–95

Product	General information			Sales		Hardware		Functions			
	Retail price	Launch date	Cumulative unit sales[a]	1995 unit sales[a]	GPS or hybrid	w/ or w/o monitor[b]	Route guidance	Route calculation	Auto route re-calculation	Voice recognition
NVX-1	$4,700	92/06	7,000 (3%)	— (0%)	GPS	w/	No	No	No	No
NVX-F10	$2,100	93/06	100,000 (41%)	— (0%)	GPS	w/	No	No	No	No
NVX-F15	$2,800	93/10	15,000 (6%)	— (0%)	GPS	w/	No	No	No	No
NVX-F1	$1,600	93/10	4,000 (2%)	— (0%)	GPS	w/	No	No	No	No
NVX-2	open price	94/02	3,000 (1%)	— (0%)	GPS	w/o	No	No	No	No
NVX-F16	$2,500	94/06	15,000 (6%)	7,000 (7%)	GPS	w/	No	No	No	No
NVX-3	$1,400	94/06	4,000 (2%)	— (0%)	GPS	w/o	No	No	No	No
NVX-B50	$1,800	94/10	9,000 (4%)	4,000 (4%)	Hybrid	w/o	No	No	No	No
NVX-4	$1,500	94/10	9,000 (4%)	4,000 (4%)	Hybrid	w/o	No	No	No	No
NVX-F16MK2	$2,500	95/02	10,000 (4%)	10,000 (10%)	GPS (w/ hybrid option)	w/	No	No	No	No
NVX-A1	$1,300	95/04	4,000 (2%)	10,000 (10%)	GPS	w/o	No	Yes	No	No
NVX-S1	$1,500	95/07	40,000 (16%)	40,000 (41%)	Hybrid	w/o	Yes	Yes	No	Optional
NVX-F30	$2,300	95/07	20,000 (8%)	20,000 (20%)	GPS	w/	Yes	Yes	No	Optional
GPX-5	$2,100	95/12	3,000 (1%)	3,000 (3%)	GPS (w/ hybrid option)	w/	Yes	Yes	No	Optional
Total			243,000 (100%)	98,000 (100%)						

Notes:

[a] All sales (in US$) were made in Japan in the after-market. All products used the NaviKen format.

[b] "w/o monitor" means that the product was sold without a monitor. A customer needed to buy a monitor (which cost US$500–US$1,000) to complete the system.

Source: Analysis of the case writer, based on research interviews.

Table 8–12 Top ten brand product comparisons, 1995

Company	Product[a]	Retail price	Launch date	1995 unit sales[a]	Hardware		Software	Functions				Total score
					GPS or hybrid	w/ or w/o monitor[b]	Digital map format	Route guidance	Route calculation	Auto route re-calculation	Voice recognition	
Pioneer	AVIC-XA1	$2,630	95/11	30,000	Hybrid	w/	Original only	Yes	Yes	No	No	13
Sony	NVX-S1	$1,500	95/07	40,000	Hybrid	w/o	NaviKen only	Yes	Yes	No	Optional	12
Matsushita	CN-V700	$1,570	95/07	50,000	Hybrid	w/o	Both	Yes	Yes	Yes	No	22
Alpine	NTV-W055V	$2,480	95/11	40,000	Hybrid	w/	Both	Yes	Yes	Yes	No	23
Mitsubishi	CU-9510	$1,490	95/05	15,000	Hybrid	w/o	NaviKen only	Yes	Yes	No	No	14
Kenwood	GPR-03EX	$1,450	95/10	15,000	Hybrid	w/o	Both	Yes	Yes	No	Yes	13
Zanavi	XA-N1	$1,480	95/06	5,000	Hybrid	w/o	NaviKen only	Yes	Yes	No	No	18
Clarion	NAX9100	$1,470	95/11	10,000	Hybrid	w/o	Original only	Yes	Yes	No	No	19
Fujitsu Ten	E500NCU	$1,650	95/11	10,000	Hybrid	w/o	Both	Yes	Yes	Yes	No	14
Nippon Denso	MV-1000S	$2,580	95/01	3,000	Hybrid	w/	Original only	Yes	Yes	No	No	22
Average												17

User test result (5 = excellent, 1 = poor)

Company	Product[a]	Easy-to-use command	Easy-to-read monitor	Easy-to-find destination	Speed of route calculation (seconds)	Accuracy of route guidance
Pioneer	AVIC-XA1	2	3	3	2 (141)	3
Sony	NVX-S1	2	3	3	2 (121)	2
Matsushita	CN-V700	5	5	4	3 (58)	5
Alpine	NTV-W055V	4	4	5	5 (16)	5
Mitsubishi	CU-9510	3	3	2	2 (110)	4
Kenwood	GPR-03EX	3	3	2	3 (57)	2
Zanavi	XA-N1	4	3	4	4 (43)	3
Clarion	NAX9100	3	5	3	4 (46)	4
Fujitsu Ten	E500NCU	3	4	2	2 (110)	3
Nippon Denso	MV-1000S	5	4	5	4 (42)	4
Average		3.4	3.7	3.3	3.1 (74)	3.5

Notes:
[a] For each brand, this table reports sales (in US$) of the best-selling after-market model in 1995.
[b] "w/o monitor" means that the product was sold without a monitor. A customer needed to buy a monitor (which cost US$500–US$1,000) to complete the system.
Source: Adapted from *1996 New and Improved Car Navigation Systems*, Naigai Shuppan Publishing, 1995.

By 1995, competition focused on the richness of the digital map databases. In October 1995, Alpine introduced another new product with a database of 11 million phone numbers built into its digital map software which a driver could use to identify his/her destination. The product sold well, giving Alpine the market leadership, as shown in Figure 8–6. Other competitors followed suit, building more advanced databases filled with large numbers of phone numbers, landmarks, and other points-of-interest information.

Fighting against heavy odds in the main models, Sony turned its product strategy back to the GPS-based model, by introducing portable navigation systems. In December 1995, Sony introduced Handy Navigation System GPX-5, the world's first detachable model. It could be used both inside and outside an automobile, targeting customers who wanted to use the system for outdoor camping, bike touring, and marine sports. The GPS-based device alone retailed for US$2,000, with an option to purchase a gyroscopic sensor to convert the system into a hybrid for an additional US$300. A customer could also add a home station kit for US$200; this could connect a navigation system to a home television and enable a consumer to plan a route before going out to drive. See Figure 8–7 for pictures of Sony's portable navigation system.

European Competition

In Europe, car navigation systems were first installed on an OEM basis in luxury automobiles in late 1994. Philips developed its first system as an optional accessory to BMW's 7 and 5-Series models in October 1994. Philips' model employed a hybrid system with GPS and dead-reckoning sensors, provided route guidance by either map, arrows, or voice, and used the CD-ROM-based digital map software developed by EGT, a NavTech U.S. subsidiary. Retailing for DM6,900 (US$4,600), the first model sold 10,000 units in 1995. In September 1995, Philips started marketing the same product at the same price through after-market channels in Germany and France, but sold only 400 units in the last three months of 1995.

In October 1994, Bosch began supplying car navigation systems for Mercedes S-Class models. Bosch's product was similar to Philips', except that it provided route guidance only with arrow signs and voice direction, with no map on the display. Bosch employed the CD-ROM-based map database developed by Etak. Retailing for DM4,000 (US$2,700), the product sold 8,000 units in 1995. Bosch also developed a model with a map on the monitor for the after-market segment in Germany and France, introducing it in June 1995, three months earlier than Philips. Retailing for DM6,500 (US$4,300), the after-market model sold 1,800 units by December 1995.

Figure 8-6 Unit market share changes in after-market/auto parts chain channel in Japan, 1994–95

January–June 1994		July–December 1994		January–June 1995		July–December 1995	
Pioneer	24%	Pioneer	29%	Alpine	24%	Alpine	29%
Sony	24%	Alpine	16%	Pioneer	21%	Pioneer	20%
Matsushita	15%	Sony	13%	Matsushita	14%	Matsushita	15%
Kenwood	9%	Matsushita	11%	Sony	8%	Clarion	10%
Fujitsu	7%	Fujitsu	8%	Clarion	7%	Kenwood	9%
Clarion	6%	Kenwood	7%	Kenwood	6%	Sony	7%
Alpine	5%	Clarion	6%	Fujitsu	6%	Fujitsu	4%
Sumitomo Denko	4%	Sumitomo Denko	6%	Sumitomo Denko	3%	Sumitomo Denko	3%
Others	4%	Others	4%	Others	10%	Others	3%

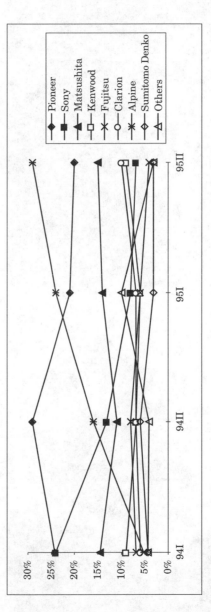

Note: This figure reports unit market shares in the auto parts chain channel, which represented 60% of after-market unit sales in Japan.

Source: Analysis of the case writer, based on research interviews.

Figure 8-7 Sony Handy Navigation System GPX-5

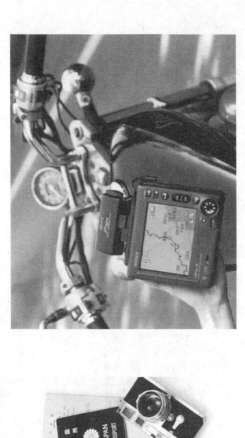

家で Home Navigation

外で Field Navigation

車で Car Navigation

Source: Company materials.

Besides the two European companies, only Sony competed in the after-market segment. Sony started test marketing its GPS-based model in France in late 1995, but sold only 300 units by April 1996. The product specification was similar to Sony's NVX-F16 and used Etak software. The GPS system pinpointed the car's current position on an LCD monitor, but did not give route guidance to the destination. It showed a driver where the destination was, but the driver had to plan the route. It was unclear whether Sony would continue marketing the tested model in Europe.

Some other companies including Alpine, Matsushita, and Pioneer were said to be planning to enter the European market in 1997–98. Luxury car manufacturers such as Jaguar and Volvo were reportedly considering OEM installation of car navigation systems. Volkswagen, Audi, and Opel were rumored to be seeking OEM suppliers of low-end models offering voice navigation with no monitor for around DM600 (US$400). Table 8–13 summarizes current and prospective competitors in Europe and the characteristics of their products.

U.S. Competition

As shown in Table 8–4 and Figures 8–1A and 8–1B, sales of one million units per year were expected in the U.S. by 2000. On the other hand, none of the models introduced to date had sold more than a few thousand units as of 1995. Car navigation systems were not yet widely known among U.S. consumers.

Industry observers believed price reductions would be critical before demand for car navigation systems would take off in the U.S. Market research revealed that few U.S. consumers would pay over US$1,000 for car navigation systems. Auto manufacturers had told car navigation makers that they needed to cut prices to as low as US$500, which is not expected until 2005 after further investments in mapping, data storage, and route guidance are completed.

Zexel, a Japanese auto parts supplier, was the first to bring car navigation systems to the U.S.[8] As an OEM, Zexel began supplying systems for GM's Oldsmobile Eighty Eight in the summer of 1994. Zexel's navigation products employed hybrid systems with GPS and dead-reckoning sensors and provided route guidance by either map, arrows, or voice. The digital map database was stored in a 170MB hard disk drive located in a car trunk. With the price tag of US$1,995, however, the product was expensive. In 1994, the most expensive car accessory in the U.S. was a US$1,200 European branded premium hi-fi

---

[8] Zexel did not sell car navigation systems either on an OEM basis or through after-market channels in Japan as of 1996.

Table 8–13 Current and prospective competitors in Europe

Current competitors

OEM

	General information				Hardware		Software	
Company	Auto maker	Retail price	Launch date	Cumulative unit sales	GPS or hybrid	Interface: map, arrow, voice	Digital map format	Software media
Bosch	Mercedes	DM4,025	94/10	8,000	Hybrid	arrow, voice	Etak	CD-ROM
Philips	BMW	DM6,900	94/10	10,000	Hybrid	map, arrow, voice	NavTech	CD-ROM

After-market

	General information				Hardware		Software	
Company	Product	Retail price	Launch date	Cumulative unit sales	GPS or hybrid	Interface: map, arrow, voice	Digital map format	Software media
Bosch	Travel Pilot	DM6,500	95/06	1,800	Hybrid	map, arrow, voice	Etak	CD-ROM
Philips	Carin	DM6,900	95/09	400	Hybrid	map, arrow, voice	NavTech	CD-ROM
Sony	NVX-160	DM5,500	95/10	300	GPS	map	Etak	CD-ROM

Prospective competitors

OEM

	General information				Hardware		Software	
Company	Auto maker	Retail price	Launch date	Expected unit sales	GPS or hybrid	Interface: map, arrow, voice	Digital map format	Software media
Mitsubishi	Volvo	—	Early '97	—	Hybrid	map, arrow, voice	TeleAtlas	CD-ROM
Bosch	VW	DM600	Early '97	—	GPS	voice	Etak	CD-ROM
Bosch	Audi	DM600	Early '97	—	GPS	voice	Etak	CD-ROM

After-market

	General information				Hardware		Software	
Company	Product	Retail price	Launch date	Expected unit sales	GPS or hybrid	Interface: map, arrow, voice	Digital map format	Software media
Alpine	NTV-W055V	DM6,000	Mid-'96	—	Hybrid	map, arrow, voice	NavTech	CD-ROM
Matsushita	—	—	Early '97	—	Hybrid	map, arrow, voice	—	—
Pioneer	—	—	Early '97	—	Hybrid	map, arrow, voice	—	—

Source: Analysis of the case writer, based on research interviews.

speaker system. Due to a lack of marketing expertise at Zexel and Oldsmobile and due to the fact that digital maps were only available for a few major cities, only 2,500 units were sold by the end of 1995.

Zexel licensed its product technology to Rockwell for after-market sales. Rockwell sold the product to rental car companies such as Avis and Hertz. The rental car companies purchased a few thousand units in total and rented the systems for a US$5 to US$7 daily upcharge. However, neither Rockwell nor the rental car companies had aggressively marketed the product.

Sony began marketing the NVX-160, the U.S. version of the Japanese model NVX-F16, in California and Florida in late 1994. Despite its lack of route guidance capability, Sony launched the NVX-160, the most advanced model in Sony's product line as of 1994, in order to be the first to market an after-market model. At a price of US$2,995, only 800 units were sold by the end of 1995.

A low-end product priced under US$1,000 was introduced in December 1995 by Amerigon, a Silicon Valley startup known for its voice recognition technology. The system was bundled with car stereos and sold under car audio brand names by manufacturers such as Alpine, Clarion, and Kenwood. The price was about US$600, although when the stereo and installation were included, the price was more like US$1,000 to US$1,500. This CD-ROM-based system, named AudioNav, did not employ GPS, relying instead on a dead-reckoning sensor alone. There was no monitor; only a voice system that used a microphone similar to the one in a cellular phone. The driver had to spell out the destination for route calculation. It was hands free, but the driver had to find a street sign or local landmark if s/he became lost. Unit sales to date are unknown.

Within a year or two Alpine and Nippon Denso were expected to supply OEM models to Honda and Toyota factories in the U.S. Pioneer, Alpine, and Matsushita were expected to enter the U.S. after-market segment, introducing modified versions of their latest domestic market models. Table 8–14 lists current and prospective competitors in the U.S. and characteristics of their products.

SUMMER 1996: RECONSTRUCTING THE GLOBAL STRATEGY

Masao Morita contemplated how to formulate its multinational marketing strategy for the fast changing car navigation systems market for the next five years. Given the different market conditions from one region to another and Sony's unsatisfactory position in each market, Morita resolved to re-evaluate the company's marketing strategy for car navigation systems and the benefits

Table 8-14 Current and prospective competitors in the U.S.

Current competitors

OEM

	General information					Hardware		Software	
Company	Auto maker	Retail price	Launch date	Cumulative unit sales		GPS or hybrid	Interface: map, arrow, voice	Digital map format	Software media
Zexel	GM/Oldsmobile	US$1,995	08/94	2,500		Hybrid	map, arrow, voice	NavTech	Hard disk (170MB)

After-market

	General information				Hardware		Software	
Company	Product	Retail price	Launch date	Cumulative unit sales	GPS or hybrid	Interface: map, arrow, voice	Digital map format	Software media
Sony	NVX-160	US$2,995	10/94	800	GPS	map	Etak	CD-ROM
Rockwell	GuideStar	US$1,995	01/95	7,000	Hybrid	map, arrow, voice	NavTech	Hard disk (170MB)
Amerigon	AudioNav	US$600	12/95	–	Dead-reckoning No GPS	voice	NavTech	CD-ROM

Prospective competitors

OEM

	General information				Hardware		Software	
Company	Auto maker	Retail price	Launch date	Expected unit sales	GPS or hybrid	Interface: map, arrow, voice	Digital map format	Software media
Alpine	Honda	US$2,000	Mid-'96	–	Hybrid	map, arrow, voice	NavTech	Hard disk (170MB)
Nippon Denso	Toyota	–	Late '96	–	Hybrid	map, arrow, voice	NavTech	Hard disk (170MB)
Bosch	Mercedes	–	Early '99	–	Hybrid	map, arrow, voice	Etak	CD-ROM

After-market

	General information				Hardware		Software	
Company	Product	Retail price	Launch date	Expected unit sales	GPS or hybrid	Interface: map, arrow, voice	Digital map format	Software media
Delco (US)	Telepath 100	US$500	Mid-'96	–	Dead-reckoning No GPS	voice	NavTech	CD-ROM
Pioneer	–	–	Early '97	–	Hybrid	map, arrow, voice	NavTech	CD-ROM
Matsushita	–	–	Early '97	–	Hybrid	map, arrow, voice	–	CD-ROM
Clarion	–	–	Early '97	–	Hybrid	map, arrow, voice	NavTech	CD-ROM
Kenwood	–	–	Early '97	–	Hybrid	map, arrow, voice	NavTech	CD-ROM

Source: Analysis of the case writer, based on research interviews.

Sony could and should provide drivers around the world. Morita needed to resolve the conflicting views within his company regarding several key issues.

Geographical Focus Issue

Some managers believed it was time to focus much more effort on markets outside Japan. One international marketing manager said:

> Both the European and U.S. markets are expected to grow as large as the Japanese market within ten years. We should preempt competitors with our own after-market models. We will be too late if we wait until these overseas markets take off. We should be the company that creates these markets as we have done at home.

In contrast, a marketing manager in Tokyo insisted that Sony should focus on re-establishing its competitive position in Japan:

> Our share is down because we have lagged behind our competitors in developing more accurate hybrid models and more sophisticated route guidance technology. The fact is, in 1996, 98% of our car navigation sales came from Japan. The growth forecasts for markets overseas are totally speculative.

The allocation of research and development (R&D) resources depended in part on Sony's geographical priorities. In 1996, Sony employed 200 highly skilled engineers dedicated to car navigation systems development, all of whom were stationed in Japan, except for one each in Europe and the U.S.

Product Choice

Given the poor performance of the NVX-160, it seemed that a simple GPS-based model at a price of US$3,000 was unlikely to appeal to drivers in Europe and the U.S. There were at least three product options for Sony: (1) launch the Handy Navigation System GPX-5, the portable GPS model most recently introduced in Japan, as a global product; (2) modify the hybrid NVX-S1 for Europe and/or the U.S.; or
(3) develop a new low-priced model for overseas markets.

A marketing manager in Tokyo emphasized the advantage of the GPX-5 as a global product:

> The portable nature of the GPX-5 should appeal to a much broader population including consumers interested in outdoor camping, bike

touring, and marine sports. Users can also use it to enjoy regular TV channels while traveling. Since the product is detachable, it is not strictly an automobile device so auto safety regulation and product liability issues may not apply. Portability also reduces the risk of theft.

The U.S. country manager, however, questioned the product's potential:

> For the product to succeed in the U.S., we need software with geocoded information specifically for camping sites, fishing locations, mountain skiing routes, and the like, all of which currently do not exist. It will cost at least US$1 million and take nine months to develop software for each recreation activity. By the time we have a variety of CD-ROMs, competition could be on a different basis. In addition, if the product is priced around US$3,000 again, it will flop. Finally, modifying the GPX-5 for the U.S. would require five engineers working on it for six months.

Another manager in Tokyo proposed to modify the NVX-S1, the hybrid model with turn-by-turn route guidance capability, for overseas markets:

> In countries where street names are clearly signed and road systems are straightforward, the current GPS-based model which only shows the driver's position on the map adds little value to drivers. We need a more sophisticated hybrid model which can be upgraded to accommodate future advances such as a real-time traffic information service and a traffic emergency warning system.

However, there were also pessimistic views regarding this product modification:

> In turn-by-turn route guidance technology, Sony lags far behind its competitors overseas. The product modification option requires Sony to reinvent its digital map software for the U.S. and European markets. When competitors launch more sophisticated route guidance systems, the present system will quickly become obsolete. Moreover, this option will incur substantial time and cost. It will take two years for our software vendor Etak to digitize U.S. and European maps for turn-by-turn route guidance. This will cost US$100 million in initial development costs and US$30 million for annual maintenance and content upgrades. This option will require 50 engineers to work with Etak in the U.S. and Europe. NavTech, Etak's competitor, will have soon digitized 100% of the U.S. and European maps for turn-by-turn guidance. We can switch from Etak to

NavTech, but we are not sure how much competitive advantage we will lose by using the same database as our main competitors.

Rejecting the above product modification options, some sales managers in the U.S. argued for developing low-end models from scratch, solely for the overseas market:

> As consumer research has shown, it is obvious nobody here will buy a US$3,000 gadget for his/her car. If we want to create a market here, we need a product designed to meet local needs. European and U.S. drivers don't need a fancy digital map nor an expensive LCD monitor and will be happy with some simple arrow and voice guidance at a price of US$1,000 or less.

The international marketing manager in Tokyo, however, strongly opposed this low-end product strategy:

> Even if a low-end stripped-down product stimulates the market in the short run, Sony will gain little in the long run. It will precipitate price competition and may shrink the market, at least in value terms. The product will not be adaptable to future developments in road infrastructure. It will diminish Sony's leadership image in car navigation systems. Furthermore, this option will need 60 of our engineers to work for a year on developing this new product. Given the competition we face at home, we cannot afford to divert them.

Standard Setting Issue

There was wide debate over the continuation of the NaviKen consortium. Some managers contended that Sony should leave NaviKen or at least develop proprietary digital map technology in parallel in order to compete head-to-head with other companies. A young manager in charge of product development stated:

> The NaviKen format was helpful early on. However, product introductions are now so frequent that we need our own digital map technology to respond quickly to the market's evolving needs. Customers appreciate a differentiated database to standardized ones. As one survey says, an average consumer owns only 1.5 CD-ROMs, and most do not use CD-ROM maps across different hardware anyway. Car navigation systems are not the same as personal computers.

In contrast, several of the digital map engineers who were heavily involved in establishing the NaviKen format in the 1980s opposed such a radical move. As one senior engineer stated:

> Such a myopic and opportunistic action may bring some market share in the short run, but hinder market development for the future. Standardized software will always benefit the consumer as well as the industry, as has been shown in the cases of CD players and VCRs. Our market research shows 80% of our customers care about software compatibility. As a market leader, Sony always tries to grow the market pie. Sony does not pursue a larger share of a shrinking market. After all we've put into establishing the NaviKen standard, why should we quit now? It is time for us to extend our effort overseas and to stimulate consumer demand as we have done in Japan.

Other managers took a compromised view. While supporting NaviKen in Japan, they proposed to establish different digital map formats for Europe and the U.S. One manager explained:

> To boost the market overseas, especially early on, we need a variety of compatible software. However, the NaviKen standard was developed for the unique Japanese road system, and is not extendible to other markets. Since the traffic infrastructures are very different from country to country, we should try to establish new product standards region by region.

Case 9

Vietnam: Market Entry Decisions

In May 1996, three U.S.-based multinational corporations (MNCs) were considering whether to enter Vietnam, and, if so, how. The world's 12th most populous nation, Vietnam was being widely discussed as a future "Asian dragon," because of the rapid economic growth and substantial inbound foreign direct investment (FDI) which had been stimulated by an ongoing series of liberalizing economic reforms in the previous ten years. Opinion was divided, however, on the political and economic future of the country, which remained a one-party communist state.

A number of U.S.-based MNCs were already operating in Vietnam, having entered immediately after the lifting of the U.S. trade embargo by President Clinton in February 1994. First to market, amid much publicity, had been PepsiCo, which, only seven hours after the lifting of the embargo, had started production in a bottling plant in which it had invested with Vietnamese and Singaporean partners, and the following evening placed advertisements featuring Miss Vietnam on national TV. Other early entrants, which had also been poised to enter at the earliest opportunity, included Motorola, Boeing, and several banks and accounting firms. These U.S.-based MNCs faced competition from many Asian and European corporations attracted by the potential growth in

This case was prepared by Assistant Professor David J. Arnold and Professor John A. Quelch as the basis for class discussion rather than to illustrate either effective or ineffective handling of an administrative situation. Company names have been disguised.

the Vietnamese market. A recent survey identified Vietnam as one of the most promising countries for future Japanese investment (see Table 9–1).

Table 9–1   Survey of Japanese corporations: Most promising countries for future investment

During the next three years	Ranking in 1995 survey	No. of 336 respondents' citings	Ranking in 1994 survey	No. of 238 respondents' citings
China	1	248	1	169
Thailand	2	122	2	75
Indonesia	3	110	4	58
U.S.	4	108	3	72
Vietnam	5	95	6	34
Malaysia	6	73	5	57
India	7	57	10	14
Philippines	8	52	10	14
Singapore	9	32	7	33
U.K.	10	24	9	19
During the next ten years	Ranking in 1995 survey	No. of 274 respondents' citings	Ranking in 1994 survey	No. of 284 respondents' citings
China	1	215	1	265
Vietnam	2	113	2	114
India	3	98	7	38
U.S.	4	83	4	85
Indonesia	5	66	5	83
Thailand	5	66	3	92
Myanmar	7	40	—	—
Malaysia	8	35	6	44
Philippines	9	31	10	19
U.K.	10	16	—	—

Source: Adapted from Export-Import Bank of Japan data.

The three MNCs had each been approached, both in their Asian offices and in the U.S., by numerous potential distributors, joint-venture partners, and consultants offering advice on market entry. The decision they faced was summarized by one consultant as follows:

It's a very difficult call. Vietnam is a large market in its own right, and it has a plentiful, well-educated, and low-cost workforce. Because it was one of the last countries to open its doors, it has been able to cherry-pick what it considers best practice from the emerging markets which have preceded it. What it has achieved so far is remarkable, especially when you remember that it's still run by the Communist Party. That's partly due to the Vietnamese, who are generally hard-working, and, especially in the south, entrepreneurial. But the government does seem genuinely committed to reform, and so far the transition has been remarkably smooth.

At the same time, there are still plenty of things about Vietnam that worry Western firms. Top of everyone's list are the corruption, the bureaucracy, and the lack of infrastructure. Also, the Communist Party has every intention of keeping firm control and retains some unnerving powers, such as the right to buy into foreign companies, or to decide the level of profits on which it will collect taxes. The pessimists had a field day in February, when the government dismantled all foreign-language billboards and painted out all foreign brand names on signs in Hanoi and Ho Chi Minh City as part of its campaign against "social evils."

It's early days yet. When you visit Vietnam, it still looks mostly undeveloped. The airports haven't been fully rehabilitated from the war, the roads are awful, and there's little sign of industrial development. But get into the city, and you'll find your hotel full of business visitors, you'll see the first tower blocks going up, the place is full of energy, and the streets are lined with small shops piled high with Western products. I've spoken to quite a few American managers who were sent here to assess the market entry situation, only to find their products already on sale all over the city. Some of them were counterfeit products, but some were genuine and had found their way here from other Asian markets.

Many companies I've spoken to are playing wait-and-see, but the market is open for business, and other firms are hoping for rich returns from getting in early.

COUNTRY PROFILE

The Socialist Republic of Vietnam was established in 1975 when, following decades of war, the country was reunified under the communist leadership of Ho Chi Minh. Vietnam had been partitioned into a communist north and a French-backed south by the 1955 Geneva Accords, following the defeat of the French colonial forces by Ho Chi Minh's army at Dien Bien Phu. Continuing tensions, and the increasing support of both Cold War military alliances, soon led to renewed war, which ended in 1975 with the withdrawal of American forces from the southern capital of Saigon (subsequently renamed Ho Chi Minh City). In 1996, all aspects of government were still controlled by the Vietnamese Communist Party and its Politburo from the capital, Hanoi in the north of the country. Ho Chi Minh City, the country's largest city, was regaining its former status as the commercial center of the nation. (See Figure 9–1 for a map of Vietnam and other parts of Asia.)

Figure 9–1   Map of Vietnam and other parts of Asia

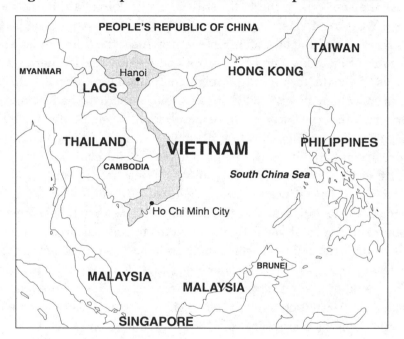

Doi moi (economic renovation) was officially launched at the Vietnamese Communist Party's 1986 Congress, and the subsequent reforms included deregulation of prices, reduction of subsidies to state enterprises, ending of the collective agricultural system, new commercial ownership laws to encourage private enterprise, new foreign investment laws, and policies directed toward the stabilization and convertibility of the Vietnamese currency, the *dong*. These reforms transformed a previously distressed economy (in 1986, inflation averaged 775%) into one of the fastest growing in the world. Economic indicators and comparative data for the principal Asian economies are reported in Table 9–2 and Figure 9–2. In 1996, the legislative program was continuing within the government's policy framework of "market socialism," which aimed to create a market-oriented economy under the control of the state.

Table 9–2   Vietnam: Economic data

	1995	1994	1993	1992
GDP (US$ million)	19,100	13,900	12,800	9,900
Real GDP growth (%)	9.5	8.5	8.1	7.8
Exports (US$ million)	5,200	4,250	3,010	2,600
Imports (US$ million)	7,520	5,850	3,900	2,550
Retail price inflation	14.2	15.5	6.5	17.8

Source: Adapted from Economist Intelligence Unit data.

Figure 9–2   Comparative performance data for Asian countries

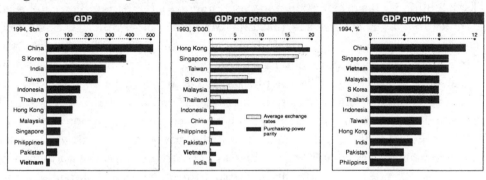

This economic growth had been fueled principally by FDI and the establishment of new private Vietnamese-owned organizations. The state-owned sector accounted for 40% of the gross domestic product (GDP) in 1995, and comprised approximately 6,000 state-owned enterprises (SOEs), half the number that had existed in 1990. To date, only three of these SOEs had been privatized (equitized). Government policy was to encourage foreign joint ventures with SOEs and to establish conglomerates in key industries following the model of the South Korean *chaebols*. By 1995, 17 such conglomerates had been established in industries including telecommunications, electricity, cement, steel, and garment manufacture. A Vietnamese government trade official described the objectives of this policy:

We are changing regulations and reducing tariffs to attract sufficient foreign investment to stimulate industrial growth, but not so much that it stifles the growth of the Vietnamese industry. The number of licenses granted in each industrial sector will be limited, and tariffs will be managed to balance imports and local production, in line with this policy.

Foreign investment commitments worth almost US$8 billion were made in 1995, twice the level of the previous year, bringing the total cumulative commitment since the launch of *doi moi* to approximately US$20 billion for over 1,300 approved projects. The total GDP of Vietnam in 1995 was US$19 billion. FDI projects in Vietnam averaged US$14 million to US$15 million of investment, compared with a US$1 million average in the People's Republic of China. Approximately US$8 billion of these commitments had been realized, of which US$4 billion was realized during 1995. The four largest sources of FDI were Taiwan (total cumulative commitment, US$3.3 billion), Hong Kong (US$2.2 billion), Japan (US$2 billion), and Singapore (US$1.6 billion), followed in rank order by South Korea, Australia, Malaysia, and France. U.S.-sourced FDI totaled approximately US$1 billion and was increasing sharply since the lifting of the trade embargo in February 1994, making the U.S. the tenth largest source of foreign investment. The major investment sectors were oil and gas, hotels and commercial real estate, telecommunications, services, and light manufacturing. In addition, Vietnam was pledged international aid worth US$2.3 billion for 1996, a 15% increase on the previous year, although many previous pledges had never materialized. The largest donor of foreign aid, which was intended primarily for infrastructure projects, was Japan.

Local private investment was running at approximately the same level as FDI, with some 20,000 private firms registered by the end of 1995. Local entrepreneurs faced a shortage of capital, given the country's low saving rate and underdeveloped banking sector. A significant contributor of both capital and human resources was the Vietnamese diaspora. The majority of the two million ethnic Vietnamese living abroad (the *Viet Kieu*) had fled from the south as the war ended in 1975 and had found refuge in North America, Western Europe, or Australasia. It was estimated that in 1994, 250,000 Vietnamese families had received a total of US$500 million from relatives living abroad. In 1994, the Vietnamese government reversed its previous policy and instituted preferential terms for *Viet Kieu* returning to their homeland, including classification as domestic residents for the purposes of taxation and the establishment of joint ventures. The greatest concentration of repatriated *Viet Kieu* was found in Ho Chi Minh City, where their entrepreneurial activities and taste for Western products contributed to that city's status as the commercial center of the nation.

Vietnam's population of 74 million, growing at 2% per annum, was the world's 12th largest and one of its most youthful: in 1995, approximately 50% of the population was aged 21 or younger. With a national literacy rate of 90%, the Vietnamese workforce was also one of the best educated among emerging markets in Asia. The recent economic growth had yet to change the living standards of the majority of the population, however. A 1994 World Bank report which praised the country's impressive economic progress also pointed out that 51% of the population lived in poverty. GDP per capita was US$235 in 1995, compared to US$2,000 in neighboring Thailand, with 4 televisions per 100 population (11 in Thailand) and 0.3 telephones per 100 population (3.1 in Thailand). These averages disguised wide variation between the major cities, where economic growth had been concentrated, and the countryside, still home to 80% of the population. This discrepancy, along with increasing pressure on agricultural land caused by population growth, was leading to significant migration to the cities. About 13% of Vietnamese lived in Ho Chi Minh City and Hanoi. Unemployment was estimated at 12%.

Vietnam joined the Association of Southeast Asian Nations (ASEAN) in July 1995.[1] Membership entailed participation in the ASEAN Free Trade Area (AFTA), one of the targets of which was to reduce tariffs on trade between member countries to a maximum of 5% by 2003, a deadline extended to 2006 for Vietnam. In the same month, Vietnam signed a cooperation agreement with the European Union (EU), which gave Vietnamese goods Most Favored Nation (MFN)[2] status in the 15 EU countries and vice versa, and included a schedule of increased European aid to Vietnam.

The restoration of full diplomatic relations with the U.S., also in July 1995, allowed the opening two months later of negotiations regarding trade normalization between the countries, including MFN status. American officials demanded as preconditions for granting of the MFN status agreement on the issue of American military personnel unaccounted for after the end of the war, and clarification of "the legal framework, intellectual property rights, trade practices, foreign exchange controls, human and labor rights."

---

[1] The other members of ASEAN are Brunei, Cambodia, Indonesia, Laos, Malaysia, Myanmar, the Philippines, Singapore, and Thailand.

[2] In a trade treaty between two countries, agreement to an MFN clause required that each country would trade with the other on terms at least as favorable as those agreed with any other country.

FORMS OF MARKET PARTICIPATION

A number of entry modes were possible for an international firm seeking to do business in Vietnam. All had to be agreed by the State Committee for Cooperation and Investment (SCCI).

The simplest arrangement was for an MNC to appoint a Vietnamese import agency and export finished product to that agent from outside Vietnam. Formerly, this would have required an international firm to deal with one of nine state-owned import organizations, but recent reforms extended the granting of import licenses to privately-owned Vietnamese firms, and an increasing number of such small distributors were eagerly seeking to represent foreign MNCs. Imported products were subject to tariffs, which had been introduced to replace import quotas as part of the *doi moi* reforms. In early 1996, these tariffs ranged from 5% to 100%, and averaged 25%, but were subject to frequent government revision and were inconsistently applied by customs officials. In addition to a license granting importer status, a separate product-specific license was required for the import or export of any item, however small, which had to be applied for with the bill of lading at least a week before the item was expected to arrive at the Vietnamese port of entry. Open licenses valid for six months for specified items could be granted to joint ventures, BCCs, or foreign-owned ventures; otherwise a license had to be obtained for each consignment.

MNCs wishing to invest in Vietnam had a variety of options. The government policy encouraged joint ventures between local SOEs and international organizations, and, in order to attract inbound investment, regulations permitted up to 70% ownership by foreign partners. The Vietnamese partner usually contributed its workforce, premises, equipment, and land use rights, the valuation of which could be problematic. The Foreign Investment Law included a buy-in stipulation, under which local parties could be granted the right to acquire an increasing share of foreign-owned ventures. In any joint venture designated by the government as an "important economic establishment" (mostly infrastructure development and energy industry projects), there was a legal requirement for the local partner to increase periodically its capital stake (and therefore equity share) in the project. A majority equity share did not bestow managerial control, however, as the law required unanimous voting by directors.

Government approval for wholly foreign-owned organizations was granted only in rare cases, typically large and complex projects, where joint ventures were not feasible. Like joint ventures, these organizations were limited to a 70-year life.

A processing contract allowed a foreign corporation to use a Vietnamese factory for production or assembly. If the products were intended for export, the foreign company could import necessary raw materials, could provide some of the equipment in the factory, and then re-export. To attract this type of venture, five Export Processing Zones (EPZs) were created, offering reduced taxation levels and ongoing investment in infrastructure. Their reputation suffered, however, from problems with power supply and water shortages, and the EPZ in Haiphong collapsed in late 1995 after the 70% owner, based in Hong Kong, declared bankruptcy. The most successful EPZ, Tan Thuan near Ho Chi Minh City, had attracted 60 projects. More recently, more projects had been established in new Industrial Processing Zones (IPZs), intended as centers for both domestic and export production. A number of consumer goods firms, including producers of cigarettes, soft drinks, and beer, had licensed manufacturers for small-scale production while awaiting approval of their joint-venture applications for larger new production facilities.

A business cooperation contract allowed a private Vietnamese enterprise and a foreign partner freedom to design their own contract, and no legal entity was established. Such an arrangement required submission to the State Committee for Cooperation and Investment (SCCI) of annual accounts, from which the SCCI calculated the profit it deemed the venture to have made, and levied taxes on the two partners at differential rates.

In 1995, the Vietnamese government published a list of major infrastructure projects which qualified for build-operate-transfer ventures. Under such an arrangement, a foreign organization would be allowed to build a property, such as a power station or a toll road, and then retain the profit from its operation for a specified time period, at the end of which it would be transferred to Vietnamese ownership without further compensation.

Finally, foreign companies could be granted a license to establish a representative office in Vietnam. The role of such offices was restricted to the promotion of international trade, or technical support for local importers or exporters, and such offices were prohibited from engaging in investment, trading, or marketing.

All forms of market participation were subject to approval by the SCCI and in many cases also required separate approval by additional government ministries or by People's Committees at the regional or city level. Consultants all warned that the granting of licenses was not only complex and time-consuming but also unpredictable, as procedures were often improvised because of the incomplete regulatory framework. One MNC, seeking to obtain a 70% stake in a joint venture, was reported to have been required to pay 120 separate fees over three years to obtain the necessary licenses, of which only 40 were required by regulations.

DOING BUSINESS IN VIETNAM

A number of additional factors were highlighted by consultants and managers, experienced in Southeast Asia, as critical to any market entry strategy.

Distribution

Potential distribution partners were plentiful but tended to concentrate only on a specified area, often as small as a few blocks in one of the major cities. The choice facing any MNC was often between a distribution organization partly or wholly owned by the government, and a young but small privately-owned distributor. The former would probably boast better connections with officials but might prove less aggressive in selling, while the latter would probably be more entrepreneurial but had yet to establish a customer base. National distribution required an extensive network of distribution partners; the Castrol oil company had to establish its own fleet of trucks to deliver motor oil to its many distribution points. The principal difficulty was described by one consultant as "telling the difference between the aggressive but competent distributor and the cowboys who will be knocking at your door as soon as you check into your hotel." He also warned that Vietnamese business tended to be based upon a

> trading culture.... Traditionally, goods have been scarce, and consumer demand could be taken for granted if you managed to get your product to the market.... The emphasis is still on moving product quickly, and negotiating over price, rather than what Western firms know as marketing or positioning. Honda has excelled at playing this game in selling motor scooters: the company appoints a large number of distributors, who then compete with each other to achieve the sales volumes they need to retain their agencies the following year. The result is that the cities are swarming with Honda motor scooters.

Corruption

Despite a government campaign and an increase in criminal convictions, corruption was prevalent at all levels in both industrial and government sectors. One experienced Asian MNC executive described Vietnam as "the worst country in Asia" in this regard, and attributed the problem to the generally low salary levels and the lack of an official schedule of fees for licenses and permits. One Vietnamese-American owner of a small Ho Chi Minh City distribution company indicated that U.S. corporations were especially challenged by this problem: "Their legislation[3] means that, if one of their managers gets caught, the liability can spread back up through the corporation. It scares them stiff, and it can put them at a real competitive disadvantage alongside Asian and European companies."

Vietnam's long coastline and mountainous frontiers facilitated smuggling of goods into the country. Around 40% to 60% of the consumer electronics piled high at streetside stores in Ho Chi Minh City were said to be smuggled, as were 100% of the highly visible foreign cigarette brands (because they were formally prohibited). U.S. products had been widely available in the major cities before the lifting of the trade embargo in 1994, including brands as varied as Kleenex (at three times the price of local brands) and Kodak (a number of Kodak processing outlets were in operation in Ho Chi Minh City as early as 1992). Executives from Castrol had reported competition from competitive brands of brake fluid which had been illegally imported as "motor oil" and thus charged only a 1% tariff instead of 35%.

Infrastructure

Years of war and economic hardship had left Vietnam with little infrastructure to support its ambitious economic reforms. The 1,000-mile trip between Hanoi and Ho Chi Minh City required five to eight days by Highway 1—the only road linking the north and south of the country—or two days by rail. Vietnam's two major ports, Ho Chi Minh City and Hai Phong, were both shallow-water harbors upriver from the sea, so large shipments had to be offloaded into smaller feeder ships at either Singapore, Hong Kong, or Kaohsiung, Taiwan. Both ports also lacked capacity and equipment to cope with booming imports, as did the country's main airports. Delays were exacerbated by product loss or damage in transit running at rates as high as 25% to 50%. Office and production premises could be subject to periodic power outages and telecommunications blackouts.

Costs

One of the major attractions of Vietnam for foreign investors was the low labor costs. Typical monthly compensation in Ho Chi Minh City and Hanoi was US$40 for an unskilled laborer (the legal minimum wage), US$100 for a

---

[3] The Foreign Corrupt Practices Act.

secretary, and US$200 for an engineer or manager. Additional employment costs were typically 50% of compensation. Rates were one-third lower outside the two major cities. Although the level of basic education was good, managerial talent was scarce. Foreign investors also faced high office rents, and the process of establishing an office was slowed by the need for land-use permits for all premises. Telecommunications costs were also high, up to US$20 per minute for calls to the U.S., for example. Both property and telecommunications costs were expected to fall with continued market development.

PROFILES OF THREE MULTINATIONAL CORPORATIONS

The three U.S. MNCs considering entry into Vietnam were all experienced in international operations, and all aspired to global leadership in their industries. Table 9–3 summarizes their international distribution arrangements.

Chemical Corporation

Chemical was the world leader in chemical adhesives and sealants for industrial applications. The company's core product range, which always formed the introductory line when entering new markets, was positioned as a replacement technology, offering superior performance-cost relative to more traditional mechanical fastenings and seals. The range of potential applications was wide, including virtually all manufacturing operations, after-market applications such as automotive servicing, and even some consumer applications. The firm marketed its specialty chemicals as low-volume, premium-priced, branded products and expected to have a diverse and fragmented customer base. This marketing strategy was built upon two major thrusts. First, sales personnel were trained to tailor their offering to the individual applications of customers. Most important, this entailed "pricing to value," which required an analysis of the long-term savings to the customer of performance improvements from switching from traditional and ostensibly cheaper technologies. Second, the firm strived to maintain technological leadership by requiring that 30% of revenues should flow from products introduced in the previous five years. In support of these two strategies, Chemical, which enjoyed a 61% gross margin, invested 32% of its 1995 revenues in sales and marketing and 7% in R&D laboratories in the U.S., Ireland, and Japan. Chemical's executives, who estimated their market share to be as high as 80% in the domestic U.S. market, viewed their major challenge as market expansion.

Table 9–3 International distribution organization of three U.S. MNCs

	Chemical Corp.	Sports Corp.	Children Corp.
Total global network			
Independent distributors	11	30	5
Joint ventures	0	11	1
Direct distribution subsidiaries	45	17	30
Asia-Pacific region			
Independent distributors	Indonesia New Zealand	Australia Indonesia New Zealand	Philippines South Korea Taiwan Thailand
Joint ventures (MNC ownership 50% or less)		Philippines (33%) Hong Kong (33%) Singapore (33%) Malaysia (33%) Thailand (28%) Taiwan (25%)	
Direct distribution subsidiaries (100% unless shown)	Australia Hong Kong Indonesia Japan Malaysia People's Republic of China (75%) Philippines Singapore South Korea Taiwan Thailand	Hong Kong India (60%) South Korea (80%) People's Republic of China (66%) Japan (51%)	Australia Hong Kong Indonesia Japan Singapore

International distribution was a strength. From its foundation, the firm had been approached by numerous distributors wishing to carry its products, and it was part of company lore that its products were crossing the Atlantic Ocean before they crossed the Mississippi River. The global distribution network had evolved independently of manufacturing operations, because of the low bulk-to-value nature of its products. By 1995, the company's manufacturing operations were located in the U.S., Puerto Rico, Ireland, Costa Rica, Japan, and Brazil, with additional operations (to meet local regulatory requirements) in India and the People's Republic of China. This logistics network could supply new markets at short notice: the ex-Soviet-bloc countries of Eastern Europe, for instance, were supplied from Ireland via a warehouse in Vienna within three days of a new distributor being appointed and/or placing an order.

Chemical favored independent distributors for market entry, because of their existing product ranges and customer base, which provided both economies of scope for the initial low-volume business, and access to industrial customers who felt no obvious need for this replacement technology. The firm emphasized training and support to distributors in the difficult selling challenge posed by its product range, and the higher margins it offered to the general industrial supply houses who made up the majority of its distributors. To encourage investment in business development, distributors were generally granted territorial exclusivity. In many cases, however, sales had reached a plateau after several years in the market, and Chemical had switched to a direct distribution subsidiary. The slowdown in sales growth was variously attributed to the lack of marketing capability by the distributor or a lack of ambition to dominate the market (distributors were often small, privately-owned organizations). In the words of the head of the firm's operations in China, "Our own people always outperform even the best distributors. They run out of steam because they don't immerse themselves in our technology and the benefits it can deliver to customers." All Chemical's 45 national distribution subsidiaries had evolved from independent national distributors.

Chemical's vice president for Asia Pacific, based in Hong Kong, had been with the company for 30 years, the last 16 in Asia. The region accounted for 13% of corporate sales revenues in 1995 and had grown 21% since 1994. Over the previous two years, Chemical's Asian operations had been restructured in response to their growing size, and, by 1995, there were four marketing sub-regions reporting to Hong Kong: Eastern Asia, which included Japan and South Korea; Greater China, comprising the People's Republic of China, Taiwan, and Hong Kong; Central Asia, including India; and Southeast Asia, including Singapore, Malaysia, Indonesia, the Philippines, Thailand, Australia, and New Zealand. The regional Hong Kong office comprised five executives and two support staff. Chemical's products would be subject to a 30% import tariff in Vietnam. The regional vice president commented:

A lot of our attention is focused on Asia these days, because of slower growth in America and Europe and because so many of our U.S. manufacturing customers are setting up here. We have an established operation here in Hong Kong, and I know we can serve Vietnam well enough from our new logistics base in Singapore. If we exported into Vietnam, using a representative office to provide technical support, our products would be three or four times the price of the local or Chinese adhesives they are using at the moment.

We have received six approaches from distributors wanting to represent us—four from Ho Chi Minh City, one from Hanoi, and one from a *Viet Kieu* working with our products in a major customer in California. Frankly, I don't know how to evaluate these potential distributors. I doubt if any of them have the sense of quality and service needed to represent Chemical and sell its products effectively. I suppose we could set up a representative office to provide technical support. We have also been approached by an SOE seeking to establish a manufacturing joint venture, but we're in India and the PRC already.

Sports Corporation

Sports Corporation, founded in 1978, enjoyed explosive growth in its youth and fashion-oriented market for sports footwear and apparel. Still under the leadership of its founder, Sports ranked second in global market share in most of its product markets. The company contracted out virtually all its manufacturing to independent suppliers in Asia and viewed its core competences as product design and marketing expertise. Sports' success depended on the ability to deliver innovative products to a fast-changing and segmented market. As a result, brand building, advertising and promotion, endorsements by sports teams and celebrities, and retail channel relations were all especially important.

The majority of Sports' products would face a 40% import tariff on entering Vietnam, although for some the rate would be only 20%. Maintaining normal margins, Sports' cheapest pair of sneakers could retail for US$35 a pair. In 1995, Sports' major competitor had established production in Vietnam under a processing contract. Although product from this plant was intended for re-export, it was thought that investment in production facilities would have a beneficial effect on the brand's market development in Vietnam. Sports executives commented that demand might prove stronger than in other emerging markets, because of the high brand awareness spread by *Viet Kieu* returning from the U.S. and other countries.

Reflecting the values of its founder, Sports sought as its international distributors "entrepreneurs with their own money on the line and a fortune to be made from rapid growth." Distributors were given territorial exclusivity and

are typically all servants of many masters. They never want one player to grow too strong. To gain market leadership, we have to get control of our own business and innovate." Despite this, Children recognized the value of independent distributors as market entry partners, given the closed character of distribution systems in many country markets. It had never entered a new country market by establishing a wholly-owned subsidiary at the outset.

Asia Pacific was the firm's smallest region in terms of sales revenue, accounting for 11% of 1995 sales, but was regarded as having the greatest long-term potential. Children's manufacturing operations, recently expanded by the installation of substantial new capacity in Indonesia, were run as a stand-alone global division which supplied the company's marketing organizations. The firm faced uneven demand due to the seasonality of gift-giving, and therefore its coordinated production schedules were inevitably skewed to suit its largest markets at the expense of the smaller ones.

Children's vice president for Asia Pacific was based at the U.S. corporate headquarters. A small team of four regional staff in Hong Kong aided Children's country managers. After an uneven history in Asia, attributed to the "complex and protectionist" distribution systems in the region, recent sales growth was strong, especially in Japan, where several previous ventures had ended in failure. The regional vice president commented:

> Some of my colleagues say it's far too early to enter Vietnam, because of the undeveloped retail sector. We need the right retail environment to support our brands, which despite our best efforts will be more expensive than the toys currently on offer. But I believe that we should appoint a distributor to start selling in Vietnam now. In fact, our best-selling products are already available in the airport duty-free shops in Ho Chi Minh City and Hanoi. Demand would be very concentrated in the two largest cities, so we could easily identify the special gift-oriented distribution channels. Also, television broadcasting is relatively advanced, so advertising would be possible from day one.[4]
>
> We have been approached by two SOEs that make toys. Their products are low quality and retail on average for US$3 a unit, compared to our US$15. However, these SOEs claim to have access to over 1,000 retail distribution points throughout the country, and the top managers in one of them seem young and aggressive. But I'd be concerned about our molds

---

[4] Total advertising spending was US$100 million in Vietnam in 1995, up from US$31 million in 1994.

being duplicated without our knowledge. We have also been asked whether we'd be interested in a processing contract, using excess capacity at one of these SOEs to assemble our toys for export. Given current labor rates, we could save US$1 a unit if we assembled some of our more labor-intensive toys in Vietnam.

Gillette Indonesia

In October 1995, Chester Allan, Gillette's country manager in Indonesia, was developing his unit's 1996 marketing plan. Once completed, it would be forwarded to Rigoberto Effio, business director in Gillette's Asia-Pacific group based in Singapore. Each year, Effio received and approved marketing plans for the 12 countries in his region, which stretched from Australia to China. Once approved by Ian Jackson, Asia-Pacific group vice president, the overall marketing plan for the region would be reviewed subsequently, along with other regional plans, by Robert King, executive vice president of Gillette's International Group.

Allan's plan projected a 19% increase in blade sales in Indonesia in 1996 from 115 million to 136 million. This seemed reasonable given a 17% increase in 1995 over the previous year. With a population of almost 200 million, Indonesia represented an important country in the portfolio of markets for which Effio and Jackson were responsible. Effio wondered whether investment spending in marketing beyond the 1995 level of 12% of sales might further accelerate market development. Given the growth rates of Gillette's business in other Asia-Pacific countries, Effio believed that a 25%–30% increase in blade sales could be achieved in Indonesia in 1996.

This case was prepared by Research Associate Diane E. Long under the supervision of Professor John A. Quelch as the basis for class discussion rather than to illustrate either effective or ineffective handling of an administrative situation. Confidential data have been disguised.

THE COMPANY

Founded in 1901, Boston-based Gillette was the world leader in blades and razors and in nine other consumer product categories—writing instruments (Paper Mate, Parker, and Waterman), correction products (Liquid Paper), men's electric razors (Braun), toothbrushes (Oral-B), shaving preparations, oral care appliances (Braun, Oral-B plaque remover), pistol-grip hair dryers (Braun), hair epilators (Braun), and hand blenders (Braun).

Gillette manufacturing operations were conducted at 50 facilities in 24 countries. A London office had been opened in 1905, and a blade factory opened in Paris the following year. The company's products were distributed through wholesalers, retailers, and agents in over 200 countries and territories.

Gillette managed its worldwide business through a combination of business and regional operational units. The North Atlantic Group manufactured and marketed Gillette's shaving and personal care products in North America and Western Europe. The Stationery Products Group, part of the Diversified Group, produced and sold Gillette's stationery products in North America and Western Europe. The Diversified Group also included Braun, Oral-B, and Jafra, each managed by a worldwide unit. The International Group, headed by Robert King, produced and marketed the shaving, stationery, and personal care products everywhere, except for North America and Western Europe. The International Group comprised three geographic divisions: Latin America; Africa, Middle East, and Eastern Europe; and Asia Pacific. Ian Jackson, group vice president based in Singapore, oversaw operations in 12 Asia-Pacific countries.

Of Gillette's 1995 sales of US$6.8 billion, blades and razors accounted for US$2.6 billion (40%). Blade and razor sales in the Asia-Pacific region were more than US$600 million. The company had consistently maintained profitable growth over the previous five years. Between 1990 and 1995, sales grew by 9% annually, net income by 17%, and earnings per share by 18%. Gillette's mission was to achieve worldwide leadership in its core product categories. In 1995, three quarters of sales came from product categories in which Gillette held worldwide share leadership. The company emphasized geographic expansion along with research and development, advertising, and capital spending as drivers of growth. New product activity and entry into and development of new markets were considered essential.

Geographic expansion required the company management to "think global, act local." Eduardo Kello, International Group business manager, explained:

> Headquarters develops new products. They are usually launched first in
> the U.S. or Western European markets, but quickly introduced in every

market worldwide. We start in a new emerging market with simple blades, we introduce the shaving concept. Later, we upgrade the market to higher value products and shaving systems. The country management in each market usually decides the mix of products to push and how to allocate marketing resources against them.

Robert King further emphasized the importance of persuading Gillette's country managers to take initiative:

Trying to drive new product activity from headquarters is like pushing on a string. The string moves much more easily if a country manager is pulling on it than if headquarters is pushing on it.

While headquarters in Boston emphasized increasing worldwide sales and distribution of higher-margin shaving systems such as Sensor, this was not feasible in many Asian markets. Only a few consumers were sophisticated and wealthy enough to be potential customers for Sensor. In Indonesia, for example, the focus was still on introducing the concept of shaving with basic Gillette products.

INDONESIA IN 1996

The Republic of Indonesia was an archipelago of more than 15,000 islands and 196 million people who spoke over 250 regional languages and dialects. (See Figure 10–1 for a map of the country.) Approximately 3,000 miles separated Sigli on Sumatra to the west from Sarmi on Irian Jaya to the east. President Suharto led the country from 1965 to 1998 and provided continuity and stability. Major economic development programs, legal reforms, and changes in domestic policies could be enacted only if supported by the president.

By 1995, Indonesia's population had reached 196 million, with 35% living in towns and 65% in rural areas. Indonesia had averaged annual gross domestic product (GDP) growth of over 7% for more than 20 years. The country traditionally exported agricultural and oil petroleum products, but economic development plans since the oil crisis of 1988 had encouraged growth in nonoil-related industries. Economic policy was laid out in five-year plans known as Repelita.[1] The goals of Repelita VI, applicable in 1996, were to maintain annual GDP growth of 6.2%, expand the manufacturing sector by 9.4% a year, and expand the nonoil/gas component of manufacturing by 10.3% a year.

---

[1] Repelita is the shortened form for the Indonesian name *Rencana pembangunan lima tahun* which meant five-year development plans.

Figure 10–1 Map of Indonesia

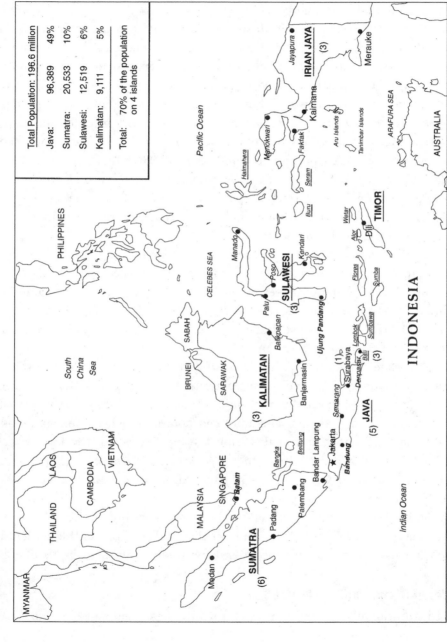

Note: Numbers in parentheses indicate number of Gillette distributors in a particular region.

Total Population: 196.6 million		
Java:	96,389	49%
Sumatra:	20,533	10%
Sulawesi:	12,519	6%
Kalimatan:	9,111	5%
Total:	70% of the population on 4 islands	

Inflation in 1996 was expected to be 12%. Over the years, liberalization of the foreign investment policy had increased private sector involvement in the economy; the central government focused on developing infrastructure in the poorer regions and on human resources.

Economic progress was manifested in increased per-capita incomes and improved standards of living for most of the population. The government stressed export-oriented industrialization to fuel growth and a demand for labor that would keep pace with population growth. During Repelita VI, it was expected that more than two million Indonesians would enter the workforce each year. The rupiah[2] had depreciated in order to maintain Indonesia's export competitiveness. The value of committed foreign investment reportedly increased from US$826 million in 1986 to US$10.3 billion in 1992 and to US$23.7 billion by June 1994.[3] In 1996, Indonesia was expected to have the highest foreign direct investment/export ratio (74%) of any major emerging market. However, only around one-half of approved foreign direct investment projects had been implemented.

Economic growth had not been consistent throughout the archipelago. Java and Bali had grown much faster than poorer regions such as Irian Jaya and East Timor; contribution of these poorer regions to the country's economy was minimal. Java and Bali accounted for 7% of the land, 60% of the population, and 75% of GDP. Four of the five major urban centers (Jakarta, Bandung, Surabaya, and Semarang) were in Java.

The average standard of living in Java and Bali was much higher than in the rest of Indonesia. An improving education system ensured that foreign companies would be attracted to the major urban areas, fueling further growth. Market research showed that consumer marketers launched their campaigns in and expected most of their sales from the top five cities (the four in Java plus Medan in Sumatra) which together accounted for 35 million of the population. About 60% of Gillette's 1995 sales were made in these five metropolitan areas.

Table 10–1 shows the percentages of households falling into each of several income classes in 1995 and projections for 2000. Also shown is the percentage of each income group who shopped regularly in supermarkets in 1995.

INDONESIAN SHAVING PRACTICES

Gillette traditionally entered a market with the basic double-edge blade. Effio

---

[2] Rupiah exchange rate in 1995 was US$1 = 2,200 rupiah.

[3] *EIU Country Profile 1995*, p. 19.

Table 10–1 Percentages of households by income sector and supermarket shopping incidence, 1995 and 2000

	Percentage of population		Percentage shopping in supermarkets: 1995
Income segment	1995	2000 (estimate)	
>$10,000	15.9	20.6	40
$5,000–$10,000	17.0	19.6	25
$2,000–$ 5,000	32.7	33.8	10
<$ 2,000	34.4	25.9	2

explained, "We lead with our strength—the shaving business. Later we leverage the distribution established for our blades on behalf of our other product lines."

Shaving was still underdeveloped in Indonesia, but the incidence of shaving was increasing (see Table 10–2). A 1995 survey of urban men over 18 years (of whom there were 40 million) indicated that 80% shaved. Those who did, shaved on average 5.5 times per month, compared with 12 times per month in Hong Kong and 26 times per month in the U.S. Tracking data indicated that, in 1993, 66% of urban adult men had been shaving with an average incidence of 4.5 times per month.

Table 10–2 Shaving incidence per month

Shaving incidence per month	Percentage of surveyed
10 times or more	15
5–9 times	34
4 times	26
3 times	10
2 times	7
1 time	8

Shaving incidence was influenced by several factors. There was increasing awareness of Western grooming practices, especially in urban areas, as a result of exposure to foreign media and the increasing presence of multinational companies and their overseas personnel. College students and graduates entering the workforce were especially important trendsetters. On the other hand, grooming products were still regarded as luxury items by many. In addition, Asian beards did not grow as fast as Caucasian or Latino beards, so shaving incidence would be lower, even in a fully developed market.

Forty percent of men who shaved used store-bought blades all or part of the time. The remainder used dry or wet knives. The average number of blades used in a year by the 20% of shavers who always used blades was 15. The average number of blades used by occasional users was four. Only 4% of men used shaving foam or lotion; 25% used soap and water, 12% used water alone, and 58% shaved dry.

GILLETTE'S OPERATION

Gillette entered Indonesia in 1971 with majority ownership of a joint venture with a local company. Gillette's razor blade plant, built in 1972, was an hour's journey from Jakarta. Gillette manufactured 75 stockkeeping units in the factory, of which 65 were shaving items. The major product was the double-edge blade for razors and cartridges. Double-edge blades accounted for 60% of the value of products manufactured. Oral-B products were a small portion of the plant's operations; the plant had just begun to "tuft" or put the bristles on the brush handles. The plant was highly automated and run by 68 full-time employees. In addition, 75 casual workers were employed on one to two-year contracts. In 1995, the plant produced 150 million blades, of which 46 million were exported. The 1996 production plan called for output of 168 million blades, of which 50 million would be exported. Production manager Eko Margo Suhartono said:

> We are looking to import new equipment and expand the line capacity to 230 million double-edge blades per year which we hope will be sufficient to meet demand for the next five years. We needed this extra capacity by 1996 but implementation has been delayed to 1997. This means, in 1996 we will have more overtime and must continue to improve plant productivity.

The manufacturing team had improved business processes as well as production efficiencies. They cut the cycle time from placement of order to product out the door from 50 to 43 days. Effio explained, "Before it would take us 7 days to make almost 3 million blades; now we only need 3 days on the floor. This is an incredible response to sales demand." Due to the demand of other MNCs for experienced workers, there was a need for continuous staff recruiting and training, and increasingly upward pressure on worker wages.

In addition, the production team carefully planned the timing of materials inputs. Due to distribution and transportation inefficiencies, the need for buffer inventories was substantial. Cartridges and handles for the razors were imported. Gillette's women's razor was launched in 1995. The razor was imported, but packaged in the country. Problems with customs clearances could impact the entire manufacturing cycle.

The plant obtained electricity from the local grid, supplemented by two backup generators. Water was drawn from a well on the property. Gillette purchased ammonia and other basic raw materials from local suppliers.

GILLETTE AND COMPETITIVE PRODUCT LINES

The Gillette brand name was synonymous with high-quality double-edge blades. In fact, the Bahasa Indonesian word for blade sounded similar to the name Gillette. In 1993, Gillette held 28% of the blade market by volume. By 1995, Gillette's unit share had grown to 48% and was expected to increase to 50% in 1996.

Gillette's policy was to make all of its products available to all of its country subsidiaries. Headquarters' persuasion and successful launches of new products in other countries were often helpful in motivating country managers to adopt new products.

Gillette's product line in Indonesia included the following:

- Three types of double-edge blades. They were the basic Gillette blue stainless blade, a premium double-edge blade (Gillette Goal Red), and an improved blue blade (Gillette Goal Blue).
- Disposables. In the U.S. and Europe, Bic dominated the market for disposable razors with plastic handles as a result of aggressive pricing. In other markets, Gillette had been able to position its disposables as a system, rather than a low-priced convenience product. In Indonesia, Gillette sold two types of disposables, the Goal II and the more advanced Blue II.
- The GII (named Trac II in the U.S.). It was the earliest shaving system from Gillette to incorporate twin blade technology, whereby the first blade lifted the hair out of the follicle for the second blade to then cut it off.
- The Contour system (named Atra in the U.S.). It had a pivoting head (as opposed to the fixed head on the GII), which enabled the twin blades to stay on the face more consistently.
- The Sensor system. Its independently sprung twin blades contributed to an improved pivoting action.

Table 10–3 provides a detailed breakdown of Gillette sales by product. Information on Gillette's gross margin as well as manufacturer, distributor,

Table 10–3 Gillette Indonesia's product line and margin structure, 1995

Products	Unit sales (million)		% of units sold made locally	Manufacturer selling price/unit[a]	Manufacturer gross margin (%)	Distributor selling price/unit[b]	Retail selling price/unit
	1995	1996 (estimate)					
A. Double-edge blades	100	108					
Gillette Blue Blade	5	5	100	0.06	47	0.08	0.11
Gillette Goal Red	80	90	100	0.11	50	0.15	0.20
Gillette Goal Blue	15	13	100	0.08	48	0.11	0.15
B. Disposables	5	10					
Goal II	4	8	100	0.21	32	0.31	0.40
Blue II	1	2	0	0.35	52[c]	0.49	0.64
C. Systems blades	10	18					
Gillette GII	2	3	20	0.45	52	0.68	0.82
Gillette Contour	5	7	20	0.55	52	0.77	1.00
Gillette Sensor	3	8	0	0.65	40[c]	0.91	1.19

Notes:

[a] In U.S. dollar equivalent.

[b] Distributors often sold (at an average 8% markup) to subdistributors or wholesalers who in turn (at an average 12% markup) sold to mom-and-pop retailers who took, on average, a further 20% markup.

[c] Represents, in the case of imported products, the difference between Gillette Indonesia's selling price and the landed transfer price.

and retailer selling prices by product line is provided. Gillette sold 115 million blades in Indonesia in 1995, of which 100 million (87%) were double-edge. In contrast, double-edge blades accounted for 70% of sales in Malaysia and only 20% in Australia. Sales of systems and disposables accounted for 30% and 50% of units sold in Australia and 25% and 5% of units sold in Malaysia. The share of Gillette Indonesia sales accounted for by the higher-margin disposables and systems was projected to increase in 1996 to around 20% of units.

As indicated in Table 10–4, Gillette Indonesia's 1995 sales of shaving products were valued at US$19.6 million. Through a combination of volume increases (19%) and price increases (20%), Gillette Indonesia management projected that this number would increase to US$27.6 million in 1996. Gillette's overall gross margin on shaving products was 46% of gross revenues (or 55% of net revenues after discounts). An income statement for Gillette Indonesia's shaving products business is presented in Table 10–5.

Gillette's main competitors were imported, low-end, double-edge blades from Eastern Europe and China. Based on market research conducted in the four major cities, Tatra, Super Nacet, and Tiger were the most often mentioned competing brands in the market. Gillette's retail prices were sometimes four times those of competitive products. Chester Allan in Jakarta explained, "Currently, most of the poorer rural shavers cannot afford Gillette products and buy low-price, low-quality brands such as Tiger and Tatra. However, with rising incomes and improved Gillette distribution and display, consumers are moving to Gillette."

Gillette's disposables faced two competitors: Bic, from the U.S. and Bagus, a locally-manufactured brand. Neither of these sold in high volumes, so the competition was not keen. The Schick division of Warner Lambert imported its higher-end products, but sales were minimal. According to Allan, "Gillette has 90% of the premium-priced segment of the market which we developed."

Gillette-brand blades commanded high awareness in the Indonesian market. Market research conducted in 1995 among Indonesian male shavers, reported in Table 10–6, showed 97% brand awareness and 55% brand used most often ratings for Gillette's Goal Red blade.

DISTRIBUTION AND SALES

Indonesian regulations prohibited a foreign company from directly importing or distributing its products. These regulations protected Indonesian distributors and resulted in inefficiencies. The American Chamber of Commerce in Jakarta estimated that 45% of retail prices in Indonesia covered distribution services.

Table 10–4   Gillette Indonesia's sales breakdown (US$ million), 1995 and 1996

Sales revenues	1995	1996*
Revenues from export sales	1.4	2.3
Revenues from in-country	21.6	29.9
Total revenues	$23.0	$32.2

In-country sales		
a. Shaving products		
Blades	10.3	11.2
Disposables	1.2	2.5
Sensor	5.6	10.4
Razors	2.0	3.0
Prep products	0.5	0.5
Total sales	$19.6	$27.6
b. Nonshave products	$2.0	$2.3

* 1996 estimated figures.

Table 10–5   Gillette Indonesia: Percentage income statement for shaving products, 1995

Gross revenue from shaving products	100%
Less trade discounts	10%
= Net revenues	90%
Less variable manufacturing costs	36%
variable selling costs (sales commissions)	2%
variable distribution costs	6%
= Gross margin	46%
Less advertising	9%
consumer promotions and merchandising	3%
general sales and administrative costs	14%
= Profit from operations	20%

To ensure distribution of products in the face of weak communications, poor traffic conditions, and lack of distribution service technology, Gillette managers and those in other MNCs had to focus on the basics of distribution over which they had little control and from which they extracted no direct profit.

Table 10–6   Indonesian male consumer awareness and usage of blades (percentage), 1995

Products in survey	Brand awareness	Ever used	Brand used most often
a. Double-edge blades			
Gillette			
Gillette Goal Red	97	85	55
Gillette Goal Blue	49	18	5
Gillette Blue Blade	14	5	1
Competitors			
Tatra	42	21	4
Super Nacet	16	4	—
Tiger/Cap Macan	59	44	11
b. Disposable			
Goal II	41	16	4
Blue II	9	3	—
c. Systems blades			
Gillette GII	12	4	1
Gillette Contour	9	4	3
Gillette Sensor	12	4	1

Note: The survey was based on a sample of 300 male adult consumers.
Source: Company records.

Gillette had originally appointed a single national distributor, but by 1993 it was apparent the arrangement was not working satisfactorily. No single distributor could provide an even depth of coverage in every district throughout the entire country. Mohammad Slamet, Gillette's national sales manager in the early 1990s, explained:

> There are many distribution issues which require on-the-spot responses. A distributor who is headquartered hundreds of miles away cannot provide a quick enough response. In addition, there often arise sensitive, purely local, issues which can only be resolved by someone familiar with the relationships, customs, and dialects of each area.

In 1993, Gillette appointed 23 distributors dispersed across the country. The new distributors were previously known to Slamet or were identified through referrals. In the year following implementation of the new system, sales rose by 60%.

A good distributor had the working capital and/or bank credit line to stock sufficient inventory and to bridge the time gap between paying Gillette and receiving payments from its customers. Second, a good distributor also had sufficient salespeople, warehouses, and reliable transportation equipment. Third, strong local connections with government officials and the trade were critical to success.

A typical distributor represented different manufacturers and product lines. Gillette's distributors were encouraged to hire people to handle only the Gillette business in the belief that such focus would result in a greater push. Gillette itself expanded its internal sales and trade relations staff to work with the new distributors.

In 1995, Nyoman Samsu Prabata was Gillette's national sales manager. Nyoman's organization comprised three regional managers (covering Western, Central, and Eastern Indonesia) who oversee a total of 12 area managers and supervisors. These managers were well compensated but were often tempted away by better offers from other multinationals as there was a shortage of general management talent in Indonesia. Nyoman's group coordinated the efforts of 23 geographically-based independent distributors and their 260 salespeople. While Gillette's distributors hired many of the sales staff and paid their base salaries, Gillette covered their commissions and other incentives for reaching targets, which averaged 20% of their total compensation.

Nyoman explained:

> The number one job of the Gillette sales team is educating the distributors and their salespeople. We have to train them how our products work, so they can demonstrate the products on their own. We have to educate them on the benefits of our products compared to both traditional shaving methods and to competitive products. We also educate them on warehousing and handling methods to reduce damage to the product.

For example, one distributor's warehouse was located in an area of Jakarta with poor transportation and prone to flooding. "A few days ago, the warehouse roof fell in under pressure from the rain. The actual damage was minimal but the operation had to stop for a day. He just would not listen to us," explained Nyoman.

In Indonesia, direct verbal confrontation was socially unacceptable. This sometimes resulted in strained relations between a distributor and an area manager festering for months without being solved. Another challenge was the different degree to which employees and consumers observed Muslim religious practices. Nyoman commented:

In Jakarta, while people are faithful followers, the attitude is a bit more casual and there is an understanding that not everyone is practicing to the same degree. However, outside Jakarta, religious practices are more closely observed. In Aceh, Sumatra, it would be an insult to wave good-bye with your left hand. In Bali, the Hindu religion is dominant so, for the "Galungan" holiday, Hindus fast for two days. For Nyepi, complete silence must be observed for one day, so any devout Hindu stays home and does not even turn on the electricity. Not only does this affect our business but I must plan ahead for holiday staffing.

Gillette gave its distributors 45 days' credit. In return, the distributors would give their customers anywhere from 30 to 60 days' credit. Nyoman said:

While we try to insist on timely payments via bank transfer, there are many times when receivables are overdue. Though the sales staff and area managers are responsible for receivables, I often have to get involved and it is important to be tough on the issue. As you move further away from Jakarta, the legal system does not provide much support, so ensuring distributors have the working capital to cover the spread between payables and receivables is critical to their selection.

In addition to the distributors who supplied wholesalers and, in turn, the extensive network of small retailers in Indonesia, Nyoman also supervised a national accounts team who negotiated sales to the major Indonesian supermarket chains, often shipping to them direct. Supermarket chains included Hero which had 54 outlets, Metro with 5 outlets, and others located in the large urban centers. These chains purchased directly from manufacturers and could handle products efficiently. In 1995, supermarkets accounted for 5% of Gillette's shaving products sales in units and 8% in value. The corresponding 1993 figures were 2% and 4%. Market research showed that higher-income, urban consumers were increasingly shopping in supermarkets. Most sales of Gillette's higher-priced shaving products were through these outlets. Competition for shelf space was intensifying. Some supermarkets were imposing slotting allowances on suppliers of up to 80% of a new product's cost to provide shelf space.

Traditional wholesalers and distributors came under pressure as a result of these trends. Many wholesalers had poor facilities, traditional goods-handling methods, and antiquated accounting—some still used an abacus to track the business. They tended to focus on turnover alone rather than in conjunction with profit margin. They were also slow to see the potential of upgrading their customers to higher-unit margin products.

Distribution coverage in Indonesia required consumer goods manufacturers like Gillette to reach more than 60,000 small kiosks and mom-and-pop stores. Gillette did not distribute through the many itinerant salespeople who traveled with their wares on bicycles from village to village. The entrepreneurial owners of the small retail outlets would respond to requests from consumers and, in turn, demand the product from their wholesalers. "Pull marketing can be effective," Slamet said. "Once the mom-and-pops start getting requests for a new product, they are willing to stock it. This is how market testing takes place," Effio explained.

COMMUNICATIONS

As indicated in Table 10–5, Gillette Indonesia spent 9% of gross sales on advertising and 3% on consumer promotions and merchandising. Ten percent of gross sales was accounted for by off-invoice allowances to the trade and other forms of trade deals. The advertising budget for shaving products in 1995 was around US$2 million.

Media advertising was targeted principally at urban male consumers. About half the advertising budget was spent on television (there were five private channels and one government owned) and half on print. Television advertising included some program sponsorships. The adult literacy rate in Indonesia was 77%, and half of Indonesian adult males read a newspaper at least once a week. The allocation of Gillette advertising was weighted toward systems and disposables to encourage consumers to trade up.

Gillette headquarters developed television advertisements for use worldwide, with the intent that local voiceovers and local package shots be superimposed. A sample Gillette print leaflet and its translation are shown in Figures 10–2A and 10–2B. Gillette Indonesia's marketing manager explained:

> We are still in the early stages of educating consumers about shaving. An ad made in Boston for the U.S. market may not have sufficient details about the basics. Nothing can be taken for granted here, especially when it comes to advertising the entry level products, the double-edge blades.

Gillette Indonesia's managers differed over the relative emphasis that advertising should place on persuading consumers to shave for the first time, increasing the incidence of shaving among existing shavers, and trading existing shavers up to higher-margin, more sophisticated shaving systems. As a compromise, the 1995 advertising budget was split equally among these three objectives. One-third of the total budget was allocated to advertising Sensor.

Figure 10–2A Gillette Indonesia's print leaflet

ENAM LANGKAH MENCUKUR LEBIH LICIN, LEBIH LEMBUT DAN LEBIH NYAMAN

Tahukah Anda ?

- Jumlah rambut yang tumbuh di wajah pria bisa mencapai 30.000 helai.
- Pertumbuhan rambut tersebut per hari rata-rata 0,38 milimeter.
- Panjang maksimum yang bisa dicapai seumur hidup sekitar 80 sentimeter.
- Dalam keadaan kering, janggut sama kakunya dengan serat lembaga yang berdiameter sama.

- **18.000 SEBELUM MASEHI** Manusia primitif mengerik rambut pada wajah mereka dengan batu dan tulang yang dipertajam, sebagaimana tergambar pada lukisan-lukisan di goa purba.

- **336 SEBELUM MASEHI** Iskandar Zulkarnaen menilahkan para prajuritnya untuk bercukur, sehingga tentara Persia tak dapat menjambak janggut mereka dalam pertempuran.

- **1698.** Kaisar Rusia, Peter Yang Agung, mengenakan Pajak atas janggut, untuk membiasakan rakyatnya mengikuti tradisi bercukur yang dilakukan masyarakat Barat.

- **1895.** King C. Gillette, asal Amerika, menemukan pisau cukur moderen yang mengubah total kebiasaan bercukur pria di seluruh dunia. Dimana-mana orang meninggalkan pisau cukur tradisional dan menggantinya dengan pisau cukur bermata ganda yang dapat diganti-ganti.

---

1. Bersihkan Wajah

Cucilah muka dengan air hangat dan sabun, lalu bilas hingga bersih. Tak perlu dikeringkan, biarkan kulit wajah dan rambut dalam keadaan basah.

2. Usapkan Gillette Foamy

Usapkan Gillette Foamy secara merata di atas permukaan yang akan dicukur.

Mencegah penguapan air dan mengurangi gesekan antara kulit dengan mata pisau. Sekaligus melembutkan kumis atau janggut yang akan dicukur.

3. Mulailah dari tempat yang Tepat.

Cukur rambut cambang, pipi, dan leher terlebih dulu. Rambut yang paling kaku tumbuh di dagu dan sekeliling bibir dan memerlukan waktu lebih lama untuk menyerap air untuk menjadi lembut.

4. Bercukurlah secara Benar.

Bercukurlah dengan tarikan yang lembut dan ringan. Usahakan untuk sesedikit mungkin melakukan tarikan. Pisau cukur Gillette dirancang untuk menghasilkan cukuran yang lebih licin, lebih lembut dan nyaman.

5. Bilaslah Mata Pisau

Di tengah kegiatan mencukur, sesekali bilaslah mata pisau cukur dengan air yang deras (misalnya dari keran) guna membuang limbah cukuran. Usai bercukur, mata pisau harus langsung dibilas dan dihentak - hentakkan sampai airnya kering.

6. Jangan Mengusap Mata Pisau.

Jangan sekalikali mengusap mata pisau dengan apa pun, karena akan merusak ketajamannya.

Gunakan cartridge yang sesuai dengan pisau cukur Gillette Anda.

Figure 10–2B English translation of Gillette Indonesia's print leaflet

SIX STEPS TO A SMOOTHER, GENTLER AND MORE COMFORTABLE SHAVE

1. Clean your face

Wash your face with hot water and soap, then rinse it until it is clean. You don't have to dry it, leave your face and hair wet.

2. Apply Gillette Foamy

Apply Gillette Foamy evenly over the surface to be shaved. It prevents water evaporation and reduces friction between the skin and the razor blade. At the same time it softens the mustache or beard which you are going to shave.

3. Start at the Right Place

First shave the sideburns, cheeks and neck. The stiffest hairs grow on the chin and around the lips and need more time to absorb water in order to become soft.

4. Shave Correctly

Shave with gentle and light strokes. Try to make as few strokes as possible. The Gillette razor is designed to produce a smoother, gentler, more comfortable shave.

5. Rinse the Razor Blade

While shaving, rinse the razor blade once in a while under running water (for example from the tap) to get rid of the whiskers. After shaving, the razor blade must be rinsed right away and shaken until dry.

6. Don't Wipe the Razor Blade

Don't ever wipe the razor blade with anything, because it will destroy its sharpness. *Use the cartridge that is right for your Gillette razor.*

Do you know?

- Up to 30,000 hairs can grow on a man's face.
- The hairs grow at an average rate of 0.38 millimeters per day.
- They can reach a maximum length of approximately 80 centimeters (32") over a lifetime.
- When it is dry, a beard is as stiff as copper fibers of the same diameter.

- **18,000 B.C.** Primitive men scraped the hair off their faces with sharpened stones and bones, as depicted in drawings in ancient caves.

- **336 B.C.** Alexander the Great ordered his soldiers to shave so that the Persian army would not be able to grab their beards in battle.

- **1698.** Peter the Great, Czar of Russia, imposed a tax on beards to get his people used to following the shaving practices of Western societies.

- **King C. Gillette**, an American, invented the modern razor, which totally changed men's shaving habits all over the world. People everywhere gave up traditional razors and replaced them with replaceable double-edged razors.

Special promotions were run in 1995 on the Sensor and Contour systems. Gift-with-purchase promotions (involving an Oral-B travel toothbrush, a toilet bag, or a trial sample of Foamy shaving cream) were targeted at upper to middle-income urban males. Promotional efforts were sometimes focused on members of executive clubs, attendees at golf tournaments, or workers in specific office buildings.

Coupons were not used in Indonesia as redemption systems through retailers were not yet in place. However, Gillette found that lucky draws with entry forms inside product packages worked well. Consumers had to send in entry forms to be included in the draws.

Gillette used similar packaging in Indonesia as in the U.S. for its more expensive systems products. The Goal II, the cheaper of Gillette's disposables, was advertised on radio. The number of blades per pack varied by outlet; twice as many were included in the pack for supermarkets as in the pack for mom-and-pop stores.

SETTING THE COURSE

As Allan reviewed his initial projections for 1996 (see Table 10–4), he wondered how rapidly the Indonesian market for blades and razors could or would expand. Should the Indonesian market be allowed to just move along at its own pace? If so, what would that pace be? Alternatively, should Gillette Indonesia invest additional resources either in advertising and promotion or in sales and distribution, to accelerate the process of market development? If so, which products should be emphasized? Would further investment be wasted if it were on concepts and products that were beyond consumers' understanding or willingness to pay?

Allan resolved to set out his objectives for Gillette Indonesia in 1996 and to develop a detailed marketing plan including an income statement projection. He knew his plan would have to satisfy Effio's objectives for Gillette's growth in the Asia-Pacific region.

Case 11

Asiaweek: Positioning a Regional Magazine

"To report accurately and fairly the affairs of Asia in all spheres of human activity, to see the world from an Asian perspective, to be Asia's voice in the world."

Asiaweek's mission statement, 1975

The mission statement laid down by Asiaweek's founders, T.J.S. George and Michael O'Neill, had appeared in every issue of the magazine since its establishment in December 1975. Asiaweek had been through good times as well as bad between 1975 and this hot, humid day in Hong Kong in June 1998, when the editorial and business managers gathered to discuss the next steps in building the magazine's brand.

Broadly speaking, Asiaweek had remained true to its mission statement, though it was not always clear what was "Asia" and the editorial message had wavered in the early 1990s. It was also losing money badly then. Subscription renewal rates were poor because of a short-term circulation focus, and top brands had stopped advertising in the magazine. The appointment of a new editorial team in 1994, a shift to a long-term strategy on circulation, and closer attention to advertising management helped to alleviate the financial problems but did not fully resolve them.

This case was prepared by Jocelyn Probert and Hellmut Schütte as the basis for class discussion rather than to illustrate either effective or ineffective handling of an administrative situation.

Jocelyn Probert is Research Analyst and Hellmut Schütte is Professor of International Management at INSEAD Europe-Asia Center.

By the late l990s there were new challenges to face. Asiaweek had become one of the top-selling English-language weekly magazines in the region, and the best-selling magazine concentrating coverage on Asia. Did this mean it had reached its limits for growth? How could Asiaweek extend its franchise and grow in the future, while remaining relevant to its Asian audience? How could—or should—it compete with global magazines like its sister publication Time, or Newsweek, both of which had extended their coverage of Asia and launched Asian editions in recent years?

The financial crisis that struck Asia in mid-1997 also had implications for Asiaweek. Advertisements were the magazine's most important source of revenue. There had been some recovery since the initial shock, but if Asian economies were going to be depressed for a long time there could be tough times ahead. Asiaweek needed to find a better balance between its advertising and circulation revenues, but how would that be possible in countries like Indonesia where the local currency had devalued so heavily?

THE ASIAWEEK STORY

Just as Newsweek was set up in the U.S. by two former journalists from Time magazine, so Asiaweek was established in Hong Kong by ex-journalists of the English-language weekly Far Eastern Economic Review. In 1975, T.J.S. George, an Indian, and Michael O'Neill, a New Zealander, announced their intention to publish a magazine for "middle-class Asians." They believed that "hundreds of thousands of people in Asia, for whom English was a second language, were not being served by any publication that covered the whole of Asian life in a coherent way."[1]

The first issue appeared on December 19, 1975. The Asiaweek formula covered the political, economic, and general news scene in Southeast Asia. Although the brief was to write stories in simple, easy to read English, the number of people in Asia in the late 1970s who were able and interested to read such an English-language magazine was not easy to estimate.

Initial circulation was just 12,000, and the magazine did not make money. Reader's Digest bought Asiaweek in 1982, but the two founders retained editorial direction. Although circulation had climbed to 60,000 by 1985, it was still a loss-making venture. In that year the New York-based Time Inc. publishing empire acquired the magazine from Reader's Digest.

T.J.S. George, who had edited the magazine between 1975 and 1981, acted as group senior editor before leaving Asiaweek in 1982. Michael O'Neill,

---

[1] Quoted in "Asiaweek Founder Dies," *The Daily News*, May 17, 1997.

Table 11-1   Time Warner's financial results: Five-year record

	1993	1994	1995	1996	1997
			US$ million		
Revenues	6,581	7,396	8,067	10,064	13,294
Operating income	591	713	697	966	1,271
Income from Entertainment group	28	176	256	290	686
Net income (loss)	−221	−91	−166	−191	246

Figure 11-1   Operating income noncash amortization of intangible assets ("Ebita"), 1997

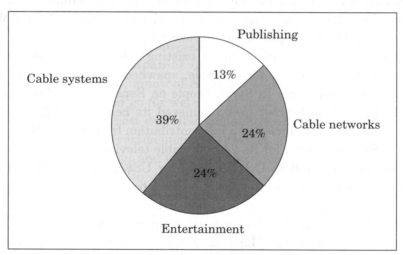

Source: *Time Warner Inc. Annual Report 1997.*

advertising. Traditionally, publishers worldwide viewed circulation as a way to attract advertising. The main goal was to get a magazine into the hands of as many people in its target audiences as possible, and then use the circulation figures as the basis on which to charge advertisers for placing their ads in it. Circulation could be "bought" through expensive direct mail campaigns or steep discounts on advertised subscription charges in order to boost a magazine's advertising rate base. Although circulation was used to establish advertising rates, total readership—calculated on the number of people who read each copy—and the quality of that audience were actually what interested the advertisers. Organizations such as the Audit Bureau of Circulation (ABC) guaranteed circulation figures, but for readership data advertisers relied on

Table 11–2 Time Warner's empire

Cable Networks	Publishing	Entertainment	Cable Systems	
Home Box Office	**Time Inc.**	**Warner Bros.**	**Time Warner Cable**	
HBO	Time	Warner Bros. Pictures	Divisions of more than	
HBO Family	People	Warner Bros. Television	100,000 subscribers	
HBO en Espanol	Sports Illustrated	Warner Bros. Television Animation	at December 31, 1997	
Cinemax	Fortune	Looney Tunes		
HBO Pictures	Life	Hanna-Barbera	**Divisions/ Subscribers**	
HBO NYC Productions	Money	Castle Rock Entertainment	**Clusters**	**('000s)**
HBO Independent Productions	Parenting	Telepictures Productions	New York City	1138
HBO Home Video	In Style	The WB Television Network	Tampa Bay	781
HBO Enterprises	Entertainment Weekly	Warner House Video	Central Florida	568
Time Warner Sports-TVKO	Cooking Light	Warner Bros. Consumer Products	Raleigh/Fayetteville	423
	Baby Task	Warner Bros. Studio Stores	Milwaukee	374
Joint Ventures	Coastal Living	Warner Bros. International Theaters	Greensboro	359
Comedy Central	Halth	Warner Bros. International Enterprises	Charlotte	356
HBO International	Hippocrates	DC Cosmics	Austin/Waco	351
HBO Ole and Brasil	People en Español	Mad Magazine	Los Angeles	341
HBO Asia	Progressive Farmer		Syracuse	309
HBO Central Europe	Southern Accents	**Warner Music Group**	Rochester	299
	Southern Living	Warner Bros. Records	Houston	295
Turner Broadcasting	Sports Illustrated For Kids	The Atlantic Group	Hawaii	294
System, Inc.	Sunset	Elektra Entertainment Group	San Antonio	293
CNN	Teen People	Sire Records Group	Columbia, SC	261
CNN Headline News	This Old House	Warner Music International	Northeast Ohio	254
CNN International	Time for Kids	Warner Chappell Music	Memphis	254
CNN*fn*	Weight Watchers	WEA Inc.	Boston	237
CNN/SI	Your Company	Ivy Hill Corp.	San Diego	227
CNN en Español	Asiaweek	WEA Manufacturing	Cincinnati	223
CNN Airport Network	Dancyu	WEA Corp.	Albany	210
CNNRadio	President	Warner Special Products	Kansas City, MO	207
CNN Interactive	Wallpaper	Alternative Distribution Alliance	Minneapolis	192
TBS Superstation	Who Weekly	Giant Manufacturing	Columbus	187
Turner Network Television	Time Life Inc.		Western Ohio	166
Cartoon Network	Book-of-the-Month Club	*Joint Venture*	Eastern Pennsylvania	
Turner Classic Movies	Warner Books	Columbia House	152	
TNT Europe	Little, Brown & Company		Green Bay	142
Cartoon Network Europe	Oxmoor House		Wilmington	133
TNT Latin America	Leisure Arts		Chicago	131
TNT & Cartoon Network	Sunset Books		Portland, OR	129
in Asia Pacific	Time Inc. New Media		Indianapolis	120
Cartoon Network Japan	Time distribution Services		El Paso	117
Atlanta Braves	Warner Publisher Services		Detroit	115
Atlanta Hawks			Jackson/Monroe, MS	109
Atlanta Thrashers	*Joint Venture*			
World Championship	American Family Enterprises		*Joint Venture*	
Wrestling			Road Runner	
Goodwill Games				
New Line Cinema				
New Line Cinema				
New Line Features				
New Line Television				

Substantially all of the assets of Home Box Office and Warner Bros. and most of Cable Systems shown above are held in Time Warner Entertainment Company, LP. Time Warner owns 74.49% of the residual equity and certain priority interests of TWE. A portion of Cable Systems is held in a partnership of which approximately two-thirds are owned by TWE.

Source: *Time Warner Inc. Annual Report 1997.*

market research organizations that conducted surveys sponsored by groups of publishers.

Until the oil shock recessions of the 1970s, magazines had always resisted discounting from their advertising rate cards. Such trading "off rate card" intensified in the U.S. during the advertising recession of the early 1990s, as advertisers played off one magazine against another for better discounts. Magazine publishers were forced to look more closely at circulation as a revenue stream in order to offset the downturn in advertising revenue. The most profitably circulated titles tended to have high newsstand sales and high newsstand prices. By raising their newsstand and subscription prices most magazines brought circulation sales up to around half of revenues.

In Asia, the general situation was different. Advertising rates among English-language publications remained much higher than they were in the U.S. because of the type of audience the ads were targeted toward: the cream of each local population. Regional magazines could command higher rates than the local media, which tended to be less developed. Circulation therefore continued to contribute only a small share of a magazine's total revenue, and strategy was driven by the advertising market, i.e., advertisers' requirements determined the countries where a magazine would want to increase its circulation and how much the magazine was prepared to invest to do so. Advertising revenues were more volatile than circulation but were earned in U.S. dollars. Circulation revenues were steady but were vulnerable to local currency movements.

One of the main readership surveys sponsored by major publishers in Asia was called Asian Profiles (AP). The market research company ACNielsen-SRG had conducted the survey every three years since 1976 in seven cities in Asia— Bangkok, Hong Kong, Jakarta, Kuala Lumpur, Manila, Singapore, and Taipei. Tokyo was excluded for cost reasons. Seoul had been dropped from the original list of eight cities after a few years for the same reason. The AP survey asked people aged 25 or over who were employed in senior positions in business, the professions, education, and government about their reading habits (which daily, weekly, or monthly newspapers and magazines they read), as well as items such as air travel, hotel stays, product ownership, and annual personal income.

The need to reach the new affluent Asian consumer and capture trends in a larger proportion of Asia's prosperous new middle class prompted an expansion of the universe of the AP survey in 1997. In addition to the 1.96 million people covered by the AP survey, researchers interviewed a sample of people representing a further 1.2 million affluent consumers aged 20 or over.

The renamed Asian Target Markets Survey (ATMS) thus represented a universe of over 3.1 million people. The reasoning was that, if magazines could show that their readership had doubled even though circulation had not increased, the advertising CPM[3] would effectively be cut in half.

ASIAWEEK RENAISSANCE

During the first few years after Time Inc.'s acquisition of Asiaweek in 1985, the Hong Kong-based magazine was left to manage its own affairs. In 1989–90, senior Time Inc. managers in New York were occupied with negotiating the merger with Warner Communications and managing the integration thereafter. Time magazine itself went through three editors in the early 1990s. Asiaweek remained a very small Asian cog in a large media wheel. Even in 1997, its total revenues were only US$36 million.

Until about 1992, Asiaweek—at that time still under the editorship of founder O'Neill—remained fiercely independent from Time magazine's operations in Asia, and was allowed to be so even while Time Inc. subsidized Asiaweek's losses. One of Asiaweek's major financial problems was the loss-making Yazhou Zhoukan, a Chinese-language version of Asiaweek—its name was a direct translation of Asiaweek—that had been launched in 1987 as a magazine for all Chinese in Asia. The problem was that a pan-Asian Chinese audience did not exist. Simplified characters were used in Singapore and on the Chinese mainland, whereas Hong Kong and Taiwan still used traditional Chinese characters, and colloquial language varied widely between Shanghai, Taipei, and Hong Kong, let alone Kuala Lumpur or Bangkok. It was impossible to write articles that sounded natural to all Chinese. In 1994, the Yazhou Zhoukan title was sold to Ming Pao, a Hong Kong-based newspaper group.

Asiaweek experimented a little with some Time-like features. For example, in 1991, it mimicked the red border of Time's cover with a green border on Asiaweek's; and in 1993, it began to produce lists of the type that other Time Inc. publications did so well—the Top 100 or Top 1,000 in a particular category—although without emphasizing them. One of its earliest lists, the ASEAN 50, which gave financial details of the 50 largest companies in the region, simply appeared as another article in the contents page without even a mention on the magazine's cover.

The editorial changes began in earnest in mid-1994, when Ann Morrison arrived from New York to take over from Michael O'Neill as editor. Her approach was "evolutionary, not revolutionary," in the words of Evan Blank,

---

[3] CPM: cost per mille (thousand) = advertising rate per page ÷ readership × 1,000.

the marketing director, who joined Asiaweek from Time International in New York in 1995. "She never wanted a reader to pick up the magazine and feel it wasn't theirs any more." There were few personnel changes, and the style of editing that had always prevailed at Asiaweek continued. This process of evolutionary change culminated in mid-1996 with a cover-to-cover redesign of the magazine. The redesign and associated costs, requiring an investment in 1996 of US$1 million, were entirely funded from the revenues of the magazine.

Also in 1995–96, Blank and Jack Maisano, a highly experienced figure in the Asian publishing world who was hired as Asiaweek's president in April 1995, began to eliminate the "deal" mentality that had infected the advertising side of the business in the early 1990s. Their task was to build the credibility of the Asiaweek brand and increase advertising volume, particularly among premium clients who had been scared away by the perceived drop in quality of the magazine.

ANALYZING THE PROBLEMS

Market Positioning

Market research data collected among the top 5% of the population in 1991 showed that Asiaweek lay in a no-man's-land between two groups of English-language publications (see Figure 11–2). On the one hand lay a group of focused, specialist titles including the Asian Wall Street Journal (AWSJ), the Far Eastern Economic Review (FEER), and BusinessWeek (the so-called "business books"), and on the other hand were Time and Newsweek, which attracted a much higher readership among both the business/professional community and the affluent elite. The question was, did Asiaweek want to position itself alongside and compete for readership with the Asian editions of Time and Newsweek, or did it want to compete in a more specialized market? Uncertain market positioning and lack of brand equity had made top companies reluctant to advertise in Asiaweek in the early 1990s. By 1997, the data (Figure 11–3) demonstrated that Asiaweek had moved strongly in the direction of Time and Newsweek. Table 11–3 shows the profile of the average Asiaweek reader, derived from the 1997 Asian Target Markets Survey (ATMS).

ASIAN IDENTITY AND BRANDING

Fundamental to the issue of market positioning was the magazine's identity and perceived value. Development strategy in the late 1990s was to establish the magazine as "the Asian authority"—it would be a big stretch to match the authority of global brands like Time, Fortune, or The Economist. The Asiaweek brand was nowhere near as well established as theirs were. Brand awareness

Figure 11–2 Asiaweek's positioning versus competitors, 1991

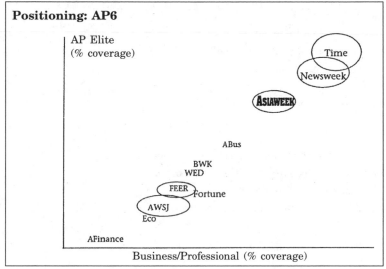

Note: Bubbles indicate 1991 Competitive Media Reporting (CMR) figures.

Source: AP6 (1991).

Figure 11–3 Asiaweek's positioning versus competitors, 1997

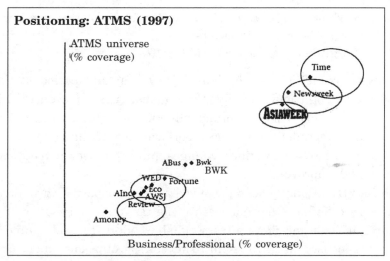

Note: Bubbles indicate 1997 CMR figures.

Source: ATMS (1997).

Table 11–3   The Asiaweek reader: A profile

Aged 25–54	92%
College educated or above	88%
Average annual household income	US$71,000
Have children aged under 18 years old	58%
Time spent reading an issue	74 minutes[a]
Readers per copy	4.9 readers[a]
Work in business	72%
Top management	18%
Opinion leaders[b]	42%
Decision makers on computers and related services for company	68%
Decision makers on telecommunications for company	60%
Average no. of business trips per year	9 trips
Average no. of hotel nights in past 12 months	26 nights
Have a credit card	84%
Have stocks/shares/bonds	47%
Have used the Internet	57%
Have a home computer	70%
Have a cellular phone	54%
Have a car	76%
Quality conscious	90%
Like to try new and different things	76%

Notes:

[a] Asiaweek subscriber survey.

[b] Have an article/book published or addressed a public conference/meeting or been interviewed by press/TV in past 12 months.

Source: Asian Target Markets Survey (ATMS) 1997.

and perceived quality had to be built up over a long period of time, and Asiaweek was young compared with these global titles or even FEER, which was over 50 years old. Whatever brand value it had achieved in the 1970s and 1980s had been degraded by the poor performance of the early 1990s. After 1995, as a result of the various changes put in place, perception of the Asiaweek brand improved.

FEER had traditionally been perceived as "the authority" in the region. Its style was very different from Asiaweek's: the language it used was drier and much more difficult for non-native English readers to understand. It was correspondent-focused in contrast to Asiaweek's group journalism (a concept developed by Henry Luce, the founder of Time magazine). That meant that stories tended to appear in FEER whenever they were filed by a correspondent, rather than deliberately being collected around a theme as was the practice at Asiaweek. FEER reached fewer people but its brand value was greater, especially during the early 1990s.

Focus groups conducted for Asiaweek tended not to see the two magazines as competitors. Perhaps that was revealing. Maybe some readers were deterred by the idea of "authority." Asiaweek had always had "its finger on the social pulse of Asia," according to Steve Marcopoto, the former president of Time Asia. It was a strong believer in photo-journalism and graphics, making it an illustrated magazine where the facts were easy to access. It was closer to a city magazine, a chronicle of the movers and shakers, with its ear close to the ground for news of goings-on in the local corridors of power.

Importantly, Asiaweek was readily perceived by its readers as being written by locals. It had been founded by Asians (New Zealand, in O'Neill's eyes, being part of Asia), even though it was now being managed by Westerners. Many of the journalists were from the Philippines or India, or elsewhere in the region, and even the few who were not from somewhere in Asia tended to have married locally and so had access to the family networks that their local colleagues naturally had. "Thanks to its Asian edition, Time magazine has come down from aeroplane level to helicopter level," commented Morrison, "but at Asiaweek we are at ground level and that is our big advantage."

This, however, did not necessarily resolve another issue: Asiaweek had been founded on the idea of "Asia" and "Asians," which perhaps was a purely Western concept. The problem was that there was still plenty of debate whether a truly Asian community existed, or indeed would ever exist. There were no pan-Asian institutions of the type that bound the European Union together. Perhaps the greatest binding element was money—which was why half of Asiaweek was devoted to business and money topics.

Many people actually wanted to read about events in their own country, but with the reassurance that what they read in the press accurately presented the situation. Regional and international magazines and newspapers could fill this role. Contrary to what people might think, censorship of the local media could actually help circulation of such titles because they were outsiders in every country. Asiaweek had gained a reputation over the years of being able to put together the full story on delicate issues about sensitive regimes.

English-language regional products such as Asiaweek and FEER, or international magazines with Asian editions and flavors such as Time and Newsweek, naturally only reached the elite in any country's population, although that segment had expanded dramatically in size over the past two decades. The AP surveys had shown that growth in the readership of English-language publications had risen by 40% since the start of the 1990s, while the AP universe had grown by 30%. People in the prosperous middle class and above, however, did not necessarily only want Asian things. They wanted good things, wherever they came from. This was another problem for Asiaweek. Was there an audience that wanted to be informed about Asia in a package that excluded both a global perspective and the local touch, i.e., a publication purely about Asia as Asia?

Asia was a collection of diverse cultures and peoples, and strong national pride sometimes made it difficult editorially to promote the magazine successfully. Newsstand sales in the Philippines, for example, would be strong if the cover story one week was about politics in the Philippines but conversely, sales at newsstands in Malaysia that same week would probably be low. If one country was featured on the front cover several weeks in a row there were likely to be complaints from readers in other countries. The 50th anniversary of India's independence was a big story in 1997, but not one that was likely to stimulate the readership in Southeast Asia. Building the Asiaweek brand was complicated by the difficulty of delivering on the cover what readers throughout the region would see as a relevant issue.

There were ways to resolve this problem some of the time. One was to run a split cover if there was enough significant material in the magazine. This meant that there were two main stories, one of which would appear on the front cover in certain countries while the other would appear as the cover story elsewhere.

A much more important way of cutting across national boundaries lay with so-called franchise issues. Franchise issues featured lists, such as the Asiaweek 1,000, the Power 50 (the 50 most influential people in Asia), Asia's best universities, its best cities, and so on. Some Time Inc. magazines like Fortune were very good at lists and Asiaweek had experimented a little in 1993, but from 1994 onward it used listings much more aggressively. They were tremendously popular with readers, and often provoked strong partisan reaction—for example, why this person was included in the list of top entrepreneurs when that person was not.

Franchise issues were also very profitable. According to the CMR report, an independent research tool widely used by publishers and advertisers, the average advertising revenue for Asiaweek in 1997 was US$595,000 per issue. The Asiaweek 1,000 issue, however, generated advertising revenue of US$1.9 million, the Business Hall of Fame US$1.1 million, and the Asiaweek Financial 500 US$1 million. The Hot Stocks 500 would attract different advertisers from those wanting to be associated with the Best Universities ranking, so lists were also a means of opening up new advertising categories. They could also be matched easily with a company's advertising cycle because the dates of their publication were announced to potential advertisers well in advance.

A very different problem for Asiaweek was when the hottest story of the week worldwide had nothing to do with Asia. Then it could only report events from the Asian perspective. One example was the death of Princess Diana in 1997. Time and Newsweek made a fortune from newsstand sales with special issues devoted to all aspects of the story; Asiaweek had just one page about it in one issue. On the other hand, the Asian financial crisis was very much Asiaweek's story. According to Blank, "We 'own' that story. We can devote more resources to that story than Time or Newsweek ever could or would."

The period when Asiaweek was redefining itself, between 1994 and 1996, coincided with a new in-house threat from Time magazine. The decision by Time International to decentralize editorial responsibility to the regions allowed each edition (Time Asia, Time Europe) to publish some of its own material, which would be available in a common pool of stories to all other editions, and to draw other articles it chose from the same common pool. Time's coverage of Asia in its Asian edition therefore expanded to a minimum of 6–8 pages, and often quite a bit more, out of 50–60 pages of print. Periodically, the cover page was also Asian, featuring Malaysian Prime Minister Mahathir or former Indonesian President Suharto. So far, however, Asiaweek had not identified any impact on its own circulation from this source.

CIRCULATION

Asiaweek had successfully increased its circulation over the years (Figure 11–4) compared with other clearly Asian titles, but it still lay far behind Newsweek and Time in terms of weekly circulation. The Asian edition of Time, for example, sold 305,000 copies a week (subscriptions and newsstand sales) compared with Asiaweek's 131,000. Nevertheless, Asiaweek's circulation in 1997 was 90% higher than in 1987, compared with Time Asia's 28% growth. The FEER had increased circulation by 35% over the same period.

The difference for Asiaweek since 1994 was in the quality of its circulation, reflected in significantly better subscription renewal rates than were achieved in earlier years. At the same time, though, only about one-fifth of Asiaweek's circulation revenue came from newsstand sales. Newsstand sales in general were much lower in Asia than in Europe. Of course, for regular readers it was much cheaper to take out a subscription: in Hong Kong, for example, the newsstand price was HK$35, whereas a 52-week subscription cost HK$478

Figure 11–4 Ten-year circulation growth, 1987–97

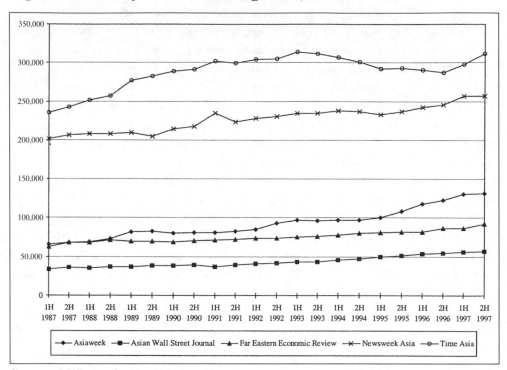

Source: ABC circulation statement.

(mid-1998 prices). Such discounting on subscriptions was common practice in the newspaper and magazine publishing world. Heavy subscription sales made it easier for Asiaweek's managers to forecast revenues, but it did suggest that not many people were prepared to put their hands in their pockets to buy it off the rack unless the cover carried a particularly relevant issue. Table 11–4 compares the newsstand prices of a variety of regional publications.

About one-third of Asiaweek's circulation came from regular bulk sales to hotels, airlines, and businesses. Bulk sales were particularly important in Hong Kong, where they accounted for about one-third of Asiaweek's circulation: the Kowloon Shangri-La and the Grand Hyatt Hotel, for example, were each taking 600 copies a week for their guests. This was the type of readership advertisers really liked. Corporate subscribers like hotels and airlines had special subscription rates that in mid-1998 gave them a 7%–8% discount from the regular rate.

Analysis of sales by country showed that Asiaweek performed relatively well in Southeast Asia against Time Asia. Table 11–5 shows Asiaweek's circulation by country in 1997, and Table 11–6 details circulation and

Table 11-4 Newsstand prices: Various publications

Issues dates		Asiaweek	FEER	ASWJ	Asian Business	The Economist (Asia ed.)	Time Asia	News-week Asia	Business Week Asia
		July '98	July '98	July '98	August '98	July '98	July '98	July '98	July '98
Hong Kong	HK$	35	40	15	38	40	38	35	35
Singapore	S$	6.25	8.50	3.50	7.00	8.00	6.25	6.25	7.00
Malaysia	RM	7.00	9.00	5.00	8.50	9.00	6.80	6.50	9.00
Indonesia	Rupiah	6,000	6,900	10,000	6,000	12,000	6,000	7,000	8,000
Philippines	Peso	65	90	50	90	100	65	65	90
Taiwan	NT$	130	160	60	120	140	120	120	130
Thailand	Baht	100	130	50	95	100	100	100	100
Japan	¥en	750	857	500	777	866	750	n.a.	840
Korea	Won	3,800	3,800	1,800	4,500	5,000	4,500	n.a.	4,000
China	RMB	35	US$5.50	25	33	55	35	33	45
India	Rupee	60	100	80	80	90	55	55	80
U.S.	US$	5.50	5.50	n.a.	6.99	n.a.	n.a.	n.a.	3.95
U.K.	£	2.95	3.50	n.a.	US$10	n.a.	n.a.	n.a.	n.a.

Source: Publication cover prices.

Table 11–5   Asiaweek circulation by country*

	Jul–Dec 1997
Southeast Asia	
Brunei	728
Cambodia	33
China, P.R.	1,689
Hong Kong	20,216
Indonesia	9,467
Laos	24
Malaysia	24,214
Philippines	21,611
Singapore	14,532
Taiwan	8,053
Thailand	9,654
Vietnam	1,255
Others	2,492
Total	113,968
North Asia	
Japan	2,187
Korea, Republic of	1,536
Total	3,723
South Asia	
Bangladesh	625
India	5,179
Nepal	439
Pakistan	1,967
Total	8,210
Australasia	
Australia	1,594
New Zealand	150
Total	1,744
North America	
Canada	582
U.S.	1,529
Total	2,111
Europe	
U.K.	298
Others	1,282
Total	1,580
Rest of world	444
Total circulation	**131,780**

* Average auditable circulation per week.
Source: Audit Bureau of Circulation (ABC) of Hong Kong.

Table 11-6 Comparative data: Circulation and advertising rates for various publications

	Asiaweek	FEER	Time Asia	Newsweek Asia	Yazhou Zhoukan	Business-Week	The Economist	AWSJ
Publishing frequency	Weekly	Weekly	Weekly	Weekly	Weekly	Weekly	Weekly	Daily
Source	ABC (HK)	ABC (HK)	ABC (U.S.)	ABC (U.S.)	Publisher	ABC (U.S.)	ABC (U.K.)	ABC (U.K.)
Period	Jul–Dec '97	Jul–Dec '97	Jul–Dec '97	Jul–Dec '97	Jul–Dec '97	Jul–Dec '97	Jul–Dec '97	Jul–Dec '97
Hong Kong	20,216	15,404	22,750	19,111	38,283	7,412	10,677	14,111
Malaysia	24,214	11,385	22,851	17,378	17,819	3,989	5,060	5,616
Singapore	14,532	7,538	27,639	27,293	13,822	7,917	10,601	7,846
Indonesia	9,467	5,234	14,047	13,321	0	2,430	1,935	3,473
Philippines	21,611	5,035	32,388	32,221	956	3,181	1,994	2,981
Taiwan	8,053	2,849	15,222	11,163	23,906	5,362	2,190	3,537
Thailand	9,654	5,386	12,106	10,060	493	1,781	3,117	4,832
Other SE Asia	6,221	3,822	14,382	14,780	355	1,844	2,763	2,060
Subtotal SE Asia	**113,968**	**56,653**	**161,385**	**145,327**	**95,634**	**33,916**	**38,337**	**44,456**
SE Asia advertising rate	Jan '98	Jan '98	Jan '98	Jan '98	Jan '98	Jan '98	Jan '98	Jan '98
4-color rate (US$)*	19,475	11,328	28,520	22,898	12,760	13,455	7,950	18,320
CPM (SE Asia)	$171	$200	$177	$158	$133	$397	$207	$412
Japan/Korea	3,723	7,451	118,878	93,491	1,312	18,307	11,539	10,762
Other Asia	8,210	4,916	37,222	26,078	1,811[3]	4,326	10,863	708
Total Asia	**125,901**	**69,020**	**317,485**	**264,896**	**98,757**	**56,549**	**60,739**	**55,926**
% circulation in Asia	96	75	100	100	99	88	100	98
Asia advertising rate								
4-color rate (US$)*	20,920	14,981	55,867	44,414	12,760	13,455	7,950	18,320
CPM (Asia)	$166	$217	$176	$168	$129	$238	$131	$328
Circulation outside Asia	5,879	23,034	0	0	826	7,470	0	1,169
Total circulation	**131,780**	**92,054**	**317,485**[1]	**264,896**[2]	**99,583**[4]	**64,019**[5]	**60,739**	**57,095**

Table 11-6 (cont'd)

	International Herald Tribune	World Executive's Digest	Reader's Digest (English)	Reader's Digest (Chinese)	Asian Business	Asia Inc.	Fortune
Publishing frequency	Daily	Monthly	Monthly	Monthly	Monthly	Monthly	Bi-weekly
Source	OJD	ABC	ABC (HK)	ABC (HK)	BPA	BPA	ABC (U.S.)
Period	Jan–Dec '97	Jul–Dec '97	Jul–Dec '97	Jul–Dec '97	Jul–Dec '97	Jan–Jun '97	Jul–Dec '97
Hong Kong	11,578	15,406	19,646	70,491	22,802	17,554	8,782
Malaysia	1,880	21,052[7]	96,321	15,903	19,168	20,225	7,820
Singapore	6,146	14,136	76,890	6,329	19,516	23,613	9,657
Indonesia	4,227	3,388	12,632	0	8,119	2,874	4,012
Philippines	3,500	20,208	142,900	0	11,344	2,934	6,818
Taiwan	2,133	1,978	5,757	182,166	5,146	1,019	2,316
Thailand	2,533	3,452	3,912	0	6,851	3,297	3,130
Other SE Asia	3,857	742	11,040	13,226	6,247	0	1,651
Subtotal SE Asia	**35,872**	**80,362**	**369,098**	**288,115**	**99,193**	**71,516**	**44,186**
SE Asia advertising rate	Jan '98	Jan '98	Jan '98	Jan '98	Jan '98	Jan '98	Jan '98
4-color rate (US$)*	14,891	11,955	26,300	20,420	13,200	14,548	11,845
CPM (SE Asia)	$415	$149	$71	$71	$133	$203	$268
Japan/Korea	8,412[6]	0	27,166	0	4,509	990	7,237
Other Asia	2,610[6]	5,418[8]	11,000	0	2,186	3,230	5,680
Total Asia	**46,894**	**85,780**	**407,264**	**288,115**	**105,888**	**75,736**	**57,103**
% circulation in Asia	99	99	100	100	100	100	87
Asia advertising rate							
4-color rate (US$)*	14,891	11,955	26,300	20,420	13,200	14,548	11,845
CPM (Asia)	$318	$139	$65	$71	$125	$192	$207
Circulation outside Asia	353	759	0	0	226	0	8,362
Total circulation	**47,247**	**86,539**	**407,264**	**288,115**	**106,114**[9]	**75,736**	**65,465**[10]

Notes: (1) Average circulation during the period: 311,387. (2) Average circulation during the period: 256,812. (3) Includes other Asia-Pacific areas. (4) Average circulation during the period: 90,720 (ABC, HK). (5) Average circulation during the period: 61,394. (6) Includes other Asia-Pacific areas. (7) Includes Brunei. (8) Includes Japan/Korea, Australia/New Zealand. (9) Average circulation during the period: 105,061. (10) Average circulation during the period: 65,103.
* Full page color bleed rates for magazines, half page four-color for newspapers.
Sources: Asiaweek, Audit Bureau of Circulation (ABC).

advertising rates for a variety of regional titles. Asiaweek's circulation in Southeast Asia was 114,000 compared with Time's 161,000. What pushed Time's sales for the entire region so much higher was its circulation in Japan and Korea, with 70,000 and 49,000 copies, respectively. Only about 4,000 copies of Asiaweek circulated in those countries. Mainly for historical reasons, including its 50-year presence in Japan, Time was the only English-language publication in those countries with a large readership. Newsweek, on the other hand, published a Japanese-language edition.

Time also had much larger circulation on the Indian subcontinent (37,000 copies compared with Asiaweek's 8,200). "We haven't tried really hard to get in," said Ann Hext, Asiaweek's director of consumer marketing, "because none of our advertisers is very interested." Asiaweek covered India within the magazine, but to give it more without upsetting other readers would probably require a second, Indian, edition. That would cost money, and India's market for readership was already very competitive. "The question is, what size do you have to be to attract advertisers wanting to reach India through magazine circulation?" Hext pondered.

Another factor inhibiting Asiaweek's circulation was its position as a "gazetted" publication in Singapore (see Appendix 11–1 for an explanation of gazetting). It was placed on restricted circulation in 1987, and the ceiling was only gradually being raised. In early 1997, circulation was still capped at 14,000, but by July 1998, the cap had been raised to 21,000. The restriction nevertheless remained in force. Time, on the other hand, had only once been gazetted for a few months in 1986–87. Asiaweek editors were encouraged to know that, even though it was restricted, circulation in Singapore was still holding its own.

Circulation in the U.S. and Europe was limited to subscribers who sought out Asiaweek. Hext knew Asiaweek could grow circulation there significantly, but it would be expensive to raise subscriber numbers to critical mass and to deliver the magazine. The marginal cost of delivery was nearly US$2 per copy, which current subscription costs just covered. There was a big debate going on about what to do. Hext thought that "if we could make money on it, it would be great. If we break even it would be just about acceptable, because we would be reaching new advertisers."

ADVERTISING

Readership, i.e., the number of people who actually read the magazine rather than subscribed to it, was a far more important measure than circulation as far as advertisers were concerned. Asiaweek's readership on the old Asian Profile survey basis was 182,500; using ATMS it was 253,500. The ATMS showed that it was the most widely read English-language weekly in Bangkok, Kuala Lumpur, and Singapore, but fell behind both Time and Newsweek in Hong Kong, Jakarta, Manila, and Taipei (Table 11–7). Naturally, certain countries and cities were intrinsically more interesting to advertisers than others. Advertising rates—and the way they changed over time—reflected what publishers thought advertisers would be prepared to pay (Table 11–8 shows a selection of rates).

In 1997, advertising sales contributed three-quarters of Asiaweek's entire revenue. Companies from Europe and the U.S. were the biggest sources of ad sales. The magazine had established itself among European advertisers—both advertising agencies and the companies themselves—since 1994 through regular visits from the advertising director to discuss political, economic, and social trends in Asia rather than Asiaweek itself. The strategy worked well. Major spenders in Asiaweek in 1996–97 included such flagship brands as Rolex, Tag Heuer, Omega, Patek Philippe, Rolls Royce, BMW, Ericsson, and Perrier. In April 1998, when Asia was deeply entrenched in crisis, the theme of current advertising director Randall Maxwell's visit to Europe was to explain what would happen as a result of the crisis.

Advertising revenues, which had hovered around US$20 million in 1992–94, rose by over 30% in 1995-96. This was better than what the "business books" like FEER and BusinessWeek had achieved, but not as good as Time and Newsweek.

Publishing industry data on advertising categories showed that in recent years consumer product companies were the major source of new growth, particularly cars, travel, watches, and cellular phones. Earlier mainstays such as corporate advertising and office equipment companies were no longer the biggest advertising categories. Hotels and airlines had replaced the cigarettes and brandy ads of earlier years. These trends confirmed the importance of Asiaweek's decision to shift its market positioning closer to Time and Newsweek, rather than toward the "business books" (as shown in Figure 11–3): it wasn't only managing directors who bought luxury watches or cell phones.

THE ASIAN CRISIS

The financial crisis that broke out in Asia in the second half of 1997 affected Asiaweek in a number of ways. Editorially, it was a great story for the magazine to cover, at length and in depth. Ann Morrison thought that the crisis was a unifying force for Asia, that the economies now realized how closely they were interrelated. "The story is about the struggle for the Asian soul," she said.

Table 11-7 Average issue readership in seven major cities

	All 7 cities		Hong Kong		Singapore		Kuala Lumpur		Taipei		Manila		Bangkok		Jakarta	
Sample size	12,401		2,035		1,787		1,729		1,703		1,764		1,753		1,630	
Total	3,134,945		893,617		310,086		296,022		390,514		405,609		545,398		293,697	
Monthly																
Asia Inc.	81,150	2.6%	24,380	2.7%	22,338	7.2%	13,078	4.4%	4,497	1.2%	7,711	1.9%	4,352	0.8%	4,795	1.6%
Asiamoney	45,763	1.5%	12,572	1.4%	4,844	1.6%	5,211	1.8%	5,757	1.5%	9,507	2.3%	5,017	0.9%	2,857	1.0%
Asian Business	137,471	4.4%	36,862	4.1%	21,013	6.8%	21,842	7.4%	11,690	3.0%	18,213	4.5%	11,676	2.1%	16,176	5.5%
Business Traveller	103,422	3.3%	30,138	3.4%	12,023	3.9%	11,825	4.0%	9,137	2.3%	16,217	4.0%	9,124	1.7%	14,959	5.1%
National Geographic	206,796	6.6%	34,055	3.8%	33,454	10.8%	53,854	18.2%	15,012	3.8%	35,434	8.7%	17,698	3.3%	17,289	5.9%
Reader's Digest (any)	678,072	21.6%	120,348	13.5%	78,739	25.4%	90,937	30.7%	130,698	33.5%	124,549	30.7%	97,002	17.8%	35,801	12.2%
Reader's Digest (Chinese)	247,171	7.9%	103,825	11.6%	7,114	2.3%	5,133	1.7%	127,692	32.7%	895	0.2%	1,253	0.2%	1,259	0.4%
Reader's Digest (English)	381,924	12.2%	25,156	2.8%	73,922	23.8%	87,332	29.5%	12,420	3.2%	123,747	30.5%	14,338	4.5%	35,007	11.9%
Reader's Digest (Thai)	86,387	2.8%	—		—		—		—		—		86,387	15.8%	—	
World Executive's Digest	97,706	3.1%	12,983	1.5%	15,851	5.1%	24,613	8.3%	4,126	1.1%	28,869	7.1%	4,740	0.9%	6,523	2.2%
Fortnightly																
Fortune	110,239	3.5%	25,496	2.9%	18,062	5.8%	18,540	6.3%	10,027	2.6%	15,729	3.9%	11,927	2.2%	10,457	3.6%
Weekly																
Asiaweek	253,467	8.1%	46,714	5.2%	33,737	10.9%	63,047	21.3%	12,491	3.2%	56,272	13.9%	22,162	4.1%	19,044	6.5%
BusinessWeek	140,596	4.5%	29,418	3.3%	20,311	6.6%	21,708	7.3%	22,883	5.9%	26,211	6.5%	7,954	1.5%	12,111	4.1%
The Economist	93,301	3.0%	29,223	3.3%	20,518	6.6%	20,618	7.0%	5,212	1.3%	6,727	1.7%	4,415	0.8%	6,588	2.2%
Far Eastern Economic Review	82,117	2.6%	20,793	2.3%	10,065	3.2%	24,692	8.3%	2,917	0.7%	8,310	2.0%	7,471	1.4%	7,869	2.7%
Newsweek	276,382	8.8%	50,080	5.6%	32,713	10.5%	43,514	14.7%	27,928	7.2%	83,026	20.5%	11,206	2.1%	27,916	9.5%
Time	306,005	9.8%	64,628	7.2%	32,806	10.6%	39,082	13.2%	34,103	8.7%	79,152	19.5%	22,007	4.0%	34,227	11.7%
Yazhou Zhoukan	111,209	3.5%	61,554	6.9%	6,956	2.2%	2,185	0.7%	39,805	10.2%	254	0.1%	133	—	322	0.1%
Daily																
Asian Wall Street Journal	85,695	2.7%	28,729	3.2%	10,743	3.5%	19,398	6.6%	5,067	1.3%	10,538	2.6%	4,125	0.8%	7,095	2.4%
Financial Times	51,290	1.6%	12,183	1.4%	8,401	2.7%	12,813	4.3%	1,591	0.4%	4,359	1.1%	6,308	1.2%	5,635	1.9%
International Herald Tribune	33,100	1.1%	9,197	1.0%	7,870	2.5%	2,858	1.0%	1,059	0.3%	7,019	1.7%	835	0.2%	4,262	1.5%
USA Today	24,249	0.8%	4,726	0.5%	1,624	0.5%	3,197	1.1%	3,866	1.0%	3,928	1.0%	4,054	0.7%	2,853	1.0%

Source: Asian Target Markets Survey (ATMS) 1997.

Table 11–8 Advertising rate trends, 1993–98

| | Advertising rate (US$/page) | | | | | | Growth |
	1993	1994	1995	1996	1997	1998	1998/1993
Asiaweek	15,015	15,615	16,865	17,710	18,595	20,920	39%
AWSJ	12,451	13,568	14,567	15,744	17,032	18,320	47%
FEER	10,298	11,276	12,234	13,335	14,268	14,981	45%
Newsweek	36,188	37,996	39,900	41,900	44,414	44,414	23%
Time	44,145	44,145	46,794	50,772	53,209	55,867	27%
	Circulation CPM (US$)						Growth
	1993	1994	1995	1996	1997	1998	1998/1993
Asiaweek	162	162	173	164	152	159	−2%
AWSJ	297	310	310	309	313	321	8%
FEER	139	148	152	163	165	163	17%
Newsweek	157	162	168	177	181	173	10%
Time	145	142	155	173	185	179	24%

Source: Publishers' rate cards, Asiaweek.

The counterforce was a rise in nationalist Asian sentiment and a crisis of identity within ASEAN and other regional institutions. "We see our target population growing with the crisis," she went on, "because Asiaweek is perceived as a homegrown magazine and it matches the spirit of Asians wanting to do things for themselves."

On the advertising side there was little impact during 1997 as advertising campaigns by the multinationals had already been planned and booked by the time the severity of the crisis became apparent in the autumn. In the first months of 1998, CMR data indicated a 22% decline in advertising revenue for all regional titles in Asia. Some publications fared better than others. The Asian Wall Street Journal was relatively unaffected because of its positioning among the financial community; Time lost 24% and Newsweek 36%. Asiaweek had initially lost 31% but since May 1998 it had seen a renewed surge of advertising—which pushed ad revenues ahead of its downward-revised projections for the year. It was not yet clear which categories of advertiser were involved. Nor was it clear whether the recovery was sustainable. The year 1998 would certainly not be as good as 1997 had been, although by the summer it seemed that Asiaweek was faring relatively well against its competitors. Prospects for 1999 were not very bright.

By mid-1998 there had been no discernible impact on the circulation side of the business. Audited data on newsstand sales were always very slow to come in, but vendors in Indonesia had been selling out on every issue covering the fall of Suharto. There was great attention paid to subscription renewals, since any fall would only show up in Asiaweek's figures in 1999–2000. Local currency movements would be a big factor in any such loss of deferred income. Indonesia was the only country where they had put the price of Asiaweek up dramatically. "With the collapse of the rupiah, for a while a 52-week subscription in Indonesia cost the equivalent of only US$10!" remarked Hext. "Of course we have to book it at that price, whatever happens to the rupiah later." Lower subscription revenue due to currency depreciations, though, was matched by declines in other costs.

Any fall in circulation would eventually have an impact on the advertising rate base. Asiaweek was working hard to maintain circulation even though the number of sponsored (bulk) copies had fallen, and it continued to guarantee its rate base of 128,000 copies. "We were actually delivering 131,000 before, so we're still giving what we promised," explained Hext. Still unclear in mid-1998 was whether advertisers would continue to value exposure to places like Indonesia that had suffered so badly. Readership in Hong Kong and Singapore had always been a valuable commodity for advertisers.

LOOKING TO THE FUTURE

To really build a brand required money, which Asiaweek did not have. Its editorial budget to produce an average 55 pages of print in each issue (rising to over 100 pages for some franchise issues) was one-tenth of Time's global editorial budget and the same amount that Time had dedicated to Asia. Self-financing requirements limited new investments, especially while there were still substantial accumulated losses to wipe out from the pre-1993 years. Ann Morrison and others were keen to offer new perspectives to Asiaweek readers, perhaps by adding views of Asia from correspondents based in Washington, London, and elsewhere. Time Inc., meanwhile, wanted Asiaweek to double its profits by the year 2000. One suggestion was to raise the cover price of the magazine in order to boost circulation revenues, although there was always the risk of hurting sales.

Asiaweek was thinking of developing line extensions like Time Inc. had done in the U.S. with Teen People and In Style. A first step was a major section on "The state of Asia's health" within a regular issue of Asiaweek in summer 1998. "We have to leverage the brand in any direction the market takes us, but at the moment we don't know what that direction is because of the crisis," said Morrison. A health magazine or a lifestyle magazine would be a possibility.

Asiaweek's own brand equity also needed reinforcing. As a second tier magazine it had always had to fight against the giants like Time and Newsweek to win advertising revenues. Evan Blank thought that advertisers preferred to go with the American titles because they were what Asians wanted to read, but he was now preparing an advertising campaign to promote Asiaweek and make both readers and advertisers feel Asiaweek was a quality publication. "We want Asiaweek to be the magazine people want to be seen reading." In the end, editorial quality was Asiaweek's own best advertisement.

A long-term issue was the question of censorship in Asia. The magazine had always thrived in countries where the local press was submissive. Maybe one day the censors would disappear. How then would Asiaweek remain relevant to and valued by its readers? What to do about China was an open question. Sixteen issues of Asiaweek had been banned by the Chinese authorities in the first half of 1997 alone, and the government in Beijing allowed only a few special categories of people to take out foreign subscriptions. Nevertheless, Chinese could be the language of the future in Asia. Should Asiaweek try a Chinese-language publication again? If not, who—and where— would its readers be in the years to come? In an ever more global world, what place did a purely regional magazine have?

Appendix 11–1 The Singapore government gazette

Singapore is the only country in Asia to restrict circulation of certain titles as a punishment for misdemeanors, rather than banning them outright for a specified period of time. Other countries like China tend to ban individual issues. Suharto had threatened an outright ban on Asiaweek in Indonesia, but had never exercised it. Magazine and newspaper editors were used to being rebuked by governments around the region for their coverage of specific stories. In one sense it was an indication that they were doing their job properly.

In Singapore, the government is highly sensitive to the maintenance of good relations between the various ethnic groups that inhabit the city-state—Chinese, Malays, and Indians—and forbids outsiders from interfering in domestic politics. The local press is closely controlled by the Singapore government. Foreign media, on the other hand, are constrained by an amendment to the Newspapers and Printing Presses Act which empowers the government to restrict the sale or distribution of any publication deemed to be engaging in the domestic politics of Singapore. Notification of such a restriction appears in the Government Gazette—hence the term gazetting. Further, another amendment to the Act requires "offshore newspapers" to apply annually for a license to circulate their titles and to post a bond against any legal actions the government may bring against them. Foreign media are required to provide coverage of Singapore as outsiders, for outsiders. The definition of what constitutes engagement in domestic politics is left vague, however, and a number of foreign publications have been punished by gazetting for their transgressions.

Asiaweek was deemed to have crossed the line into the forbidden territory of domestic politics in its coverage of Operation Spectrum, a security sweep in 1987 in which a number of Catholic priests and others were detained without trial under the internal security law. For refusing to publish the government's official reply in its entirety Asiaweek was gazetted and its circulation reduced from 10,000 copies to 500 copies per issue. An apology from Asiaweek and the transfer to Hong Kong of the correspondent responsible for the reporting (which prompted the correspondent in question to resign) resulted in circulation being raised first to 5,000 copies and then 7,500 copies per week. The gazette remained in force, however, the 7,500 limit on circulation remained until March 1995, when another perceived transgression of the terms of the Act provoked a verbal warning that Asiaweek's circulation would be cut to 3,000 copies. The restriction did not appear in the Government Gazette, however, and since then Asiaweek's circulation has been allowed to rise steadily from 7,500 copies to 21,000 copies in July 1998. This means that each individual copy of Asiaweek must be numbered, and the editors must request the right to increase its circulation. In practice, that right has been granted each time it has been asked for in recent years. Nevertheless, Asiaweek remains a gazetted title.

Other publications to have fallen foul of the Act include Asian Wall Street Journal, which temporarily decided to cease circulation completely in Singapore rather than distribute the very limited number of copies permitted by the Gazette; Far Eastern Economic Review, which also decided to cease circulation but was caught by another amendment to the Act which allowed gazetted foreign publications to be reproduced, without the original publisher's permission, as long as they carried no advertisements— the FEER now has restricted circulation in Singapore; The Economist, which was temporarily gazetted in 1994 for its attitude to the Singapore government's response to the magazine's coverage of the prosecution of an editor under the Official Secrets Act for early release of economic data; and the International Herald Tribune, which in 1994 provoked court action by members of the Singapore government despite an apology from the paper, for an opinion piece which implied criticism of an un-named country's judiciary. The International Herald Tribune quickly faced more libel proceedings for another opinion piece referring to other members of the Singapore government. Plaintiffs in both court cases won substantial damages from the newspaper, which was not, however, gazetted.

Blair Water Purifiers India

"A pity I couldn't have stayed for Diwali," thought Rahul Chatterjee. "Anyway, it was great to be back home in Calcutta." The Diwali holiday and its festivities would begin in early November 1996, some two weeks after Chatterjee had returned to the U.S. Chatterjee worked as an international market liaison for Blair Company, Inc. This was his eighth year with Blair Company and easily his favorite. "Your challenge will be in moving us from just dabbling in less developed countries (LDCs) to our thriving in them," his boss had said when Chatterjee was promoted to the job last January. Chatterjee had agreed and was thrilled when asked to visit Bombay and New Delhi in April. His purpose on that trip was to gather background data on the possibility of Blair Company entering the Indian market for home water purification devices. Initial results were encouraging and prompted the second trip.

Chatterjee had used his second trip primarily to study Indian consumers in Calcutta and Bangalore and to gather information on possible competitors. The two cities represented quite different

This case was prepared by Professor James E. Nelson for educational purposes rather than to illustrate either effective or ineffective decision making. Some data as well as the identity of the company are disguised.

The author would like to thank students in the Class of 1996 (Batch 31), Indian Institute of Management, Calcutta, for their invaluable help in collecting all data needed to write this case. He would also like to thank Professor Roger Kerin, Southern Methodist University, for his helpful comments toward the writing of this case.

Please address all correspondence to: James E. Nelson, University of Colorado at Boulder, College of Business Administration, Campus Box 419, Boulder CO 80309-0419, U.S.

Reprinted from Asian Case Research Journal, Vol. 2, 29–51. Copyright © 1998 by John Wiley & Sons (Asia) Ltd.

metropolitan areas in terms of location, size, language, and infrastructure—yet both suffered from similar problems in terms of water supplied to their residents. These problems could be found in many LDCs, providing a favorable environment for home water purification systems.

Information gathered on both visits would be used to make a recommendation on market entry and on elements of an entry strategy. Executives at Blair Company would compare Chatterjee's recommendation to those from two other Blair Company liaisons who were focusing their efforts on Argentina, Brazil, and Indonesia.

INDIAN MARKET FOR HOME WATER FILTRATION AND PURIFICATION

Like most aspects of India, the market for home water filtration and purification took a good deal of effort to understand. Yet despite expending this effort, Chatterjee realized that much remained either unknown or in conflict. For example, the market seemed clearly a mature one, with four or five established Indian competitors fighting for market share. Or, was it? Another view portrayed the market as a fragmented one, with no large competitor having a national presence and perhaps 100 small, regional manufacturers, each competing in just 1 or 2 of India's 25 states. Indeed, the market could be in its early growth stages, as reflected by the large number of product designs, materials, and performances. Perhaps with a next generation product and a world-class marketing effort, Blair Company could consolidate the market and stimulate tremendous growth—much like the situation in the Indian market for automobiles.

Such uncertainty made it difficult to estimate market potential. However, Chatterjee had collected unit sales estimates for a ten-year period for three similar product categories—vacuum cleaners, sewing machines, and color televisions. In addition, a Delhi-based research firm had provided him with estimates of unit sales for Aquaguard, the largest selling water purifier in several Indian states. Chatterjee had used the data in two forecasting models available at Blair Company along with three subjective scenarios—realistic, optimistic, and pessimistic—to arrive at the estimates and forecasts for water purifiers shown in Table 12–1. "If anything," Chatterjee had explained to his boss, "my forecasts are conservative because they describe only first time sales, not any replacement sales over the ten-year forecast horizon." He also pointed out that his forecasts applied only to industry sales in larger urban areas, which was the present industry focus.

One thing that seemed certain was that many Indians felt the need for improved water quality. Folklore, newspapers, consumer activists, and

Table 12–1 Industry sales estimates and forecasts for water purifiers ('000 units) in India, 1990–2005

Year	Unit sales estimates	Unit sales forecast		
		Realistic scenario	Optimistic scenario	Pessimistic scenario
1990	60			
1991	90			
1992	150			
1993	200			
1994	220			
1995	240			
1996		250	250	250
1997		320	370	300
1998		430	540	400
1999		570	800	550
2000		800	1,200	750
2001		1,000	1,500	850
2002		1,300	1,900	900
2003		1,500	2,100	750
2004		1,600	2,100	580
2005		1,500	1,900	420

government officials regularly reinforced this need by describing the poor quality of Indian water. Quality suffered particularly during the monsoons because of highly polluted water entering treatment plants and because of numerous leaks and unauthorized withdrawals from water systems. Such leaks and withdrawals often polluted clean water after it had left the plants. Politicians running for national, state, and local government offices also reinforced the need for improved water quality through election campaign promises. Governments at these levels set standards for water quality, took measurements at thousands of locations throughout the nation, and advised consumers when water became unsafe.

During periods of poor water quality, many Indian consumers had little choice but to consume the water as they found it. However, better educated, wealthier, and more health conscious consumers took steps to safeguard their family's health and often continued these steps all year round. A good estimate of the number of such households, Chatterjee thought, would be around 40 million. These consumers were similar in many respects to consumers in middle and upper middle-class households in the U.S. and the European Union. They valued comfort and product choice. They saw consumption of material goods as a means to a higher quality of life. They liked foreign brands and would pay a higher price for such brands, as long as purchased products outperformed competing Indian products. Chatterjee had identified as his target market these 40 million households plus those in another 4 million households who had similar values and lifestyles, but as yet took little effort to improve water quality in their homes.

Traditional Method for Home Water Purification

The traditional method of water purification in the target market relied not on any commercially supplied product but on boiling. Each day or several times a day, a cook, maid, or family member would boil two to five liters of water for ten minutes, allow it to cool, and then transfer it to containers for storage (often in a refrigerator). Chatterjee estimated that about 50% of the target market used this procedure. Boiling was seen by consumers as inexpensive, effective in terms of eliminating dangerous bacteria, and entrenched in a traditional sense. Many consumers who used this method considered it more effective than any product on the market. However, boiling affected the palatability of water, leaving the purified product somewhat "flat" in taste. Boiling was also cumbersome, time-consuming, and ineffective in removing physical impurities and unpleasant odors. Consequently, about 10% of the target market took a second step by filtering their boiled water through "candle filters" before storage. Many consumers who took this action did so despite knowing that water could become recontaminated during handling and storage.

Mechanical Methods for Home Water Filtration and Purification

About 40% of the target market used a mechanical device to improve their water quality. Half of this group used candle filters, primarily because of their low price and ease of use. The typical candle filter comprised two containers, one resting on top of the other. The upper container held one or more porous ceramic cylinders (candles) which strained the water as gravity drew it into the lower container. Containers were made of plastic, porcelain, or stainless steel and typically stored between 15 and 25 liters of filtered water. Purchase costs depended on materials and capacities, ranging from Rs350 for a small plastic model to Rs1,100 for a large stainless steel model (35 Indian rupees were equivalent to US$1 in 1996). Candle filters were slow, producing 15 liters (one candle) to 45 liters (three candles) of filtered water every 24 hours. To maintain this productivity, candles regularly needed to be removed, cleaned, and boiled for 20 minutes. Most manufacturers recommended that consumers replace candles (Rs40 each) either once a year or more frequently, depending on sediment levels.

The other half of this group used "water purifiers," devices that were considerably more sophisticated than candle filters. Water purifiers typically employed three water processing stages. The first removed sediments, the second objectionable odors and colors, and the third harmful bacteria and viruses. Engineers at Blair Company were skeptical that most purifiers claiming the latter benefit actually could deliver on their promise. However, all purifiers did a better job here than candle filters. Candle filters were totally ineffective in eliminating bacteria and viruses (and might even increase this type of contamination), despite advertising claims to the contrary. Water purifiers generally used stainless steel containers and were sold at prices ranging from Rs2,000 to Rs7,000, depending on manufacturers, features, and capacities. Common flow rates were one to two liters of purified water per minute. Simple service activities could be performed on water purifiers by consumers as needed. However, more complicated service required units to be taken to a nearby dealer or an on-site visit from a skilled technician.

The remaining 10% of the target market owned neither a filter nor a purifier and seldom boiled their water. Many consumers in this group were unaware of water problems and thought their water quality acceptable. However, a few consumers in this group refused to pay for products that they believed were mostly ineffective. Overall, Chatterjee believed that only a few consumers in this group could be induced to change their habits and become customers. The most attractive segments consisted of the 90% of households in the target market who boiled, boiled and filtered, only filtered, or purified their water.

All segments in the target market showed a good deal of similarity in terms of what they thought important in the purchase of a water purifier. According to Chatterjee's research, the most important factor was product performance in terms of sediment, bacteria, and virus removal, capacity (either in the form of storage or flow rate), safety, and "footprint" space. Purchase price was also an important concern among consumers who boiled, boiled and filtered, or only filtered their water. The next most important factor was ease of installation and service, with style and appearance rated almost as important. The least important factor was warranty and availability of finance for purchase. Finally, all segments expected a water purifier to be warranted against defective operation for 18 to 24 months and to perform trouble free for five to ten years.

FOREIGN INVESTMENT IN INDIA

India appeared attractive to many foreign investors because of government actions, begun in the 1980s, during the administration of Prime Minister Rajiv Gandhi. The broad label applied to these actions was "liberalization." Liberalization had opened the Indian economy to foreign investors, stemming from recognition that protectionist policies had not worked very well and that Western economies and technologies—seen against the collapse of the Soviet Union—did. Liberalization had meant major changes in approval requirements for new commercial projects, investment policies, taxation procedures, and, most importantly, attitudes of government officials. These changes had stayed in place through the two national governments that followed Gandhi's assassination in 1991.

If Blair Company entered the Indian market, it would do so in one of three ways: (1) joint-working arrangement, (2) joint-venture company, or (3) acquisition. In a joint-working arrangement, Blair Company would supply key purifier components to an Indian company that would manufacture and market the assembled product. License fees would be remitted to Blair Company on a per unit basis over the terms of the agreement (typically five years, with an option to renew for three more). A joint-venture agreement would have Blair Company partnering with an existing Indian company expressly for the purpose of manufacturing and marketing water purifiers. Profits from the joint-venture operation would be split between the two parties per the agreement, which usually contained a clause describing buy/sell procedures available to the two parties after a minimum time period. An acquisition entry would have Blair Company purchasing an existing Indian company whose operations then would be expanded to include the water purifier. Profits from the acquisition would belong to Blair Company.

Beyond understanding these basic entry possibilities, Chatterjee acknowledged that he was no expert in legal aspects attending the project. However, two days spent with a Calcutta consulting firm had produced the following information. Blair Company must apply for market entry from the Foreign Investment Promotion Board, Secretariat for Industrial Approval, Ministry of Industries. The proposal would go before the Board for an assessment of the relevant technology and India's need for the technology. If approved by the Board, the proposal then would go to the Reserve Bank of India, Ministry of Finance, for approval of any royalties and fees, remittances of dividends and interest (if any), repatriations of profits and invested capital, and repayment of foreign loans. While the process sounded cumbersome and time-consuming, the consultant assured Chatterjee that the government usually would complete its deliberations in less than six months and that his consulting firm could "virtually guarantee" final approval.

Trademarks and patents were protected by law in India. Trademarks were protected for seven years and could be renewed on payment of a prescribed fee. Patents lasted for 14 years. On balance, Chatterjee had told his boss that Blair Company would have "no more problem protecting its intellectual property rights in India than in the U.S.—as long as we stay out of court." Chatterjee went on to explain that litigation in India was expensive and protracted. Litigation problems were compounded by an appeal process that could extend a case for easily a generation. Consequently, many foreign companies preferred arbitration, as India was a party to the Geneva Convention covering Foreign Arbitral Awards.

Foreign companies were taxed on income arising from Indian operations. They also paid taxes on any interest, dividends, and royalties received, and on any capital gains received from a sale of assets. The government offered a wide range of tax concessions to foreign investors, including liberal depreciation allowances and generous deductions. The government offered even more favorable tax treatment if foreign investors would locate in one of India's six Free Trade Zones. Overall, Chatterjee thought that corporate tax rates in India probably were somewhat higher than in the U.S. However, so were profits—the average return on assets for all Indian corporations in recent years was almost 18%, compared to about 11% for American corporations.

Approval by the Reserve Bank of India was needed for repatriation of ordinary profits. However, approval should be obtained easily if Blair Company could show that repatriated profits were being paid out of export earnings of hard currencies. Chatterjee thought that export earnings would not be difficult to realize, given India's extremely low-wage rates and its central location to wealthier South Asian countries. "Profit repatriation was really not much of an issue, anyway," he thought. Three years might pass before profits of any magnitude could be realized; at least five years would pass before substantial profits would be available for repatriation. Approval of repatriation by the Reserve Bank might not be required at this time, given liberalization trends. Finally, if repatriation remained difficult, Blair Company could undertake cross trading or other actions to unblock profits.

Overall, investment and trade regulations in India in 1996 meant that business could be conducted much more easily than ever before. Hundreds of companies from the European Union, Japan, Korea, and the U.S. were entering India in all sectors of the country's economy. In the home appliance market, Chatterjee could identify 11 such firms—Carrier, Electrolux, General

Electric, Goldstar, Matsushita, Singer, Samsung, Sanyo, Sharp, Toshiba, and Whirlpool. Many of these firms had yet to realize substantial profits but all saw the promise of a huge market developing over the next few years.

BLAIR COMPANY, INC.

Blair Company was founded in 1975 by Eugene Blair, after he left his position in research and development at Culligan International Company. Blair Company's first product was a desalinator, used by mobile home parks in Florida to remove salts from brackish well water supplied to residents. The product was a huge success and markets quickly expanded to include nearby municipalities, smaller businesses, hospitals, and bottlers of water for sale to consumers. Geographic markets also expanded, first to other coastal regions near the company's headquarters in Tampa, Florida, and then to desert areas in southwestern U.S. New products were added rapidly as well and, by 1996, the product line included desalinators, particle filters, ozonators, ion exchange resins, and purifiers. Industry experts generally regarded the product line as superior in terms of performance and quality, with prices higher than those of many competitors.

Blair Company's sales revenues for 1996 would be almost US$400 million, with an expected profit close to US$50 million. Annual growth in sales revenues averaged 12% for the period 1992–96. Blair Company employed over 4,000 people, with 380 having technical backgrounds and responsibilities.

Export sales of desalinators and related products began at Blair Company in 1980. Units were sold first to resorts in Mexico and Belize and later to water bottlers in Germany. Export sales grew rapidly and Blair Company found it necessary to organize its International Division in 1985. Sales in the International Division also grew rapidly and would reach almost US$140 million in 1996. About US$70 million would come from countries in Latin and South America, US$30 million from Europe (including shipments to Africa), and US$40 million from South Asia and Australia. The International Division had sales offices, small assembly areas, and distribution facilities in Frankfurt, Tokyo, and Singapore.

The Frankfurt office had been the impetus in 1990 for the development and marketing of Blair Company's first product targeted exclusively at consumer households—a home water filter. Sales engineers at the Frankfurt office began receiving consumer and distributor requests for a home water filter soon after the fall of the Berlin Wall in 1989. By late 1991, two models had been designed in the U.S. and introduced in Germany (particularly to the eastern regions), Poland, Hungary, Romania, the Czech Republic, and Slovakia.

Blair Company executives watched the success of the two water filters with great interest. The market for clean water in LDCs was huge, profitable, and attractive in a socially responsible sense. However, the quality of water in many LDCs was such that a water filter usually would not be satisfactory. Consequently, in late 1994, executives had directed the development of a water purifier that could be added to the product line. Engineers had given the final design in the project the brand name, "Delight." For the time being, Chatterjee and the other market analysts had accepted the name, not knowing if it might infringe on any existing brand in India or in the other countries under study.

DELIGHT PURIFIER

The Delight purifier used a combination of technologies to remove four types of contaminants found in potable water—sediments, organic and inorganic chemicals, microbials or cysts, and objectionable tastes and odors. The technologies were effective as long as contaminants in the water were present at "reasonable" levels. Engineers at Blair Company had interpreted "reasonable" as levels described in several World Health Organization (WHO) reports on potable water and had combined the technologies to purify water to a level beyond WHO standards. Engineers had repeatedly assured Chatterjee that Delight's design in terms of technologies should not be a concern. Ten units operating in the company's testing laboratory showed no signs of failure or performance deterioration after some 5,000 hours of continuous use. "Still," Chatterjee thought, "we will undertake a good bit of field testing in India before entering. The risks of failure are too large to ignore. And, besides, results of our testing would be useful in convincing consumers and retailers to buy."

Chatterjee and the other market analysts still faced major design issues in configuring technologies into physical products. For example, a "point of entry" design would place the product immediately after water entry to the home, treating all water before it flowed to all water outlets. In contrast, a "point of use" design would place the product on a countertop, wall, or at the end of a faucet and treat only water arriving at that location. Based on cost estimates, designs of competing products, and his understanding of Indian consumers, Chatterjee would direct engineers to proceed only with "point of use" designs for the market.

Other technical details were yet to be worked out. For example, Chatterjee had to provide engineers with suggestions for filter flow rates, storage capacities (if any), unit layout, and overall dimensions, plus a number of special features. One such feature was the possibility of a small battery to operate the filter for several hours in case of a power failure (a common occurrence in India and many other LDCs). Another might be one or two "bells or whistles" to tell cooks, maids, and family members that the unit indeed was working properly. Yet another might be an "additive" feature, permitting users to add fluoride, vitamins, or even flavorings to their water.

Chatterjee knew that the Indian market would eventually require a number of models. However, at the outset of market entry, he probably could get by with just two—one with a larger capacity for houses and bungalows and the other a smaller capacity model for flats. He thought that model styling and specific appearances should reflect a Western, high-technology school of design in order to distinguish the Delight purifier from competitors' products. To that end, he had instructed a graphics artist to develop two ideas that he had used to gauge consumer reactions on his last visit (see Figure 12–1). Consumers liked both models but preferred the countertop design to the wallmount design.

Figure 12–1 Wallmount and countertop designs

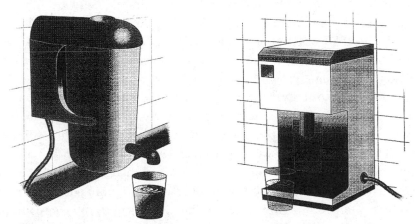

COMPETITORS

More than 100 companies competed in the Indian market for home water filters and purifiers. While information on most of these companies was difficult to obtain, Chatterjee and the Indian research agencies were able to develop descriptions of three major competitors and brief profiles of several others.

Eureka Forbes

The most established competitor in the water purifier market was Eureka Forbes, a joint-venture company established in 1982 between Electrolux

(Sweden) and Forbes Campbell (India). The company marketed a broad line of "modern, lifestyle products" including water purifiers, vacuum cleaners, and mixers/grinders. The brand name used for its water purifiers was "Aquaguard," a name so well established that many consumers mistakenly used it to refer to other water purifiers or to the entire product category. Aquaguard, with its ten-year market history, was clearly the market leader and came close to being India's only national brand. However, Eureka Forbes had recently introduced a second brand of water purifier called "PureSip." The PureSip model was similar to Aquaguard except for its third stage process which used a polyiodide resin instead of ultraviolet rays to kill bacteria and viruses. This meant that water from a PureSip purifier could be stored safely for later usage. Also in contrast to Aquaguard, the PureSip model needed no electricity for its operation.

However, the biggest difference between the two products was how they were sold. Aquaguard was sold exclusively by a 2,500-person sales force that called directly on households. In contrast, PureSip was sold by independent dealers of smaller home appliances. Unit prices to consumers for Aquaguard and PureSip in 1996 were approximately Rs5,500 and Rs2,000, respectively. Chatterjee believed that unit sales of PureSip were much smaller than unit sales for Aquaguard but growing at a much faster rate.

An Aquaguard unit typically was mounted on a kitchen wall, with plumbing required to bring water to the purifier's inlet. A two-meter long power cord was connected to a 230-volt AC electrical outlet—the Indian standard. If the power supply were to drop to 190 volts or lower, the unit would stop functioning. Other limits of the product included a smallish amount of activated carbon, which could eliminate only weak organic odors. It could not remove strong odors or inorganic solutes like nitrates and iron compounds. The unit's design did not allow for storage of treated water and its flow rate of one liter per minute seemed slow to some consumers.

Aquaguard's promotion strategy emphasized personal selling. Each salesman was assigned to a specific neighborhood and was monitored by a group leader who, in turn, was monitored by a supervisor. Each salesman was expected to canvass his neighborhood, select prospective households (e.g., those with annual incomes exceeding Rs70,000), demonstrate the product, and make an intensive effort to sell the product. Repeated sales calls helped to educate consumers about their water quality and to reassure them that Aquaguard service was readily available. Television commercials and advertisements in magazines and newspapers (see Figure 12–2) supported the personal selling efforts. Chatterjee estimated that Eureka Forbes would spend about Rs120

Figure 12-2   Aquaguard newspaper advertisement

million on all sales activities in 1996 or roughly 11% of its sales revenues. He estimated that about Rs100 million of the Rs120 million would be spent in the form of sales commissions. Chatterjee thought the company's total advertising expenditure for the year would be only about Rs1 million.

Eureka Forbes was a formidable competitor. The sales force was huge, highly motivated, and well managed. Moreover, Aquaguard was the first product to enter the water purifier market and the name had tremendous brand equity. The product itself was probably the weakest strategic component—but it would take much to convince consumers of this. And, while the sales force offered a huge competitive advantage, it represented an enormous fixed cost and essentially limited sales efforts to large urban areas. More than 80% of India's population lived in rural areas, where water quality was even lower.

Ion Exchange

Ion Exchange was the premier water treatment company in India, specializing in treatments of water, processed liquids, and wastewater in industrial markets. The company began operations in 1964 as a wholly-owned subsidiary of British Permutit. Permutit divested its holdings in 1985 and Ion Exchange became a wholly-owned Indian company. The company presently served customers in a diverse group of industries, including nuclear and thermal power stations, fertilizers, petrochemical refineries, textiles, automobiles, and home water purifiers. Its home water purifiers carried the family brand name, Zero-B (Zero-Bacteria).

Zero-B purifiers used a halogenated resin technology as part of a three-stage purification process. The first stage removed suspended impurities via filter pads, the second eliminated bad odors and taste with activated carbon, and the third killed bacteria using trace quantities of polyiodide (iodine). The latter feature was attractive because it helped prevent iodine deficiency diseases and permitted purified water to be stored up to eight hours without fear of recontamination.

The basic purifier product for the home carried the name, "Puristore." A Puristore unit typically sat on a kitchen counter near the tap, with no electricity or plumbing hookup needed for its operation. The unit stored 20 liters of purified water. It was sold to consumers for Rs2,000. Each year the user had to replace the halogenated resin at a cost of Rs200.

Chatterjee estimated that Zero-B had captured about 7% of the Indian water purifier market. Probably the biggest reason for the small share was a lack of consumer awareness. Zero-B purifiers had been on the market for less than three years. They were not advertised heavily nor did they enjoy the sales effort intensity of Aquaguard. Distribution, too, was limited. During Chatterjee's visit, he could find only five dealers in Calcutta carrying Zero-B products and none in Bangalore. Dealers that he contacted were of the opinion that Zero-B's marketing efforts would soon intensify—two had heard rumors that a door-to-door sales force was planned and that consumer advertising was about to begin.

Chatterjee had confirmed the latter point with a visit to a Calcutta advertising agency. A modest number of ten-second TV commercials would soon be aired on Zee TV and DD[1] metro channels. The advertisements would focus on educating consumers with the position, "It is not a filter." Instead, Zero-B is a water purifier and much more effective than a candle filter in preventing health problems. Apart from this advertising effort, the only other form of promotion used was a point-of-sale brochure that dealers could give to prospective customers (see Figure 12–3).

On balance, Chatterjee thought that Ion Exchange could be a major player in the market. The company had over 30 years' experience in the field of water purification and devoted in excess of Rs10 million each year to corporate research and development. "In fact," he thought, "all Ion Exchange really needs to do is to recognize the market's potential and to make it a priority within the company." However, this might be difficult to do, given the company's prominent emphasis on industrial markets. Chatterjee estimated that Zero-B products would account for less than 2% of Ion Exchange's 1997 total sales, estimated at Rs1,000 million. He thought the total marketing expenditures for Zero-B would be around Rs3 million.

Singer

The newest competitor to enter the Indian water purifier market was Singer India Ltd. Originally, Singer India was a subsidiary of The Singer Company, located in the U.S., but a minority share (49%) was sold to Indian investors in 1982. The change in ownership had led to the construction of manufacturing facilities in India for sewing machines in 1983. The facilities were expanded in 1991 to produce a broad line of home appliances. Sales revenues for 1996 for the entire product line—sewing machines, food processors, irons, mixers, toasters, water heaters, ceiling fans, cooking ranges, and color televisions— would be about Rs900 million.

During Chatterjee's time in Calcutta, he had visited a Singer Company showroom on Park Street. Initially he had hoped that Singer might be a suitable partner to manufacture and distribute the Delight purifier. However, much to his surprise, he was told that Singer now had its own brand "Aquarius" on the market. The product was not yet available in Calcutta but was being sold in Bombay and Delhi.

A marketing research agency in Delhi was able to gather some information on the Singer purifier. The product contained nine stages and was sold to consumers for Rs4,000. It removed sediments, heavy metals, bad tastes, odors, and colors. It also killed bacteria and viruses, fungi, and nematodes. The

---

[1] The names of television channels commonly available in many Indian cities.

Figure 12–3   Zero-B flyer

ZERO B
PuriLine

Because good health and good times go together

Water contamination is the cause of 80% of diseases. Zero-B Puriline ensures safe drinking water – free from bacteria which cause diarrhoea, dysentery, gastroenteritis, cholera, typhoid, etc. and also Polio, Coxsackie and ECHO viruses.

3 stage purification process – virtually maintenance free

Zero-B Puriline has a special synthetic filter which removes suspended impurities in the water.

The BAC unit removes bad odour, taste and colour.

And the purifying medium eliminates disease causing bacteria and viruses on contact.

AUTOGUARD

The Autoguard stops the water flow as soon as the purifying medium gets exhausted, indicating the time for replacement and thus ensuring pure and safe drinking water at all times.

ResiProtec

– the power that resists re-entry of bacteria and viruses in purified water and thus ensures safe drinking water for hours.

Zero Electricity – Safe Water 24 hours a day

Zero-B Puriline doesn't use electricity. So don't worry about damage due to power failures and voltage fluctuations.

Approved by reputed organisations

"... it is concluded that the Zero-B filter used according to the instructions will satisfactorily disinfect water both for viruses and bacteria so that it is microbiologically safe for human consumption."

– *King Edward VII Hospital, Midhurst, West Sussex, UK.*

Also certified in Singapore, U.K., Venezuela, Kenya, Nairobi, China, Argentina and the Sultanate of Oman.*

* Test certificates can be made available on request.

Zero-B is a Registered Trademark of

ION EXCHANGE
THE POWER
BEHIND WATER **(INDIA) LTD**

Pioneers & leaders in water treatment

Consumer Products Division
502 Veer Savarkar Marg, Prabhadevi, Bombay 400 025.
Tel.: (91) 22-4306329/4301736. Tlx: 011-74458 IONX IN.
Cable: IONTREAT . Fax: (91) 22-4377712/4301840.

Branches at:
● Bangalore: 2271030 ● Baroda: 335507 ● Calcutta: 402406 ● Delhi: 5432860
● Hyderabad: 225745 ● Lucknow: 239348 ● Madras: 8253293 ● Pune: 779061.

purifier required water pressure (8 PSI minimum) to operate but needed no electricity. It came in a single counter top model that could be moved from one room to another. Life of the device at a flow rate of 3.8 liters per minute was listed as 40,000 liters—about four to six years of use in a typical Indian household. The product's life could be extended to 70,000 liters at a somewhat slower flow rate. However, at 70,000 liters, the product must be discarded. The agency reported a heavy advertising blitz accompanying the introduction in Delhi—emphasizing TV and newspaper advertising, plus outdoor and transit advertising as support. All ten Singer showrooms in Delhi offered vivid demonstrations of the product's operation.

Chatterjee had to admit that photos of the Aquarius purifier shown in the Calcutta showroom looked appealing. And, a trade article he found had described the product as "state-of-the-art" in comparison to the "primitive" products now on the market. Chatterjee and Blair Company engineers tended to agree—the disinfecting resin used in Aquarius had been developed by the U.S. government's National Aeronautics and Space Administration (NASA) and was proven to be 100% effective against bacteria and viruses. "If only I could have brought a unit back with me," he thought. "We could have some test results and see just how good it is." The trade article also mentioned that Singer hoped to sell 40,000 units over the next two years.

Chatterjee knew that Singer was a well-known and respected brand name in India. Further, Singer's distribution channels were superior to those of any competitor in the market, including those of Eureka Forbes. Most prominent of Singer's three distribution channels were the 210 company-owned showrooms located in major urban areas around the country. Each sold and serviced the entire line of Singer products. Each was very well kept and staffed by knowledgeable personnel. Singer products also were sold throughout India by over 3,000 independent dealers, who received inventory from an estimated 70 Singer-appointed distributors. According to the market research agency in Delhi, distributors earned margins of 12% of the retail price for Aquarius while dealers earned margins of 5%. Finally, Singer employed over 400 salesmen who sold sewing machines and food processors door-to-door. Like Eureka Forbes, the direct sales force sold products primarily in large urban markets.

Other Competitors

Chatterjee was aware of several other water purifiers on the Indian market. The Delta brand from S & S Industries in Madras seemed a carbon copy of Aquaguard, except for a more eye pleasing counter top design. According to promotional literature, Delta offered a line of water related products—

contaminants that were peculiar to particular regions. For example, Calcutta and much of the surrounding area suffered from iron contamination, which no filter or purifier now on the Indian market could remove to a satisfactory level. Water supplies in other areas of the country were known to contain objectionable concentrations of calcium, salt, arsenic, lead, or sulfur. Most Indian consumers would need one or the other of the additional modules, but very few would need both.

Market Entry and Marketing Planning Recommendations

Assuming that Chatterjee recommended proceeding with the field test, he would need to make a recommendation concerning mode of market entry. In addition, his recommendation should include an outline of a marketing plan.

Licensee considerations. If market entry were in the form of a joint-working arrangement with a licensee, Blair Company's financial investment would be minimal. Chatterjee thought that Blair Company might risk as little as US$30,000 in capital for production facilities and equipment, plus another US$5,000 for office facilities and equipment. These investments would be completely offset by the licensee's payment to Blair Company for technology transfer and personnel training. Annual fixed costs to Blair Company should not exceed US$40,000 at the outset and would decrease to US$15,000 as soon as an Indian national could be hired, trained, and left in charge. Duties of this individual would be to work with Blair Company personnel in the U.S. and with management at the licensee to see that units were produced per Blair Company's specifications. Apart from this activity, Blair Company would have no control over the licensee's operations. Chatterjee expected that the licensee would pay Blair Company royalties of about Rs280 for each unit sold in the domestic market and Rs450 for each unit that was exported. The average royalty probably would be around Rs300.

Joint venture/acquisition considerations. If entry were in the form of either a joint venture or an acquisition, financial investment and annual fixed costs would be much higher and depend greatly on the scope of operations. Chatterjee had roughed out some estimates for a joint-venture market entry, based on three levels of scope (see Table 12–2). His estimates reflected what he thought were reasonable assumptions for all needed investments plus annual fixed expenses for sales activities, general administrative overheads, research and development, insurance, and depreciation. His estimates allowed for the Delight purifier to be sold either through dealers or through a direct, door-to-door sales force. Chatterjee thought that estimates of annual fixed expenses for market entry via acquisition would be identical to those for a joint venture.

Table 12–2 Investments and fixed costs for a joint-venture market entry

	Operational scope		
	Two regions	Four regions	National market
1998 market potential (units)	55,000	110,000	430,000
Initial investment (Rs'000)	4,000	8,000	30,000
Annual fixed overhead expenses (Rs'000)			
Using dealer channels	4,000	7,000	40,000
Using direct sales force	7,200	14,000	88,000

However, estimates for the investment (purchase) might be considerably higher, the same, or lower. It depended on what was purchased.

Chatterjee's estimates of Delight's unit contribution margins reflected a number of assumptions—expected economies of scale, experience curve effects, costs of Indian labor and raw materials, and competitors' pricing strategies. However, the most important assumption was Delight's pricing strategy. If a skimming strategy was used and the product sold through a dealer channel, the basic module would be priced to dealers at Rs5,500 and to consumers at Rs5,900. "This would give us about a Rs650 unit contribution, once we got production flowing smoothly," he thought. In contrast, if a penetration strategy was used and the product sold through a dealer channel, the basic module would be priced to dealers at Rs4,100, to consumers at Rs4,400, and yield a unit contribution of Rs300. For simplicity's sake, Chatterjee assumed that the two additional models would be priced to dealers at Rs800, to consumers at Rs1,000, and would yield a unit contribution of Rs100.

To achieve unit contributions of Rs650 or Rs300, the basic modules would employ different designs. The basic module for the skimming strategy would be noticeably superior, with higher performance and quality, a longer warranty period, more features, and a more attractive appearance than the basic module for the penetration strategy. Positioning, too, most likely would be different. Chatterjee recognized several positioning possibilities: performance and taste, value for money/low price, safety, health, convenience, attractive styling, avoiding diseases and health related bills, and superior American technology. The only position he considered "taken" in the market was that occupied by Aquaguard—protect family health and service at your doorstep. While other

Uzbekistan government, Chairman Kim and his senior managers had to answer the challenges facing the automobile business and, at the same time, review Daewoo's overall strategy in Uzbekistan.

COMPANY BACKGROUND

Founded in 1967 as a small textile trading company, the Daewoo Group was one of the world's largest industrial enterprises. Consisting of 31 domestic companies and 454 overseas subsidiaries and branch offices with more than 250,000 employees worldwide as of June 1997, the Daewoo Group was engaged in trading; in domestic and overseas construction; in shipbuilding; and in the manufacture of motor vehicles, heavy machinery, telecommunications equipment, consumer electronics, home appliances, textiles, and other products. Daewoo also had investments in financial and telecommunications services, and operated hotels worldwide. The Daewoo Group recorded total sales of US$68 billion in 1996 and ranked 24th on the *Fortune* Global 500. Figure 13–1 summarizes the sales and export growth of Daewoo, and Table 13–1 breaks down Daewoo's overseas business network by region and by line of business.

Figure 13–1 Daewoo's total sales and exports (US$ billion), 1970–97

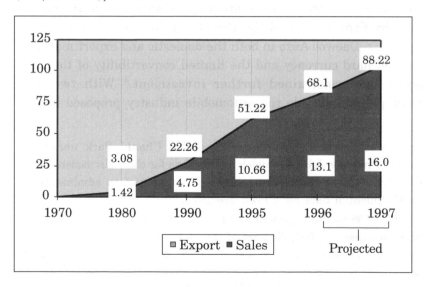

Table 13–1 Daewoo's overseas business network (as of June 1997)

a. Overseas network by region

	Subsidiaries	Branches	R&D centers	Construction sites	Total	Cumulative investment (US$)*
Asia	135	68	3	29	235	1,390 million
Africa/Middle East	24	27		40	91	315 million
CIS	25	13	2		40	270 million
Eastern Europe	37	6		1	44	571 million
Western Europe	36	9	5		50	364 million
Americas	54	20	3	1	78	394 million
Total	311	143	13	71	538	3,304 million

b. Overseas network by lines of business

	Subsidiaries	Branches	R&D centers	Construction sites	Total	Cumulative investment (US$)*
Trade	138	86			224	910 million
Construction	41	21		71	133	676 million
Electronics/ telecommunications	74	24	9		107	680 million
Automotive industry	20	1	2		23	767 million
Heavy industry	11	5	2		18	100 million
Finance	13	4			17	125 million
Others	14	2			16	46 million
Total	311	143	13	71	538	3,304 million

* Investment amount = equity investment + loans to the subsidiaries.

As of June 1997, Daewoo had investments in 380 projects in over 85 nations. Daewoo expected to increase its global network to 1,000 locations by the year 2000. Unlike many multinationals, more than half of Daewoo's overseas investments since 1991 had been concentrated in emerging markets, which the management thought had the greatest potential in the 21st century. By meeting the development needs of these emerging markets, Daewoo hoped to fully realize its commitment to "mutual prosperity."

Fully operational overseas investment programs included electronics and home appliances manufacturing in the U.K., France, Spain, Poland, Mexico, Uzbekistan, and Kazakhstan. Daewoo also had investments in major vehicle and component production plants in Poland, Romania, the Czech Republic, Uzbekistan, India, China, the Ukraine, Vietnam, the Philippines, Iran, and Indonesia.

By the year 2000, Daewoo aimed to be among the world's top ten companies in automobiles, electronics and home appliances, heavy equipment manufacturing, shipbuilding, and telecommunications services. Chairman Kim had founded the company at the age of 31 and still exercised intimate leadership over key strategic issues in all 31 subsidiary companies. His entrepreneurial spirit, hard work, and business insights made him an important role model among younger Koreans. He authored the book, *It's a Big World and There's Lots to be Done*, published in August 1989. The Korean edition sold one million copies in record time. The English translation was published in 1992 under the title, *Every Street is Paved with Gold*. Chairman Kim spent more than 260 days abroad every year, always worked more than 130 hours a week, and had never taken a vacation throughout his career.

COMPANY HISTORY

Daewoo Corporation was founded in 1967 as a producer and exporter of textile products. The company became the parent of what was known in 1997 as the Daewoo Group, which comprised 31 companies. Exports grew from US$580,000 in 1967 to US$40 million in 1972. In that year, the company became the second largest Korean exporter and was awarded the "Order of Industrial Merit, Gold Tower" by the Korean government.[2] Daewoo Corporation went public in 1973 and diversified into construction, financial services, and apparel manufacturing, in each case by acquiring financially distressed companies. Predicting the imposition of textile import quotas by the U.S. government, Chairman Kim strongly pushed for maximum textile exports. As a result, when

---

[2] Korea's total exports were less than US$2 billion in 1972.

the quotas were allocated among suppliers based on their shares of exports into the U.S., Daewoo Corp. benefited by reselling a portion of its quota, as well as by making profits on its own export sales. According to a senior Daewoo executive:

> With the quota premium alone, we could have bought ten top-of-the-line 20-story office buildings in downtown Seoul every year. With that much money on hand, we decided instead to pursue our entrepreneurial ambition and contribute to our country by doing real business.

Taking advantage of that success, Daewoo diversified further into heavy machinery industries in the late 1970s. It was the Korean government that pushed for this diversification. Due to the worldwide recession and the energy crisis, the Korean government's industrial restructuring drive toward heavy machinery and petrochemicals faced great challenges. A senior Daewoo executive explained:

> Once we became famous thanks to a couple of successful turnarounds, the government and the financial community consistently pushed us to do more acquisitions. Some people criticized us for the acquisition drive, but we were compelled to acquire many of the current Daewoo companies. We turned Korea Heavy Industries into a profit in our first year running its operations in 1976, and dedicated the Okpo shipyard (currently the main facility of Daewoo shipbuilding) in 1981. We also acquired the 50% stake in GM Korea in 1978.

By 1979, Daewoo was Korea's biggest exporter and one of the five largest conglomerates in Korea. By 1981, the number of Daewoo overseas offices had grown to 65. In 1982, consumer electronics and telecommunications were added to Daewoo's business portfolio. Daewoo Telecom's 16-bit personal computer Model D became a popular choice in the U.S. market under the Leading Edge brand. Expansion into emerging markets including several former communist nations laid the foundation for Daewoo's continued growth. Daewoo played a leading role in developing Korea's economic (and diplomatic) relations with Libya, Sudan, Iran, China, and Russia throughout the 1970s and 1980s. Korea's first commercial office in Eastern Europe was established by Daewoo in East Berlin in 1988, followed by other Daewoo offices in Prague in 1989 and Moscow in 1990. A refrigerator plant was dedicated in China in 1988. Daewoo formed the first Korean–Chinese joint venture in 1989 to produce color-picture tubes. Throughout the 1990s, Daewoo continued its leading role in building economic relations with Poland, Romania, and North Korea.

Chairman Kim and the Daewoo people attributed the growth to their hard work and willingness to take on new challenges. Overcoming a variety of environmental threats and administrative challenges during the high-growth period, Daewoo built a refined and flexible management system supported by the entrepreneurial initiative of front-line managers rather than by management and planning processes. Industry insiders also explained Daewoo's growth in terms of its financial expertise, its use of governmental subsidies for turnarounds, and its exploitation of opportunities in both the domestic and international financial markets.

Above all, an international orientation had been the engine of Daewoo's growth. Having started as a trading company, Daewoo had developed competencies in international trade and finance from the outset. When Daewoo became one of the biggest Korean conglomerates in the early 1980s, its managers discovered that the 40-million domestic market was too small to fuel Daewoo's continued growth. So, international expansion was inevitable. Moreover, some of Daewoo's export goods were more technically sophisticated than the domestic market could absorb at that time. A senior Daewoo executive in the textile business stated:

> When we considered introducing some of the apparel products developed for export into the domestic market in the early 1980s, we realized that many of the incumbent firms would be driven out of the market. We decided to pursue the larger overseas market rather than try to steal shares from our weaker competitors in Korea. As we built our credential in international markets, our business partners offered bigger deals in a wider variety of businesses.

Table 13–2 lists the principal Daewoo Group companies in Korea, and Table 13–3 lists the principal overseas Daewoo subsidiaries.

Overseas automobile investments were central to Daewoo's globalization and growth strategy in the 1990s. Faced with stiff competition in a slow growth domestic market, Chairman Kim took charge of the automobile business and led the series of overseas automobile investments detailed below. In addition to the automobile projects, overseas investments were also initiated in electronics and telecommunications services. Daewoo was running mobile communications services in China and Uzbekistan. Local banks and financial institutions were established in 18 nations. Daewoo's bid for Thomson Multimedia was still on

Table 13-2 Major Daewoo Group companies (domestic)[a]

	1996 sales (US$)	Company	Business fields and products
Trading	$19.4 billion (automobile-related; $12.5 billion)	Daewoo Corporation (General Trading Division)	Trading, financing, resource development, investment, project organization, logistics
Construction & hotels	$7.2 billion	Daewoo Corporation (Construction Division)	Architectural works, civil works, plants, R&D, development programs, design engineering
		Keangnam Enterprises, Ltd.	Architectural works, civil works, plants, engineering and consulting
		Kyungnam Metal Co., Ltd.	Aluminum extrusion, curtain walls, frames, profiles, fabrication of aluminum sash
		Daewoo Development Co., Ltd.	Hotels and museum
Heavy industry & shipbuilding	$5.1 billion	Daewoo Heavy Industries Ltd. (General Machinery Division)	Diesel engines, construction equipment, machine tools, factory automation, defense products, materials, precision machines, aerospace products, machinery & equipment
		Daewoo Heavy Industries Ltd. (Shipbuilding Division)	Shipbuilding, offshore platforms, specialty vessels, repair & conversion, offshore workshops, drilling rigs, steel structures, industrial plants
		Korea Industrial Systems Co., Ltd.	Computer numerically controlled equipment
Automotive industry[b]	$4.5 billion	Daewoo Motor Co., Ltd.	Vehicle manufacturing (passenger cars, buses, trucks)
		Daewoo Heavy Industries Ltd. (Public Motors Division)	Minivehicle production
		Daewoo Automotive Components Ltd.	Alternators, cranking motors, ignition coils, distributors, brake systems, catalytic converters, steering systems, FWD axles, compressors, car air-conditioner, components, radiators
		Daewoo Precision Industries Ltd.	Automotive components, materials nuclear fuel components, machinery, pneumatic tools, defense industry products
		Koram Plastics Co., Ltd	Rim bumpers, battery cases
		Korea Automotive Fuel Systems	Automotive fuel systems
		Daewoo Motor Sales Co., Ltd.	Vehicle sales

Table 13-2 (cont'd)

	1996 sales (US$)	Company	Business fields and products
Electronics & telecommunications	$4.2 billion	Daewoo Electronics Co., Ltd	TVs, VCRs, microwave ovens, audio systems, home appliances
		Daewoo Electronic Components Co., Ltd.	E-tuners, Hybrid-ICs, DYs, capacitors (film, aluminum, electrolytic, tantalum), FBTs, thermistors, relays, keyboards, and SAW Filters
		Orion Electric Co., Ltd.	Monochrome CRTs, electron guns, color CRTS, electron gun parts, computer monitors, flat panel display devices (LDC, PDP, and ELD)
		Orion Electric Components Co., Ltd.	Color CRT manufacturing and sales
		Daewoo Electric Motor Industries Ltd.	Motor manufacturing
		Daewoo Telecom Ltd.	Computers, peripherals, system integration, telecommunications systems
		Daewoo Information Systems Co., Ltd.	System integration, system products, system services
Finance & services	$1.2 billion	Daewoo Securities Co., Ltd.	Brokerage, underwriting, overseas investment, settlement and standing proxy, dealing, mergers & acquisitions
		Daewoo Economic Research Institute	Advanced analysis of economic factors
		Daewoo Capital Management Co., Ltd.	Korea fund advisor, investment advisor, portfolio manager
		Korea Financial Service Co., Ltd.	Factoring
		The Diners Club of Korea	Credit cards
		Dongwoo Management Co., Ltd.	Building maintenance
		Daewoo Venture Capital Co., Ltd.	Technical & financial support to small & medium-sized enterprises

Notes:

[a] This figure is the annual consolidated sales by domestic companies.

[b] Daewoo's automobile-related sales by overseas subsidiaries were estimated to be US$8.6 billion as of 1996.

Table 13–3   Major Daewoo Group subsidiaries (overseas)

	Western Europe	Business fields and products
U.K.	Daewoo Worthing Technical Center	Car design and engineering
	Daewood Electronics U.K.	Home appliances mfg.
France	Euro Daewoo	Heavy machinery
	Daewoo Cars	Car sales
	Daewoo Electronics Mfg.	Home appliances mfg.
	Daewoo Orion	CRT mfg.
	Daewoo Automobile France	Car sales
Germany	Daewoo Automobile Germany	Car sales
	Daewoo Motor Engineering	Car engineering
	Euro Daewoo	Heavy equipment sales
	Eastern Europe	
Poland	Daewoo-FSO Motor	Passenger car mfg.
	Daewoo Motor Polska	Commercial vehicles mfg.
	Centrum Daewoo	Car sales
	Daewoo Electronics Poland	Home appliances mfg.
Romania	Daewoo Automobile Romania	Passenger cars mfg.
	Daewoo Mangalia Heavy Industries	Shipbuilding and repair
	Daewoo Romania Bank	Banking
Czech Republic	Daewoo AVIA	Commercial vehicles mfg.
Hungary	Daewoo MBM	Bearing production
	Daewoo Bank	Loans, trusts
	Daewoo Securities	Securities brokerage
	Daewoo Leasing	Leasing
	CIS	
Uzbekistan	Uz–Daewoo Auto	Passenger cars mfg.
	Uz–Daewoo Electronics	Home appliances mfg.
	Uz–Daewoo Bank	Banking
	Uz–Daewoo Textile	Cotton fabrics
	Uz–Daewoo Telecom	Telecommunications services
Kazakhstan	Daewoo Almaty Electronics	Home appliances mfg.
	Kazaktelecom	Telecommunications services
Ukraine	Auto ZAZ	Passenger cars mfg.
	Dniepr–Daewoo	Telecom equipment mfg.

Table 13–3 (cont'd)

Asia		Business fields and products
China	Daewoo China	Holding company
	FAW–Daewoo Automotive Engines	Engine, transmissions
	Shandong–Daewoo Automotive Components	Automotive components
	Daewoo Cement Plant	Cement production
	Guilin Daewoo Bus	Buses
	Daewoo Heavy Industries Yantai	Excavator mfg.
	Beijing Lufthansa Center	Hotel, office, apartments
	Yanbian Daewoo Hotel	Hotel
	Guilin Sheraton Hotel	Hotel
	Shanghai Business Center	Business center construction
	Heilongjiang Electronic Technology	Telecommunications services
Vietnam	Daeha Business Center	Hotel, offices, apartments
	Daewoo Hanel Electronics	Home appliances mfg.
	Orion Hanel Picture Tube	CRT manufacturing
	Vietnam Daewoo Motor	Passenger car mfg.
	Firstvina Bank	Banking
	Saidong Industrial Zone Development	Plant site development
India	Daewoo Motors India	Passenger cars mfg.
	Daewoo Securities India	Securities brokerage
	Daewoo Power India	Power plant construction

Africa and Middle East		
Iran	Kerman Motor	Passenger cars mfg.
Morocco	Rabat Hilton Hotel	Hotel
Sudan	International Tire Manufacturing	Tire
	Port Sudan Spinning Mill	Cotton yarn
Algeria	Algiers Hilton Hotel	Hotel
Nigeria	Daewoo Nigeria	Construction
Angola	Oil Exploration Project	Oil exploration

Latin America		
Mexico	Daewoo Electronics Mexico	Color TV mfg.
	Decomex	Home appliances sales
	Dehamex	Home appliances mfg.
	Daewoo Electro-Components Mexico	Components mfg.
	Daewoo Orion Mexicana	CPT mfg.

Table 13–3   (cont'd)

	Latin America	Business fields and products
Chile	Decsa	Home appliances sales
Peru	Oil Exploration Project	Oil exploration
Colombia	Deco	Home appliances sales

	North America	
U.S.	Daewoo Motor America	Car sales
	Daewoo International America	Trading
	Daewoo Electronics America	Home appliances sales
	Daewoo Securities	Securities brokerage
	Daewoo Machinery	Heavy equipment sales

hold.[3] As of June 1997, Daewoo had invested US$3.3 billion in more than 380 overseas projects. Chairman Kim anticipated US$15 billion worth of overseas projects by 2005. According to the plan, Daewoo would employ 250,000 foreign workers at 1,000 overseas subsidiaries and branches that would help generate a group total of US$177 billion in revenues by 2000.

Daewoo's Automobile Business: 1972–92

Daewoo Motor Company (DMC) is the automobile subsidiary of Daewoo Group. In 1972, General Motors had set up an automobile plant (GM Korea) as a joint venture with a Korean local partner. Daewoo acquired the local partner's 50% share of GM Korea in 1978 and assumed management responsibility. The company was renamed Daewoo Motor Company in 1983. DMC was the market leader in the domestic compact car market (considered the "luxury" end of the market at that time in Korea) and was second in the domestic subcompact car market until the mid-1980s. As a partner in GM's "world car" project, Daewoo

---

[3] In February 1996, the Chirac government announced a privatization plan for Thomson S.A., the French conglomerate comprising Thompson CSF (defense and electronics), Thomson SGS (semiconductor), and Thomson Multimedia (TMM: consumer electronics and telecommunications equipment). TMM had acquired 100% of GE's Audio & Video Division including GE's 100% share of RCA in 1987. In 1996, Daewoo announced its plan to bid and was selected as the final bidder for TMM. The deal was put on hold due to the pressure of domstic politics in France. If Daewoo succeeded in the bid, it would become the biggest consumer electronics company in the world.

invested US$1.1 billion to set up a new production line for the Pontiac Lemans (a 1500cc subcompact) targeted at both the U.S. and Korean markets, and started production in 1986. Exports to the U.S. began in April 1987. Domestic sales of the Lemans were encouraging at first, but exports were fewer than expected. According to a DMC executive, Daewoo gradually saw the need to pursue a more independent strategy:

> GM considered DMC as just one more factory in its worldwide network serving the Korean domestic market (60,000 vehicles/year) and providing low-cost vehicles for the U.S. market (40,000 vehicles/year). However, DMC wanted to pursue a larger market opportunity. The relationship soured and Daewoo set up a minicar plant with cooperation from Suzuki in 1988. In 1991, the new plant located in Changwon started to produce the Tico (with an 800cc engine) and the Damas (a light commercial vehicle) based on the design platform of the Suzuki Alto.

By mid-1991, the divergence of interests between Daewoo and GM had become acute, and industry insiders began to forecast the possible breakup of the joint venture. Meanwhile, in the late 1980s, domestic competition became tougher. Hyundai, Daewoo's biggest domestic rival, introduced new compact (2000cc, Sonata) and subcompact (1500cc, Excel) models with enhanced features, thanks to continued research and development (R&D) investment and technical assistance from Mitsubishi. Hyundai launched the Excel and the Sonata in the U.S. market in 1986 and 1988, respectively. Kia, which had been a small number three manufacturer with a limited product line until the mid-1980s, was permitted by the Korean government to enter the passenger vehicle segment in 1984. Kia introduced subcompact and compact cars in 1986 and 1990, respectively. Ford and Mazda had equity stakes and technology licensing agreements with Kia. Kia's 1300cc subcompact model (Pride) was exported to the U.S. market as the Ford Festiva. Under the trade liberalization program, import tariffs and sales taxes on vehicles imported into Korea were scheduled to be lowered gradually. In the face of stiff competition, market growth was expected to slow down due to growing traffic congestion on the roads, increasing parking charges, and reduced tax incentives for buyers. Figure 13–2 shows trends in automobile ownership in Korea.

Faced with mounting competitive pressures, DMC had several problems. A labor strike in 1986 that lasted three months diluted the launch of the Lemans. Another strike in 1990 was also timed to coincide with a model change, and further hurt DMC's market position. The Changwon minicar plant did not suffer from labor disputes, but market demand for its minicars did not meet

Figure 13–2 Trends in automobile ownership in Korea

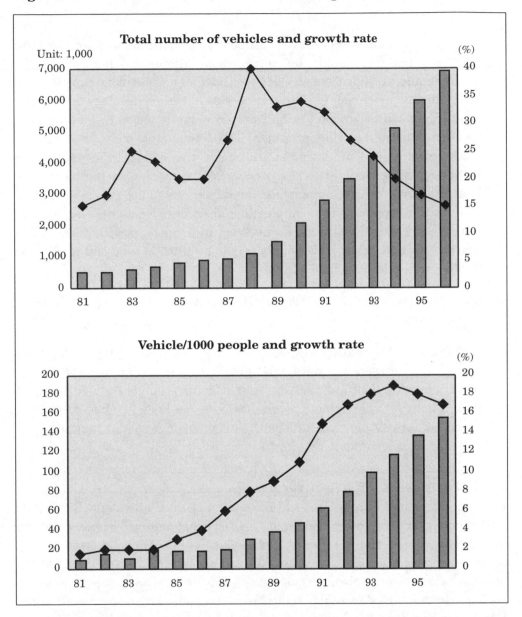

expectations due to the increasing consumer preference for bigger cars. One analyst in Seoul stated:

> During the turnaround of Daewoo Shipbuilding Company in the late 1980s, DMC did not get enough top management attention, which drives the resource allocation process at Daewoo. DMC management underestimated how quickly its domestic rivals were closing the technology gap. DMC focused on short-term profits and only invested enough to give periodic face-lifts to the existing products. DMC tended to rely on technical assistance from GM rather than make the effort to develop new technologies internally; this threatened DMC's position as the technology leader among Korean automobile manufacturers. Faced with mounting competitive pressure from domestic competitors with redesigned and improved product lines and the prospect of a breakup with GM, DMC's market position looked increasingly fragile by 1992. Morale and production quality were also deteriorating.

This analysis was not shared by DMC managers. According to a DMC executive in Seoul:

> I agree that the market response for the 1992 model was lower than expected. However, we were not ignorant of the need for technology investment. As the joint venture with GM increasingly seemed likely to limit the growth of our automobile business, we knew we had to prepare to be technologically self-sufficient. The problem was the magnitude of investment commitment required to achieve this.

The Globalization Drive Since 1992

In 1992, Chairman Kim decided to take charge of DMC's strategy. Relying on his previous turnaround experience at Daewoo Shipbuilding Company, he first mandated closer cooperation between DMC and other Daewoo Group companies and developed new foreign markets for existing models. An aggressive grass-roots sales campaign was launched to place Daewoo cars with all Daewoo employees and their relatives and friends. Financing assistance to DMC was provided by the entire network of Daewoo companies. Second, Chairman Kim initiated major new product development efforts. Three new passenger vehicle projects were started in fall 1993, each led by young general managers, and the organization was reshaped to meet the challenge. Following the breakup of the joint venture with GM in the winter of 1992, Chairman Kim merged the minicar plant operation into DMC. While searching for a technology cooperation partner, DMC bought automobile R&D firms in Worthing, U.K. (new model design and development) and Munich, Germany (engine development), which would be the basis for a global R&D network in collaboration with the existing R&D centers both in and outside of Korea.[4] Third, Chairman Kim set out to restore employee morale. He met all 12,000 DMC employees in 100 group meetings, which helped him secure support for implementing the changes needed to restore DMC's competitive edge.

Globalization was crucial to this effort. Chairman Kim believed that Daewoo had a unique strength in international operations (in comparison with other domestic competitors and foreign companies) and built his strategy on this. He exploited foreign markets with existing products and set up sales beachheads that would ensure sufficient demand to generate the scale economies needed for the next generation of models. After initiating exports to Western Europe in early 1995, DMC achieved 1% market share in the U.K. within 10 months. This confirmed Chairman Kim's belief in Daewoo's ability to penetrate new markets. Beyond the sales generated, Daewoo acquired invaluable learning about the automobile export market. Responses from emerging markets were even more favorable. Beginning with a knock-down plant in India (where Daewoo acquired existing facilities owned by Toyota and a local company) and the Uz–Daewoo Auto project in Uzbekistan, Daewoo acquired RODAE (the biggest automobile plant in Romania) in 1994 and FSO (the biggest automobile plant in Poland formerly owned by the government) in 1995. The Uzbekistan project encouraged other emerging market governments to work with Daewoo. Between 1992 and 1997, Daewoo also invested in production facilities in Vietnam, Indonesia, the Philippines, the Czech Republic, Iran, and China. Daewoo's corporate size (sales of US$65 billion in 1996), its financing capacity, and its global business network facilitated these transactions. Figure 13–3 and Table 13–4 detail Daewoo's automobile operations in Korea and overseas.

Daewoo sold 636,000 vehicles worldwide in 1995, and 857,000 in 1996. Around half of the sales outside Korea were made in emerging markets, the other half in developed markets. DMC was the 18th largest auto producer in 1996 with US$12 billion sales and 27,000 employees, but aimed to be in the top ten by 2000. In that year, DMC expected to produce 2.5 million vehicles, valued at US$40 billion. DMC's domestic production capacity goal of one million vehicles was accomplished with the dedication of Daewoo Motor's Kunsan plant in 1997.

---

[4] Daewoo was also planning to open an R&D center in the U.S. as of July 1997.

Figure 13-3 Companies affiliated with Daewoo's automobile production

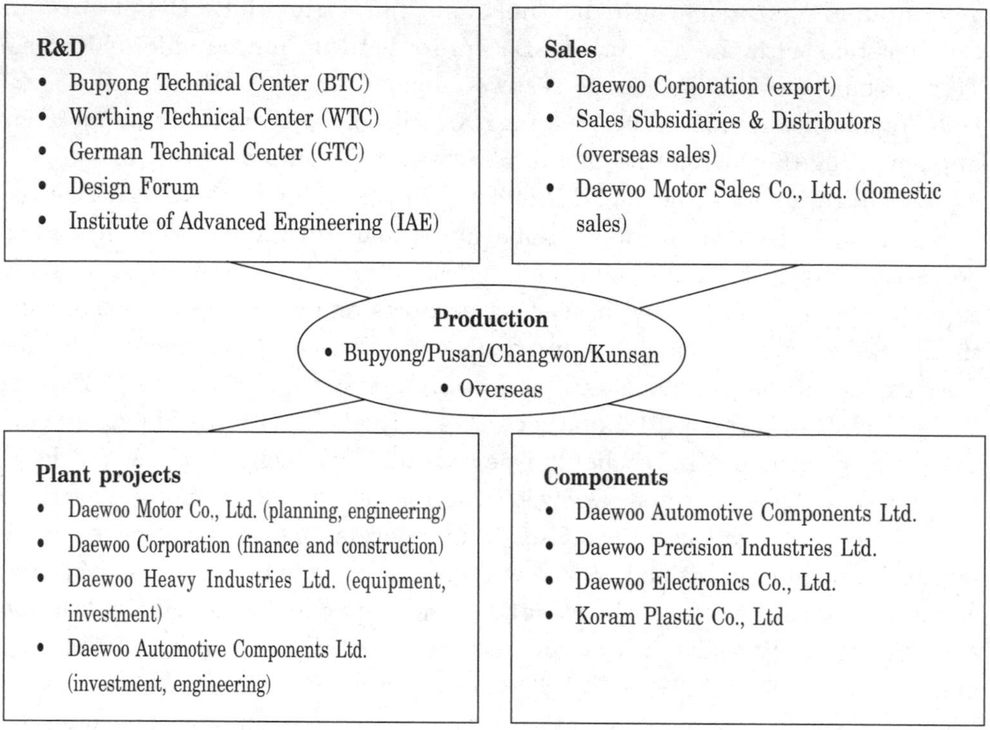

R&D
- Bupyong Technical Center (BTC)
- Worthing Technical Center (WTC)
- German Technical Center (GTC)
- Design Forum
- Institute of Advanced Engineering (IAE)

Sales
- Daewoo Corporation (export)
- Sales Subsidiaries & Distributors (overseas sales)
- Daewoo Motor Sales Co., Ltd. (domestic sales)

Production
- Bupyong/Pusan/Changwon/Kunsan
- Overseas

Plant projects
- Daewoo Motor Co., Ltd. (planning, engineering)
- Daewoo Corporation (finance and construction)
- Daewoo Heavy Industries Ltd. (equipment, investment)
- Daewoo Automotive Components Ltd. (investment, engineering)

Components
- Daewoo Automotive Components Ltd.
- Daewoo Precision Industries Ltd.
- Daewoo Electronics Co., Ltd.
- Koram Plastic Co., Ltd

Some industry experts raised concerns about this drive for scale. Given the over-capacity in the global automobile industry, they argued that fewer than ten automobile companies could survive in the 21st century. However, Chairman Kim was confident that Daewoo's global strategy to achieve the necessary scale economies would work. He stated:[5]

> For the last 20 years, there have always been concerns about over-capacity in the global automobile industry. Daewoo is creating new demand in the emerging markets of Eastern Europe, the former CIS countries, and Asia.[6] With the rapid industrial development and the growth of consumer buying power, Daewoo can benefit from being the first mover in these markets. Of course, Daewoo will also pursue opportunities in developed country

---

[5] *The Monthly Chosun*, February 1995.

[6] The CIS (Commonwealth of Independent States) included the independent republics that formerly comprised the Soviet Union.

Table 13–4 Daewoo's domestic and overseas automobile operations

a. Domestic plants

Location	Products	Capacity (1997)
Bupyong	Passenger cars	500,000
	KD (knock-down kits)	200,000
Pusan	Buses	6,000
Changwon	Minicars/light commercial vehicles	240,000
Kunsan	Passenger cars	300,000
	Trucks	20,000

b. Overseas plants

Country	Plant	Products	Capacity (by 1998)
Poland	DW–FSO	Passenger cars (local model)	120,000
		Commercial vehicles	40,000
	DMP	Passenger cars	20,000
		Commercial vehicles	45,000
Romania	RODAE	Passenger cars	200,000
Czech Republic	Avia	Commercial vehicles	25,000
Uzbekistan	Uz–Daewoo	Passenger cars	150,000
		Mini-commercial	50,000
India	DDML	Passenger cars	160,000
		Commercial vehicles	10,000
China	Guilin	Buses	5,000
Iran	KMC	Passenger cars	25,000
Philippines	TAMC	Passenger cars	10,000
	FDIC	Large buses	500
Vietnam	Vidamco	Passenger cars	25,000
		Large buses	2,000
Indonesia	PT. SD	Passenger cars	3,000

c. Domestic and export sales, 1994–96

Location	Product	1994	1995	1996
Domestic[a]	Passenger cars	284,734	233,555	278,617
	Commercial vehicles	24,863	20,886	21,460
	Sub-total	*309,597*	*254,441*	*300,077*

Table 13–4 (cont'd)

Location	Product	1994	1995	1996
Export[b]	Passenger cars	107,283	262,185	348,545
	Commercial vehicles	3,640	3,044	5,168
	KD[c]	—	15,672	118,199
	Sub-total	*110,923*	*280,901*	*471,912*
Total		420,520	535,342	771,989

Notes: [a] Domestic sales in Korea.
   [b] Exports of finished vehicles from Korea.
   [c] Exports of knock-down kits from Korea.

markets. There, we will define unique market niches and adopt differentiated marketing strategies. Our U.S. market launch in 1998 will show the way. To seize the opportunity in emerging markets, Daewoo is acquiring existing plants in those countries. We cannot rely on direct exports of finished vehicles because they will inevitably come up against trade barriers. Acquisitions save time and money for both sides. The capital-intensive nature of the automobile industry is such that it takes around US$1,000 fixed cost per unit of annual production to build a new plant; with careful renovation of existing plants, a large part of this cost can be saved. Daewoo's expanded market base will be the basis for achieving the necessary scale economies.

To remain competitive in the international market, we have to commit to an annual product development investment of US$1 billion across five platforms. We need 300,000 to 400,000 unit production for each platform (including the variants such as convertibles and wagons), totaling two million units of annual production. At this level of production, per unit R&D cost can be kept under US$500. This is why leading automobile makers are maintaining production output of over two million vehicles per year. To maintain consumer interest, Daewoo is planning to introduce two or three new models every year. We launched the Lanos (a 1500cc subcompact) and the Nubira (an 1800cc or 2000cc subcompact) in 1996, and the Leganza (a 2200cc or 3000cc compact) in 1997. Export of these new models will begin in late 1997. Overseas plants will soon switch their production lines to these new models.

As of July 1997, more industry insiders were accepting the logic of Daewoo's move toward globalization. As one put it:

Korea's domestic automobile market is too small for three producers (Daewoo, Hyundai, and Kia). With the expected market entry of Samsung in 1998 (based on a technology licensing agreement with Nissan) which will add capacity to produce 200,000 vehicles a year, competition in the domestic market will intensify further. At the same time, tariff and nontariff barriers on foreign cars coming into the domestic market will be lowered. Korean producers are losing their cost advantage due to rising wage and land costs. Exports to emerging markets will be restricted by protective trade policies to nurture their industrialization goals. Overseas production is therefore essential. Without it, even the export of components will become economically infeasible in the near future. Current overseas moves by Hyundai and Kia prove this point.

As of July 1997, Daewoo's three new models were enjoying strong sales in Korea. Both the Lanos and the Leganza broke the first month sales record for a new model, and DMC was regaining market leadership. The Leganza was launched in the U.S. in 1998.

HISTORY OF THE UZ–DAEWOO AUTO PROJECT

Daewoo and the Uzbekistan Economy

Uzbekistan was liberated from the former Soviet Union in August 1991. Under President Kharimov's strong leadership, Uzbekistan is actively pursuing industrialization. Located in the middle of the historic Silk Road trading route in Eurasia, Uzbekistan has a rich heritage of Islamic culture and is geographically positioned to serve as a distribution center of Central Asia. Table 13–5 and Table 13–6 report key economic indicators of Uzbekistan, while Figure 13–4 shows a map of Uzbekistan. The population of 22 million is well-educated; the adult literacy rate is 95%, 80% of the adult population have secondary education, and 16% have higher education. Uzbekistan is the world's fourth largest producer of cotton (1.5 million tons/year) and has important deposits of gold (70 tons/year: 95% of former CIS annual production), natural gas (40 billion cubic meters/year: 5% of former CIS annual production), copper, molibdenum, zinc, and tungsten. Uzbekistan is agriculturally self-sufficient (mainly through rice). Soviet assembly plants in machinery, aircraft production, and steel refining had created a skilled labor force. The political environment is stable. Though still experiencing high inflation and a shortage of hard currency, Uzbekistan has the best record of macroeconomic stability among the former CIS countries in Central Asia. According to Mr. V. Golishev, the presidential economic advisor:

Table 13-5 Key economic indicators for Uzbekistan

		1994		1995				1996			
		3 Qtr	4 Qtr	1 Qtr	2 Qtr	3 Qtr	4 Qtr	1 Qtr	2 Qtr	3 Qtr	4 Qtr
Industrial production	Monthly av.										
General index	1990 = 100	93.4	130.7	72.7	82.2	99.4	n.a.	n.a.	n.a.	n.a.	n.a.
Cement	1,000 tons	428	328	261	276	322	280	211	305	307	248[a]
Mining											
Lignite	1,000 tons	336	298	221	234	269	278	232	239	253	190[a]
Natural gas	mil. cu metres	3,313	4,207	4,406	3,968	3,544	4,066	4,526	3,879	3,564	4,069[a]
Crude petroleum	1,000 tons	326	402	437	430	439	464	402	432	398	461[a]
Employment											
Industry	1,000	1,100	1,084	1,120	1,110	1,110	1,070	1,050	1,035	1,020	n.a.
Unemployment, registered		19.3	21.2	27.6	32.8	28.4	26.4	28.9	32.9	33.4	n.a.
Wages											
Monthly earnings	Soum	480	600	973	1,475	1,551	2,118	2,244	3,350	3,920	n.a.
Construction											
Dwellings completed	1,000	6.9	6.4	2.4	5.6	6.4	5.1	2.0	5.9	8.7	n.a.
Foreign trade	Qtrly totals										
Exports	US$ mil.	449.2	1,276.3	449.0	779.7	577.8	1,243.5	453.4	518.1[b]	n.a.	n.a.
of which: CIS		224.1	998.9	478.7	442.5	255.6	252.7	109.5	109.6[b]	n.a.	n.a.
Imports	US$ mil.	648.2	790.7	517.9	592.8	488.8	1,148.4	603.4	559.8[b]	n.a.	n.a.
of which: CIS		375.2	378.3	220.0	273.5	316.8	307.3	187.0	205.2[b]	n.a.	n.a.

Notes: [a] October only.
[b] Total for April–May.
Source: OECD.

Table 13–6   Former Soviet Republics: GDP and GDP per head (at purchasing power parity)

	1989	1990	1991	1992	1993	1994	1995	1996
Armenia—GDP								
$ bn	17.6	17.0	16.1	7.9	6.9	7.3	8.0	8.6
per head ($)	5,062	4,804	4,469	2,143	1,853	2,051	2,124	2,275
Azerbaijan—GDP								
$ bn	21.8	20.0	20.7	13.8	10.9	8.7	7.4	7.6
per head ($)	3,076	2,804	2,872	1,866	1,474	1,163	986	1,005
Belarus—GDP								
$ bn	49.9	50.4	51.4	47.7	43.8	37.7	34.8	36.5
per head ($)	4,879	4,910	5,006	4,631	4,228	3,645	3,365	3,525
Estonia—GDP								
$ bn	7.7	7.4	6.8	6.2	5.8	5.8	6.1	6.4
per head ($)	4,896	4,670	4,334	3,988	3,803	3,836	4,067	4,349
Georgia—GDP								
$ bn	24.1	21.4	17.8	10.9	7.7	5.6	5.5	6.2
per head ($)	4,420	3,919	3,275	2,005	1,405	1,032	1,005	1,139
Kazakhstan—GDP								
$ bn	71.9	74.6	72.4	64.7	56.0	43.0	40.1	41.4
per head ($)	4,327	4,477	4,304	3,827	3,316	2,523	2,416	2,507
Kyrgyz Republic—GDP								
$ bn	11.0	11.9	11.2	9.7	8.3	6.3	6.0	6.5
per head ($)	2,550	2,706	2,524	2,164	1,842	1,364	1,311	1,372
Latvia—GDP								
$ bn	14.5	14.6	13.6	9.1	8.0	8.2	8.3	8.6
per head ($)	5,437	5,471	5,118	3,462	3,070	3,209	3,288	3,463
Lithuania—GDP								
$ bn	33.0	33.9	30.0	19.2	13.7	14.2	14.9	15.8
per head ($)	8,945	9,121	8,031	5,141	3,681	3,813	4,025	4,255
Moldova—GDP								
$ bn	15.9	16.2	13.9	10.2	10.3	7.2	7.2	6.8
per head ($)	3,666	3,722	3,195	2,336	2,362	1,666	1,661	1,563
Russia—GDP								
$ bn	856.7	875.4	865.0	759.9	711.9	636.4	626.2	601.4
per head ($)	5,815	5,918	5,835	5,124	4,805	4,301	4,227	4,066
Tajikistan—GDP								
$ bn	9.9	10.2	9.7	7.0	5.2	4.5	4.0	3.4
per head ($)	1,915	1,920	1,770	1,248	916	781	693	577

Table 13–6 (cont'd)

	1989	1990	1991	1992	1993	1994	1995	1996
Turkmenistan—GDP								
$ bn	10.0	10.7	10.5	10.2	9.5	7.7	6.8	6.7
per head ($)	2,798	2,903	2,815	2,675	2,413	1,930	1,627	1,522
Ukraine—GDP								
$ bn	216.5	217.6	206.6	191.3	168.4	132.4	119.2	109.5
per head ($)	4,181	4,197	3,978	3,668	3,227	2,551	2,308	2,138
Uzbekistan—GDP								
$ bn	44.6	47.5	49.1	46.0	45.0	43.1	42.6	41.9
per head ($)	2,219	2,312	2,351	2,122	2,058	1,928	1,892	1,847

Sources: IMF; World Bank, *Statistical Handbook of States of the Former USSR*; UN Economic Commission for Europe, *Bulletin for Europe*, Vol. 44, 1992; EIU calculations.

During the first stage of economic reform (from independence to mid-1994), Uzbekistan created a new commercially based legal framework and started market reforms. During the second stage (from mid-1994 to 1996), macroeconomic stabilization was the main objective. While Russia experienced a 50% decline in GDP from 1990 to 1996, Uzbekistan's GDP fell only 18% and the country achieved 1.6% GDP growth in 1996. The national budget deficit has been less than 3.5% each of last two years. Inflation in 1996 was 5.6% per month (half of the 1995 level), and is expected to drop further in 1997. The labor market is stable with 4% unemployment despite the 1.5%–2% population growth each year. Now, the government is pursuing a stabilization policy together with privatization and price reform. We are also promoting the formation of small and medium-sized businesses through a variety of ownership structures. To attract foreign investment, additional tax and customs duty concessions are planned.

Some Western analysts were more cautious, pointing to the large current account deficit, growing external debt burden, continuing restrictions on currency convertibility, regulatory controls on banking transactions, and the legacy of the communist bureaucracy, all of which discouraged importers and investors, particularly small and medium-sized businesses.

A senior Daewoo executive involved in the Uzbekistan automobile project commented:

Figure 13–4 Map of Uzbekistan

Source: *Financial Times*.

In emerging markets, we always find that there is an opportunity on the other side of any threat. If everything were fine, these countries wouldn't need us. We jump into difficult markets and take advantage of the opportunities they present while managing the risk. By working hard, we build credentials with our partners (whether they are government officials or entrepreneurs) and find the best solutions for mutual prosperity. By being the first mover, we are in a better position to obtain cooperation. As a country becomes richer, it doesn't have to concede as much to later entrants.

After gaining independence from the Soviet Union, Uzbekistan needed managerial talent, financial capital, and technology to realize its growth potential. Because Uzbekistan had to specialize in the production of cotton and other raw materials when it was part of the Soviet Union, it had relied on Russia for most capital goods and consumer durables. President Kharimov's ambition was to turn Uzbekistan into a strong economic power in Central Asia through industrial development and export promotion. This required foreign investment. However, multinationals from the developed countries were concerned about political risk, macroeconomic instability, and various regulatory barriers. Siemens, Lufthansa, and Cargill had business interests in Uzbekistan, but none of them had been willing to commit to substantial investment. Japanese firms that had been active investors in developing countries in the 1960s and 1970s were also reluctant. It was Daewoo that first answered the call.

Daewoo's unique commitment to Uzbekistan was described by Golishev, the presidential economic advisor:

Daewoo was the first foreign company to commit to a large-scale manufacturing plant in Uzbekistan. My country needs long-term, reliable partners, not casual partners in pursuit of a quick profit. The speedy entrepreneurial decision making of Daewoo management and the leadership of President Kharimov helped to overcome the bureaucratic obstacles. For example, it took only 24 months to build the Uz–Daewoo plant while it usually took at least three years to build an automobile plant in Korea. The Uz–Daewoo plant became the leading symbol of Uzbekistan industrial development. The day the plant opened was declared a national holiday (Uzbekistan–Korea Friendship Day). Today, Daewoo's presence is not limited to automobile production. Daewoo is increasing its role in other key industries such as cotton, electronics, and telecommunications.

The Uz–Daewoo Auto Project

President Kharimov visited Korea in June 1992 and expressed interest in Daewoo's Changwon auto plant. Daewoo signed a 50:50 joint-venture agreement with Uzautoprom[7] in August 1992 to build an automobile plant in Uzbekistan which would manufacture 200,000 vehicles annually including 100,000 Nexias, 50,000 Ticos, and 50,000 Damas. Figure 13–5 shows pictures and specifications of these models.[8] Construction of the Uz–Daewoo automobile plant began in 1994, and once completed in July 1996, it became the first modern automobile factory in Central Asia. Uz–Daewoo Auto would reach full-scale production by the end of 1997. Two-shift production commenced in February 1997, and three-team two-shift production was scheduled to begin in October 1997.

Located 350 kilometers from Tashkent and next to the rail link in Andijan, the plant offered good logistics. Previously, the plant had been used as a tractor assembly factory with 550 employees. The refurbished plant followed the same design as the Changwon plant in Korea. See Figure 13–6 for a plant diagram.

Production of the Damas, Tico, and Nexia models started on March 15, June 3, and June 17, 1996, respectively. Uzbekistan engineers and technicians (all of whom were trained at the Changwon and Bupyong plants in Korea) were in charge of production. Among the 3,200 workers at the factory, only 25 expatriate personnel were sent from Korea. Most of the local employees were in the 20–30 age range with a technical school background. Some had previously worked in the old tractor factory. Jobs at the new plant were highly prized, even though the average worker earned the equivalent of US$200 a month. Table 13–7 documents the production and sales record while Table 13–8 provides data on the long-term operating plan of Uz–Daewoo Auto.

The total project investment was US$658 million of which shareholders' equity was US$200 million and debt was US$458 million. The Uzbekistan government provided 50% of the equity capital through Uzautoprom, and Daewoo Corp. provided the other 50%. Of the US$458 million debt, US$396 million was sourced through foreign loans (US$222 million by the suppliers' credit of Daewoo Corp. and US$174 million by the National Bank of

---

[7] Uzautoprom is the Automobile Manufacturing Association of Uzbekistan and is fully controlled by the Uzbekistan government. Hence, the project was effectively a joint venture between the Uzbekistan government and Daewoo.

[8] These brand names were the same as those used in Korea. Performance characteristics and specifications of the vehicles were almost identical, with minimal local adaptation.

Figure 13–5 Pictures and specifications of vehicles produced by Uz–Daewoo Auto

NEXIA

GLE
- 1.5 SOHC engine
- Flush 13-inch wheel covers
- Power steering (option)
- Air conditioning (option)
- AM/FM stereo radio & cassette
- Power windows   • Power antenna

GL
- 1.5 SOHC engine
- Front bucket seats, sliding & reclining
- Floor mat, carpet   • Door pocket
- Door lock, manual   • Speaker(FRT/RR)
- Variable speed wipe   • Digital clock
- Remote trunk lid release, electric

TiCO

DLX
- Back glass - heated
- Driver's side map pocket
- AM/FM Stereo, Digital clock
- Speaker(LH/RH)   • Manual antenna
- Air conditioning (option)
- Manual transmission (5-speed)

GLE
- Front bucket seats, sliding & reclining
- Full flat seat   • Ventilator
- Manual transmission (4-speed)
- Door lock, manual
- Wiper speed   • Cigar lighter

Both DLX and STD with 800cc 3 cylinder gasoline engine.

DAMAS

MINI BUS DLX
- Wheel ctr cap   • Headrest
- Air conditioning (option)
- Windshield washer - combined with wiper
- Back glass - heated   • AM/FM stereo. ETR
- Driver's side map pocket   • Manual antenna
- Speaker LH/RH (on door side)
- Capacity: 7 person

MINI BUS DLX
- Door key - driver & codriver
- Front driver's seat, sliding
- Headrest (front - separate - slim)
- Air conditioning (option)
- Seatbelt warning - driver
- Capacity: 450kg

VAN
- Mud flap FRT & RR
- Head lamp - round (halogen)
- Door lock, manual, FRT
- Glove box   • Locking fuel lid

All models with: Both DLX and STD with 800cc 3 cylinder gasoline engine.

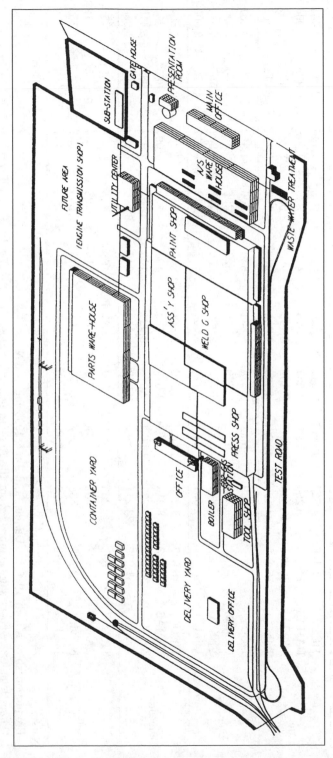

Figure 13–6 Uz–Daewoo Auto: Plant diagram

Table 13–7 Uz–Daewoo Auto: Sales and production through July 1997

| | | Total | 1996 | 1997 | 1997 (monthly data) | | | | | | |
					1	2	3	4	5	6	7
Production[a]	TICO	18,607	4,764	13,843	1,686	2,041	1,641	2,552	2,157	2,231	1,535
	DAMAS	14,420	8,664	5,756	1,012	415	493	992	1,077	1,026	741
	NEXIA	35,111	12,229	22,882	2,984	3,496	2,418	4,313	3,545	3,616	2,510
	Total	68,138	25,657	42,481	5,682	5,952	4,552	7,857	6,779	6,873	4,786
Sales[b]	TICO	17,426	4,525	12,901	1,247	1,888	1,822	2,302	1,745	2,213	1,684
	DAMAS	14,105	8,266	5,839	1,031	576	472	836	1,148	870	906
	NEXIA	33,601	11,345	22,256	2,152	3,192	2,980	4,054	3,281	3,030	3,567
	Total	65,132	24,136	40,996	4,430	5,656	5,274	7,192	6,174	6,113	6,157
Inventory[c]	TICO		239	n.a.	678	831	650	900	1,312	1,330	1,181
	DAMAS		398	n.a.	379	218	329	395	324	480	315
	NEXIA		884	n.a.	1,716	2,020	1,458	1,717	1,981	2,567	1,510
	Total		1,521	n.a.	2,773	3,069	2,437	3,012	3,617	4,377	3,006
Domestic	TICO	16,833	4,220	12,613	1,240	1,851	1,654	2,257	1,739	2,208	1,664
	DAMAS	13,923	8,214	5,709	1,024	570	454	808	1,094	865	894
	NEXIA	30,453	10,777	19,676	2,076	3,029	2,105	3,751	2,624	2,681	3,410
	Total	61,209	23,211	37,998	4,340	5,450	4,213	6,816	5,457	5,754	5,968
Export	TICO	593	305	288	7	37	168	45	6	5	20
	DAMAS	182	52	130	7	65	18	28	54	5	12
	NEXIA	3,148	568	2,580	76	163	875	303	657	349	157
	Total	3,923	926	2,998	90	265	1,061	376	717	359	189

Notes:
[a] Production since March 1996 for Damas, and June 1996 for Tico/Nexia.
[b] Domestic sales + export sales (shipped from the Andijan factory). Sales since August 1996 for all three models.
[c] Inventories at the factory at the end of the year or month (inventories at dealers' are not included).

Table 13–8   Uz–Daewoo Auto's long-term operating plan, 1996–2000

a. Long-term production plan (units: 1,000 vehicles)

		1996	1997	1998	1999	2000	Others
Tico	STD	1	11	11	13	15	A/C: 35%
	DLX	4	27	27	32	35	
	(Total)	5	38	38	45	50	
Damas	STD	1	1	4	5	5	A/C: 6%
	DLX	5	9	23	27	30	
	Van	2	4	11	13	15	
	(Total)	9	15	38	45	50	
Nexia	GL	5	29	30	36	40	A/C: 66%
	GLX	7	43	44	54	60	
	(Total)	12	72	74	90	100	
Total		26	125	150	180	200	Export 50%

Note: A/C = air conditioning

b. Local content plan (% of value)

	1996	1997	1998	1999	2000
Tico/Damas	20%	30%	40%	60%	70%
Nexia	10%	20%	30%	40%	60%

c. Local content plan (parts added by year)

	Locally-supplied parts
1996	seat, bumper, instrument panel (T/D), paint, trim part, wiring harness, brake/fuel pipe, blow molding, tuner, small plastic parts, small press parts
1997	glass, muffler, fuel tank, carpet, insulation (T/D), large press parts, large plastic parts, battery, regulator, fastener
1998	tire, brake disc, mirror, weatherstrip, speaker, instrument panel (Nexia)
1999	engine parts, transmission parts, combustion switch, knuckle, brake hose, seat belt, speedometer, head lamp, parking brake lever
2000	heater, caliper, brake system, shock absorber

Uzbekistan) and the equivalent of US$62 million was sourced through a local loan prepared by Asaka Bank. The Uzbekistan government provided a payment guarantee for Daewoo's US$222 million suppliers' credit. Following the "Uzbekistan cabinet decree on Uz–Daewoo Auto," the Uzbekistan government not only infused investment money but also provided administrative support for the project. A deputy prime minister was appointed to oversee and expedite the construction of the factory. The Uzbekistan government granted a five-year exemption for income tax, value-added tax, and customs duty on imported components, and promised to protect Uz–Daewoo's privileged position in the domestic market for two years.[9]

As of July 1997, Daewoo was meeting the expectations of the Uzbekistan government. The plant was credited with creating more than 10,000 new jobs, including jobs in construction, in auto dealerships, and in 10 local component companies established since 1996. A bank was set up to provide financial support for international trade and automobile sales. Technology transfer was achieved through the technology licensing agreements and the personnel exchange program for employees of Uz–Daewoo Auto and local component manufacturers. All of the 3,200 employees completed a three-month training program in Korea; they were followed by dealer technicians and component manufacturer technicians. According to a senior executive in charge of the Daewoo Human Resource Development Institute in Korea:

> Both parties learnt from each other. Our Uzbekistan friends learnt technology and hard work in Korea, and both parties benefited from the international exposure. I heard that, one day, President Kharimov asked an Uzbekistan technician to say a few words in Korean when he visited the plant.

Uz–Daewoo's production capacity was scheduled to reach 300,000 units by the year 2000. In 1996, 26,000 vehicles were produced. The production goal for 1997 was 125,000 vehicles. Of these, 60,000 were expected to be exported to the Central Asian republics and Russia (30,000 for each), and 50,000 were expected to be sold in Uzbekistan. The remaining 15,000 would be held in factory and dealer inventories. Of the 40,000 units actually produced by July 31, 30,000 were sold domestically and 10,000 were exported.

The plant ran two shifts of 250 working days a year, which could produce 40 vehicles per hour (20 Nexia, 10 Tico, and 10 Damas). Suppliers were selected ahead of production. By July 1997, six Korea–Uzbekistan joint ventures had been set up to work with Uz–Daewoo Auto, and small stamping parts were produced by wholly-owned Uzbekistan companies. Uz–Daewoo was

---

[9] The value-added tax was 18% in Uzbekistan. The Uzbekistan government imposed a 5.26% customs duty on auto imports from Russia and other former CIS countries and 60% customs duty on auto imports from non-CIS countries.

working closely to source components from other Daewoo plants such as RODAE of Romania and Daewoo–PSO of Poland. Imported parts and components were sent from Korea to the Andijan plant by ship and train. Deliveries took 40 days. Local component sourcing was gradually increasing. In 1997, local content was expected to be 40% by value, including interior seats, bumpers, switchboards, and other components. By the year 2000, the value of locally-made components was to reach 70%.[10]

In addition to the Uz–Daewoo Auto plant, Daewoo had many other investments in Uzbekistan. Cumulative investments totaled US$1 billion by July 1997. Daewoo was the first Korean company to establish a trade office in Tashkent. Uz–Daewoo Electronics, a joint venture between Daewoo and the Uzbekistan government, was established in 1994, and, by 1997, manufactured 400,000 television sets and video camera recorders (VCRs), which were sold in Uzbekistan and Russia. In telecommunications, Daewoo provided 210,000 TDX lines to the Fergana region of Uzbekistan and was preparing for telephone and global satellite-delivered mobile telecommunications services. Daewoo also established the Uz–Daewoo Bank and was participating in the construction of railroads between China and Central Asia, as well as various natural resource development projects. Table 13–9 summarizes the history of Daewoo's operations in Uzbekistan, and Table 13–10 lists Daewoo's business activities in Uzbekistan. According to Daewoo executives, there was a certain complementarity between Daewoo and Uzbekistan. President Kharimov was impressed by Korea's history of government-led high-growth economic development in the 1960s through the 1970s, and hoped that Uzbekistan might be able to replicate this experience. Daewoo's extensive experience in emerging markets was also valued by Uzbekistan officials. Daewoo's many lines of business and its sheer size also helped. According to a Western businessman in Tashkent:

> Size helps in Uzbekistan. Small companies are often frustrated by the regulations and bureaucracy. Given the limited currency convertibility and the various development needs, Daewoo's multiple lines of business help a lot. For example, it seems that Daewoo can buy cotton with local currency earnings and export it, which is impossible for me to do. While other firms are still hesitant to invest, Daewoo has a myriad of business opportunities to offer to Uzbekistan because the company operates in so many fields.

---

[10] Local content referred to the proportion of locally-made components and parts to the total value of the finished goods.

Table 13–9   History of Daewoo's operation in Uzbekistan

June 1992	Uzbekistan President I. Kharimov visited Korea
July 1992	Chairman Kim visited Uzbekistan
August 1992	Automobile joint-venture contract signed between Daewoo and Uzbekistan government
September 1992	Daewoo Corp. opened trading office in Tashkent
May 1993	Electronics joint-venture plant established
June 1994	Korean President Y.S. Kim visited Uzbekistan
February 1995	Uzbekistan President I. Kharimov visited Korea
May 1995	Trading joint venture (KOSMO) established
June 1995	Uzbekistan Prime Minister visited Korea
October 1995	US$100 million cotton import contract signed
March 1996	Telecommunications joint-venture plant established
May 1996	Mobile Telecommunications (GSM) joint venture established
July 1996	Opening ceremony of Uz–Daewoo automobile joint-venture plant (the day was declared a national holiday in Uzbekistan)
May 1997	Daewoo Bank opened
June 18, 1997	Daewoo textile plant opened
June 24, 1997	Uzbekistan Telecommunications Minister visited Korea
December 11, 1997	Automobile parts plant scheduled to open

Decision Making and Negotiation

Critical issues regarding the Uz–Daewoo Auto project and other Daewoo businesses in Uzbekistan were negotiated directly between President Kharimov and Chairman Kim. The two leaders had developed a great mutual respect since the start of the project. President Kharimov was believed to consider Chairman Kim and Daewoo his most important economic development partner. It was Chairman Kim's strong entrepreneurial leadership that helped Daewoo open the new market and made things happen. According to a senior Daewoo executive involved in the Uzbekistan operation:

> Chairman Kim always initiates our business deals and takes charge not only of strategic decisions but also of operational details. Experienced aides in the corporate office and operating divisions provide analysis reports to aid him in his decision making. However, it is usually Chairman Kim who senses the opportunities and judges the business prospects of each. He really thinks that every street is paved with gold. After a project has progressed to a certain stage, he focuses on key strategic issues and

Table 13–10   List of Daewoo businesses in Uzbekistan (as of July 1997)

Total investment amount: US$1 billion
Total number of expatriate managers: 75
Total number of local employees: 6,000

Name:	Daewoo Corp., Tashkent office
Business:	Trading office of Daewoo Corp. (trading and investment arm of Daewoo Group)
Figures:	US$900 million sales in 1996
Employment:	1 expatriate, 14 local
Plan:	Increased cotton trade (US$150 million in 1996, US$500 million in 2000), investment in cotton plantation (30K hectares/25K ton in 2000), US$500 million investment in ginning plant (50K ton capacity)
Name:	KOSMO
Business:	International trade JV (trading electronics and automobile parts)
Figures:	US$3.1 million sales in 1996
Employment:	1 expatriate, 14 local
Plan:	US$22 million sales in 2000
Name:	Daewoo Textile Co.
Business:	Cotton yarn plant (13K ton/year: first case of 100% ownership by a foreign investor), 70% of output is for export, existing textile plant was renovated
Figures:	US$60 million investment, US$40 million export
Employment:	10 expatriate, 800 local
Plan:	Expansion into spinning, dyeing, and apparel manufacturing, vertical integration of cotton-related operations
Name:	Uz–Daewoo Auto Co.
Business:	Automobile JV, 3 passenger car lines (Nexia 100K units, Tico 50K units, Damas 50K units), CKD assembly of bus and truck (bus 1K units, truck 110 units), 8 JVs for parts and 3 local firms under technology license
Figures:	US$658 million investment, 200K production capacity
Employment:	25 expatriate, 4,000 local
Plan:	Increasing local content from 40% (1987) to 80% (2000), establishing national sales and service network
Name:	Uz–Daewoo Electronics Co. (36% stake for Uzbekistan government)
Business:	TV, VCR, car-audio
Figures:	US$20 million investment, US$100 million sales in 1997 (expected): 30% for export
Employment:	7 expatriate, 660 local
Plan:	Extending local sales network (currently 14 outlets in Tashkent, 24 outside Tashkent), increasing local content

Table 13–10   (cont'd)

Name:	Daewoo Telecom, Tashkent office
Business:	Trading TDX system and telecommunications equipment
Figures:	TDX 210K lines (nationwide)
Name:	Asloka–Daewoo Co. (49% owned by the Uzbekistan government)
Business:	Manufacturing, installation, and maintenance of TDX system (since August 1996)
Figures:	US$20 million investment, TDX 200K lines/year
Employment:	5 expatriate, 200 local
Plan:	Exporting 30% of output to CIS countries, main provider of National Telecommunications Network Plan (2 million lines over 15 years)
Name:	Uzbekistan Mobile Telecom System (division of Daewoo Corp.)
Business:	GSM cellular phone network (US$50 million investment), local telephone network in Fergana region (JV contract signed in July 1996: US$192 million investment), long distance provider (1 out of 3 providers: 2 others are Russian firms)
Name:	Uz–Daewoo Bank
Business:	Universal banking (mainly serving government-invested firms and Daewoo-related firms) (Daewoo Securities 55%, Uzbekistan partner 10%, EBRD 25%, Koram Bank 10%)
Figures:	US$20 million investment by Daewoo
Plan:	Expanding service boundaries, expanding asset base up to US$60 million by 2000

Currently Planned

Business:	Business center (400-room hotel, 22-floor office building, department store), foreign residential units
Situation:	JV agreement signed in July 1997, construction scheduled to start in December 1997

Academic cooperation between Uzbekistan National Academy and Daewoo Research Institutes (Economics, Advanced Engineering)

---

delegates operational issues to the corporate staff and local subsidiary managers. As the project matures further, the local subsidiary takes more of the initiative. Whenever necessary, Chairman Kim intervenes and deals with a problem, but the process is quite simple. With only a couple of phone calls or faxes, he cuts to the heart of the problem and identifies a solution. He also benefits from the wisdom of experienced executive assistants and front-line managers, but the process mainly involves very brief informal discussions. I've never seen him sit through a lengthy internal presentation. This business style is reflected in the simple internal reporting process of Daewoo. The direct experience of front-line managers is appreciated more than an ornate analysis written from behind a desk. Strategy is important. But it should be no more than a direction for the whole company. Bureaucratic haggling and sticking to routine procedures are the biggest enemies of progress in Daewoo. Having started as a trading company, Daewoo still values flexibility and deal making rather than building and running routinized operating systems.

Another senior Daewoo executive assisting Chairman Kim in managing overseas operations stated:

In emerging markets, the window of opportunity is not always open. Timing is often critical. Detailed environmental surveys or market research are important, but not always obtainable and often used for internal battles to make excuses or to avoid responsibility. In addition, market research studies often focus on the existing state-of-affairs, underestimating or ignoring future potential. We negotiate the environment. Chairman Kim visits the investment site, negotiates the deal personally, and makes an up-or-down decision. In this process, Chairman Kim carefully evaluates the business prospects and develops solutions. Once faced with a decision, he spends enormous energy verifying investment information from various sources. In the Uz–Daewoo Auto project, he visited Uzbekistan more than ten times in a six-month period before he made the final decision to sign the agreement. This is one of the reasons why we have been able to penetrate so many emerging markets.

Some outsiders including business scholars, consultants, and business reporters criticized this entrepreneurial style. According to them, Daewoo relied too much on the entrepreneurial leadership of Chairman Kim, leaving little room for systematic management. There was also a concern that Daewoo was expanding much too fast and widely without sufficient core competencies and financial base. An investment banker in Seoul provided an interesting affirmative view:

When I first looked into Daewoo's investment decision processes, I was frustrated. Formal feasibility studies were often considered "ornamental" by the front-line managers and even by some of the financial managers. One Daewoo executive once told me that formal investment analysis is never sufficient to assess a project's feasibility without the benefit of business intuition. Now, I have a better understanding of Daewoo's way of doing business. First, Daewoo applies excellent project financing skills to its overseas investments. For example, in the Uz–Daewoo Auto case, Daewoo provided 50% of the equity capital over three years, and the debt was arranged with a payment guarantee from the Uzbekistan government. So, Daewoo could inject the initial portion of equity capital and reinvest the earnings from the project later on. Daewoo's financing terms and risk management approaches are quite creative. I've also found that the core of Daewoo's investment information is strictly confidential due to the nature of deals in emerging markets. This is one of the reasons why Daewoo's investment decisions may seem improvised to outsiders.

According to a Daewoo executive who had helped Chairman Kim coordinate Daewoo's global operations for many years:

> We use quantitative analyses in our feasibility studies, but we do not rely solely on them in making our investment decisions. Daewoo's experience in emerging markets is very useful. Published data on emerging markets are not reliable and, due to political and economic volatility, are quickly outdated. Critical information bearing on the deal may come from the key players, but in many cases, they do not have the complete picture either. So, we learn as we go. For example, Daewoo and the Uzbekistan government invented a new approach to currency convertibility and import duties. Local experts can tell you something, but it is not a simple matter of retaining a consultant. Often, there is no base case for comparison. Strict confidentiality is essential, so only a limited number of people can be involved in the deal. As the deal is negotiated, mutual trust builds and we gain access to better information with the help of our ever-improving credentials. In this process, we can negotiate the details of the business environment in which we are going to operate. So, planning which market to enter while standing in front of a map of the world is impossible. Sometimes, we worry that there might have been better alternatives. However, it is impossible to know everything about every country in the world.

MARKETING

Market Size

A senior Daewoo manager involved in the deal commented on the size of the potential market and its relationship to the initial plant size and product mix:

In the late 1980s when Uzbekistan was still a part of the Soviet Union, there were one million cars on the road in Uzbekistan. The typical Russian car used to sell in Uzbekistan for 6,000 rubles when the average worker earned 250 rubles per month.[11] Around 80,000 new cars were sold each year. A European Union study in 1996 suggested that Uzbekistan could absorb 4,000 imported cars per year based on the gross national product (GNP) per-capita level. Considering the average age of cars on the road and a 10% annual replacement rate, annual demand for new cars in Uzbekistan should be 100,000 units. With 80% of the 14 million adults in Uzbekistan holding a driver's license, the long-term market potential is much larger. Considering an annual market demand for two million cars in the whole CIS region, we thought that 100,000 car exports to the neighboring countries were feasible. President Kharimov had initially suggested a 100,000-vehicle-capacity plant to produce the Tico and Damas models during his visit to the Changwon minicar plant. Daewoo subsequently offered to build a 200,000-vehicle-capacity plant. Originally, we planned to produce 40,000 Rabo (a small truck based on the Tico body), 60,000 Damas vans, 80,000 Tico cars, but we subsequently changed our product mix to 50,000 Damas, 50,000 Tico, and 100,000 Nexia when we considered the market preference for larger, C-Class cars.

As of 1995, there were 834,000 passenger cars and 266,000 trucks in Uzbekistan. The average age of vehicles on the road was nine years. Ninety-five percent of the vehicles had been made in Russia. Table 13–11 shows the mix of cars on the road according to vehicle size class.

Table 13–11   Mix of cars on the road*

Mix of cars on the road: 1996		Forecast mix of new car sales: 1997
Class A	7,000 (0.9%)	1.5%–2%, Tico has 100% share
Class B	88,000 (11.8%)	15%, Oka, Tavria
Class C	611,000 (81.7%)	80%, VW Golf, Fiat (Turkey), Nexia
Class D	12,000 (1.7%)	2%–3%, Mercedes, BMW, Opel
Class E	29,000 (3.9%)	1%–2%, Mercedes, BMW

* Across the whole CIS region, demand for C-Class cars was 81% of the total while A-Class cars represented only 2%.

Source: Interview with Mr. Yusupov, general director of Uz–Daewoo Auto.

---

[11] The typical Uz–Daewoo Auto employee earned 10,000 soum a month in mid-1997.

Sales, Distribution, and Service

Table 13–7 shows the sales and production history of Uz–Daewoo Auto. Of the 42,000 vehicles produced by the end of July 1997, 26,000 vehicles were sold for cash, 4,000 vehicles were sold via bank transfer, and 1,300 vehicles were exported. A further 2,980 vehicles were in manufacturer inventory, and 5,800 vehicles were in dealer inventory. Ninety percent of the exports were to Russia, while the other 10% went to Kazakhstan, Kyrgystan, and Belarus.

At the company-owned flagship retail dealership in Andijan, the sales manager reported that 45 vehicles had been sold in May 1997, up from 20 in April. In a typical day, 50–60 customer prospects visited the dealership. No trade-ins were negotiated. All new cars carried a one-year warranty. The four salespeople were paid salaries with no sales commission. Two spare parts salespeople also worked at the dealership. Daewoo was not closely involved in domestic marketing. Uz–Daewoo Auto was in charge of production, nationwide promotion, and sales to dealers, and Uzautosanoat was in charge of distribution.[12] Due to high inflation (5%–6% per month in 1997), Uz–Daewoo changed its price schedule every month subject to government approval. Table 13–12 reports the retail price tags at the flagship dealer. Table 13–13 shows the comparative cost structure for Tico and Nexia cars produced in Uzbekistan.

Table 13–12 Retail sticker prices on July 29, 1997*

	Local currency (cash)	Local currency (bank transfer)	US$/export
Nexia GL: Basic model	$13,000	$15,600	$9,026
Nexia GL: Fully loaded model	$17,400	$20,880	$10,626
TICO: Basic model	$6,790	$8,830	$4,800
TICO: Fully loaded model	$7,960	$10,350	$5,540
DAMAS: Basic model	$9,110	$11,840	$5,900

* Table 13–14 shows the exchange rate trends in more detail.

According to a Daewoo manager involved in the Uzbekistan operation:

---

[12] Uzautosanoat was an automobile sales and distribution company wholly owned by the Uzbekistan government. A ministerial level official was appointed the CEO of the company.

Table 13–13 Comparative cost structure (%) for Tico and Nexia produced in Uzbekistan, July 1997

	Tico	Nexia
Factory price	100.0	100.0
Cost of goods sold	71.1	72.1
Administrative cost	9.6	8.6
Transportation & others*	6.0	6.0
Profit margin	13.3	13.3
Interest on loans from Daewoo	7.1	7.1
Construction fee to Daewoo	8.2	8.2
3% royalty to Daewoo	3.0	3.0

* Transportation costs for imported parts were US$3,200 per container for 2,000 containers per month (at full production).

The retail price tags don't tell you the whole story. The high inflation and continuous devaluation of the soum against the U.S. dollar create an arbitrage opportunity. If you can buy in U.S. dollars (at the official rate), you should earn an arbitrage profit due to the discrepancy between the official rate and the black market rate.

In Uzbekistan, Uz–Daewoo Auto had appointed 40 direct dealers, who in turn had appointed 150 subdealers. Eighteen of the direct dealers were wholly owned by Uzautosanoat. Most of the dealers were former automotive service stations. Dealers earned a 5% retail sales margin on the Nexia and a 10% margin on the Tico and Damas. New dealers received discounts on purchases of their initial inventory. Outside Uzbekistan, Uz–Daewoo had appointed 22 dealers in Russia and other CIS countries. Of these, five were wholly owned, and six were partly owned by Uzautosanoat. By mid-1997, 1 billion soum and US$4 million had been spent to establish the distribution and service network. Uz–Daewoo and Uzautosanoat were planning to expand them. Further expansion of the service network would emphasize private service centers. Around 200 service centers were to be set up in Uzbekistan, and 50 of them were to be supplied with parts and components through Uzautosanoat. Dealer sales managers and service technicians received training provided by Daewoo in Korea as part of the personnel exchange program.

Uz–Daewoo Auto advertised daily on Uzbekistan's national television network. One advertisement showed the Nexia's maneuvering and performance

Figure 13–14 Exchange rate trend: Soum/U.S. dollar*

	Official rate	Market rate	Market rate/Official rate (%)
1996			
January	36.2	44.2	122
February	36.4	45.5	125
March	36.4	47.9	132
April	36.9	49.3	134
May	37.7	51.3	136
June	37.8	51.5	136
July	37.9	53.2	140
August	38.6	56.1	145
September	39.7	63.4	160
October	42.3	75.5	178
November	49.5	103.1	208
December	52.9	109.5	207
1997			
January	55.6	118.0	212
February	56.7	126.6	224
March	58.0	138.5	239
April	59.3	150.0	253
May	60.1	144.2	240
June	61.8	142.8	231
July	64.2	141.3	220

* In January 1996, one U.S. dollar was equivalent to 36.2 soum at the official rate (and 44.2 soum at the market rate).

capabilities in a circus arena, dodging the animals. Uz–Daewoo Auto's television advertising was part of an overall corporate image-building campaign by Daewoo, which would cost US$1 million in 1997—almost one-quarter of all paid television advertising in Uzbekistan.

Competition

The Uzbekistan government was pushing Uz–Daewoo Auto to increase exports to generate hard currency. However, Daewoo claimed that sluggish domestic sales growth had limited the achievement of scale economies, and kept unit costs high. Smugglers from neighboring countries also restricted export sales. As long as the black market exchange rate of soum/U.S. dollar was almost twice the official rate, export sales through official channels were problematic.

In the absence of tight border controls, it was impossible to prevent smugglers from neighboring countries from bringing in U.S. dollars, converting them into soum at the black market rate, and then smuggling Uz–Daewoo cars back to their countries.

Daewoo had hoped that Uz–Daewoo Auto would be a useful production base for the growing Russian market. In Russia, imported cars from Uzbekistan had to pay a 5.26% tariff while those from Korea and other non-CIS countries paid 60%. Value-added tax in Russia was 20% (18% in Uzbekistan); the sales tax differential was absorbed by Uz–Daewoo Auto on officially exported cars. It cost US$480 to transport a Nexia (US$420 for a Tico) from Uzbekistan to Moscow.

Autovaz, the largest Russian automobile manufacturer which had formerly produced Rada, was producing and selling the VAZ2109 (1500cc) and the VAZ2110 (a new 1500cc model). Its production capacity was 900,000 vehicles a year, of which 600,000 were assigned for sale in the Russian domestic market. Table 13–15 shows price comparisons between Russian cars and Uz–Daewoo cars.

Table 13–15 Comparable retail car prices in Russia

Russian cars			Uz–Daewoo cars		
Producer	Model	Price[a]	Producer	Model	Price
Autovaz	OKA	US$3,000	Uz–Daewoo	Tico	US$6,000
Tavria	Tavria	US$3,000			
Autovax	VAZ2109	US$9,496	Uz–Daewoo	Nexia	US$12,000[b]
	VAX2110	US$11,870			

Notes:

[a] U.S. dollar prices were as of July 27, 1997, at the official exchange rate.

[b] On the black market, the Nexia could retail for $8,000 if payment was made in U.S. dollars. The VAZ2109 sold for US$8,500 on the black market.

According to Mr. Yusupov, general director of Uz–Daewoo Auto, competition in the export market was tough and getting tougher:

The Nexia is better equipped to compete in the export market. Traditionally, Russian and Uzbekistan consumers prefer C-Class cars (with engine sizes between 1500 and 1800cc) due partly to rough road conditions. Uz–Daewoo should consider shifting the production mix in favor of the

Nexia. Ford is planning a 50,000-vehicle-capacity plant to make Ford Escorts in Belarus; the retail price will be around US$10,000–US$12,000. Opel (the German subsidiary of General Motors) has a strategic alliance with Autovaz to introduce the Astra in 1998 which will be made in a 50,000-vehicle-capacity plant. Moscvich is also working on an alliance to produce Renault cars. Kia is planning a 50,000-vehicle-capacity CKD plant in Kaliningrad, Russia. There will be a flood of C-Class cars. Moreover, these competitors are spreading the word that the Nexia is no longer in production in Korea. Uz–Daewoo will be in trouble if Daewoo doesn't enable us to introduce a new model.

Daewoo managers also acknowledged the increasing competitive challenge, but viewed the situation differently:

At present, Russian-made cards do not match Uz–Daewoo cars in terms of quality or performance. It will take some time before the competitive pressure materializes. Autovaz will only be doing joint CKD production of Opel's Astra and Calibra at the end of 1998. It will be another year before they start producing Opel engines for those cars. There are many strategic alliances on paper, but as yet, no cars are rolling off production lines. Actions speak louder than words, and these deals always take longer than expected to bear fruit. Of course, Daewoo is preparing for the challenges. We will start producing state-of-the-art models (which are still under development) from 2000. The new model line will cover C, D, and E-Class cars. The Uz–Daewoo plant is designed to be able to shift to production of these new models.

Hard Currency Problem

Due to the shortage of hard currency in Uzbekistan, the convertibility of the soum was strictly limited. Because the Uz–Daewoo project was designed to generate hard currency through exports, the Uzbekistan government gave Daewoo a higher priority in hard currency allocation for plant construction and component imports.[13] However, currency convertibility and repatriation of the earnings were ongoing challenges, and constrained further investment. Daewoo arranged foreign loans (under suppliers' credit) from Western banks and institutions for its Uzbekistan projects, but recognized that it would take

---

[13] Due to limited hard currency reserves and a growing current account deficit, the Uzbekistan government allocated hard currency for each business.

time for those projects to generate hard currency earnings. From the outset, Daewoo had been trying to alleviate this problem through becoming involved in the cotton business. From simple cotton exports, Daewoo was planning to expand its business into cotton plantations and spinning. Detailed operational decisions dealing with raw material allocation and pricing were still pending, but the business prospects were bright.[14] According to a Daewoo manager involved in the cotton business, a new textile industry complex in Uzbekistan that included the whole value-added processes, from spinning to apparel manufacturing, could generate US$15 billion worth of annual exports within ten years.

Management Challenges

When construction work started on the plant, a task force was appointed by Chairman Kim to implement the Uz–Daewoo project. Kwan-Ki Lee (also the chairman of Uz–Daewoo Auto) was in charge of the team. Overall Daewoo operations in Uzbekistan were coordinated by Daewoo Corporation and reported to Chairman Kim. However, managing an operation in a remote foreign environment was still a daunting task. Early on, the telecommunications infrastructure was not reliable: in 1993, it could take 30 minutes to send a five-page fax from Seoul to Tashkent. Chairman Kim visited Uzbekistan whenever necessary. Lee and his staff were spending half their time in Uzbekistan and usually traveled on weekends to save time. Due to the variety of Daewoo's businesses in Uzbekistan, the company was planning to appoint a senior executive stationed there to coordinate all Uzbekistan operations. Due to both the cultural and physical distance between Tashkent and Seoul, life in Uzbekistan was still a challenge for Korean managers. All 20 Uz–Daewoo Auto expatriates in Uzbekistan had their families in Korea. There was no reliable international school in Uzbekistan. At first, they could only obtain Korean food through monthly shipments from Daewoo's Seoul office. Managing cross-cultural conflict was also a challenge. It took great patience and understanding to persuade Uzbekistan workers to adopt attitudes of hard work and competitiveness.

CONCLUSION

Preparing for his upcoming visit to Uzbekistan, Chairman Kim reviewed the progress of Daewoo's cooperative ventures there and reflected on the role that

---

[14] Due to the importance of cotton to the Uzbekistan economy, the Uzbekistan government was in charge of quantity allocation and pricing of the cotton trade.

cooperative ventures with other companies and with national governments had played in the growth in Daewoo. Uz–Daewoo Auto was facing several challenges. Faced with the pressure from the Uzbekistan government for increased export sales, Uz–Daewoo had to meet various competitive challenges in both the domestic and export markets. Smugglers from neighboring countries were a major obstacle to export sales. Several multinational companies planning entry into Uzbekistan were criticizing the benefits Daewoo had earned as a first mover. While hard currency shortages and limited convertibility constrained further investment, the Uzbekistan government was offering Daewoo two new investment projects outside the automobile sector. Chairman Kim had to resolve these issues as he sought to advance Daewoo's overall strategic relationship with Uzbekistan.

Newspaper Crisis:
The Cut-throat Price War

THE HONG KONG NEWSPAPER INDUSTRY

Hong Kong has about 20 Chinese-language daily newspapers. The top five sellers are *Oriental Daily News*, *Apple Daily*, *Sing Pao*, *Tin Tin Daily News*, and *Ming Pao*. Apart from *Apple Daily* which was launched in June 1995, the other four have had a long history in the market. *Oriental Daily News* started publication in January 1969, *Sing Pao* in May 1939, *Tin Tin Daily News* in November 1960, and *Ming Pao* in May 1959.

The target readers of Chinese newspapers can be divided into two major groups: mass market and niche market. *Oriental Daily News*, *Apple Daily*, *Sing Pao*, *Hong Kong Daily News*, and *Tin Tin Daily News* all target the mass market, a segment favored by advertisers. *Ming Pao*, *Hong Kong Economic Journal*, and *Hong Kong Economic Times*, on the other hand, serve more specific market segments. The first is directed at the middle-class and higher-educated individuals while the latter two specialize in local financial news. They all have their own regular readers.

The cost of a Chinese-language daily newspaper falls into three types: distribution, newsprint, and operational costs. For each copy of

This case was prepared by Dr Susan Tai as the basis for class discussion rather than to illustrate either effective or ineffective handling of an administrative or business situation.

Please address all correspondence to: Susan Tai, H.C., Assistant Professor, Department of Business Studies, The Hong Kong Polytechnic University, Hung Hum, Kowloon, Hong Kong.

Reprinted from Asian Case Research Journal, Vol. 1, 163–175. Copyright © 1997 by John Wiley & Sons (Asia) Ltd.

a Chinese-language daily newspaper, on average, $0.50[1] is given to the distribution agent and $1.50 to the newsstands, making the distribution costs of each paper about $2. Other than the distribution costs, the average newsprint and operational costs are estimated to be between $6 and $8. Thus, the average cost of one copy ranges from about $8 to $10 (Table 14–1). Before the price war, all Chinese-language newspapers were priced at $5, so the revenue gained from the sale of each newspaper was less than its costs. Therefore publishers relied heavily on advertising for additional revenue which represented a large part of the total income. The volume of advertisements is, in turn, determined by the circulation figures of a newspaper. At the outbreak of the price war in December 1995, some publishers preferred to cut their prices in order to maintain high circulation figures and to keep their readers from switching to a cheaper publication.

Table 14–1 Unit revenues and costs of a typical newspaper in Hong Kong

Revenues	$
Revenue from newspapers sold	5.00
Advertising revenue	4.00
Costs	
Production	7.48
Distribution	2.075
Loss per unit before the price war	0.555

Source: The Newspaper Society of Hong Kong, cited in Chan & Lam, 1996.

There are many unfavorable factors that create tough times for the newspaper industry. Negative factors in recent years include newsprint costs which have soared about 30% and shrinking advertising revenue mainly due to a drastic reduction in the number of China property advertisements. The total advertising revenue for all newspapers in the first three months of 1995 was $974 million, down 10.1% from the previous year (Survey Research Group Limited). The price of all Chinese-language daily newspapers rose from $4 to $5 in October 1994 which affected the desire of readers to purchase more than one newspaper. Newspaper sales were also deteriorating.

---

[1] All currencies in Hong Kong dollars unless otherwise stated.

Two Chinese-language newspapers, *Hong Kong Today* and *Wah Kiu Yat Po* closed on November 26, 1994 and January 12, 1995, respectively. A few Chinese newspapers operated just at the margin and some smaller papers could follow *Wah Kiu*'s lead. Meanwhile, the proximity of Hong Kong's handover in 1997 was expected to exert some unpredictable impact on the freedom of news reportage. Thus, the general atmosphere of the newspaper industry market was highly unfavorable for a new contender. However, *Apple Daily* took a bold step into this market on June 20, 1995 and successfully attacked the market leader—*Oriental Daily News* directly. Hong Kong has a very dense population which can support substantial advertising. Therefore it is a very competitive market. This is exactly what makes Hong Kong so attractive to publishers and is also the reason why the territory is one of the world's most competitive markets.[2]

THE SUCCESSFUL ENTRY OF *APPLE DAILY*

Apple Daily is a mass-market product with a planned circulation of 200,000 copies originally and an initial investment of $300 million. Advertisers were generally unwilling to expand their budgets to sustain another mass-circulation daily that may only extend their reach by another 1% or 2%. However, *Apple Daily* after nine months had already achieved a circulation of nearly 300,000 copies and ran second in popularity in the Chinese newspaper industry. *Apple Daily* decided to invest further to raise its full daily capacity to 400,000 copies. It also declared that it would be within striking distance by early 1996 to challenge *Oriental Daily News* for the number one spot. Although the paper was initially suffering a daily loss of $50,000, it was expected to break even soon after its production capacity was upgraded in the middle of 1996.[3]

To understand the factors behind the successful launch of *Apple Daily*, one needs an insight into Jimmy Lai, the founder of Next Media Group. Lai's first brush with fame came as the boss of Giordano, a fashion chain store in Hong Kong, when he donated proceeds from the sales of T-shirts emblazoned with pro-democracy slogans to student protesters in Tiananmen Square in 1989. While many have fallen silent in the aftermath of June 4, Lai had maintained a strong anti-communist stance. Lai insulted the Chinese premier in his *Next Magazine* and hence *Apple Daily* fell out of favor with the Chinese authorities.

---

[2] "Out with the old, in with the new," *Asian Advertising and Marketing*, March 24, 1995.

[3] "Bite of the big apple," *South China Morning Post*, November 25, 1995.

While Lai's anti-communist stance may have helped him sell papers, it affected negatively his business investments.[4]

Those who worked with Lai have described him as intelligent, hard-working, and down-to-earth. He was also noted for his generosity. Senior journalists at *Apple Daily* were reportedly on a yearly salary of $675,000, and section heads earned as much as $1.5 million or more a year. Lai took a hands-on approach when it came to the day-to-day running of *Apple Daily*, chairing the daily editorial meetings. He said that his contributions to the meetings were limited to suggestions as to what should go on the front page. To guarantee feedback from his readers, Lai started a focus group made up of ordinary people who are paid to come into the office to tell the editors what they think of the paper.[5]

Product

Apple Daily offered sufficient exclusive news and good editorials to tempt readers away from the top-read *Oriental Daily News* and *Sing Pao* newspapers.[6] For example, the team in charge of city crime consists of more than 90 reporters and photographers working round-the-clock. Hong Kong celebrities often slam the newspaper because they are distressed by the details of their private lives being splashed across the pages of the paper.[7] *Apple Daily* responds to the demands of customers by providing timely news items which are tightly-edited, concisely-written in colloquial text and highlighted by big headlines, full color photos, and innovative graphic designs, all strongly influenced by *USA Today,* a popular newspaper in the U.S. To compete with its rivals, *Apple Daily* provides a broader editorial content and contains more pages despite high newsprint costs (Table 14–2).

Price

Apple Daily, which was not a member of the Newspaper Society of Hong Kong, argued that newspapers should have the freedom and flexibility to decide how to price their products. During the first month of its launch, the nominal price of *Apple Daily* was $5 but readers only paid the discounted price of $2 if they presented a coupon which had been enclosed in *Next Magazine* and *Easy*

---

[4] Ibid.

[5] Ibid.

[6] *Asian Advertising and Marketing*, March 24, 1995.

[7] *South China Morning Post*, November 25, 1995.

Table 14–2 Editorial content of the top three Chinese-language newspapers

Editorial content	Apple Daily	Oriental Daily News	Sing Pao
Main news			
Local	6	4	$4\frac{1}{2}$
International	2	2	2
China	2	1	$1\frac{1}{2}$
South China Special	1	—	—
Sports	1	1	1
Business/Finance/Property	8	$4\frac{1}{2}$	4
Entertainment	4–6	3	3
Horse racing	3–8	$3\frac{1}{2}$	3
Supplement	6	6	6
Total pages	33–40	25	25

Finder, both sister publications of *Apple Daily*. This was accompanied by a series of promotional campaigns, for instance, a free apple was given to customers with each newspaper purchased at 7-Eleven convenience stores. After the promotional month, *Apple Daily* resumed its price of $5 until the price war broke out.

Distribution

In Hong Kong, most people prefer buying newspapers from newsstands to taking out subscriptions. The retail sale of newspapers has been extended to convenience stores, supermarkets, and newspaper kiosks within Mass Transit Railway stations. The most common distribution channel is the distribution agents, who first take the newspapers from the newspaper publishers and then act as wholesalers to perform the bulk-breaking function by assigning the newspapers to smaller distributors in each district. They then redistribute the newspapers to the hawkers in newsstands and kiosks. Sole-agent circulation is similar to distribution agent circulation, except that the sole agent performs the functions of distribution agents and smaller distributors by delivering the newspapers to newspaper hawkers.

On the first day of its launch, *Apple Daily* alleged that five major Chinese-language newspapers formed a cartel with the specific aim of hindering the circulation of *Apple Daily* in retaliation for its promotional price of $2. The refusal of all agents, except one, to distribute the paper forced *Apple Daily* to set up its own distribution network and acquire its own vehicles for the distribution of newspapers. In general, newspaper hawkers earned $1.50 for selling a copy of a Chinese-language newspaper. However, they were able to earn $4.50 for each copy of *Apple Daily*. Therefore, *Apple Daily* was successful in setting up a distribution network during its launch. Later, the distribution network changed slightly when the redemption coupons ran out. But sellers could still earn $1.75 for every copy of *Apple Daily* versus only $1.50 for other newspapers. *Apple Daily* also adopted a "return paper" policy which was not used by most of the other newspapers (except *Sing Tao Evening Daily* and *Hong Kong Evening Daily News*). Under this policy, the hawkers were allowed to return the unsold copies of *Apple Daily* to the distribution agent for $3. Although during the price war the retail price of *Apple Daily* fell to $4, the hawkers' earnings for each returned copy remained unchanged.

Promotion

The launch of *Apple Daily* was also accompanied by a $600,000 television commercial featuring Jimmy Lai surrounded by masked men firing arrows at him and a tag line that read: "An apple a day keeps the lies away." It also offered free apples and T-shirts to create customer awareness and induce product trial. Besides the heavy advertising and promotional program during the first launch of *Apple Daily*, the company also provided a series of guarantees to vendors and advertisers. *Apple Daily* guaranteed newspaper vendors that they would be able to triple their profit as it would offer $4.50 for sales in the first month of its establishment while other papers only offered $1.50. It also guaranteed the advertisers and advertising agencies that its circulation would not be less than 200,000 copies, and claimed that its advertising rate was the cheapest among all the top-selling Chinese-language newspapers. If its circulation fell below 150,000 copies, the gross rate would be reduced by 50%. If the circulation fell below 100,000 copies, the advertising would be free.

As a result, *Apple Daily* sold like hot cakes on its first day of publication, as buyers snapped up the initial print run of 220,000 copies. It grabbed at least a 10% to 15% share of Hong Kong's Chinese-language newspaper market in its first two months of operation. Its circulation surged past the 300,000 mark, just six months after its launch. Most major Chinese-language newspaper titles suffered a dramatic double-digit decrease in readership six months after the launch of *Apple Daily*, according to *Survey Research Hong Kong*.[8]

THE CUT-THROAT PRICE WAR

As an immediate action to counter its aggressive new rival, C.K. Ma, the publisher of *Oriental Daily News (ODN)*, responded by giving out prizes worth $10 million to readers and imitated the style and content of *Apple Daily*. *ODN* also acquired additional printing facilities and accumulated a huge amount of newsprint. Once all the new facilities were in place, the paper struck back by cutting its price to $2 on December 9, 1995 for an indefinite period.[9] In comparison with other Chinese-language newspapers, *ODN* claimed to have the most variety of content in its Supplement Section. To satisfy customer needs, it also showed a great improvement in both soft and hard news. It also included a new section, *Oriental Finance*, which offered a detailed analysis of news on real estate and international finance. From December 3, 1995, a free coupon was printed on the front page of *Oriental Sundae* (a sister publication of *ODN*) which was published every Sunday. The readers could present the coupon to redeem a copy of the newspaper at newsstands, 7-Eleven, and Circle K convenience stores as well as TV service kiosks inside the Mass Transit Railway stations on the same day.

After a series of promotional programs and discount pricing, *ODN* succeeded in obtaining a new circulation record in the Hong Kong newspaper market—838,487 copies on December 16, 1995. However, the revenue of *ODN* was reduced by more than $3 million per month. Although the discount price led to a tremendous loss of revenue, it had regained its market leader position. The market share of major Chinese dailies and the list of press industry events during the price war are reported in Tables 14–3 and 14–4, respectively.

Apple Daily

After the outbreak of the price war, *Apple Daily* quickly reduced its price from $5 to $4 on December 10, 1995. It also provided a price guarantee to consumers by claiming that the retail price of $4 would be maintained until July 1, 1997. Its circulation dropped from its peak of 310,000 copies to 275,000 copies

---

[8] "*Apple Daily* eating away at readers of rival papers," *Media: Asia's Media & Marketing Newspaper*, March 15, 1995.

[9] Chan, R. and P.L. Lam, "The price war in the broadsheet market: The Hong Kong experience," *Pricing Strategy & Practice*, 4: 26–31, 1996.

Table 14–3 Market share of major Chinese dailies in Hong Kong

Chinese daily	Average daily sales in 1994[a]	Average daily sales in 1995 before the price war[b]	Average daily sales one week after the price war[c]
Oriental Daily	400,000	300,000	500,000–830,000
Apple Daily	Not yet launched	300,000	250,000–270,000
Sing Pao Daily	200,000	210,000	n.a.
Tin Tin Daily	175,000	n.a.	n.a.
Hong Kong Daily	105,000	100,000	200,000–270,000

Notes:

n.a. = Figures not available.

[a] Estimates by *Ming Pao Daily*, December 12, 1995

[b] Estimates by Standard Chartered Securities.

[c] Estimates by individual dailies.

Source: Chan & Lam, 1996.[10]

gradually. On February 27, 1996, Jimmy Lai sold a 27% stake in his Giordano fashion company for nearly $188 million. He was almost certain to put most of it in a fighting fund to defend his publishing group in a price war.

Sing Pao, Hong Kong Daily News, and Tin Tin Daily News

Sing Pao, Hong Kong Daily News, and *Tin Tin Daily News* followed the lead of *ODN* by cutting their prices to $2 (December 10, 1995), $1 (December 11, 1995), and $2 (December 12, 1995), respectively. They were forced to make cuts in their prices to stop the decline of their circulation. Had they not taken this action, advertisers might have switched to *ODN* or *Apple Daily*. As a result, all the discounted newspapers showed an increase in both circulation and sales figures. The $1 or $2 newspaper price was so low that it could not even cover the fees paid to the distribution channels.

The actions of *Sing Pao* and *Tin Tin Daily News* were aimed at maintaining their market position, while *Hong Kong Daily News* wanted to dramatize the event by reducing its price to only $1, which was its selling price in 1983. After the price cut, the circulation of *Hong Kong Daily News* more than doubled. On December 14, 1995, *Tin Tin Daily News* introduced an additional edition of its newspaper, which updated local and world news between 2 a.m. and 7 a.m. and was distributed to the newsstands at 10 a.m.

---

[10] Ibid.

Table 14–4 Significant events in the press industry from December 1995 to March 1996

Date	Events
December 9, 1995	*Oriental Daily News* reduced its newspaper price from $5 to $2.
December 10, 1995	*Apple Daily* reduced the publication price to $4 and pledged it would not change its press price until 1997.
	Sing Pao Daily News announced a price cut to $2.
December 11, 1995	*Hong Kong Daily News* announced it would reduce its cover price from $5 to $1.
December 12, 1995	*Tin Tin Daily News* cut its cover price to $2.
	TV Daily News declared immediate closure.
December 16, 1995	*Express News* and *United Daily News* folded.
December 19, 1995	*Hong Kong Economic Journal* announced it would stop its Sunday publication.
December 28, 1995	*South China Economic Journal* was shut down.
January 4, 1996	The Newspaper Society of Hong Kong reported that the five newspapers which had cut their prices had lost $110 million since the outbreak of the price war.
January 6, 1996	Culturecom Limited, publishers of *Tin Tin Daily News*, laid off about 100 staff and sacrificed *Ching Sun Chow Hon*.
January 12, 1996	*Hong Kong Daily News* increased its cover price to $2.
February 9, 1996	*Apple Daily* said it would lay off 16 members of its staff.
February 14, 1996	*Tin Tin Daily News* announced it would raise its price to $3.
March 18, 1996	A new newspaper, *Mad Dog Daily*, was introduced into the market.

Through such innovative measures and the effect of its discounted price, *Tin Tin Daily News* increased its circulation by almost three times during the price war.

Ming Pao, *The Hong Kong Economic Times*, and *Hong Kong Economic Journal*

These newspapers vowed to stay out of the war and believed that they were in a different market from the mass-market newspapers. It was reported that *Hong Kong Economic Journal* had even shown an increase in its sales volume during the early part of the price war. On the whole, these newspapers improved the quality of their content to prevent the loss of readership. For example, *Ming Pao* increased the number of journalists in every section and invited readers to make suggestions on its editorial content.

The Aftermath—Casualties and Winners

Within a few weeks of the price war breaking out, several less financially-endowed players that could not afford to cut their prices closed down due to the decline in their readership. They were *TV Daily News*, *Express News*, *United Daily News*, and *South China Economic News* which were closed on December 12, 16, and 28, 1995, respectively. These publications shared some common characteristics: they had low circulation figures, were losing money, and had a long history. For example, *United Daily News* had only 20,000 regular daily sales and lost between $4 million and $5 million each month. *TV Daily News*, the only Chinese-language entertainment broadsheet, had been in the market for 26 years. Although these victims had their own reasons for leaving the market, they had been directly or indirectly affected by the outbreak of the price war. For instance, the sales of *Express News* dropped 15% within a week of the price war.

The brutal effects of the price war and record high newsprint costs mauled the profitability of the listed Hong Kong newspapers. The stock prices of *Tin Tin Daily News* and *Hong Kong Daily News* dropped by 27% while that of *Oriental Daily News* dropped by 16% just one week after the outbreak of the price war. The stock prices of the other newspapers which maintained their newspaper prices were reduced from between 5% and 18%. As for *Apple Daily*, its daily losses jumped from $500,000 to $800,000.

The beneficiaries of the price war were definitely the readers who had to only pay $2 or $1 for a paper which sold for $5 before the price war. The quality of the newspaper content and the number of pages were increased due to the keen competition. Some newspapers upped the stakes by offering large discounts on their rate cards on condition that advertisers did not include key competitors in their buying schedule. Others increased the level of discounting from between 5% and 15% previously to 10% and 30% during the war. The escalating war came amid a decline in the overall circulation figures and a slump in newspapers' share of the advertising expenditure pie from 35.2% in 1994 to 29% in 1995. Although some publications claimed their circulation had doubled or even tripled, advertisers were cautious because the additional readers may not have been the target audience they were seeking. However, Raymond Wong Yuk Man, a well-known commentator in political affairs, saw the price war in the territory in a different light. He believed that the newspaper price war opened up opportunities for new entrants.[11]

FINDINGS OF SURVEYS

Two surveys were conducted during the price war to find out its effect on consumers and vendors. The consumer survey was carried out in March 1996, just about three months after the outbreak of the price war. The total number of useful questionnaires returned was 136 and the demographic profile is listed in Table 14–5. The vendor survey took place in April 1996 and the test group was chosen from different districts on Hong Kong island and in Kowloon. The total number of questionnaires used for analysis was 100.

Table 14–5 Respondents' profile in the consumer survey

Marital status
Single: 54.4%   Married: 45.6%

Sex
Male: 47.8%   Female: 52.2%

Occupation
Managerial: 3.7%   White collar worker: 20.6%   Blue collar worker: 26.5%
Technical: 13.2%   Professional: 4.4%   Housewife: 19.9%
Student: 7.3%   Businessman: 4.4%

Education level
Under Form 5: 28.7%   Form 5:   44.9%
Matriculation: 8.8%   Tertiary education: 17.6%

Age
15–19:   3.7%   20–24: 19.9%   25–29: 30.9%   30–34: 17.6%
35–39: 15.4%   40–49: 11.8%   50–59: 0.7%

Total family income per month (US$1 = HK$7.8)
Under $8,000:   11.7% $8,001–$15,000:   24.3%
$15,001–$25,000:   33.8% $25,001–$40,000:   19.9%
More than $40,000: 10.3%

Reasons for Newspaper Choice

Of the respondents, 85.4% admitted to buying the discount-priced newspapers. Among them, 36.8% of the respondents bought the newspaper for its better quality, 46.2% bought it out of habit, and 17.1% were influenced by the

---

[11] "Mad but not crazy," *Asiaweek*, March 15, 1996.

discount price. If all the newspapers had been sold at the same price, 87.2% responded that they would still buy the same paper that they did. However, 12.8% reported that they would not continue to purchase the discount-priced newspapers.

Selection Criteria for a Chinese-language Daily Newspaper

All the eight top-scoring criteria for choosing a Chinese-language daily newspaper were concerned with the content of a newspaper (Table 14–6). "Infotainment" (information plus entertainment) was the most popular trend of the Hong Kong newspaper market. Its aim was to imitate the success of *Next Magazine*, the top-selling magazine in Hong Kong. For example, *Apple Daily*, *Oriental Daily News*, and *Sing Pao* had already made "infotainment" the core of their newspaper content. The majority of the respondents (78.8%) only bought one copy of a Chinese newspaper. The majority of the respondents (40%) perceived the most ideal price of a copy of a Chinese-language daily newspaper to be $3, followed by $4 (31%), and then $5 (18%).

Table 14–6 Selection criteria for a Chinese-language daily newspaper

Selection criteria	Mean score
Updated information	1.58
Reliability in reportage	1.66
Variety in content	1.72
Objectivity in reportage	2.00
Interesting news	2.18
Entertainment	2.29
Exclusivity in reportage	2.42
Gossip	2.58
Price	2.59
Ease of purchase	2.69
Reputation	2.76
Color	2.81
Paper quality	2.85
Column design layout	2.96
Headline news on front page	3.07

Note: Most important = 1; least important = 5.

The majority of the paper vendors (80%) found that the price war affected their business. On average, the sales of discounted newspapers increased by 27%, and there was a decrease of 20% in the sales of those which did not offer discounts. Despite the fact that the net profit of the vendors had increased by 12.5% in the short run, about half of the vendors were worried about the prospect of the press industry as they found it difficult to sell newspapers not engaged in the price war. About 30% of the vendors perceived the price war to be the result of market domination while another 30% saw it as revenge against *Apple Daily*'s promotional pricing. Most vendors were afraid that if the market was dominated by one publisher their business would be badly affected. The most appropriate price was $4 from the point of view of the vendors. Vendors also thought that the price war would not last very long.

Medicine East

In December 1994, Ye Peng Chao, general manager of Medicine East Private Limited, was wondering what he should do to achieve greater consumer acceptance of the Medicine East concept and to expand the company's franchise program.

Medicine East was formed to provide customers with the best of Eastern and Western healthcare products and services at reasonable prices. The company had ten outlets in Singapore operating under the Medicine East label and sought expansion locally and regionally. A franchise program was developed and embarked in early 1993 to facilitate more rapid expansion.

THE COMPANY

History

Medicine East was a unique retail concept developed to make available the rich tradition of Chinese remedies and tonics as well as the best of Western pharmacy to both retailers and consumers. In 1993, the Chinese medical hall business, like many other traditional small and medium-sized retailing businesses, was facing difficult times. Many saw the need to upgrade the business concept and operations. The company was formed as a franchise project to revitalize and reposition the traditional Chinese druggist operations through the introduction of

---

This case was prepared by Geok Theng Lau and Kelvin Quee Siew Lai as the basis for class discussion rather than to illustrate either effective or ineffective handling of an administrative situation.

Geok Theng Lau is Associate Professor at the National University of Singapore. Kelvin Quee Siew Lai is an officer at the Singapore Productivity and Standards Board.

a modern store format, modern retail management systems, more aggressive and integrated retail marketing and promotional activities, as well as product innovation. Interested retailers would be brought through the franchising process so as to effect the transfer of know-how and to exploit scale economy in product purchasing, product development, marketing activities, and implementation of computerized management information system.

Medicine East was initiated for two primary reasons: (a) the recognition by its founding members of the potential in creating a modernized Chinese medical hall to meet the changing expectations and needs of today's consumers; and (b) the announcement of the Retail Sector Development Plan by the government in which grants would be offered for the development of franchises.

The idea to modernize the herbal trade was born in 1991 in a meeting among three men who later became partners of the company. The three partners were Tee Khiang Ng who was closely involved in his family business of importation of Chinese herbal products; Michael Chia, who operated seven Chinese medical halls owned by family members; and Ye Peng Chao, who was the general manager of a major Western pharmaceutical company and was involved directly in its expansion. The three men felt they had the right blend of experience to make the venture a success. They approached the National Productivity Board—the government's franchise division—to subsidize consultancy services for product research, design, and marketing.

Concept and Operation

Medicine East aimed to provide the best of Eastern and Western healthcare. With the use of modern and professional retail techniques, Medicine East hoped to apply this new retail concept to enhance the appeal and competitiveness of traditional medical halls in meeting changing customer needs.

Essentially, the scheme was based on a total healthcare concept to transform the Chinese medical hall into a modern specialty store. These stores would offer a retail mix featuring the best of both Chinese herbal products and Western healthcare products.

"We hope the scheme will appeal to many of the 700 Chinese medical halls in Singapore who will consider it as a means of streamlining their operations to meet the challenges of a rapidly changing retail environment and higher customer expectations," said Chao.

The franchise scheme sought to assist and upgrade as many Chinese medical halls as possible. These Chinese medical hall owners would be able to capitalize on direct benefits from economies of scale and a more systematic approach to retailing with Medicine East's support. At the same time, participants would continue to preserve their authority and exercise their innovations.

Central purchasing would be another key advantage in terms of getting better prices. Coupled with a computerized point-of-sale system linked to accounting and inventory systems, these modern retail management concepts would result in accurate and timely information that would increase business efficiency.

Other benefits included the adoption of a modern store design that would ensure a consistent image and a store layout that would reflect the new concept and yet retain the traditional flavor of the Chinese medical hall. Store environment would be enhanced with air-conditioning, better lightway, and piped-in music to improve customer comfort. Layout would be improved to facilitate easy customer movement. Proper signs would identify product categories to assist customers to locate their products. Service counters would also provide advice and better customer service.

In terms of product mix, franchisees could increase competitiveness through a selective expansion of their product range and a good mix of herbal and non-herbal related products. The latter might include personal care and skin cosmetics and selected toiletries. In addition, a unique mix would be derived from the development of exclusive house brands of herbal products.

"Medicine East hopes to add value to the business by updating the overall approach to retailing. Modern retail concepts will enhance store layout, product display, and improve store management. Innovativeness will be the key in making our services and products more relevant to meet today's customer needs," commented Chao.

Other key areas of efficiency included integrated advertising and promotional activities, logistics, staff training, and other aspects of store management. Franchisees could look forward to providing additional services and benefits which included dispensing of herbal mixtures and prescriptions from a Chinese physician, recommendations on product usage, and better quality control of herbal products. Credit card facilities would also be available to add to consumer convenience.

Medicine East differed from Western pharmacies which carried a few Chinese patent medicines, and from Chinese medical halls which carried a few Western medicines in its range of products from both sides. Half of each store would be given over to traditional Chinese health products and herbs, and the other half to Western medicines (see Figure 15–1 for a typical store floor plan).

Figure 15–1 Medicine East's typical store floor plan

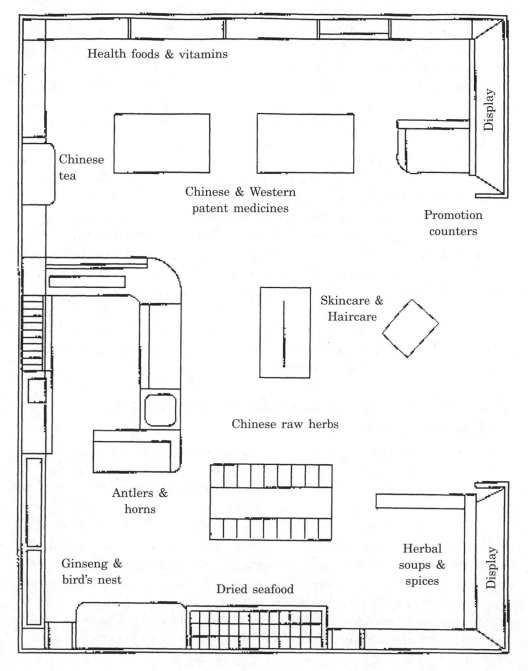

Health foods & vitamins

Chinese
tea

Chinese & Western
patent medicines

Display

Promotion
counters

Skincare &
Haircare

Chinese raw herbs

Antlers &
horns

Ginseng &
bird's nest

Dried seafood

Herbal
soups &
spices

Display

Three versions of Medicine East stores were possible: (a) stores with Western trained pharmacists dispensing prescribed Western drugs and selling Chinese prepackaged herbs and tonics as well as toiletries and personal and beauty care products, (b) stores with trained Chinese physicians dispensing Chinese herbs and tonics and selling Western over-the-counter (OTC) drugs as well as toiletries and personal and beauty care products, and (c) stores with no pharmacists or Chinese physicians, but selling only Western OTC drugs, prepackaged Chinese herbs and tonics as well as toiletries and personal and beauty care products.

Studies had indicated that consumers were receptive toward the modernization of the traditional Chinese medical halls. Retailers and their suppliers had also taken a positive attitude toward these changes.

"Chinese medical halls have been an invaluable part of our retail scene for generations. Competitive prices and good location have contributed to their success. Medicine East hopes to combine the respected traditions of this trade with modern retail management expertise to add a new dimension to the business. We also hope that many will respond constructively as the success of the franchise will have positive effects on the market potential for herbal products and remedies. Medicine East will hopefully increase the relevance and appeal for Chinese herbal products and their associated methods of treatment to meet changing consumer demands," said Chao.

PHARMACEUTICAL AND HEALTH AND BEAUTY CARE INDUSTRY
Estimated Market Size

The size of the retail business in pharmaceutical and medicinal goods, cosmetics, and toiletries in Singapore was unclear. The 1996 data in Table 15–1 were provided by the Department of Statistics in their report for wholesale and retail trade.

The figures probably did not include a large portion of businesses generated by the Chinese medical halls since they might be classified under a different category of business. Experts estimated the value of business generated by about 700 Chinese medical halls in Singapore to be around S$1 billion (including exports). About 40% of this business were accounted for by bird's nests and ginseng. While the sales of about 130 Western pharmaceutical retailers were growing rapidly, the sales of the Chinese medical halls had been declining.

Table 15–1 Wholesale and retail trade, 1996

No. of establishments	1,222
Employment	
Proprietors/partners	1,052
Others	3,789
Total	4,841
Sales turnover	S$773.69 million
Operating expenditure	
Cost of goods sold	S$529.42 million
Remuneration	S$70.07 million
Others	S$125.72 million
Total	S$725.21 million
Operating surplus	S$55.60 million
Value-added	S$130.57 million

Consumer Behavior

Consumers of pharmaceutical and health and beauty care products could be divided into two main groups: those who patronized the Chinese medical halls and those who patronized Western pharmacies and drugstores. Those who patronized Chinese medical halls consisted of: (a) the older consumers who purchased herbs and herbal products, and (b) the younger, more price sensitive consumers who patronized Chinese medical halls for their lower prices of Western healthcare products. Those who patronized Western pharmacies and drugstores were (a) the middle-aged, English-educated consumers, and (b) the younger, brand and quality-conscious consumers.

More consumers were buying from Western pharmacies and drugstores despite the higher prices and inconvenient locations of some stores. Many of these consumers felt that the Western pharmacies and drugstores provided value-added services such as professional advice and recommendations of appropriate products. These outlets were also felt to have better store ambiance and comfort, and carry a better range of products. There appeared to be a greater confidence in perceived product quality, safety, and effectiveness of Western brand names. These consumers were also influenced by advertisements by Western pharmaceutical and health and beauty care retailing chain stores and outlets.

"Chinese medical halls are losing customers, especially the younger consumers who do not appreciate herbal products," said Chao. "If the medical halls do not modernize, they will disappear one day." To survive, many of them had diversified into selling everything else from watches to detergent, becoming, in fact, provision shops. Many younger consumers associated the medical halls with older people and they did not feel comfortable entering these outlets. The outlets also often did not carry the products they looked for. Further, many of the Chinese medical hall operators and personnel did not know how to communicate and interact with these younger consumers. Most personnel did not even know how to speak English. Many of these Chinese medical halls also carried the strong smell of the Chinese medicine and herbs which they sold, and the young consumers felt "put off" by this odor which they were not accustomed to.

Overall, Singaporeans were becoming more affluent and were willing to spend more for their health and personal care and grooming. Many Singaporeans were becoming more health conscious and were reportedly taking health food supplements. The development of such health supplements and diet food segments had greatly surpassed the health food section, the former estimated to grow around 20% per year while the latter was estimated to grow less than 10% per year. Singaporeans' level of health awareness was rising but still low compared to the Americans and Australians. This explained the popularity of multi-vitamins among consumers who had little knowledge of health. Health foods, on the other hand, were predominantly organic and low in sugar and salt. The misconception that health food tasted bad, together with the short shelf life and high price, made health food unpopular to the mass market. To be true to organic qualities, health foods must be void of preservatives and were therefore difficult to improve in terms of taste without affecting health benefits. The only category among health foods that was taking off was snacks such as health bars and fruit.

People were also becoming more knowledgeable about personal care and grooming and were using various toiletries and personal care products. The toiletries market was a comparatively mature one and manufacturers were producing more specialized products to be targeted at very specific target segments, especially in saturated sectors like the shampoo business. The number of brands of health supplements, toiletries, and personal care products had increased tremendously during the last five to ten years.

Singapore's drug bill, however, was still the lowest among all Asian countries, based on 1992 estimates. In 1991, Singapore spent 0.18% of its gross national product on drugs compared to South Korea's 0.91% or the Philippines' 1.14%. One reason was that doctors here were careful not to prescribe expensive drugs since Singaporeans had to pay for the medicines they received. In other countries such as Japan, the cost of medication was covered by insurance.

Market Players and Competitors

In Singapore, there were a few big players and many small players in the retailing of pharmaceutical and/or health and beauty care products. The big players were Guardian, Apex, and Watson. The smaller players consisted of the neighborhood stores.

Apex was owned by United Engineers and had over 20 outlets in Singapore. Their outlets tended to be situated in shopping centers or within department stores or supermarket chains. Many Apex stores had qualified pharmacists dispensing drugs.

Watson was a recent player, having entered the Singapore market in 1988. It was owned by Hong Kong's Hutchinson Group and had 28 outlets in Singapore. Watson did not have qualified pharmacists in its stores, but concentrated on OTC drugs, health and beauty care products, toiletries, gift items, food items, and other related products.

Guardian had a total of 47 pharmacies and health and beauty shops. Thirty-nine of the stores were full-service pharmacies, managed by qualified pharmacists and providing dispensing services and patient counselling as well as selling OTC items. The remaining stores were health and beauty shops which had a wide range of OTC and other items but no full dispensing services. The company served 14,000 customers and provided late night dispensing in eight of the pharmacies. Guardian had the advantage of having its own trading arm—Accord Marketing Services—to provide marketing and distributing services. Accord was responsible for distributing a wide range of pharmaceuticals, healthcare products, home nursing equipment, fine toiletries, and lifestyle products from other agency lines as well as developing and marketing Guardian's own house brand of pharmaceutical products and Nature Life—a brand of natural health supplements. Manufactured overseas to Guardian's specifications, these house brand products were either imported as finished products or repackaged in-house. Through Accord Marketing Services' extensive network which covered medical specialists, hospitals, pharmacies, supermarkets, department stores, and Chinese druggists, the house brand products and other services products had been successfully marketed together with other leading brand names in Singapore.

The 700 medical halls in Singapore sold mainly Chinese herbs and tonics, both loose as well as prepackaged ones. Some of these stores had Chinese physicians to attend to patients and dispense Chinese herbs and tonics. Many of these medical halls were selling more common Western OTC drugs (such as Panadol), health supplements, and personal and beauty care products. Many neighborhood retail and grocery outlets as well as the traditional Indian and

Malay sundry stores were selling some common toiletries and personal and beauty care products as well as a limited range of OTC drugs and health foods.

One prominent player in the Chinese medicine business was the Chinese medicine chain, Eu Yan Sang. The chain was started by Tong Sen Eu, the son of Kwong Pai Eu who left Guangdong province, China, in the 1870s to work as a grocery shop assistant in Penang and later amassed a fortune in tin mining. When Tong Sen Eu died, the ownership of Eu Yan Sang was divided into 13 parts among his sons with a stipulation that any decision about the company had to be unanimous. Naturally, this led to lots of friction. By 1990, the company had nine shops and a flagship medical hall in South Bridge Road. The business became more difficult and profit margin from the medical business was slim at 9%, despite the efforts to adopt a new marketing strategy. In 1990, the company was sold to Lum Chang Holdings which was interested primarily in the company's real estate. In early 1993, Lum Chang decided to sell the flagging medicine business to Richard Yee Ming Eu and his three cousins, thereby returning the business to the Eu family. The company had been producing easy-to-use prepackaged soups and herbal prescriptions in capsule and even teabag forms. The company planned to increase production with a new manufacturing plant in Malaysia and to raise exports.

Another major player in the Chinese medicine retailing business was Medical Alliance Corporation (MAC), another franchise concept to upgrade the old medical halls through collective purchasing power, development of house brands, clever packaging, and better quality control. MAC was formed in December 1992 by a group of 40 people from complementary and related business in the Chinese medical trade. It was headed by Kien Fu Chen, a 72-year-old trained Chinese physician who owned a Chinese medical hall. Its first franchise model was launched in November 1993; and a second shop was converted the next month with better lighting, signage, and air-conditioning. Both shops experienced double-digit growth in the first month of operations after conversion, with the second shop reporting a 30% increase in sales turnover. Appendix 15–1 gives more information on the MAC franchise.

THE MEDICINE EAST FRANCHISE PACKAGE

The Medicine East franchise is detailed in Appendix 15–2. It was the view of Medicine East that the Chinese medicine retail outlets in Singapore would develop ultimately into two main types:

1. One that would retain the traditional format that might include offering the services of a Chinese physician. The product mix would

focus on herbal product prescriptions or dispensing. It would be positioned strongly as a specialty store dealing in traditional Chinese herbal products and remedies although the management might be upgraded and modernized.

2. The other would be the retail-oriented whole store format. Although these stores might include the services of the Chinese physician, the product mix would mainly be prepackaged herbal products, herbal tonics, and Western healthcare products. This group would continue to retain the position of a specialty healthcare store but with a more diversified and complete healthcare products for the modern consumers (an analogy of this store format would be that of a Chinese "Watson" store).

It was this second type of store that Medicine East aimed to develop through its new concept. The main target group of franchisees would be the existing Chinese medical halls and the secondary target group would be the pharmacists, Chinese physicians, and members of the healthcare profession interested in retailing, while the remaining target group would be entrepreneurs with keen interest in healthcare retailing.

Franchisees would also be given 20 hours of classroom and shop floor training in areas such as product knowledge, franchise operations, store management and display, and customer service.

Potential Franchisees

The main criteria for the selection of franchisees adopted by Medicine East partners were as follows:

1. Past experience and knowledge of healthcare products or in the pharmaceutical industry or medical halls.
2. Availability of stores in good locations, ideally to be situated in a public housing new town; heavy human traffic flow and young families would also be considered.
3. Potential franchisees must be committed to the retailing of healthcare businesses.
4. Financial resources which included the initial fee of about S$10,000 to S$30,000 for a franchise term of three years, renovation costs, and other operating expenses. The franchise term also included a 4% royalty from monthly sales revenue of participating outlets. In return, they would enjoy savings through bulk purchases.

Management of the Franchise

Medicine East adopted the approach that in the management of the franchise and franchise outlets, it must have the right people to work with the franchisees. Strong emphasis was placed on a partnership relationship between the franchisor and the franchisees. The system of control was rather flexible and the implementation of rules was mainly through persuasion rather than forced implementation.

Progress So Far

In March 1993, a prototype store was opened. The store acted as a model for other future stores. It was also a test store to see how consumers in Singapore would react to the store concept and format. Unless there was a Chinese physician at hand, Medicine East had decided to concentrate on prepackaged products such as tonic soups, herbal teas, raw herbs such as ginseng and bird's nest products as well as seafood tonics such as abalones and dried scallops. Chinese patent medicines would be kept to a minimum because of the difficulty of verifying their authenticity and safety.

The first franchise, operated by a dispensing pharmacist, opened in 1993. The store did well and reached its sales turnover target six months earlier than planned. This was followed by several other converted medical halls.

One such traditional medical hall was Mun Hin Tong. It joined the Medicine East franchise in 1994. With more than 20 years as a traditional medical hall, it had not been easy for it to make the change to the Medicine East format. However, Mun Hin Tong had come to the conclusion that times had changed. It knew that it had to complement its experience with modern management systems and new retailing formats to cater to the new generation of consumers. Mun Hin Tong reported that after its conversion, it not only retained its regulars but also attracted the younger and English-educated customers. Its customers also did not bargain any more. It got a wider and clearer selection of good, genuine quality products. In fact, the merchandise was more than three times its product range in the past. Its sales had also increased by 100% since conversion.

THE FUTURE

Chao wondered what strategy he should develop to encourage more owners of traditional medical halls to join the Medicine East franchise. He also wondered what marketing strategy he should develop to further enhance the Medicine East concept in order to attract and retain customers, given strong competition from Western pharmacy outlets and MAC.

Medicine East was also considering expansion of its franchise to countries like Taiwan, Malaysia, and Indonesia. The plan was to develop both local and regional retail markets. The company would also develop more house brand products and go into the distribution business. In a highly competitive but limited market within Singapore, it was essential that the franchise development be geared toward internationalization so that its business potential could be fully exploited. Chao wondered how he should go about expanding internationally into the region. Which country or countries should he focus on? What should the organizational structure to support such an expansion be like?

Appendix 15–1   MAC franchise

The formation of Medical Alliance Corporation (MAC) involved a cross section of the Chinese medical trade expertise, manufacturers, retailers, wholesalers, importers, and exporters in the medical field. Its franchise concept was a strategy synergy to upgrade old medical halls through collective purchasing power, development of house brands, clever packaging, and better quality control. It was headed by Kien Fu Chen.

Experience and expertise
Realizing the need to revitalize the medical hall business, MAC offered more than 650 traditionally-operated medical halls the opportunity to tap its experience drawn from generations of operating Chinese medical halls. It also offered the retail management expertise of its consultants and cost-effectiveness through bulk purchases.

Better prospects and improved façade
Its first two franchise stores experienced double-digit growth in the first month of operation after conversion. Before the shops were converted, product display was in disorder and there was no organized system in place. The shops were now air-conditioned and had better lighting and signage.

New challenge
MAC offered a comprehensive management program to help new franchisees to upgrade their inventory system, retail space, and display concept.

The right focus
MAC advised its franchisees on how to improve on product mix and make use of limited shelf space for more profit-generating products. It purchased for customers the right products they needed. Given the right product mix,

Appendix 15–1 (cont'd)

franchisees would be able to enjoy economies of scale through bulk purchases from agents.

An "old friend" nearby

Another important feature of the MAC franchise was the imparting of skills of highly personalized service to customers. Its philosophy was to remain within friendly housing estates. Adopting a traditional Chinese shopfront with the hundred drawers, dark wood finishing, and the prominent logo, an MAC shop was easy to identify.

Quality assurance

MAC had acquired a 50% stake in Wan Tong Foodstuff Trading which provided manufacturing and packaging support for MAC's products. This ensured that quality products were manufactured.

Benefits of an MAC franchisee

1. A franchisee had the incentive of owning the business while having the expertise of MAC at his disposal. A franchisee would still be the decision maker and MAC would be there to assist.

2. A franchisee might use MAC's recognized and trusted name and corporate style.

3. A franchisee would have experts to guide him through the startup period, avoiding problems experienced by new business owners. A comprehensive set of manuals covering operations, store layout, and systems would be made available.

4. MAC would also help with the renovation of the shop including interior design of the wall cabinets and shelves, product placement, and merchandising. MAC would be on hand from the drawing board, to negotiations with the contractors, up to adding the finishing touches to the shop.

5. A franchisee would benefit from purchasing a wide range of merchandise sourced and selected by MAC at a much reduced wholesale price.

6. Training would be provided for the franchisee and staff to upgrade service quality and efficiency. Programs included classroom sessions conducted by experienced business experts. Topics covered were retail store operations, pricing strategies, product categories, and customer service.

7. MAC had communication consultants to implement strong publicity programs to promote MAC. A franchisee would be supported by strong

Appendix 15–1 (cont'd)

advertising and promotions run by MAC and would also get guidelines and support on the opening of the MAC store.

8. A franchisee would also have access to MAC's ongoing market research, as well as the latest developments on the improvement of products and service such as bar-coding systems for stock.

Appendix 15–2 Franchise information for Medicine East

Franchise mission

To establish a partnership with existing retailers to revitalize and reposition the Chinese medical hall business, and realize its potential to its fullest.

Retail mission

To provide its customers with the best of Eastern and Western healthcare products and services at reasonable prices.

Steps to maximize the potential of the Chinese medicine retail business

1. Based on comprehensive research and the support of consultants, the need for a new direction for the Chinese medical hall business was identified.

   A new concept in Chinese medicine and healthcare product retailing would be introduced to pursue this new direction.

   a. A new name

   Medicine East was developed to integrate Chinese medical halls which joined this franchise chain. This name would spearhead the modernization of the business and build an exclusive identity for the franchise. Medicine East would introduce a new and exciting concept in Chinese medicine retailing.

   b. A new store format

   A new store format would integrate valued traditions within a modern retail environment to increase customer appeal and serve a wider customer base which would include both the Chinese and English educated.

   Stores would be air-conditioned and brightly lit to provide a more comfortable environment. All stores would enjoy a consistent and readily identifiable image to build greater consumer awareness and familiarity. These would also have promotion and dispensary counters. The stores would carry both Eastern and Western healthcare products. Some of the categories of products included: Chinese herbal soup-packs and spices,

Appendix 15–2 (cont'd)

speciality food tonics like ginseng and bird's nest, Chinese herbal teas, herbal jellies, and cooling drinks, Western OTC products, skin and haircare products, and oral hygiene products.

2. The franchise chain would benefit from collective strength and economies of scale. The key areas included:

   a. Central purchasing

   Through bulk purchasing, better profit margins, credit terms, and conditions of purchase might be secured. These included consignment arrangements, controlled selling prices, display incentives, and promotional support.

   b. Regular advertising and promotions

   Joint advertising and in-store promotional activities would be planned and carried out. The cost of such activities might become highly cost-effective for all members of Medicine East. A regular and well-planned awareness building program would contribute to consumer awareness, acceptance, and patronage.

   c. Training—professional trainers would conduct comprehensive training programs

   A training program on product knowledge and selling skills would be implemented for the staff of the retail stores to raise the level of professionalism and customer service. This would lead to greater consumer satisfaction and confidence in the store.

   Some of the training programs included:

   i.   handling common problems encountered in a Chinese medicine shop and prescribing remedies.
   ii. pricing, packaging, and preparation of herbal products for sale within the store.
   iii. pricing, display, operation, documentation, administration, and maintenance of the retail outlets.
   iv. product quality, safety, mechanism of action and contraindications.

3. Market growth can be achieved by the following methods:

   a. Educating the consumers

   Consumer education program might be carried out for the benefit of the trade. These programs might include public seminars on the proper use of Chinese medicine and tonics; brochures and articles might be developed on the value of Chinese medicines. These might be targeted at the Chinese and

Appendix 15–2   (cont'd)

English-educated consumers to increase the awareness of Chinese medicine as natural, safe, and effective remedies for many conditions.

b. Providing comprehensive Eastern and Western healthcare products and services—the "one-stop" healthcare store

Through the new retail format, merchandising would be undertaken on a modular basis. The format would allow the flexibility of incorporating Western healthcare products and services. This would allow retailers to change the product mix to meet changing consumer demands.

Special services might also be rendered. At some outlets, a pharmacist to provide dispensing services and/or a Chinese physician who provided treatment and consultation services might be present.

Cathay Pacific Airways

At its new, plush headquarters at Chek Lap Kok Airport called Cathay Pacific City, Cathay Pacific's senior management was discussing the strategies that would successfully take the airline through the Asian economic crisis and into the new millennium. Cathay Pacific Airways (CX) had embarked on an ambitious five-year three-phase project in 1994, starting with the launch of a new corporate logo and image. Improvements were made to its service and fleet in the last two phases. However, as the economic storm raged on, CX's competition upped the ante and passengers became more particular with how they spent their money. In addition, various health hazards—bird flu and red tide—lessened tourist arrivals in Hong Kong. Internally, CX had to battle with a union crisis regarding revised remuneration packages for its flight attendants and pilots.

The senior management was wondering whether the 1994-planned project was sufficient to withstand the unpredicted onslaught of crisis after crisis, and provide CX with a sustainable competitive edge in and outside of Hong Kong. Or, should more be done?

HISTORY

In the mid-1940s, two enterprising adventurers, American Roy C. Farrell and Australian Sydney de Kantzow, began their import-export trade with a refurbished war-surplus aircraft carrying cargo between

---

This case was prepared by Swee Hoon Ang and Siew Meng Leong as the basis for class discussion rather than to illustrate either effective or ineffective handling of an administrative or business situation.

Swee Hoon Ang and Siew Meng Leong are Associate Professor and Professor respectively at the National University of Singapore.

Copyright © 1999 by Swee Hoon Ang and Siew Meng Leong.

Shanghai and Australia. As demand for Australian consumer goods flourished, an offer was made to buy out the company, which the entrepreneurs rejected. This curtailed their freedom to operate in the city, and prompted the move to Hong Kong where CX was later founded on September 24, 1946. Farrell and de Kantzow did not have a name for their new enterprise then. After much debate, a name that captured the romance and adventure associated with travel in the Far East was chosen—Cathay Pacific Airways.

Over the next 50-odd years, CX became one of the leading Asian airlines in the world. In the 1980s, the airline industry experienced a spectacular boom. Coupled with the prospering Asian economy, CX substantially increased its flights to various Asian destinations and beyond. During the first half of the 1990s, when many carriers were hit by the oil crisis, the continued growth of the Asian economy saw Asian airlines remaining profitable. CX engaged in several cost-cutting measures to rationalize its operations. It moved some functions outside its home base. It also launched a new program to offer more personalized service to cater to the differing needs of customers.

In 1994, CX started a three-phase program to strengthen its foothold as a leading Asian airline. It invested some \$450 million[1] in Cathay Pacific City at Chek Lap Kok Airport. This included three 10-story office towers, a 23-story staff hotel, engineering stores, a safety-training facility, and a simulator building for 14 full-flight simulators. Today, covering a global network of 48 destinations, CX operates a fleet of 59 aircraft that is among the youngest and most technologically advanced in the world. It includes Boeing 777 and 747, Airbus A330 and A340, and six dedicated freighter aircraft.

ORIGINAL POSITIONING

CX's original corporate identity dated back to "a time when air transport was the preserve of business travelers and wealthy, mostly Western leisure travelers." CX was only a small regional carrier then. Competition in the airline industry was less intense, and the target market was obvious. However, over time, competition intensified and competitors began developing new corporate identities. The need for CX to revamp its identity became more apparent.

Although CX's previous advertising generated very high awareness, its positioning (as an Asian airline) was not distinct. There was a divergence between the airline's image, product, and the needs and wants of its key markets. CX was catering to an expanding Asian market, and thus felt a

---

[1] All denominations are in U.S. dollars unless otherwise stated.

pressing need to project greater clarity about its origins as an Asian airline to their key markets.

As Asia accounted for most of CX's total passengers (from 69% in the late 1980s to over 75% in 1993), it seemed obvious to CX that this was the target market. Moreover, it had a growth rate projected then to be four times that of the world average by the World Travel Organization. Said Tim Fitzsimmons, CX's general manager for marketing and sales, "Passengers from Hong Kong and south China represent over 20% of our market, Taiwanese passengers represent 17%, and Japanese 16%. These markets are mature and maturing, and contain an increasingly significant segment which is the Asian traveler who is product, value, and image conscious." Thus, CX developed a new marketing strategy that catered to these key markets—the Asian traveler who traveled to and from, and within Asia. CX also identified a smaller target segment that included many of their most loyal customers—the high-frequency Western traveler who was typically based in Asia.

NEW CORPORATE IDENTITY

With the new focus on primarily Asians, CX found that it had to develop a new corporate identity that reflected the growing importance of the Asian traveler—a brand that would appeal to these customers.

A new logo was sought. Design firm Landor Associates was appointed to develop CX's new corporate identity. It conducted research in CX's six key markets of Hong Kong, Tokyo, Taipei, Sydney, Singapore, and London. The results showed that of the three designs proposed by Landor, the Asian-inspired brushwing emerged the favorite. Playing a big part in this campaign, the brushwing, a single L-stroke of a calligrapher's brush, suggested the wing of a bird in flight. It represented the fusion of Asian culture and flight. Compared with other airlines included in the testing, the brushwing fared better due to its "visibly refreshing, very distinctive, and pleasing appeal." Although a bird motif was common in airline logos, respondents thought that the brushwing design was unique and original because it was executed in calligraphy.

Besides expressing CX as an Asian yet international airline, the brushwing embodied speed and an energetic flight—a reflection of CX's dedication to excellence in flying. Moreover, since calligraphy is created by the human hand, not machinery, and cannot be mass produced, this motif was chosen as it symbolized CX's devotion to high standards of caring, personal service.

HEART OF ASIA

An aggressive marketing communications campaign was used to launch CX's new corporate identity. Called "Heart of Asia," the campaign was born out of CX's position in Asia. The big idea was selected after an extensive worldwide research by McCann-Erickson. Developed by a Hong Kong team, it played on the physical location of CX's home town—a position that CX could unmistakably lay claim to. CX is the Heart of Asia on three levels. First, on a geographical level, Hong Kong is located at the center of Asia. It is the gateway to China, and has a four-hour flying time to Singapore and Tokyo. Further, with Asia having over half the world's population, CX could claim it is within a five-hour flying time from Hong Kong to half the world. Second, on an emotional level, CX wanted to emphasize its Asian service—"service with a heart." Finally, on a physical level, Hong Kong, being CX's base, is the heart of Asia with its energy, physical convenience, new airport, and relationship with regional sister airline, Dragonair. As Dragonair flies to several Chinese cities and towns, CX could capitalize on the convenience it offered for travel to China.

The project comprised three phases. Phase I (1994–95) focused on repositioning CX. This involved an extensive advertising campaign. Phase II (1995–97) emphasized product leadership and the upgrading of facilities, for the business and economy classes. This involved physical improvement in the aircraft as well as services rendered. Finally, Phase III (1997–99) concentrated on service leadership. This involved staff training as well as the provision of services outside the aircraft.

Phase I

Called Operation Better Shape, Phase I focused on promoting the new logo and building up the image of CX, and to a lesser extent, the core product and service benefits that CX offered. Launched on September 8, 1994, it comprised both print and television advertisements, as well as outdoor and radio advertising, direct mailing, and point-of-sale and below-the-line materials to promote the new CX logo. Figure 16–1 shows the new logo used on its passenger ticket jackets. The creative brief aimed to convey that with over 50 years of experience in Asia, CX was able to provide a better travel experience with top quality service.

The advertisements. Ad agency McCann-Erickson was chosen to spearhead the campaign. The ads were designed to be integrative and seamless in projecting CX's modern Asian image. The calligraphic motif in the logo was

Figure 16–1   New logo: The brushwing

Source: Courtesy of Cathay Pacific.

carried through in the print ads. The first print ad, a teaser ad called Heartbeat, showed a brushstroke of a heartbeat (see Figure 16–2). In the new corporate colors of green, red, and white, the ad described the new corporate slogan of Heart of Asia.

Figure 16–2   Teaser ad: Heartbeat

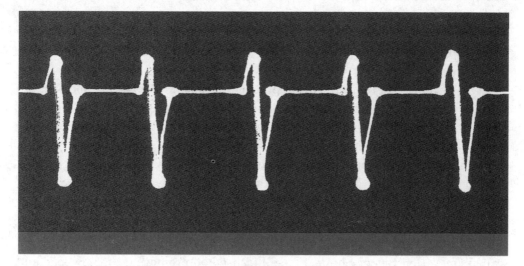

Source: Courtesy of Cathay Pacific.

Continuing with the integrative nature of the campaign, the inaugural television commercial, Drums, featured the varied talents of modern and traditional drummers from CX's Asian destinations. The heartbeat was translated into a drumbeat to create a sense of energy and passion. The pop soundtrack was by renowned Japanese composer, Ryuichi Sakamoto, famous for the movie theme, *The Last Emperor*. Shooting took place in nine locations, from Tokyo to Bali, and from Seoul to Kuala Lumpur, to capture the energy and spirit of modern Asia. In the opening scene, a sense of inspiration was conveyed by the drummer standing on a mountain peak. The passing to a new image of leadership and modernity was symbolized by the next scene which showed a drummer on top of Central Plaza, then Asia's tallest building. Importantly also, the visual colors of green and red—CX's corporate colors— were consistently embedded throughout the commercial in the color of the scenery, clothes, and drums. One scene showed the unveiling of a plane with the new livery against the sunrise, together with the drumbeat in the background, symbolizing the dawn of a new era of more enjoyable air travel on CX.

The first print ad that was launched shared the "beat" as the TV commercial and the brushstroke character of the new logo. It showed a calligraphic visual of a heartbeat as seen on a heartbeat monitor. This was accompanied by outdoor advertising posters of the heartbeat along major roads in Hong Kong including the cross-harbor tunnel. Other print ads followed which described CX's core values. One called Asia's Largest Network showed a brushstroke fishnet flung into the sea from a Chinese boat. The copy stated, "From our home at the heart of Asia we offer the most extensive network around the region and also on to 15 cities in China with our sister airline Dragonair. Cathay Pacific." Another, called Flexibility, featured a brushstroke visual of bamboo with a single word headline—"Flexibility". The copy read, "In Asia, flexibility is strength. And with over 650 flights a week to and from Hong Kong no one gives you more strength in Asia than Cathay Pacific. The Heart of Asia." Each print ad described a core Asian value that CX wanted to be identified with.

After a series of such calligraphic prints, CX launched a new set that included more "life-like" pictures. This included one called "Warm Welcome" which showed a steaming Chinese teapot with cups (Figure 16–3), and another "Harmony" which showed a pair of fish (Figure 16–4).

Media. The media plan targeted delivery of 2,000 million viewings to adults worldwide between September and December 1994. This included airing the TV commercial on local television in 20 countries, and a further 47 countries via satellite TV. The print ads appeared in 266 newspapers and magazines.

Phase II

During Phase II of the campaign, CX planned for and sought to carry out some $260 million worth of enhancements to its fleet, especially for economy and business-class passengers. In June 1996, CX began equipping its economy class fleet with six-channel, seat-back personal TV sets offering Hollywood and Asian movies of different genre—comedy, action, romance—as well as lifestyle

Figure 16–3   Print ad: Warm Welcome

Source: Courtesy of Cathay Pacific.

Figure 16–4 Print ad: Harmony

Source: Courtesy of Cathay Pacific.

and children's programs. This was in response to a research finding which indicated that its economy-class passengers placed a very high value on personal inflight entertainment.

Business-class passengers are the most keenly fought-after markets in the airline industry. CX spent a major part of the enhancements for this segment. Following a focus group study of cabin attendants, frequent fliers, and business travelers, CX included more personal leg space for the business-class passenger. A new look for its business class was also created by introducing a simple trolley and additional cabin staff, so as to provide a first-class style of service. The ratio of cabin attendants to passengers was increased so as to provide more personalized and flexible, and more prompt and less hurried, service. CX also focused on improving its staff training, inflight entertainment, and route-specific food, drinks, and even entertainment, with an emphasis on Asian cuisine that was of a greater choice and authenticity. For instance, inflight slippers and Japanese meals were offered on all direct flights to Japan, while satay (Malay version of shish kebab) was served with cocktails on Kuala Lumpur/Penang flights. Entertainment came in the form of more Asian language choices.

Phase III

In September 1997, Cathay Pacific launched a groundbreaking new phase to its "Heart of Asia" campaign. Service Leadership, the softer side of the airline, was to help differentiate CX from its competition in the longer term, and build on its brand image as a highly sophisticated international airline with a deep commitment to delivering genuine Asian service. Its principal aim was to make passengers feel right at home when they fly CX. CX believed that when it comes to good service, people make the difference. Thus, it wanted not only to transform the style but also the substance of its service. Staff training, compensation and benefits programs, and management culture were examined to see how they could enhance the vital but less tangible, personal aspects of customer service.

To provide a "modern Asian" service style, CX surveyed what passengers perceived as excellent service. They found that passengers considered good service to be personal, genuine, respectful, and non-discriminatory. They also expected CX's staff to be fair, knowledgeable about their product, consistent, and to work with warmth and spontaneity. The qualities of efficiency and professionalism were also cited as important.

To stand out from competition, CX's new service advertisements avoided the usual smiling cabin attendants interacting with happy customers. Instead, the new ads were unusual and fun. In one commercial, the CX heroine calmed a frantically bouncing football to impress upon its audience the skills of CX staff to reduce the stress of business travel. Another ad featured a lady interacting with a paper airplane and globe to represent CX's global network. In yet another, a staff member played with a feather and that symbolized its soft and gentle service.

CX offered membership programs which rewarded loyal frequent flyers with special benefits. The Marco Polo Club is CX's loyalty club and it rewarded members with service-related benefits. To qualify as a member, passengers must travel a certain number of kilometers with the airline. In return, members received benefits such as lounge access, a service hotline, priority wait-listing, extra baggage allowances, and discounts at selected hotels and restaurants. There are four tiers of membership: Diamond, Gold, Silver, and Green Card; relating to the number of kilometers traveled annually, and the service benefits vary for each tier.

In Seoul and Manila, CX offered CityCheck downtown check-in services for their business travelers. CityCheck allowed passengers to check in on the day of their flight, receive their boarding card, and pay the airport departure tax. This facilitated a speedy and trouble-free journey to the airport. In the U.K., to make airport transfer as smooth as possible, CX offered a free limousine service to full-fare first and business-class passengers. In Hong Kong, CX's Telecheck service enabled business travelers with hand-carry baggage only to check in by telephone. In addition, all CX passengers traveling with hand luggage only could make use of the No Bag Check-in service. CX also introduced a Return Check-in service for passengers traveling between Hong Kong and Bangkok, Singapore or Manila, to save them queuing time on their return journey. The lounge provided by CX offered a business service center, shower facilities, a TV area, an extensive buffet, and a relaxation room with sleeper sofas and electronic massage chairs (first-class lounge only).

Once on board, passengers also enjoyed a high standard of service and comfort; seats configured to allow as much personal space as possible, world-class entertainment, quality food, inflight phones, and fax facilities. In addition, CX's baggage delivery system had three levels of priority: First Priority baggage for first-class passengers and Diamond Card members of the Marco Polo Club, Priority Baggage for business-class passengers and Gold and Green Card members of the Marco Polo Club, and finally all other passengers' luggage.

CX Stay-A-While accommodation packages offered substantial savings on walk-in hotel rates, and were available worldwide in conjunction with CX flights. They were designed to suit both business travelers and holiday makers, and offered a variety of convenient city-center locations and out-of-town resorts, from deluxe to budget prices.

Personal televisions located in the seat arm were now provided in all classes across almost all of CX's fleet. Passengers could enjoy a greater choice of inflight audio-visual programming, and the airline continued to make improvements.

On some of CX's aircraft, passengers could access "Cathay Interactive" in English, Chinese, Japanese, or Korean, on their personal TVs. They could select information on duty free and gift items, destinations, holiday packages, the Marco Polo Club, the Passages frequent flyer program, PC-based games, and other services.

In addition, CX bought new aircraft that were more comfortable, cost-effective, and well-matched to the airline's intercontinental and regional routes. The ongoing fleet replacement program would continue up to year 2003, and already the new aircraft had won praise from passengers.

CX also heavily promoted Hong Kong as a major tourist destination, and a convenient place for stopovers. Hong Kong is a city that is both traditional and high-tech, a shoppers' and food paradise, and a city of nightlife. CX flew to over 45 cities on five continents, and offered the most convenient connections from Hong Kong to 28 major cities across the region. CX also promoted Hong Kong as the gateway to China. From Hong Kong, passengers could choose from over 45 daily flights to China on seven other airlines.

TRACKING RESEARCH

A tracking study was conducted in 1996 on the effectiveness of the marketing communications campaign along the following dimensions—advertising awareness, total airline awareness, image, "Asian" qualities, favorite airline status, and logo recognition. The results showed that advertising awareness improved by 12% from 1994 to 1996. In particular, such improved awareness was registered by intercontinental travelers, with regional travelers maintaining their level of awareness before and after the campaign. Hence, by end 1996, intercontinental travelers overtook regional travelers in awareness of the ads.

However, total airline awareness fell from 70% in 1993 to 67% in 1996, despite the massive campaign. Intercontinental travelers had lower airline awareness of CX compared to regional travelers who exhibited levels between 70% to 90% since 1993.

The image results for CX indicated that it was increasingly being perceived as an expensive airline. In the midst of price competition in the airline industry, CX strived to focus on non-price elements such as service upgrade.

On how well CX possessed various "Asian" qualities, the tracking study showed that CX rated favorably (above six on a nine-point scale), indicating that the campaign had repositioned it successfully as an Asian airline. Overall, the greatest change in its Asianization was observed in 1994–95, but not in 1995–96. However, differences between regional and intercontinental travelers were again observed. The Asian image of CX was more evident to intercontinental travelers at the end of the campaign from 1995 to 1996 than earlier.

CX's standing as the favorite airline for worldwide destinations declined over the years. Only in 1996 did proportionately more regional travelers view CX as the favorite airline for travel to/from/within Asia.

Finally, tests showed that recognition of its brushwing logo almost doubled from 32% to 61% from 1994 to 1996. However, recognition of its former logo was still high at over 70% even in 1996, two years after the new logo was introduced.

OTHER OPINIONS

Indeed, opinions regarding the makeover were mixed. There is a fine line between making the identity too Asian and thus alienating international passengers, and making it too European and failing to capitalize on CX's Asian heritage for positioning purposes. One of Hong Kong's best known designer felt that the identity lacked exoticism of the region and is too north European. Another designer liked the color, which represented good luck. However, he remarked that the icon went halfway in attempts to be Asian—a fault that might be due to the ethnic mix and background of CX's board.

THE ASIAN CRISIS

In retrospect, the handover of Hong Kong to China on July 1, 1997 marked the start of a turbulent period for Asia. A day after the handover, Thailand devalued its baht which started a chain reaction in the surrounding Asian economies. The Asian flu saw tumbling currencies, rising interest rates, unprecedented corporate losses and closures, and increased retrenchment and unemployment. Intraregional travel declined as Asian consumers stayed home or traveled domestically for leisure. For the first six months of 1998, Hong Kong's tourism industry lost HK$1.8 billion compared to 1997. Japanese and Korean tourism to Hong Kong plummeted almost 60%.

The crisis and the airline industry. The crisis had taken its toll on Asian airlines. Previously, airlines could offer cheap economy tickets and yet make profits on volume. They could reap substantial profits from business and first-class passengers. With the crisis, bargains were still available, if not more attractive, but the cheap fare was now not just in economy, but also business class, taking away the deep profits that Asian airlines used to enjoy.

According to the Center for Asia-Pacific Aviation, the yield (the price an average passenger pays to fly one mile) of 19 major Asian airlines as a group fell 10% between 1997 and end-1998. Although 7 of the 19 carriers made operating profits totaling $2.2 billion, these earnings were slashed by the currency exchange rates that pushed the group into the red—down 175% from their performance a year before. Table 16–1 shows the change in earnings of some regional airlines since the start of the crisis.

Table 16–1   Earnings change, 1997–98

Airlines	Earnings change 1998	1999 (estimate)
Cathay Pacific	−132%	n.a.
China Airlines	57%	n.a.
Korean Air	n.m.	−91%
Malaysian Airlines	−51%	−77%
Qantas	17%	5%
Singapore Airlines	1%	−18%
Thai Airways	34%	−20%

Note: "n.m." means not meaningful.
Source: Salomon Smith Barney, Hong Kong.

Except for Singapore Airlines, and the Australian and New Zealand carriers, the other airlines suffered badly. Some of the catastrophes included:

- Garuda: The national airline of Indonesia ceased all flying to the U.S. in October 1997.
- Korean Air: Although it posted a 1998 profit, this was because it sold six aircraft and laid off 10% of its staff. Some routes were canceled, including the Cheju-Beijing route, which was cut just a week after KAL began the service. As recent as April 1999, analysts had been optimistic of KAL as the Korean economy picked up and the won appreciated.

- Philippine Airlines: It went into bankruptcy and shut down for several months, resuming gradually certain flights after local investors stepped in.
- EVA: This Taiwanese airline saw its profit fall by 92%, although its air cargo business remained strong.
- Malaysian Airline System: The flag carrier of Malaysia began 1999 with a new policy of paying for fuel in Malaysian ringgit rather than in U.S. dollars so that it could reduce costs. It also cut six international routes in January, including service to Macao and Vancouver, Canada. It lost about $200 million in 1998.
- Thai Airways: This airline managed to make a narrow profit in the last quarter of 1998. It negotiated with Airbus and Boeing to postpone a $360 million worth of airline orders.

More trouble was on the cards. Although the airlines had canceled many aircraft orders, there were new planes scheduled to be delivered in 1999. This would result in 10.1% more seats to fill in 2000 than in 1997. In Hong Kong, although tourist arrivals had improved slightly in late 1998, the economy was still contracting and domestic demand still weakening. CX was expected to lose revenue from Hong Kong passengers. Mark Simpson, research chief at Nomura Securities, did not expect the situation to stabilize for CX until 2000 or 2001. He also pointed out that CX was vulnerable to the weak yen and sagging demand in Japan, one of its most important markets, and to changing business mix as the cost-conscious spurn first and business class on short-haul Asian routes. Indeed, its 1998 results showed that routes to Japan and Southeast Asia were the most affected by the crisis. Although long-haul services to Europe and North America performed better, they were also affected.

The Asian doldrums saw CX suffering its first loss in 1998 since 1963—a whopping HK$542 million. Table 16–2 shows the key financial and operating statistics from 1990 to 1998. In 1996 and 1997, CX made profits of HK$3.81 billion and HK$1.69 billion, respectively. The disappointing results in 1998 reflected the full impact of the Asian crisis on its operations. CX's overall passenger load factor for 1998 was down 0.7 percentage points from 1997 to 67.5%. Average yield was HK45.2 cents per revenue passenger kilometer, down by 18.9% as there was a reduction in the number of business and first-class passengers. Cargo revenue also suffered a similar fate. Its turnover of HK$7.04 billion was 9.5% down from 1997. Part of this decline was due to serious startup difficulties experienced at the Chek Lap Kok Airport. This resulted in substantial revenue losses in July and August 1998. All in, turnover for 1998 was HK$26.7 billion, a 12.9% decrease from 1997.

Table 16-2 Key financial and operating statistics

	1990	1991	1992	1993	1994	1995	1996	1997	1998
Traffic turnover (HK$ million)	19,155	20,130	22,258	22,598	25,643	28,827	30,530	29,633	25,572
Revenue from passenger services (HK$ million)	15,823	16,459	18,284	18,321	20,027	22,128	23,680	21,851	18,532
Revenue from cargo services (HK$ million)	3,332	3,671	3,974	4,277	5,616	6,699	6,850	7,782	7,040
Profit (HK$ million)	2,995	2,950	3,008	2,293	2,388	2,978	3,809	1,694	(542)
Earnings per share (HK cents)	104.6	103.0	105.0	80.0	83.4	104.0	119.6	49.5	(16)
Revenue load factor (%)	74.3	71.0	70.4	68.9	70.4	70.8	72.6	69.5	67.1
Passenger load factor (%)	75.9	73.6	73.5	70.0	71.3	71.6	74.0	68.2	67.5
Cargo load factor (%)	64.0	62.0	60.0	63.3	66.1	67.0	66.9	72.9	65.2
Destinations at year end (number)	38	39	41	42	42	44	45	48	48
Staff number at year end (number)	12,764	12,747	13,240	13,857	14,216	14,744	15,757	15,747	13,971
Aircraft departures (000's)	38	38	41	46	49	52	55	56	59
On-time performance* (%)	71.5	70.2	69.1	74.0	79.0	77.3	78.0	81.8	80.3

* Defined as departure within 15 minutes.

In August 1999, CX announced its interim results for 1999. It turned in a profit of HK$108 million for the first six months despite the massive flight cancelations due to a pilot strike in June (see story on page 336). However, this profit was bolstered by disposal of some HK$322 million worth of investments and profits of HK$47 million from associated companies. Turnover rose 1.4% to HK$13,167 million, while passenger numbers declined by 1%. The passenger and cargo load factors at mid-1999 were 67.1% and 68.8%, respectively, with yields of HK$0.46 and HK$1.80. On-time performance improved with 85.9% of flights departing within 15 minutes of schedule. Its net debt equity ratio stood at 0.57 times, with a profit margin of 0.8%.

HEALTH SCARES

The Year of the Tiger—the year the Chinese believe is to be feared—lived up to its ferocious reputation for Hong Kong in 1998. Apart from the economic flu, Hong Kong also experienced several health hazards. The first was the bird flu outbreak which began in April 1997. It did not get much public attention until December, when 18 cases were reported, 6 fatal. Most of these victims appeared to have contracted the virus from live chickens. The virus, H5N1, was said to have come about because of the mixing of local chickens with those from China. Chinese officials had failed to report an outbreak of the virus in the mainland in February and March that killed 1.7 million birds. In Hong Kong, 4,500 chickens died in April.

This outbreak saw panic in several countries, especially Taiwan. Posters warning of the virus were posted at Taiwanese airports that urged travelers bound for Hong Kong to minimize public activities, to avoid contact with birds, and to seek immediate treatment for illnesses. Taiwan airport customs and port police were also ordered by the Council of Agriculture to tighten inspections of luggage from Hong Kong. Such warnings saw several hundred visitors from Taiwan and Japan canceling planned visits.

Compounding this problem was the red tide disease which followed shortly after the bird flu scare. In the first two weeks of its outbreak, some 50 Hong Kongers had food poisoning, suspected to be caused by ciguatoxic fish. The waters of some fish farms were reportedly to have been choked with dead fish, resulting in fish carrying poisonous algae. People affected showed symptoms of numbness of the mouth and the limbs, vomiting, diarrhea, alternate bouts of fever and chills, and pains of the joints and muscles. With lessons learned from the bird flu, the Hong Kong government advised the public to be extra cautious of big coral reef fish and to avoid shellfish. However, unlike the bird flu which appeared to be a one-off incident, the red tide seemed recurring. In March 1999, evidence of the red tide was again detected off the Hong Kong coast.

HIGH AIRPORT COSTS

Another problem associated with Hong Kong was the high operating cost of the new airport. The landing fees at Chek Lap Kok were, on average, twice as high as in Singapore, 64% higher than at the former Kai Tak Airport, and the third highest in the world after Narita in Tokyo and the Kansai Airport in Osaka. Airlines were complaining about the high costs. Among others, Swissair, United Airlines, and Northwest Airlines, reduced their flights to Hong Kong. Said one senior airline official, "It is a competitive world market and if you really want to attract more air services then you have to price accordingly. When you see that Chek Lap Kok is charging double that of Changi in Singapore, then if there is any discretion on the part of airlines, they are going to go where it is less costly."

INTERNAL STRIFE

On top of these external problems, CX also had to contend with internal disputes between its union and management. Following the economic crisis, CX management resorted to cost-cutting measures. One asked its 4,600-odd cabin-crew employees to choose among three options: flying four more hours per month for a 3.5% pay raise, accepting a pay freeze, or allowing themselves to be laid off. Most attendants favored the package of increased pay and working hours. What could have been smooth negotiations turned out to be a long-drawn affair when CX management required individual acceptance of the agreement and would not have the union accept on behalf of the flight attendants. This infuriated the unionists who accused CX management of undermining collective bargaining power—something which CX said did not exist under Hong Kong labor law. To support their fellow unionists, the pilots' union also joined in the fray. This came to a showdown in May–June 1999 when pilots reported sick and did not show up for work over the pay dispute. Some 500 flights were canceled over the three weeks. Interim measures were undertaken where CX chartered flights with other airlines. By mid-June, an agreement was reached and flight schedules resumed normalcy. The strike cost CX HK$500 million.

HIGH PRICE

In terms of price, analysts believed that the economic crisis had not helped CX. Unlike SIA which was able to take advantage of Singapore's weakened currency, CX had less pricing flexibility because of the Hong Kong dollar's peg to the U.S. dollar. Complained a Hong Konger, Poo Hee Young, "I think all Hong Kong people would like to support our own airline ... if everything else were equal. However, Cathay Pacific is driving us away by charging exorbitant airfares." Apparently, although published fares among competing airlines were comparable to CX's, they offered attractive packages and off-season discounts, while CX seldom did. Says Young, "Why would anyone in his right mind choose to pay nearly double to fly Cathay Pacific when the service, time schedule, and safety record of the other carriers are just as good?"

COMPETITION

Moreover, CX had to compete with both Asian and non-Asian airlines for its Asian as well as international flights. Among its more formidable competitors were Lufthansa and Singapore Airlines (both ranked among the top five airlines by *Fortune* magazine in 1998), British Airways, United Airlines, and Japan Airlines. CX was 10th in the same global ranking.

Singapore Airlines (SIA), CX's main competitor, joined the Star Alliance in April 2000. Star Alliance was set up in 1997 by United Airlines, Lufthansa, Air Canada, Scandinavian Airlines, and Thai Airways to harness their international services and expand their global reach. This came after the establishment of two strategic alliances. In June 1997, SIA, Air New Zealand, Ansett Australia, and Ansett International announced the largest airline alliance in Asia Pacific. In November the same year, SIA announced an alliance with Lufthansa. As part of the alliance, Lufthansa would use Singapore as its primary hub for Southeast Asia and Australia, while SIA would use Frankfurt as its hub for continental Europe. Both alliances also involved code-sharing facilities.

Another of SIA's strategies was to go beyond merely being an international airline. It wanted to become a global group of airlines and airlines-related companies, by acquiring stakes in them. During the Asian crisis, SIA looked to acquire part of South African Airways and Thai Airways. However, not all SIA's attempts at building a global group of airlines were successful. Failed attempts included a bid for Qantas in 1992, a joint venture with India's Tata group in 1998, and buying a 25% stake in China Airlines in 1999. It also sought to purchase a 50% stake of Ansett Airlines for A$500 million for a stronger lock on the "Kangaroo route" to Australia, although the purchase did not eventually materialize.

Another SIA strategy was its continued provision of excellent service. In line with the electronic age, SIA offered electronic ticketing for some flights. Ticketless, passengers did not have to worry about losing their tickets. They made a booking, showed up at the check-in counter on the day of the flight, paid by credit card and collected the boarding pass. In 1998, SIA introduced a slew of improvements for all classes. An International Culinary Panel comprising world renowned chefs, food writers, and culinary experts was set up to tap the connoisseurs' expertise to provide exquisite dishes. SIA wanted to show that gourmet food could be served in planes as well. For first-class flights exceeding seven hours, sleeper suits comprising a top pullover and matching pants were provided. A SkySuite allowed seats to recline to a full, flat bed for the extra comfort. For visitors to Singapore, a complimentary mobile cellular phone was provided. Business-class passengers got roomier seats for extra personal space and comfort, while economy-class passengers were provided with better inflight entertainment. Krisworld, SIA's inflight entertainment, offered over 60 entertainment options in every seat of all Megatop 747s, Jubilee 777s, and Celestar 340s.

SIA's policy of steady aircraft fleet renewal saw it continue to operate one of the most modern passenger fleets in the world. As at March 1998, the average aircraft age was five years two months.

Such strategies saw SIA's passenger revenue, cargo revenue, and operating profit climb by 4.6%, 14.7%, and 15.5%, respectively in 1998 over 1997.

STEPS TAKEN BY CX

In light of the economic and health crises and competition, CX took a number of steps to improve its competitiveness. These included the removal from service of seven older Boeing 747-200 aircraft and six more B747-300 aircraft in 1999. It would continue to reduce its unit operating cost from HK$2.57 per available ton kilometer in 1997 to HK$2.25 in 1998.

Despite these cost-cutting measures, CX was cognizant that it should not compromise on investing for the future. An extensive investment program aimed at improving its products and services was underway. This included accepting delivery of ten new Boeing and Airbus aircraft during 1999. This, coupled with the removal of the older aircraft, would make the overall fleet younger and more efficient to operate.

CX also positioned itself to meet widening global competition by becoming a founder member of the new oneworld alliance along with American Airlines, British Airways, Canadian Airlines, and Qantas Airways. Figure 16–5 shows a picture used in the promotional materials for oneworld. CX also launched a new frequent flyer program, Asia Miles, with these partners. It was designed to be one of the most comprehensive in Asia. Besides the conventional way of earning miles by flying, buying air tickets, and staying at selected hotels,

Figure 16–5   Picture used in promotional materials for oneworld alliance

Source: Courtesy of Cathay Pacific.

members could also earn through banking and making phone calls. Unlike the now-defunct "Passages," which was a partnership among CX, Singapore Airlines, and Malaysian Airlines, Asia Miles allowed the economy-class passengers in addition to business-class passengers to earn miles. To complement CX's existing Marco Polo Club, all members were automatically enrolled in Asia Miles. Currently, Asia Miles is well ahead of its target to attract 350,000 members during its first year.

CX's new range of services also extended to cyberspace. In September 1999, it launched a new Internet booking service accessible through its website. Easy and convenient, customers could buy air tickets 24 hours a day from anywhere in the world. This service initially applied to all CX flights out of Hong Kong and selected flights from destinations such as Bangkok, Brisbane, Frankfurt, London, Manila, San Francisco, Singapore, Sydney, Taipei, and Tokyo. Customers could choose to have their tickets delivered to them by courier or held at their airport of departure. In selected markets, they could use the electronic ticketing service where printed tickets were not needed and they only needed to present their passports for check-in. In some cases, tickets could be purchased through the Internet booking page as little as three hours before a flight's scheduled departure time.

After the turbulent two years, CX announced in July 1999 the launch of a new ad campaign to show its commitment to Hong Kong through both good and bad times. Titled "Four Seasons," the ad showed that Hong Kong had always endured periods of winter, but that spring and summer would always come around. It underlined CX's commitment to Hong Kong and ended with the title "Same team. Same dream." The print ads featured CX's brushstroke style. However, unlike earlier print ads, the latest ads also featured other graphic elements such as color photographs.

A Ray of Hope

Besides these corporate and communication changes, CX hoped that the future of Hong Kong and Asia would become brighter. A ray of hope illuminated from Disney's Magic Kingdom for Hong Kong as it was to host Asia's newest theme park. The project was expected to cost $1.3 billion and was to be located on the outlying Lantau island. When news broke that Hong Kong and Disney were negotiating to build the theme park, CX's share price saw a big surge.

However, some market analysts were not confident that this spelled the end of the dry run. The theme park was not expected to be operational until 2006. Even then, the additional one to two million people that it would attract overseas translated to only about 4.5% increase in passenger numbers for CX. Most would be short hauls as not many would be expected to come from Paris, Florida, California, or Tokyo to see Disney's theme park in Hong Kong.

Conclusion

As they wished upon a star, CX's management hoped that their dreams would come true to turn around CX and see it through the Asian crisis as a stronger airline.

Sources

"Asian Airlines Hit Hard by Recent Economic Crisis," *USA Today*, March 16, 1999, p. 11E.

"BA Chief Wants Cut in HK Landing Fees," *The Straits Times*, March 23, 1999, p. 54.

"Cathay Pacific Suffers Loss of HK$542 Million in 1998," *BusinessWorld*, March 17, 1999.

"Cathay Pacific Workers Stage Sit-in," *The Asian Wall Street Journal*, February 1, 1999, p. 4.

"Cathay Staff Demand Talks," *Hong Kong Standard*, February 1, 1999.

"Fish Farms on Alert as Red Tide Returns," *South China Morning Post*, March 6, 1999, p. 4.

"Health Hazard," *Far Eastern Economic Review*, January 15, 1998, p. 17.

"Hong Kong Looks to the Magic Kingdom for Economic Spell," *Canberra Times*, March 22, 1999, p. 9.

Information from Singapore Airlines website.

"Overpriced Airline," *South China Morning Post*, March 15, 1999, p. 22.

Press releases from Cathay Pacific.

"Ready for Takeoff?" *Asiaweek*, March 26, 1999, pp. 64–5.

"SIA Confirms Deal on Ansett Stake," *The Straits Times*, March 26, 1999, p. 77.

"Tourists Told SAR Safe After Bird Flu Fears," *South China Morning Post*, December 20, 1997.

Amway Japan Limited

In April 1997, overlooking the cherry trees in full bloom outside his office at Amway Japan Limited (AJL) in Tokyo, Bruce L. Stephens, president of AJL, pondered how to reverse the first performance decline the company had experienced since entering the Japanese direct selling market in 1979.

Established as the tenth overseas subsidiary of Amway Corporation of Ada, Michigan, AJL had grown to become the most successful company in the Amway group, accounting for 30% of its worldwide estimated retail sales of US$6.8 billion in 1996. In fiscal year (FY) 1996, AJL's net sales were up 19.2% to ¥212.2 billion (US$1.9 billion), net income grew 21.8% to ¥28.1 billion (US$257 million).[1] The number of its core distributorships expanded 11.6% to exceed the all-time record of one million.[2] Table 17–1 summarizes AJL's recent performance.

This case was prepared by doctoral candidate Yoshinori Fujikawa of Harvard Business School and Dr. Patrick Reinmoller of Japan Advanced Institute of Science and Technology under the supervision of Professors David J. Arnold and John A. Quelch as the basis for class discussion rather than to illustrate either effective or ineffective handling of an administrative situation. Some figures and names have been disguised for security and competitive reasons.

[1] Exchange rate was approximately ¥109 = US$1 in 1997.

[2] Amway used "distributorship" as an official counting unit for its distributor membership. Under this counting method, a single person, a married couple, and parent–child team were considered as one "distributorship." In practice, the terms "distributorship" and "distributor" were used interchangeably.

Table 17–1 Selected financial and company data, FY 1992–96[a]

	FY 1992	FY 1993	FY 1994	FY 1995	FY 1996	FY 1996[d] (US$ thousand)	sales (%)	FY 1992–FY 1996 CAGR* (%)
Income statement data (¥ million except for per share amounts)								
Net sales	123,253	130,028	157,556	177,991	212,196	1,946,752	100.0	14.5
Cost of sales[b]	36,087	37,319	43,576	47,515	55,588	509,982	26.2	11.4
Gross profit	87,166	92,709	113,980	130,476	156,608	1,436,771	73.8	15.8
Operating expenses								
Distributor incentives[c]	31,908	34,001	42,652	47,885	57,044	523,339	26.9	15.6
Distribution expenses	7,653	7,773	8,324	8,853	9,839	90,266	4.6	6.5
Selling and administration expenses	15,188	16,810	19,616	24,022	28,355	260,138	13.4	16.9
Total operating expenses	54,749	58,584	70,592	80,760	95,238	873,743	44.9	14.8
Operating income	32,417	34,125	43,388	49,716	61,370	563,028	28.9	17.3
Other income	3,487	2,485	2,557	1,733	1,309	12,009	0.6	–21.7
Income before income taxes	35,904	36,610	45,945	51,449	62,679	575,037	29.5	14.9
Income taxes	19,373	20,759	25,341	28,387	34,598	317,413	16.3	15.6
Net income	16,531	15,851	20,604	23,062	28,081	257,624	13.2	14.2
Net income per share	110.49	105.94	137.70	154.13	187.83	1.72		14.2
Cash dividends per share	50.00	60.00	140.00	190.00	125.00	1.15		25.7
Shares outstanding (thousand)	149,625	149,625	149,625	149,625	149,502	149,502		0.0
Balance sheet data (¥ million except for per share amounts)						(US$ thousand)		CAGR (%)
Inventory	10,300	9,900	11,000	11,400	12,500	114,679		5.0
Working capital	57,000	62,300	68,900	43,600	27,000	247,706		–17.0
Total assets	93,000	102,000	116,500	121,800	116,200	1,066,055		5.7
Total shareholder's equity	64,700	72,300	79,200	77,900	63,900	586,239		–0.3
ROA	18.4	16.3	18.9	19.4	23.6	23.6		6.4
ROE	27.2	23.1	27.2	29.4	39.6	39.6		9.8
Other data								CAGR (%)
Number of employees	746	769	871	960	1,044			8.8
Number of core distributors	752,000	861,000	896,000	980,000	1,093,000			9.8
Number of direct distributors	4,600	4,800	5,900	7,100	8,500			16.6
Core distributor renewal rate	67.6%	71.1%	72.8%	71.8%	73.0%			1.9

* Compound annual growth rate.
[a] Fiscal year ended August 31. For example, FY 1996 was from September 1, 1995 to August 31, 1996.
[b] Approximately 65% of AJL's cost of sales for FY 1992–FY 1996 represented purchase of products from Amway Corporation (Ada, Michigan) which AJL paid in yen. Prices of these products were determined with an implicit U.S. dollar/yen exchange rate which AJL calculated to be ¥91/US$1 until FY 1996 and which was changed to ¥107/US$1.
[c] Distributor incentives, principally in the form of bonus payments to distributors based on performance, fluctuated with the sales volume.
[d] The U.S. dollar amounts were calculated at the approximate rate of exchange prevailing on August 31, 1996, of ¥109/US$1.
Source: *Amway Japan Limited Annual Reports 1994–96.*

AJL's first-half results in FY 1997, however, showed net sales declining to ¥96.3 billion, down 11.6% from the first half of the previous year, and net income down 27.6% to ¥11.6 billion. AJL's revised year-end forecasts projected 1.3% annual sales growth which would bring net sales to ¥215 billion, and 6.8% decline in net income to ¥26.2 billion.

Stephens, a 1966 Harvard MBA, joined Amway Corporation in 1990 as general manager of Amway GmbH in Germany and became president of AJL in 1991. He had previous experience in the Asian operation of U.S. firms including PepsiCo, RJR Tobacco, Seagram, and Tupperware. Having succeeded in doubling AJL's sales during the five years of his presidency, Stephens now needed to develop a strategy not only for rebuilding growth in the second half of FY 1997, but also for achieving AJL's long-term goal of sales of ¥300 billion by FY 2000.

DIRECT SELLING INDUSTRY

The direct selling industry was growing at 8% annually, with worldwide sales of US$72 billion in 1995, and more than 20 million people in the world engaged in direct selling, on either a part-time or full-time basis. In 1996, Japan was the largest market, with sales of US$30 billion and two million distributors, followed by the U.S. with US$18 billion sales and seven million distributors. Table 17–2 provides an overview of the industry, with particular details on Japan and the U.S.

Direct selling was a face-to-face method of selling to the consumer, not relying on fixed retail stores, product advertising, or direct mail. Salespeople called on consumers to show sample products and to obtain orders. The goods were then supplied by the company, either directly to the consumer or through the salespeople. Direct selling was considered as particularly suited to high-quality household and personal products that benefited from detailed explanation or demonstration. Direct selling was usually distinguished from direct marketing, which comprised mail-order retailing, telemarketing, television direct response, and electronic shopping.

Direct selling companies employed several different approaches: door-to-door, person-to-person, and party plan. Traditional direct sales programs were often described as "door-to-door" business. The person contacting customers typically worked for the company as a sales representative. Closely supervised by the company, the individual was usually assigned a limited geographic territory and specific hours in which to sell the company's products. Normally, the salesperson only sought to sell to customers and would not recruit others

Table 17–2 World direct selling industry, 1995

Country	Sales (US$ million)	Distributors ('000)	Country	Sales (US$ million)	Distributors ('000)
Japan	30,320	2,000	Netherlands	130	34
U.S.	16,550	6,300	Belgium	128	14
Germany	2,630	191	New Zealand	117	68
Mexico	2,000	900	Hong Kong	109	105
Brazil	1,950	850	Chile	108	80
Taiwan	1,770	2,000	Sweden	100	30
U.K.	1,474	450	Singapore	99	35
Korea	1,330	157	Poland	92	165
Italy	1,320	400	Portugal	83	34
France	1,100	250	Norway	80	8
Argentina	1,014	350	Finland	79	8
Australia	1,000	400	Turkey	75	110
Canada	844	600	Philippines	74	420
Spain	691	84	India	60	10
Malaysia	510	350	Hungary	59	116
Thailand	448	250	Uruguay	46	29
South Africa	300	100	Israel	45	8
Switzerland	196	6	Denmark	35	4
Austria	190	6	Slovenia	28	5
Indonesia	160	600	Czech Republic	22	19
Peru	160	100	Greece	22	24
			Ireland	22	6

Sales by major product groups	U.S.	Japan
Personal care products (cosmetics, skin care, etc.)	38.8%	41.0%
Home/family care (cleaners, cookware, etc.)	34.4%	19.1%
Services/miscellaneous/others (long distance calls, etc.)	10.3%	n.a.
Wellness (vitamins, etc.)	9.2%	17.3%
Leisure/educational (books, games, etc.)	7.3%	22.6%

Locus of sales	U.S.	Japan
In the home	59.0%	44.0%
Over the phone	15.9%	n.a.
In a workplace	14.8%	12.0%
At a public event (fair, exhibition, shopping mall, etc.)	4.3%	6.0%
Other locations	6.0%	38.0%

Sales approach (% of sales)	U.S.	Japan
Individual/one-to-one selling	64.9%	n.a.
Party plan/group sales	32.1%	n.a.
Customer placing order directly with firm	1.6%	n.a.
Others	1.4%	n.a.

Demographics of salespeople	U.S.	Japan
Female/male	79%/21%	85%/15%
Part-time/full-time	89%/11%	90%/10%

Sources: World Federation of Direct Selling Associations; US Direct Selling Association; and Japan Direct Selling Association.

to form a distributor network. Avon employed such a method, selling cosmetics through its army of "Avon Lady" representatives.

In contrast, the "person-to-person" method relied upon independent businesspeople acting as distributors for household or nutritional product companies such as Amway, Nu Skin, and Shaklee. The distributors purchased products wholesale from the manufacturer and sold them to end customers, who were typically their friends, families, and acquaintances. The method was also known as "network marketing" or "multilevel marketing," since the independent distributors often sponsored subdistributors, who in turn recruited others to expand their sales network. A distributor's compensation included margins on any direct sales to customers and a percentage of the sales of the entire sales group that s/he sponsored.

In the "party plan" method, the salesperson, frequently called a counselor, consultant, or advisor, demonstrated products to a group of customers in the home of one customer. The hosting customer commonly received a commission, some free gifts, or extra price discounts. The sales associate usually followed up with customers to see if they needed more products, might be interested in hosting their own party, or even would like to represent the company. Some salespersons were employees of the company; others were independent. Tupperware (kitchenware) and Mary Kay (cosmetics) were known for this method.

AMWAY CORPORATION AND AMWAY JAPAN LIMITED

Amway, one of the largest direct selling companies in the world, operating in more than 70 countries and territories in 1996 with worldwide estimated retail sales of US$6.8 billion, triple its sales in 1990. In 1996, Amway ranked fifth among the world's household products companies. Table 17–3 summarizes Amway's global expansion and ranking. The Amway group included Amway Corporation, headquartered in Ada, Michigan, and 44 international affiliates including the two publicly-held companies, Tokyo-based Amway Japan Limited (AJL), which generated US$1.9 billion, and Hong Kong-based Amway Asia Pacific Ltd., which recorded sales of US$717 million in Australia, New Zealand, Malaysia, Thailand, Taiwan, Macao, Hong Kong, and China. Amway's largest markets included North America, Japan, Korea, and Italy. Approximately 70% of Amway's worldwide sales were generated outside North America and 50% from Asian markets.

Amway Corporation was founded in 1959 by Jay van Andel and Richard M. DeVos, with the vision "to be the best business opportunity in the world." Starting with their first product, L.O.C. (Liquid Organic Cleaner) and the

Table 17–3 Amway worldwide expansion and sales ranking, 1996

1962	Canada		Panama	1993	Argentina
1971	Australia		Italy	1994	Czech Republic
1973	U.K.		New Zealand		Turkey
1974	Hong Kong	1986	Spain		Slovakia
1975	Germany	1987	Thailand	1995	Slovenia
1976	Malaysia		Guatemala		Uruguay
1977	France	1990	Mexico		El Salvador
1978	Netherlands	1991	Korea		Honduras
1979	Japan		Hungary		Chile
1980	Switzerland		Brazil		China
1982	Taiwan	1992	Portugal	1996	Costa Rica
1983	Belgium		Indonesia		Greece
1985	Austria		Poland		Columbia

Source: Amway Corporation, *1996 Annual Review.*

Ranking	Company	Headquarters	Sales (US$ billion)
1	Unilever	U.K.	22.5
2	The Procter & Gamble Company	Cincinnati, OH	20.5
3	L'Oreal	France	9.4
4	Colgate-Palmolive Company	New York, NY	7.8
5	**Amway**	**Ada, MI**	**6.8**
6	Kao	Japan	6.4
7	Henckel KGaA	Germany	5.4
8	Shiseido	Japan	4.9
9	S.C. Johnson Wax	Racine, WI	3.8
10	The Estee Lauder Companies	New York, NY	3.2
11	Joh. A. Benckiser GmbH	Germany	3.2
12	Reckitt & Coleman	U.K.	3.1
13	**Avon Products**	**New York, NY**	**2.9**
14	Wella AG	Germany	2.3
15	The Clorox Company	Oakland, CA	2.2
16	Sanofi	France	2.2
17	Revlon, Inc.	New York, NY	2.1
18	Lion	Japan	2.1
19	Beiersdorf AG	Germany	2.0
20	**Pola**	**Japan**	**1.9**
21	Kanebo	Japan	1.9
22	Sara Lee Corporation	Chicago, IL	1.8
23	Bristol-Myers Squibb Corporation	New York, NY	1.7
24	LVMH	France	1.7
25	Alberto-Culver Company	Melrose Park, IL	1.5
26	Ecolab, Inc.	St. Paul, MN	1.5
27	The Dial Corporation	Phoenix, AZ	1.4
28	The Gillette Company	Boston, MA	1.3
29	Johnson & Johnson	New Brunswick, NJ	1.2
30	**Mary Kay, Inc.**	**Dallas, TX**	**1.0**
31	**Nu Skin International**	**Provo, UT**	**1.0**
32	LG Household & Health Care	Korea	0.9
33	Pacific Corporation	Korea	0.9
34	The Limited	Columbus, OH	0.8
35	Natura Cosmetics	Brazil	0.8

Note: Bolded companies employed direct selling methods.

Source: *Household and Personal Products Industry (HAPPI)*, Internet Homepage, 1997.

subsequently introduced laundry detergent, SA8, the cofounders offered a small circle of their friends the opportunity to become independent distributors using their direct sales approach, later known as the Amway Sales and Marketing Plan.

Growth was rapid, and the number of products grew to 150 by 1970. By 1997, distributors marketed 400 Amway brand products in the U.S., ranging from home care, housewares, personal care, to nutrition products. Research, development, and manufacture of products were mainly carried out in Ada, with additional production facilities located in California, China, and South Korea. In the U.S. market, Amway also marketed 6,500 non-Amway brand name items through catalogs as well as a variety of services including voice messaging and long distance phone services. Amway's overseas affiliates mainly imported Amway products from the U.S., but in some cases also sold locally sourced products.

The core of the Amway direct selling method was the large network of independent distributors which expanded to over 2.5 million worldwide in 1997. They were introduced into the Amway business by other distributors, and sold Amway products using the Amway Sales and Marketing Plan. Under the Plan, they earned income from the markup of products, a performance incentive based on a percentage of their sales volume, and other incentives based on the sales volume of those they sponsored.

Amway Corporation was privately held by the DeVos and van Andel families. Major strategic issues were governed by the Policy Board, composed of the co-founders and their eight children. The Board was created in 1992 as an outgrowth of the founders' two-man Policy Committee. The day-to-day affairs of Amway's global operations were directed by Chairman Steve van Andel and President Dick DeVos, the eldest sons of the two founders. The two second-generation leaders shared the office of Chief Executive, leading a Global Senior Management Team in which Stephens of AJL participated.

Throughout its history, Amway had remained closely linked to its founders and their families. Every employee and distributor worldwide participated in a program to learn the company history and "founding families" business philosophy, known as "Founders' Vision, Mission, Fundamentals, and Values" (see Figure 17–1).

Amway Japan Limited (AJL) was founded in 1977 and began operations in 1979 as the exclusive distribution vehicle in Japan for Amway Corporation. AJL was a publicly-traded company on Tokyo's Over-the-Counter (OTC) Exchange since 1991, and became the tenth Japanese company to be listed on the New York Stock Exchange in 1994. The co-founders of Amway Corporation and the

Figure 17–1 Founders' Vision, Mission, Fundamentals, and Values

FOUNDERS' FUNDAMENTALS

Rich DeVos and Jay Van Andel built the Amway business on the following principles, which they and their families believe constitute a sound foundation for a meaningful life.

FREEDOM
Freedom is our natural state and most conducive environment in which to live, work, achieve, and grow. It allows for our belief in God and for the opportunity to build a meaningful, purposeful life. The Amway business recognizes, supports, and expands our freedom, which is both personal and economic. Thus, it is our responsibility to ensure, protect, and sustain our freedom.

FAMILY
The family is our primary social structure, providing love and nurturing, heritage and legacy. The family provides us with a consistent set of values, and a framework for growth and the ability to thrive as individuals. The Amway business respects and supports the family, as evidenced by the Amway Policy Board and the prominence of "family" in Amway distributorships.

HOPE
Hope gives us the power to transform our lives in positive ways. It is a force that allows us to envision dreams, establish goals, and achieve great things. By offering hope, we open windows of possibility for others, and it is why Amway speaks so meaningfully to the needs of people around the world.

REWARD
Reward involves the shared action of giving and receiving. Reward helps us grow, either as the giver or the recipient, and there are many ways we are rewarded. At the most basic, it is to be acknowledged and loved as a person. To be rewarded also means to be recognized for one's commitments, valued for one's contributions, and compensated for one's efforts. Reward helps productivity flourish by providing both closure for one action and impetus for a new action. Reward is integral to the Amway business as we help each other grow as people and as entrepreneurs.

VISION

To be the best business opportunity in the world.

VALUES

These are the essential and enduring standards, not to be compromised, by which we operate the Amway business.

PARTNERSHIP
Amway is built on the concept of partnership, beginning with the partnership between our founders. The partnership that exists among the founding families, distributors, and employees is our most prized possession. We always try to do what is in the long-term best interest of our partners, in a manner which increases trust and confidence. The success of Amway will reward all who have contributed to its success.

INTEGRITY
Integrity is essential to our business success. We do what is right, not just whatever "works." Amway's success is measured not only in economic terms, but by the respect, trust, and credibility we earn.

PERSONAL WORTH
We acknowledge the uniqueness created in each individual. Every person is worthy of respect, and deserves fair treatment and the opportunity to succeed to the fullest extent of his or her potential.

MISSION

Through the partnering of Distributors, Employees, and the Founding Families, and the support of quality products and service, we offer all people the opportunity to achieve their goals through the Amway Sales and Marketing Plan.

ACHIEVEMENT
We are builders and encouragers. We strive for excellence in all we do. Our focus is on continuous improvement, progress, and achievement of individual and group goals. We anticipate change, respond swiftly to it, take action to get the job done, and gain from our experiences. We encourage creativity and innovation.

PERSONAL RESPONSIBILITY
Each individual is responsible and accountable for achieving personal goals, as well as giving 100 percent effort in helping achieve corporate or team goals. By helping people help themselves, we further the potential for individual and shared success. We also have a responsibility to be good citizens in the communities where we live and work.

FREE ENTERPRISE
We are proud advocates of freedom and free enterprise. Human economic advancement is clearly proven to be best achieved in a free market economy.

Source: Company material.

members of their families owned over 80% of AJL's shares. In 1996, AJL was the largest direct selling company in Japan and also the third largest foreign firm in Japan, after IBM Japan and Coca-Cola Company Japan (see Table 17–4).

AMWAY BUSINESS

The Amway business was based on a direct selling system in which distributors promoted and delivered a variety of Amway products to customers on a person-to-person basis. Amway products were exclusively distributed by AJL, not sold at regular retail stores, and there were no media advertisements for promoting particular products.

Amway Product

AJL started its operation with a small product line of household cleaners and detergents. In 1983, three hair care products and three nutritional supplements were added as the first products jointly developed by Amway Corporation and AJL. The cosmetics line, branded Artistry, followed in 1986. The "big ticket items" selling at over ¥150,000 (about US$1,400), such as Amway Queen Cookware and Amway Water Treatment System, had functioned as a major drive for the recent sales expansion.

During the 1990s, the product line expanded rapidly. In 1997, AJL marketed some 140 items in the four product categories including Personal Care (which accounted for 32.4% of FY 1996 sales), Housewares (29.5%), Nutrition (23.8%), and Home Care (10.2%). Table 17–5 illustrates the sales performance of each category from FY 1992 to FY 1996.

New products had played an important role in AJL's growth. New products, defined as products introduced during the preceding two years, accounted for a substantial share of AJL's total sales, ranging from 25% to 40% every year. Recent successful new products included Skin Care products in the line of the Artistry brand cosmetics, Amway Water Treatment System, and Triple X, an all inclusive dietary supplement. These products led their respective product categories in sales and collectively accounted for 47% of sales in 1996 (see Table 17–5).

In 1997, approximately 65% of AJL's entire product line was imported from Amway Corporation, usually with the package design and product formula modified to suit Japanese consumer culture and lifestyles. In addition, AJL also developed some products solely for the Japanese market, in cooperation with other suppliers. Example of such joint product development included a kitchen knife set developed with Henckels of Germany, and the Amway Induction Range and a coffee maker developed with Sharp Corporation.

Table 17–4 Ranking of direct selling companies and foreign firms in Japan

a. Top 20 direct selling companies in Japan by sales, FY 1995 and FY 1996

Ranking	Company	Main business	FY 1996 sales (¥ million)	FY 1995 sales (¥ million)	Growth (%)
1	**Amway Japan Limited**	**Household products**	**212,196**	**177,991**	**19.2**
2	Duskin	Dust-control product, rental	176,668	172,843	2.2
3	Yakult	Beverage	150,569	160,252	20.4
4	Gakushu Kenkyusha	Books, tutorial materials	113,328	117,372	23.4
5	Miki Corporation	Health food	100,662	102,540	21.8
6	Pola Corporation	Cosmetics	100,260	102,200	21.9
7	Brother Sales Ltd.	Sewing machines	96,638	94,917	1.8
8	Taihei	Food	69,175	68,647	0.8
9	Yamahisa	Household products	64,680	60,204	7.4
10	Janome Sewing Machine	Sewing machines	60,339	62,667	23.7
11	Asahi Solar	Household products	55,500	41,446	33.9
12	Charle	Underwear	50,335	50,299	0.1
13	Shinko Sangyo	Household products	49,706	46,810	6.2
14	Noevir	Cosmetics	45,446	43,059	5.5
15	Nu Skin Japan	Cosmetics	41,505	23,000	80.5
16	Chandeal	Underwear	40,000	32,000	25.0
17	Maruhachi Mawata	Bedding products	38,249	35,074	9.1
18	Nippon Menard Cosmetics	Cosmetics	36,000	37,000	22.7
19	Fuji Yakuhin	Medical drugs, cosmetics	35,958	30,854	16.5
20	Herbalife of Japan	Health food	34,000	8,200	314.6

Source: Teikoku Data Bank.

Table 17–4 (cont'd)

b. Top 10 foreign companies in Japan, by income, FY 1996

Ranking	Overall ranking*	Company	FY 1996 declared income (¥ million)	Annual growth (%)
1	24	IBM Japan	117,048	146.1
2	52	Coca-Cola Company Japan	65,778	−0.9
3	65	Amway Japan Limited	57,958	19.9
4	123	Isuzu Motors	33,225	n.a.
5	144	Motorola Japan	28,972	50.6
6	181	American Life Insurance Company	23,600	23.9
7	182	Nestle Japan	23,515	0.8
8	187	McDonald's Japan	22,565	25.4
9	188	Alcan Aluminum Limited	22,562	n.a.
10	190	Banyu Pharmaceutical	22,519	1.6

* Ranking among all firms including Japanese companies.

Source: *Shukan Diamond*, July 1997.

Table 17–5 Net sales by product category and best-selling products

a. Sales by Product Category, FY 1992–FY 1996

Category	Main products	FY 1992	FY 1993	FY 1994	FY 1995	FY 1996	FY 1996 (US$ million)	Sales (%)	CAGR FY 1992–96
				(¥ million)					
Home Care	Laundry, kitchen and household detergents, metal cleaner, air fresheners, car care, etc.	22,300	21,800	21,500	22,400	21,600	198	10.2	–0.8
Housewares	Amway Queen Cookware, Amway Water Treatment System, etc	25,400	26,600	46,500	50,600	62,700	575	29.5	25.3
Nutrition	Nutritional supplements, coffee, pastas, etc.	32,300	33,700	37,000	42,400	50,400	462	23.8	11.8
Personal Care	Cosmetics, toiletry products, fashion jewelry, fashion goods, etc.	38,000	41,900	46,000	55,500	68,600	629	32.3	15.9
Others	Starter kit, sales slips, sales forms, etc.	5,300	6,000	6,600	7,100	8,900	82	4.2	13.8
Total sales		123,300	130,000	157,600	178,000	212,200	1,947	100.0	14.5

Source: Company materials.

b. Top Five Best Sellers, FY 1994–FY 1996

FY 1994 product	Category	FY 1995 product	Category	FY 1996 product	Category
1 Water Treatment System	Houseware	1 Skin Care	Personal Care	1 Skin Care	Personal Care
2 Queen Cookware Set	Houseware	2 Water Treatment System	Houseware	2 Water Treatment System	Houseware
3 Acerola C	Nutrition	3 Queen Cookware Set	Houseware	3 Queen Cookware Set	Houseware
4 Dish Drops (1 liter)	Home Care	4 Triple X	Nutrition	4 Triple X	Nutrition
5 Wheat Germ E	Nutrition	5 A.W.P.	Personal Care	5 Base Make	Personal Care
Top five sales (¥ million)	48,317	Top five sales (¥ million)	81,664	Top five sales (¥ million)	98,934
% total sales	31	% total sales	46	% total sales	47

Source: Company materials.

Amway Distributors

Amway distributors contracted with AJL on an annual basis. AJL's distributor contract renewal rate had stayed at about 70% in the 1990s, much higher than the industry average of 50%. In FY 1996, approximately 1.6 million people in Japan were Amway distributors, 1.1 million of whom renewed and remained as AJL's "core distributors" for FY 1997.

New distributors joined Amway by signing a contract provided by an existing Amway distributor. Through the contracting, distributors were connected to each other in a vertical relationship between the sponsoring distributors, dubbed "up-lines," and the new distributors, called "down-lines." Distributors were rewarded for the sales generated by their down-lines in addition to their own sales. The only up-front investment required to become a distributor was the purchase of a starter kit at ¥8,400 (approximately US$77), which included Amway business manuals. Each distributor remained an entrepreneurial salesperson who could decide how to participate in the Amway business, with the only requirement being observance of the Amway Code of Ethics and Rules of Conduct, shown in Table 17–6.

Amway distributors could buy Amway products at a discount, typically 30% off the suggested retail price. Approximately 70% of the 1.1 million core distributorships were categorized as "consumer-type distributors," who maintained their distributorship solely for this discount privilege. These distributors rarely participated in meetings or events, and contacted the up-line distributors or AJL, except for placing orders. Half the orders were placed through up-lines and half directly with AJL.

Distributors could also earn income from their sales of Amway products to end consumers and/or from the sales of their sponsored down-line distributors. In 1997, about 30% of the AJL's core distributorships were categorized as "business-type distributors," who conducted marketing and sponsoring activities. A business-type distributor's source of income consisted of the following: (1) the markup on products sold, about 30% of the suggested price; and (2) a performance incentive calculated on a sales volume, ranging from 3% to 25% of the sales.

Various non-pecuniary incentives and rewards were also provided for the business-type distributors, who were explicitly ranked according to their sales achievements. Amway offered ten achievement levels worldwide, symbolized by different names and ornamental pins, such as Diamond Direct Distributors and Crown Ambassadors. Each time the distributors moved up the ladder, their success was officially recognized within the distributor community. For example, their photos and sales records were shown on the monthly distributor

Table 17–6 Amway Code of Ethics and Rules of Conduct

Amway Code of Ethics

The basic precept of the Amway business is "Do unto others as I would have them do unto me."

1. The distributors must understand that their behavior has considerable effects not only on their own business but also on other distributors, and must always act responsibly with well-rounded character and sincerity.

2. The distributors must sincerely represent only the truth when introducing Amway products and the Amway business to prospects.

3. The distributors must, among other things, take great care of customers. If complaints concerning the products arise from any customer, the distributors should promptly address such complaints in accordance with Amway's rules and with a modest attitude.

Amway Rules of Conduct

The Rules of Conduct stipulate the rules relating to the Amway business and to the conduct of distributors. The distributors must faithfully observe and act in accordance with the Rules of Conduct in order to develop the Amway business in a sound manner.

The detailed rules are described under the following headings:

Rule 1:   Application for Distributorship
Rule 2:   Team and Renewal of Distributorship
Rule 3:   Sales of Amway Products
Rule 4:   Sponsoring Activities and Sponsor's Responsibility
Rule 5:   Recognition of Distributor Qualification
Rule 6:   Meetings and Other Business Activities
Rule 7:   Use of Amway's Tradename, Trademarks, and Writings
Rule 8:   Distributorship in case of Marriage or Divorce
Rule 9:   Inheritance and Testamentary Gift of Distributorship
Rule 10: Requalification of Distributorship (Rules of Inactivity)
Rule 11: Termination and Expiration of Distributorship
Rule 12: Penalty

Source: Company materials.

magazine, AMAGRAM. Moving up in the hierarchy also created further opportunities to be publicly commended, ranging from an invitation to a party with the founding families to an opportunity to speak at junior distributor conferences or to participate in international conventions, usually held in resorts at places such as Hawaii and Guam.

Distributors who achieved a level higher than Direct Distributors (DDs) grew to 8,500 in FY 1996 from 5,500 in FY 1994. The DD status was given to distributors who had achieved certain volume levels, which typically required sales network of approximately 150 down-line distributors. Their motives varied across DDs. Some wanted supplemental part-time income; others wanted to gain financial independence from their previous jobs; and still others wanted the social recognition and personal contacts that an Amway business could offer. Although their skills and personal investments in operating the business varied from distributor to distributor, annual gross income of an average DD was estimated to be ¥5 million (US$46,000). Some highly successful DDs earned as much as ¥25 million (US$230,000) a year.

Business-type distributors regularly contacted AJL for placing orders and participating in various events. Up-line distributors usually combined several of their down-lines' orders into a single batch order. The regularly organized rallies, conventions, and other events functioned as motivation vehicles. These events typically included successful distributors' speeches, new product explanation, and narration of the Amway mission and values. All the elements helped to create a highly emotional atmosphere, stimulating further endeavor.

Legal and Public Relations Issues

Amway's business, especially its Sales and Marketing Plan, was often described as "multilevel marketing" or "network marketing." Its multiplicative model of sales expansion based on distributors' sponsoring activities had drawn legal and social attention in several major markets including the U.S. and Japan. It had on occasion been confused with the "pyramid scheme," fraudulent money making.

During the 1970s, the U.S. Federal Trade Commission (FTC) investigated a number of sales plans, including Amway's, as a result of consumer and distributor losses at the hands of a number of direct selling businesses, including some which imitated Amway. In 1979, the FTC ruled that Amway's plan was not a questionable practice. The major reasons why the FTC ruled in Amway's favor included: distributors earned income based on the actual sales of their network; distributors could not make money from recruiting per se; distributors were not forced to buy a high volume of inventory; and the company was willing to buy back the unsold products so that the distributor would not suffer any major financial losses.

In Japan, the "Door-to-Door Sales Law" regulated direct sales practices, mail-order businesses, and chain sales transactions. The law was first enacted in 1976 and was revised in 1984, 1988, and 1996. In addition, there existed another law known as the "Law on the Prevention of Endless Chain Schemes," enacted in 1979, which prohibited pyramid schemes. During the 1970s, a number of companies employing "pyramid schemes" caused social problems when they abused their sales systems and Japanese consumers incurred large financial losses. Although AJL's business was legitimate under these Japanese laws, there remained some public confusion between Amway and pyramid schemes. Table 17–7 summarizes various consumer and distributor survey results.

AJL's Role in Amway Business: Helping Distributors to Grow Their Business

AJL provided distributors a wide variety of support to help them to grow their business. Major activities included customer services, distributor relationship, logistics, marketing, and public relations. Figure 17–2 illustrates AJL's organization chart in 1997.

Customer Service and Customer Satisfaction (CS)

CS Department, which belonged to Distributor Relations Division, was primarily responsible for handling incoming calls and claims from Amway distributors and end users. A customer free dial service was initially centralized at Tokyo headquarters but, by the mid-1990s, the task was decentralized into eight regional CS centers. In 1996, these CS centers received approximately 1.2 million incoming calls, about 90% from distributors and 10% from end customers. Many of the consumer-type distributors and end consumers regarded AJL as more competent and trustworthy than their up-line distributors. About 60% of the inquiries were product related and 40% business related.

About 130 operators in Tokyo and an additional 180 in regional centers responded to the calls. About 30% were engaged in analysis of the call data. The data were grouped by product categories or demographics. Monthly purchase data were also added to the database. However, if the contracts were not renewed at the end of each year, all data would be cleared and no follow-up efforts were made. One CS manager explained, "It is very hard to follow up although mail questionnaires are sent to people who have decided to leave Amway. Their sales data are erased after one month."

The concern of the CS Department was how to reduce the number of claims and how to handle the calls more efficiently. Further distributor education could be one way of reducing the number of minor inquiries, which were

Table 17-7   Consumer and distributor survey results

a. Consumers' image toward Amway, 1996

Response	%	Comments
Favorable	33%	Quality products
Neutral	35%	Direct sales, American company
Unfavorable	32%	Pyramid sales, expensive products

b. Consumers' awareness and purchase experience of Amway by age and sex

Age & sex	Aided awareness (%)		Ever purchased (%)	
	1995	1996	1995	1996
Total	57	68	25	28
Male	45	57	11	14
Female	70	79	41	43
Male				
20–29 years old	51	63	10	13
30–39	61	82	19	20
40–49	43	50	10	13
50 and older	22	53	7	9
Female				
20–29 years old	74	83	32	37
30–39	82	93	50	55
40–49	69	66	47	46
50 and older	55	66	34	36

c. Consumers' awareness and purchase experience by direct selling companies

Companies	Aided awareness (%)		Ever purchased (%)	
	1995	1996	1995	1996
Amway	57	68	19	16
Avon	56	57	15	15
Charle	57	60	16	15
Japan Healthy Summit	n.a.	3	13	12
Miki Shoji	35	36	8	8
Nihon Forever Living	n.a.	1	6	6
Noevir	72	76	n.a.	3
Nu Skin	10	13	2	2
Pola	92	92	1	1
Shaklee	6	6	n.a.	0
Tupperware	51	51	n.a.	0
X-1	3	3	0	0

Table 17-7 (cont'd)

d. Distributor satisfaction survey

Satisfied with Amway products?	Current user (%)		Current non-user (%)	
	1995	1996	1995	1996
Satisfied with quality	88	87	64	61
Satisfied with price	69	82	45	41
Overall satisfaction	74	71	42	40

Want to buy Amway products?	Current user (%)	
	1995	1996
Want to buy	55	56
Don't know	23	25
Don't want to buy	22	19

Source: Company materials.

usually covered in the catalogs and other printed materials. One CS manager explained, "The constant top ten questions could effectively be answered by distributors. However, a complicated question could only be handled in more individualized conversation."

In order to address the increasing number of inquiries, an automatic system, called VPS (voice-processing-system), was developed. In 1996, about 400,000 of all incoming calls were answered by VPS. The system was capable of responding to simple questions and also taking orders. Other information technologies were also at the experimental stage of application. AJL established an Amway homepage in 1996 for providing distributors with more information on product and distributor support activities. Another technology at developmental stage was satellite broadcasting, through which visual information and data were broadcast to regional offices and distributor centers. For example, the 1996 National Convention in Tokyo was broadcast to all the regional offices. Inter-departmental communication was also expected to improve dramatically when groupware software such as Lotus Notes were introduced within a year to connect CS to other AJL divisions and departments. However, according to a CS manager, the CS database would remain accessible only to CS managers. CS Department would maintain its primary role to analyze data and customize the results before CS managers report specific issues to other divisions or departments.

Figure 17-2 AJL organization chart, April 1997

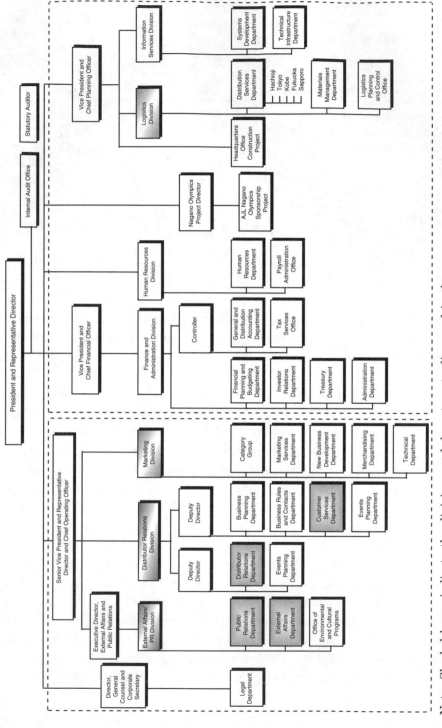

Note: Shaded boxes indicate the divisions and departments discussed in the case.

Source: Company materials.

Distributor Relations (DR)

The DR Department, which was also a part of Distributor Relations Division, served as an interface between AJL and business-type distributors who were above the Direct Distributor level (collectively called DDs). In 1996, there were 106 DR staff and 30 DR coordinators to provide information, counseling, and recognition to 8,500 DDs.

DR staff members organized large-scale meetings for training DDs in the Amway business and its business ethics and philosophy. AJL devised various education programs for distributors at every stage of their advancement to the next ranking. In 1996, about one thousand such meetings were organized throughout Japan.

DR coordinators organized smaller-scale individual meetings, serving a consulting function for each distributor. Coordinators conducted business analysis on issues such as how much sponsoring should be done for the particular distributor group, how much sales should be generated for the specific time frame, and so forth. DR coordinators also tried to provide specific action plans to improve an individual distributor's performance.

The DR Department was also responsible for organizing a number of events such as tours, rallies, and seminars, which totaled several thousand a year ranging from a national convention to small gatherings at the local level. These events served the purpose of providing recognition and motivation to the distributors. The distributors were commended publicly for their sales achievements.

Logistics

The Logistics Division was responsible for quick and accurate order processing, packing, and delivery of Amway products. In FY 1996, AJL handled a daily average of 19,000 orders (4.6 million for the year). Every order on average resulted in six cartons to be shipped. During the 1990s, total quality control programs had shortened the delivery lead time from three to five days to one to two days. In addition to routine picking and packing tasks, AJL's six nationwide Regional Distribution Centers (RDCs) performed the quality control function for the Amway products, including those imported from the U.S. Japanese customers were well-known for their sensitivity to even slight tears of the packaging.

Marketing

The Marketing Division planned and implemented AJL's marketing strategies, new product development, and merchandising. While the DR Division primarily served the upper-level business-type distributors (DDs and above), the Marketing Division focused on lower-level business-type distributors and consumer-type distributors. Its function was to provide distributors useful information about new product introduction, product promotions, sales system improvement, and schedules for seminars and events through periodicals.

More strategic tasks included conducting segmentation analysis and formulating target marketing plans. Until the 1990s, AJL had not collected or utilized distributors' profiles and purchase data extensively. However, AJL had built a distributor database by the mid-1990s and rolled out "Targeted Marketing Initiatives" in 1996. Through segmenting the data, AJL tried to refine its understanding of distributors' buying habits and to provide them more customized information for their particular areas of interests.

The preliminary segmentation study was started in FY 1993 together with a leading consulting company. The immediate finding of the detailed data analysis was that distributors in different demographic groups tended to focus their sales efforts on very different product categories: some specialized in the Nutrition category while others focused on selling beauty and fashion-related products in the Personal Care category, and the like. The preliminary segmentation study distinguished the nine different distributor segments as shown in Table 17–8.

A successful example of "Targeted Marketing Initiatives" included the launch of Club Artistry program in 1996. Distributors received gifts and other rewards such as resort hotel stays based on their purchase volumes of skin care products. After analyzing the segmentation data, AJL offered the Club invitation only to the younger female distributors who had been heavy purchasers of Artistry products. The launch of the Club was an immediate success. Within days, about 250,000 distributors joined the Club, prompting AJL to close membership temporarily.

Another example was the launch of Invictus, a line of high-quality skin care products for men. The launch program for Invictus was tailored to the pre-identified younger male distributor segment. AJL tested a new communication media in the launch process by redesigning the monthly magazine AMAGRAM. Several modified versions of the AMAGRAM were designed so as to target different distributor demographics such as single male, single female, and young families. According to a marketing manager, this new media proved to generate more favorable feedback and sales productivity than other media such as direct mailing of product leaflets.

Table 17–8   AJL's distributor segments, FY 1997 (estimated)

Segment	Description	Sales (%)
DD and above	• Business-type distributors with DD and above achievements	30.7
Below DD and consumer-type distributors	• Other lower-level business-type distributors and consumer-type distributors	69.3
1. GMS (General merchandising) store type)	• Highest productivity • Balanced product categories • Mostly young family with children	15.0
2. PC/NT (Personal Care + Nutrition)	• Second highest productivity • Close to business-type distributors • Relatively young	11.3
3. HC/NT (Home Care + Nutrition)	• Family oriented • Potential in home/family products	2.8
4. HC/PC (Home Care + Personal Care)	• Largest number of distributors • Young family • Potential for children's items	10.1
5. HC (Home Care specialists)	• High disposable income • Conservative lifestyle • Need for reliable information	2.2
6. PC (Personal Care specialists)	• Youngest segment • High potential in personal use items • 94% female, 46% single	7.8
7. NT (Nutrition specialists)	• Belief in only Nutrition products • High potential in items for young male and aging population	2.9
8. Others	• Gift related • Other unsegmented distributors	17.2

Source: Company materials.

Public Relations and External Affairs

There were two departments in the PR&EA Division. The Public Relations Department aimed at improving Amway's image in the mass media and Japanese society, while the External Affairs Department was responsible for establishing good relations with the government and other public organizations.

During the 1980s, several pyramid scheme companies collapsed, causing a series of consumer problems including substantial financial loss and suicides of the program members. The fraudulent nature of the pyramid schemes was explained by the mass media as an example of direct selling. AJL's rapid growth during the 1980s started to gain Japanese consumers' attention and attract suspicion. However, until PR was established as a formal department in 1987, AJL made little effort to publicize the company. Both the positive and negative reputation of Amway had been formed mainly through word-of-mouth.

While the growing network of distributors helped to diffuse some information about Amway, some tended to promote a partial image of Amway, emphasizing the quick and easy money making aspect of the business. As a result of AJL's inaction during the period, Japanese consumers, and media in particular, developed skepticism about Amway. Some distributors' misconduct, such as coercive recruitment of down-line distributors, was occasionally covered by the press.

In 1989, so widespread was skepticism that AJL undertook its first corporate advertising after ten years of operation in Japan. However, some major newspapers and TV networks did not accept AJL's requests for advertisement until the mid-1990s. The *Asahi Shimbun*, the nation's leading newspaper with a readership of about five million, had refused Amway's advertisement, influencing other media to maintain their closed door policies toward AJL. The Newspaper Advertising Review Council (NARC), for example, continued to give an "X" rating to AJL, meaning that acceptance of AJL advertisements depended on the judgment of the leading companies in the industry.

The public listing of AJL on the Tokyo OTC Exchange and New York Stock Exchange boosted its corporate image, and its first advertisement in the *Asahi Shimbun* appeared in December 1996. The first campaign featured the message "Real Amway" with pictures of a baby, a kitchen, and fruit stressing the superior quality of Amway's traditional cleaning products such as L.O.C. and SA8 (see Figure 17–3). The following texts appeared on the advertisements:

"Our business—direct selling—is communication between people."

"The way we do ... it is to develop high-quality products which are directly sold to the people by our distributors."

"Distributors who buy for themselves are the majority ... there are also couples who enjoy running their business to realize their dreams."

Figure 17–3   AJL's corporate advertisement example

Source: Company materials.

AJL's advertisement in the *Asahi Shimbun* helped to convince other newspapers and magazines to change their stances. Amway frequently bought tie-up spaces in major business magazines and wrote comprehensive texts on the company and its business. The tie-up pages were similar in design to regular editorial articles but different in some aspects: Every page was headed or footed with a remark that the contents were provided by the company for promotional purposes. Press conferences and news releases were also used to diffuse corporate information, with particular emphasis on sound financial results. Presentations were often conducted for stock analysts of major security houses and financial media.

As a part of its PR strategy, AJL also actively sponsored various events, including sports, environmental activities, and art performances. In the past, AJL sponsored the Japanese tours of major orchestras such as the American Symphony Orchestra and the New York Philharmonic. Contemporary American art had been exhibited in several major Japanese museums. "Porgy and Bess" and Yo Yo Ma concerts were also sponsored by AJL. Amway had also sponsored the 1998 Winter Olympic Games in Nagano. Environmental issues were also addressed through Amway Nature Center which frequently conducted fund raising campaigns in the form of Amway distributors' purchase of the Center's goods, for example, T-shirts and pencils, for use at Amway meetings and conferences.

CHALLENGES AND OPPORTUNITIES IN 1997

1997 Decline

AJL's disappointing first half results in FY 1997 reflected downturns in all four product categories. Category by category analysis had revealed, however, that approximately 70% of the total sales decline was due to a fall in sales of housewares. Housewares suffered far more than the other three, with sales down 25.9% to ¥24.9 billion, led by declines in sales of Amway Queen Cookware and the Amway Water Treatment System. Home Care category sales showed the second biggest decline, down 10.5% to ¥9.7 billion. This partly reflected AJL's strategic decision during the second quarter of FY 1996 to reduce the price of certain Home Care products for competitive reasons. Sales in Personal Care, the largest category, declined 5.2% to ¥33.3 billion, reflecting a decline in sales of Artistry cosmetics and skincare. Sales in the Nutrition category meanwhile dipped 1.8%, as a decline in sales of Triple X was almost offset by a rise in sales of new products such as herbal food supplements.

Challenge for the Future

Stephens was concerned with the following issues: (1) fluctuating distributor motivation; (2) growing dissatisfaction with Amway products; (3) increasing difficulty in controlling distributor network; and (4) changing market environment.

Fluctuating distributor motivation. Historically, AJL had relied greatly on several top distributors. The top five distributors and their downlines were believed to account for a substantial portion of AJL's total sales in 1996. In 1996, the company's top distributor, Kaoru Nakajima, pursued the Double Crown Ambassador DD, the highest recognition level of Amway distributors which nobody had ever achieved worldwide. Working with his down-line distributors, Nakajima tried to achieve a particular sales goal within a certain time frame so that he and his entire down-line would be invited to his commendation ceremony at New York's Radio City Music Hall. After successfully accomplishing the goal and enjoying the trip to New York City, the group was said to slow down their sales effort in 1997.

The reduced level of distributor motivation was reflected in a decrease in the rate at which existing distributors were sponsoring new distributors. This in turn had a negative impact on sales, particularly, of expensive durable items such as the Amway Queen Cookware and the Amway Water Treatment System, because these were the items that new distributors typically bought when they first joined Amway to get large savings.

Growing dissatisfaction with Amway products. AJL had put an emphasis on introducing high-quality products. Stephens explained, "(AJL) tended to believe in the high-quality image of our products. However, the price-value tradeoff of our products is becoming a great concern among distributors and leaders as indicated in the distributor satisfaction survey." (See Table 17–7 for the distributor satisfaction survey results.)

Distributors' dissatisfaction with AJL's high prices was also prompted by an increasing awareness of the gap between AJL's and other foreign Amway affiliates' pricing, due to easy access to international pricing information through the Internet. Distributors also became sensitive with the relatively higher price of Amway products as competitors such as Nu Skin and Shaklee had introduced similar personal care or nutrition products at lower prices.

In addition, AJL had to cope with a rise of approximately 21% in product procurement prices from Amway Corporation effective September 1, 1996. The price adjustment was mainly a result of continuing depreciation of the yen against the U.S. dollar since 1995. While finance executives saw AJL in a very strong position to absorb the increased import prices, it had caused a deterioration in its operating margins (see Table 17–1).

Increasing difficulty in controlling distributor network. With an ever-expanding distributor network, it had become more difficult to control some distributors' misconduct, such as coercive recruiting of or selling to their down-lines. They were the primary reason for the increasing number of AJL-related inquiries to various consumer organizations, as a result of which the image of AJL had remained unfavorable (see Table 17–9).

Table 17–9 Product inquiries and complaints

a. Inquiries from distributors to AJL, FY 1990–FY 1996

FY	Amway business	Amway product	Total
1990	278,741	18,869	297,610
1991	328,614	29,874	358,488
1992	305,408	32,297	337,705
1993	354,510	41,006	395,516
1994	517,511	219,751	737,262
1995	630,337	240,971	871,308
1996	729,009	269,587	998,596

Note: FY 1990–FY 1993 figures include only Distributor Inquiry Center. FY 1994–FY 1996 figures include both Distributor and Customer Inquiry Centers.
Source: Company materials.

b. Number of inquiries and complaints to consumer center, 1993–95

	1993	1994	1995
Total	233,999	273,931	342,073
Multilevel marketing	5,341	6,658	9,738
Amway	1,013	1,419	1,520
AJL's share in multilevel marketing (%)	19.0	21.3	15.6
AJL's rank in multilevel marketing	1st	1st	1st

Note: Figures were based on the number of calls. No distinction was made between inquiries and complaints.
Source: Japan Consumer Information Center.

Stephens asserted that AJL's extraordinary success in the Japanese market had made the company a target for some journalists, although he also acknowledged that:

We cannot hope to solve the problem if we lay all the blame on hostile journalism. AJL must do whatever we can to prevent social problems arising from distributors by establishing healthy systems and continuing to provide extensive education programs.

However, as a senior executive of DR Division stated, "Distributors are not Amway employees after all. They joined Amway because they wanted to operate their business as entrepreneurs who are free from any formal control. I am not sure how much Amway should and can control the individual distributor's conduct. In addition, eliminating these activities was virtually impossible with the existing AJL's distributor support staffing. It has become more difficult to adequately communicate with and effectively deliver education programs to an increasing number of distributors."

Recently, increasing Internet postings had exacerbated this problem. With major web browser software, the keyword "amway" would bring Internet users to a mixed list of official Amway websites as well as the skeptics' homepages which attacked Amway. Respecting free speech rights, AJL did not take any explicit counter measures to address such negative postings on the Internet.

Changing market environment. Stephens also saw both threats and opportunities in ongoing change in the Japanese market environment. Table 17–10 shows some selected demographic and macroeconomic figures.

"Japan is experiencing a period of great political, economic, and social changes. Remarkable changes in people's values and judgment criteria are arising from a variety of aspects: low birth rates, aging of the population, changes in lifestyles, shifts in purchasing behavior, rising share of female labor force, changes in employment patterns, and growing interest in healthy lifestyles ...

The distribution sector saw a definite change in consumer behavior, and as a result, new styles of sales such as nonstore sales and consumer participation-type direct selling have come to draw significant public interest. Door-to-door sales still account for only about 2% of total retail sales, but are growing while the retail industry as a whole is not.

Current trends of increasing corporate restructuring and diminishing life-time employment system indicate continuing oversupply in the labor market. Many women want a business career but do not want, or cannot get, traditional salaried employment opportunities. Many older people will have a need or want for additional income after retirement from regular employment. There still exists a potential for new distributors to be served by AJL.

Table 17–10   Selected demographic and macroeconomic data

a. Unemployment rate, 1993–96

	1993	1994	1995	1996
Male	2.4%	2.8%	3.1%	3.3%
Female	2.6%	3.0%	3.2%	3.3%

Source: Management and Coordination Agency.

b. Demographic change in Japan, 1980–2000

	1980	1990	2000
Elderly people (over 65)	9.1%	12.0%	17.0%
Household with elderly people	22.7%	26.4%	—
Birth rate (per 100 persons)	1.36	1.00	1.11
Number of children/females	1.75	1.54	1.60

Source: Japan Direct Selling Association.

c. Retail and direct selling industry, 1994–96

	1994	1995	1996	CAGR
Total retail industry (¥ billion)	144,823	144,677	145,920	0.4%
Direct selling industry (¥ billion)	3,130	3,230	3,340	3.3%
Direct selling/total retail	2.2%	2.2%	2.3%	

Source: Japan Direct Selling Association.

Price slashing became common among the distribution industry as discount and convenience stores began to spread quickly. This trend became even more pronounced as a result of the increasing corporate overseas outsourcing and government deregulation.

Price slashing has now taken root in Japanese society as a long-term trend. People's worship of high-priced, high-quality products seems now a thing of the past."

In 1997, AJL also had to cope with the effects of revisions to Japan's Door-to-Door Sales Law which came into force in November 1996. Varying interpretations of the revised law had created uncertainties among distributors about whether they were in full compliance. Lack of clarification of the new law's implications to Amway business significantly inhibited their sales efforts. The incomplete understanding of the revision especially impacted negatively on sales of expensive durable products over ¥20,000, to which the new law was believed to be applied.

Strategic Options: Penetration or Productivity

While trying to address these issues, Stephens also emphasized the importance of leveraging the core strength AJL had long accumulated:

> ... as we face these challenges, we are going to keep our focus firmly fixed on preserving and strengthening the full power of our most important single asset, which is our partnership with our distributors.... A strong, positive relationship exists between AJL and distributors, based on the Amway Sales and Marketing Plan. Continued increases in the number of renewed distributors have succeeded in establishing the most extensive network of its kind in Japan. Furthermore, the renewal rate of distributors has been over 70% for the past years. This is a very high level relative to other direct selling companies not only in Japan, but also worldwide. Distributors' strong loyalty to AJL and our products further strengthens the distributor network.

Although Stephens was confident that the ongoing "Targeted Marketing Initiatives" would contribute to further growth of the company, he pondered how to maximize the potential AJL possessed with its distributor network. Since AJL's direct day-to-day contacts with distributors ranged from order processing, delivery, inquiry calls, to field meetings, AJL had unlimited opportunities to cultivate value from each of such direct interaction with distributors.

Stephens saw three levers for boosting AJL's sales in the future: (1) sponsoring, (2) retention, and (3) productivity.

First, "sponsoring" was to increase the number of distributors further. The growing number of distributors had been the engine of AJL's success to date. Given the potential of direct selling in the ongoing change of the Japanese market, sticking to the proven strategy seemed still to be the way to go.

Second, AJL could generate sales further by improving "retention." Although AJL's distributor renewal rate of 70% was already much higher than the industry average, this figure also meant that half million distributors out of 1.6 million left Amway in 1996. Focusing on this large group of non-renewing people could provide room for sales improvement. Little effort had been made to follow up those leaving, as a senior DR executive said: "You cannot bother somebody who is upset with something by asking questions about it."

Finally, AJL could also pursue future growth by increasing "productivity," that is, sales per distributor. As a marketing manager emphasized, the network of 1.1 million core distributors with 70% renewal rate might have been "already huge enough." Concentrating on tapping sales productivity of the established distributor network could be the key to further growth.

Having analyzed the complex situation AJL faced in 1997, Stephens devised a little diagram to straighten up his strategic thinking. As shown in Figure 17–4, it had two dimensions: one was labeled "penetration" strategy; the other was "productivity." Stephens saw three strategic options for AJL: (1) penetration growth, (2) productivity growth, or (3) both. Stephens needed to come up with a clear strategic direction based on a thorough analysis of both pros and cons of each strategic choice.

STAYING THE COURSE

Stephens declared his determination to develop AJL's strategy for delivering growth both in the near term and the longer term as follows.

> First, we are taking specific steps to cope with the special challenges we face in FY 1997 and to rebuild growth in the second half of the year.
>
> Second, we are simultaneously continuing to make the investments we need to make to further reinforce the core strengths of our business for the future. These core strengths are our direct selling system, which is the bedrock of our business; our partnership with our more than one million core distributorships, which is our most important single asset; and our broad and diverse product line-up targeted at the Japanese market and meaningfully differentiated from competing products.
>
> And third, we are continuing aggressively to exploit all available means to leverage our core strengths to the maximum possible extent.
>
> We are not taking any easy options for short-term gain. We are continuing to make the investments we need to make to secure our future.
>
> We are staying the course.

Figure 17–4 Strategic options

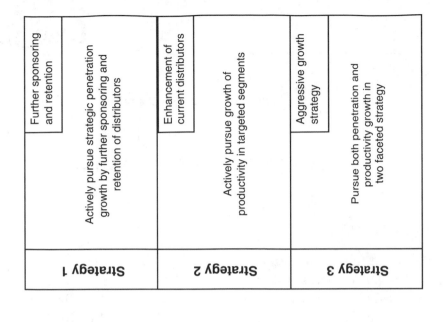

Strategy 1	Further sponsoring and retention	Actively pursue strategic penetration growth by further sponsoring and retention of distributors
Strategy 2	Enhancement of current distributors	Actively pursue growth of productivity in targeted segments
Strategy 3	Aggressive growth strategy	Pursue both penetration and productivity growth in two faceted strategy

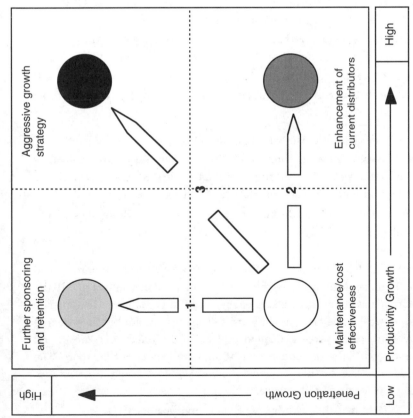

Source: Company materials.

Primula Parkroyal Hotel: Positioning and Managing for Turnaround

Primula Parkroyal Kuala Terengganu (PPR), a hotel on the northeast coast of Peninsular Malaysia, was going through a strategic change exercise, after a new management took over in 1996. In June 1997, Rodney Hawker, PPR's general manager, was working on the 1998 marketing plan for the hotel. As input into this marketing plan, he needed to decide what target customer segments to focus on, and how the hotel should be positioned to compete effectively with other hotels in Kuala Terengganu as well as with hotels elsewhere. The Asian financial crisis was beginning to unfold with dropping arrival numbers. The situation was further aggravated by the intense

This case was prepared by Aliah Hanim M. Salleh and Jochen Wirtz as the basis for class discussion rather than to illustrate either effective or ineffective handling of an administrative situation. Primula Parkroyal has approved this case for publication and the disclosure of the hotel's name.

Aliah Hanim M. Salleh and Jochen Wirtz are Associate Professors at the Universiti Kebangsaan Malaysia and the National University of Singapore, respectively.

The authors gratefully acknowledge Rosiati Ramli, Zakiah M. Mohamed, and Zaleha Abd. Shukor, who together with the main author, conducted all the interviews for this case and drafted an earlier version in Bahasa Melayu. The data collection was funded by a Universiti Kebangsaan Malaysia research grant for a case research project, headed by Dr. Nik Rahimah Nik Yacob, and the write-up was partially funded by the National University of Singapore. The authors would also like to thank Siew Lien Sim for the research assistance provided with the writing of this case.

competition from the many new resorts and hotels that had mushroomed in the state during the past four years. Furthermore, PPR's service levels and staff morale needed to be improved. Against this backdrop, Hawker had the objective of reinstating the hotel as the premier quality hotel in Kuala Terengganu.

MANAGEMENT TAKEOVER AND REFURBISHMENT

The hotel is located on a beach off the South China Sea in Kuala Terengganu, the capital of Terengganu, a northeastern state of Peninsular Malaysia. Terengganu is an oil-rich state with a population of about 850,000, comprising mostly Malay Muslims. PPR was one of the first four-star hotels to be built along the eastern coast of Peninsular Malaysia in the 1980s. As of 1997, PPR had a total equity of RM1.6 million,[1] and total assets of RM3.1 million. However, under the ownership of a state government agency, it incurred millions of ringgit in accumulated losses. The state government aimed at making the hotel profitable as well as at improving the state's tourism infrastructure.

In March 1996, Southern Pacific Hotel Corporation (SPHC) took over PPR's management. SPHC had won a "12-plus five-year contract" to manage the hotel, after successfully outbidding several other large hotel management operating companies from the Asia-Pacific region. Hawker asserted that a unique factor favoring SPHC's interest in PPR was Terengganu's unspoilt beaches, waterfalls, lakes, and untapped potential as an attractive tourist destination in Malaysia. This was seen relative to Penang and Langkawi, both of which were expected to reach saturation as tourist destinations. PPR was also the only hotel in Kuala Terengganu which enjoyed both a resort image (with its beach location) as well as a business image (being so close to town).

In managing the strategic change of the hotel, SPHC focused on the following key priorities: upgrading the quality of the hotel's physical facilities, remarketing and positioning the hotel, training staff, and changing the work culture. Permodalan Terengganu Berhad (PTB), the Terengganu state government's investment arm, became the owner just before the management takeover. Under the terms of a profit-sharing agreement between PTB and SPHC, PTB financed an initial RM11 million to be used by SPHC for physically upgrading and refurbishing the hotel. In recognition of the need to motivate its staff to deliver quality services, rebuilding a new staff canteen was the first

---

[1] RM = Ringgit, Malaysia's currency. The exchange rate was US$1 = RM3.8 at the end of 1998.

renovation work done. Other works included renovating 72 guestrooms in the double-story wing with access to the beach, and 150 deluxe rooms in the hotel's 11-story tower block. A new tea lounge was opened, adjoining the reception area and coffeehouse facing the beach. The entire swimming pool area was also relandscaped, befitting a world-class business resort hotel.

COMPETITION

Table 18–1 shows PPR's main competitors in the vicinity of Kuala Terengganu, and Table 18–2 presents their market shares. The tables show PPR's strong position in terms of positioning (i.e., excellent city and beach front location), quality of service, and facilities (the only four-star hotel). This strong positioning also translated into a 41.7% share revenue of the total market in Terengganu.

MARKET SEGMENTS

PPR targeted the following segments: commercial guests (30.1% of room nights), individual travelers (29%), government (17.1%), conference (13.7%), and tour groups and sports (15.2%) (Table 18–3). Table 18–4 shows the food and beverage (F&B) revenues by segment for May 1997. An internal report indicated that PPR enjoyed a lion's share of the commercial market in Terengganu, giving it a higher average yield than its competitors. This report forecast a 16.8% growth in this segment for 1998.

Guests of SPHC hotels in the Asia-Pacific region could obtain special discounts and other privileges through the Pacific Privilege Card membership program. This Pacific Privilege market was PPR's largest supporter in its private (individual travelers) segment. While this program was low-yielding, it produced volume. The private segment was anticipated to become the hotel's biggest segment over time. PPR planned to increase its share with a "low-season promotion drive" and intensive customer database marketing.

The conference market was primarily supported by the Malaysian government. This segment was projected to increase by 30%. A sales executive based in Kuala Lumpur and Kuala Terengganu was in charge of promoting PPR as a conference destination focusing on the government segment. To cushion reductions in government spending due to the Asian crisis, promotions were mostly targeted at senior departmental officers, who were less restricted in their hotel choice.

Table 18–1 Comparative characteristics of Primula Parkroyal versus competitors

	Sutra Beach Resort	Seri Malaysia	Permai Park Inn	Primula Parkroyal
Location	38 km from town center; beach front	In town	5 km from town center	3 km from town center, beach front
No. of rooms	120 chalets/rooms	145 rooms	131 rooms	150 deluxe rooms, 27 suites & 72 guest/family rooms
Affiliation/owner	SPR Management	Gateway Inn Management	Kemayan Resorts	SPHC/ Permodalan Terengganu Bhd.
Market segment mix	Private, corporate, government, groups	Groups, private, government	Corporate, government, travel agents/ tour groups	Corporate, government, travel agents/ tour groups
Service positioning	3.5-star deluxe resort, medium priced	2.5-star "value-for-money" budget hotel chain	3-star town hotel, "bed & breakfast" image	4-star beach cum business resort
1997 occupancy rate (est.)	40%	55%	50%	49%
Rooms sold: 1997 (est.)	16,790	30,113	23,908	44,805
Average room rate 1997 (est.)	RM125.00	RM80.00	RM92.00	RM137.91
F&B outlets/ conference facilities	• *Merang* restaurant • *R-U Tapai* lounge • Conference hall (350 pax) • Karaoke lounge	• *Sekayu* café (a-la carte except Friday & Sunday • Lunch	• Café-in-the-Park • Conference hall (250 pax)	• *Bayu* lounge • Cascade Grill • *Rhusila* coffeehouse • 1 ballroom • 7 meeting rooms
Physical facilities & services	• Business center • Tennis court • Souvenir shop • Swimming pool	• Business center • Swimming pool • Shopping arcade • Gymnasium • Tea/coffee-making facilities in rooms	• Retail stores	• Business center • *Koko Nut Klub* • Swimming pool • Health center • Tennis & volleyball • Laundry & ironing • Tea/coffee-making facilities in rooms

Sources: Primula Parkroyal internal reports and authors' observations during site visits.

Table 18-2 Market share among competing hotels/resorts, March–December 1996

Hotel	No. of rooms	Capacity (room nights/year)	Rooms sold	Occupancy rate (%)	Average room rate	Room revenue (RM)	Actual share Rooms (%)	Revenue (%)
Primula Parkroyal	247	75,582	34,453	46	130.04	4,480,268	34.2	41.7
P. Park Inn	131	40,086	18,039	45	87.81	1,478,369	17.9	13.8
Seri Malaysia	150	45,900	24,327	53	68.33	1,743,781	24.1	16.2
Sutra Beach Resort	100	30,600	10,710	35	116.00	1,242,360	10.6	11.5
Tanjung Jara Beach	115	35,190	13,372	38	135.00	1,805,220	13.2	16.8
Total	743	227,358	100,901	44.38	106.54	10,749,998	100.0	100.0

Source: Primula Parkroyal 1997 business plan.

Table 18–3 Summary of room revenues for January–December 1997 (planned)

	1997 budget
No. of rooms available	90,885
No. of rooms occupied	44,805
Occupancy (%)	49.3
Average tariff (RM)	137.91

Customer segment	Rooms occupied		Average tariff (RM)	Room revenue (RM)
Commercial				
Corporate	8,590	19.2%	153.10	1,315,100
Corporate conference	2,270	5.1%	126.09	286,220
Others	2,615	5.8%	148.51	388,350
Subtotal	13,475	30.1%	147.66	1,989,670
Private				
Rack	255	0.6%	227.88	58,110
F.I.T.'s	9,555	21.3%	149.15	1,425,100
Other discounts	3,165	7.1%	125.42	396,950
Subtotal	12,975	29.0%	144.91	1,880,160
Others				
Govt. – F.I.T.'s govt.	7,190	16.0%	135.69	975,600
Conference	3,860	8.6%	137.05	529,000
Sports	1,625	3.6%	117.05	190,200
Embassies & others	515	1.1%	185.00	17,575
Tour groups	5,165	11.6%	115.57	596,900
Subtotal	18,355	40.9%	130.05	2,309,275
Total	44,805	100.0%	137.91	6,179,105

Note: F.I.T. stands for frequent independent travelers.
Source: Primula Parkroyal internal management report.

ROOM SALES

According to Cik[2] Norshidah, one of three sales personnel working in the Marketing and Sales Department, sales were conducted by SPHC's Kuala Lumpur head office, which collectively promoted the Parkroyal chain. Room sales were the responsibility of the Rooms Division, headed by Clive Murray.

---

[2] Cik is the Malay equivalent of the title Miss.

Table 18-4 Room and F&B revenues by segment for May 1997

Customer segment	No. of clients	Room-nights	Percentage	Room revenue (RM)	F&B revenue (RM)
Commercial					
Corporate	658	489	11.00	77,074.71	13,357.82
Corporate conferences	970	488	10.59	50,938.76	5,847.02
Subtotal	1,628	977	21.59	128,013.47	19,204.84
Private					
Private individuals	1,268	729	15.83	107,169.69	27,796.45
Other discounts	907	593	12.87	41,342.11	13,030.61
Subtotal	2,175	1,322	28.7	148,511.8	40,827.06
Government-related					
Govt. conferences	1,176	625	13.57	62,940.12	17,587.53
Govt. groups	16	8	0.17	1,080.00	0.00
Government	650	437	9.49	65,298.63	9,087.21
Embassies	9	5	0.11	790.00	584.33
Subtotal	1,851	1,075	23.34	130,108.75	27,259.07
Others					
Tour groups	807	359	7.79	36,284.53	2,830.95
Tour agents	195	110	2.39	13,593.87	6,679.12
Sports	1,192	521	11.31	44,159.38	17,661.43
Internal use	228	165	3.58	0.00	734.26
Daily use	0	0	0	1,165.00	288.53
Long-term use	101	73	1.58	8,863.60	1,471.52
Employee offers	7	5	0.11	0.00	97.12
Subtotal	2,530	1,233	26.76	104,066.38	29,762.93
Total	8,184	4,607	100.00	510,703.40	118,063.90

Source: Primula Parkroyal internal management report.

As rooms can be sold at steep discounts, SPHC used both occupancy rates and average room rates to measure the yield of its rooms. Adlin Masood headed the Public Relations Department, which planned and executed cultural, sports and social events and the hotel's public relations activities throughout the year. Adlin's work supported not only room sales, but also helped bring in the crowds for the F&B outlets as well as service the conference and tour group guests.

Out of RM11.7 million in total operating revenue planned for 1997, RM6.18 million were expected to come from room revenues (Table 18–3). Seventy-seven per cent of room revenues would be net contribution, which compared to an actual net contribution of 70% for the January to May 1997 period. A breakdown of room and F&B revenues, for each customer segment for May 1997 is provided in Table 18–4.

PPR's beach location fronting the South China Sea made it vulnerable to seasonal fluctuations in demand. During peak holiday periods of June, July, and August, the occupancy rate was expected to reach 62%–63% (with average room rates of RM143). In contrast, demand could go as low as 31%–34% (with average room rates dipping to RM125) in the off-peak monsoon season of December, January, and February (Table 18–5). During the peak season, the occupancy rate could reach 100% on weekends and public holidays.

According to Hawker, PPR's occupancy rate had not increased very much since the management takeover. Table 18–5 compares the 1997 planned occupancy and average room rates against 1996 figures. The sales and marketing expenses for January to May 1997 are shown in Table 18–6.

HOTEL OPERATIONS

PPR's business was organized into two main departments, which operated as separate profit centers: Rooms Division, which included the front office operation, and Food and Beverage Department.

Rooms Division and Front Office Operations

The hotel's front office operations were managed by Encik[3] Radi. This department was responsible for managing room reservations and setting room prices, as well as for arranging every activity their guests engaged in throughout their stay. The department received room reservations either directly from individual guests, tour operators, or event sponsors. Other functions of the department included managing the reception counter and room services, porter and concierge services, and recreational support. The Rooms

---

[3] Encik is the Malay equivalent of the title Mr.

Table 18–5 Monthly average room occupancy rates, January–December 1997 (planned)

| | 1997 | | 1996 | |
| | Occupancy | Average rate | Occupancy | Average rate |
Month	(%)	(RM)	(%)	(RM)
January	31.3	125.22	n.a.	n.a.
February	33.8	125.44	n.a.	n.a.
March	43.0	135.85	26.9	134.47
April	51.8	135.70	43.6	123.42
May	58.6	140.87	46.6	142.23
June	63.0	142.66	47.9	127.04
July	62.3	142.97	49.8	122.29
August	60.2	143.47	56.4	128.03
September	58.3	143.08	31.6	131.25
October	56.5	141.52	51.6	132.20
November	38.3	134.93	47.4	131.36
December	36.4	125.07	35.3	126.64

Source: Primula Parkroyal internal management report.

Table 18–6 Sales and marketing expenses (cost center)

Sales and marketing expenses	Jan–May 1997 (RM)
Salaries & related expenses	70,216
Staff benefits	11,987
Promotional expenses	50,261
Other expenses	92,027
Total	224,491

Source: Primula Parkroyal internal management report.

Division's income statement is shown in Table 18–7, with the main cost item being staffing (21.1% of gross room revenue).

Radi was fully aware that personal interaction with his front office staff was the key driver of guest satisfaction. He strongly believed that his staff needed to be developed and trained to increase service levels, especially as no formal front office training had been conducted since 1992 under the previous

Table 18–7   Income statement for Rooms Division (Jan to May 1997)

Room P&L	RM	Revenue (%)
Room income	1,827,807	100.0
Staff expenses		
Salaries & wages	212,565	11.6
Overtime	9,129	0.5
Employee benefits	165,216	9.0
Subtotal	386,910	21.1
Other expenses	161,242	8.9
Total expenses	548,152	30.0
Net contribution	1,279,655	70.0

Source: Primula Parkroyal management internal report.

management. Radi felt that job rotation, for example, between reception and reservation personnel, as well as cross-training (in other Malaysian Parkroyal hotels), could be carried out to develop skills and enrich jobs. Also, there was a need to motivate and retain his front office staff, to contain the high turnover rates in the department. He noted that staff motivation was low, and turnover and absenteeism were high. Radi had 35 front office staff at the end of 1997.

Another key area of concern was more effective management of room capacity. In particular, the occupancy rate had to be increased throughout the year, but especially so during the low season (the monsoon months). Also, since 83% of the hotel's room nights were currently occupied by Malaysians, Radi believed that more efforts should be made to attract Malaysian tour groups, rather than tying up high promotional expenses in attempting to bring in more foreign tourists.

Food and Beverage Department

Harry Thaliwal, a Malaysian with a Swiss qualification in hotel management, was appointed the F&B manager. Previously, he was attached to Parkroyal properties in Sydney and Kuala Lumpur. With 75 staff reporting to him, Thaliwal was responsible for the kitchen, four F&B outlets, conference facilities, and banquet services.

In general, F&B outlets contribute about 30%–35% of a hotel's operating revenue. In the past, lunch buffets were offered only when the occupancy rate was considered high enough to sustain it. Thaliwal saw the potential to attract locals and other tourists not residing at PPR to the hotel for the breakfast, lunch, tea, and dinner/supper buffets. With the introduction of a new set of menus for the buffets, PPR managed to attract a significant number of non-hotel guests, which pushed its F&B's contribution to over 50% of total operating revenue. Of the F&B clientele, 60% were non-hotel guests. Some 20% of breakfast buffets, 40% of lunch and dinner buffets, and 90% of the "hi-tea" and supper buffets were consumed by non-hotel guests. The department's P&L statement is presented in Table 18–8.

Table 18–8 Profit and loss statement for Food & Beverage Department (Jan to May 1997)

	RM
Revenues	1,809,670
Less cost of goods sold	(679,517)
Gross revenues	1,130,153
Expenses	
Total wages	460,314
Employee benefits	230,285
Other expenses	193,293
Total expenses	883,892
Net profit (loss)	246,261

Source: Primula Parkroyal internal report.

As banquet services accounted for about 50% of F&B revenue, more effective planning and marketing of the hotel's banquet services, F&B outlets, and conference rooms were planned. To facilitate more efficient booking of banquets, Thaliwal introduced a system for managing event scheduling, and ruled that all requests on quotations were to be answered within 24 hours of a client's inquiry. Also, on-the-job training of the chefs and their cross-training with Kuala Lumpur's Parkroyal were conducted. This was necessary, as the menus had not been altered for the past 12 years before the management change.

Thaliwal also observed that a significant number of waiters and waitresses were reluctant to interact with foreign guests, mostly due to a lack of confidence in their English language proficiency. Also, an adequate sense of urgency to respond to guests' requests had to be instilled. Improving service standards had become a key challenge. Viewing customer complaints seriously, Thaliwal introduced lucky draws to encourage guests to fill in comment cards as a continuous system of soliciting customer feedback. Analyses of customer comments were made regularly to keep service standards in line with the guests' expectations.

Thaliwal implemented many changes, which targeted at upgrading service quality. They included restructuring of job positions by promoting several staff to supervisory levels, enriching jobs by deploying staff for both room service and reception duty, and cutting manpower and energy costs by merging the coffeehouse with bar operations. A karaoke lounge located at the hotel rooftop was replaced by a banquet room, as the former was under-utilized and was incurring losses.

Thaliwal also implemented a proper inventory and storage system for hotel supplies (including food and beverage items). The system was designed to ensure sufficient supplies, particularly of fresh produce, to meet the daily needs of all F&B outlets, and to avoid excessive overstocking of certain room supplies. The use of kitchen supplies was tightly controlled by himself and the chief chef. The ordering process for new hotel supplies also needed a revamp. Thaliwal terminated all contracts requiring tenders for food and room supplies. Also, tenders for hotel supplies were now open every six months, in contrast to the previous system of once in three months. The suppliers of food and room materials were evaluated on price, quality, and services rendered.

Upon PTB's request, which ran all its operations based on Islamic principles, income from alcoholic beverages was treated separately from income from other hotel operations. As Table 18–9 illustrates, the special accounting treatment was made to "cleanse" the hotel revenues (Islamic principles prohibit profiteering from the sale of liquor). Therefore, PTB's share of the profit generated from alcoholic beverages was not absorbed into PTB's group profits. Instead, this portion was given on a yearly basis to Baitulmal, a public welfare agency.

HUMAN RESOURCE DEVELOPMENT

SPHC appointed Encik Rohaizad as manager of the Human Resources Department (HRD) three months after the management takeover. He found himself in the following situation: low levels of staff training, absence of staff exposure to other hotels' operations and services, and high absenteeism (Table 18–10). Rohaizad saw changing the work culture as his top priority, with the need to instill service orientation and a high level of work ethics across the ranks. Staff size was trimmed from 350 to 315 after the management takeover.

To upgrade skills and advance career development, training programs were conducted at three levels. At the preliminary stage, training targeted at

Table 18–9   Profit from liquor sales (May 1997)

	RM
Revenue	
Liquor sales	21,295
Less cost (33.27% of liquor sold)	(7,085)
Gross revenue	14,210
Expenses	
Management/license fees (2% of liquor revenue)	426
Portion of F&B expenses relating to liquor sales	
(4.6% of F&B expenses)	9,071
Total expenses	(9,497)
Liquor profit (GP)	4,713
less incentive fee (6% of GP)	(283)
Transfer to liquor profit reserve	4,430

Source: Primula Parkroyal internal report.

Table 18–10   Human resource statistics (July–December 1996)

	Jul	Aug	Sep	Oct	Nov	Dec
Employee strength	292	304	305	301	305	308
Days absent	65	66	128	78	88	125
Employee turnover	24	17	6	13	9	3
New employees	17	30	8	7	12	6

Source: Primula Parkroyal's HRD records.

instilling knowledge of the hotel's service offerings, service orientation, and higher work ethics was conducted. The next level focused on customer complaint handling and related skills training. Lastly, for middle management and above, specific courses, such as management accounting and industrial relations, were conducted. Despite the training, changing work culture and attitude remained imperative. For instance, during the last rainy season, among the ten employees that were sent to the Penang Parkroyal Hotel for cross-training, four returned before the training was completed.

Besides problems with employees' work attitude, Rohaizad also found difficulty in recruiting hotel personnel in the predominantly Muslim state. This was possibly due to the Muslim religious code that prohibits Muslims from serving or consuming alcoholic drinks. Rohaizad believed that the people's low level of awareness of the various employment benefits, such as free meals and transport to and from work, also contributed to their reluctance to work in the hotel/catering industry. Rohaizad conducted career lectures and participated in exhibitions aimed at Terengganu youths and secondary school graduates, to source for new personnel.

Hawker pondered the formulation of the 1998 business plan. The worsening economic crisis made it crucial for Hawker to decide on the positioning of the hotel, to identify PPR's primary target segments, as well as to develop strategies that could smoothen the severe seasonal demand fluctuations. Also, work attitudes and culture of staff had to be critically assessed should a high-quality positioning be aspired.

The following websites may provide useful information for the case analysis:

- Primula Parkroyal—http://www.sphc.com.au/hotels/parkroyl/pprimula. html
- Asia Travel Hotels and Resorts Reservation Service—http://asiatravel.com/malaysia/primula/index.html
- Introduction to Terengganu—http://terengganu.gov.my/intro.htm
- Information on Tourism in MalayyTa—http://tourism.gov.my/
- Malaysia Home Page— http://www.visitmalaysia.com
- SPHC Home Page—http://www.sphc.com.au

IPC

"Local commitment, global connections. Local expertise, global development." So reads the title page of the *1996 Annual Report* of Singapore's IPC Corporation. Following a turbulent 1996, which saw sales drop by 48%, this was the company's answer, its new vision for the coming year. No sign of turmoil, no inkling of self-doubt; only a resilient attitude, the sign of a firm ready to take a "bold step forward."

It was a similar "bold step" by Chief Executive Officer Patrick Ngiam that brought the company into existence in 1976. Leaving the safe and familiar path of his family's seafood business, Ngiam decided to put his engineering background to good use, launching himself into the personal computer business. Together with his brother, Patrick formed a firm in the early 1980s to make a product that was at best, a luxury with an uncertain albeit potentially bright future.

With the bold entry into an emerging industry, the Ngiam brothers propelled their brainchild IPC into a massive growth spurt over the next 15 years. By 1995, IPC had sales of $1.5 billion from the four corners of the globe and had rapidly grown to become one of the leading Asian firms in the PC industry. A sudden slide starting in 1996, however, reduced IPC to barely half of its former self, leading it to refocus its activities on the Asia-Pacific region. This reorientation caused the firm to lose 48% of its sales, its stock price to plummet, and total assets to shrink from over $1 billion to less than $400 million in 1997. Would IPC be able to face the challenges of this drastic downsizing to achieve its target of becoming "an internationally

---

This case was prepared by Ishtiaq Mahmood and Kulwant Singh, Assistant Professor and Associate Professor at the National University of Singapore, respectively. This case was prepared for teaching purposes only.

All denominations are in Singapore dollars unless otherwise stated.

Copyright © 1999 by Ishtiaq Mahmood and Kulwant Singh.

renowned developer of total solutions in the information technology (IT) arena?"

THE PC INDUSTRY

IPC's entry into the PC market coincided with major growth in the global PC industry. The innocuous introduction of the first personal computer in the mid-1970s quickly led to the emergence of one of the largest, technologically dynamic, economically important, and rapidly growing industries in history (Table 19–1 provides summary information on the PC industry).

In addition to rapid growth, the PC industry was characterized by a high degree of fragmentation, intense levels of competition, and high rates of technological change. Even the five largest players, such as Compaq, Dell, IBM, Gateway, and HP had only between 8% and 12% of the world market share. On the other hand, there was an emerging trend for greater concentration, with the top five to ten firms capturing an increasing share of industry sales. As the PC increasingly approached commodity status, a high degree of standardization of the PC architecture and of most components, widely available components, and easy assembly allowed relatively easy entry into the market. Many firms with limited technological abilities continued to enter the market and compete in local markets on the basis of price, only to fail when technological change occurred. Product cycles were very short, often less than one year, and prices declined rapidly and steeply within weeks of introduction. It was an accepted norm in the industry that as much as 80% of the total industry profits made on a particular product would be earned within the first four to six months of its introduction. Firms that missed this window had few opportunities to make profits and would be stranded with costly and rapidly depreciating inventories.

As even the large, market-leading firms utilized similar components in their products, customers increasingly resisted premiums for brand names. Instead, only products that led the market in performance, in incorporating the latest hardware improvements, or in being customized to specific needs were able to command temporary price premiums.

Most basic research in the industry was conducted by major component manufacturers and leading PC firms. Most prominent among these component manufacturers were Intel and Microsoft, who each held monopoly positions in their markets. Most software and hardware advances in the PC industry were driven by new product introductions by these two firms. Industry observers noticed that most firms in the PC industry served as suppliers or distributors

Table 19–1 PC industry statistics

a. Worldwide shipment trends

Year	Units (millions)	% growth	Year	Units (millions)	% growth
1990	23.99	—	1996	67.53	21.3
1991	25.98	8.3	1997	80.39	19
1992	30.46	17.2	1998	94.61	17.7
1993	37.12	21.9	1999	109.7	15.9
1994	44.18	19	2000	124.1	13.2
1995	55.67	26			

Source: IDC Asia Pacific.

b. Asia-Pacific PC unit shipments

	1Q 1997 ('000)	1Q 1998 ('000)	Change (%)
Indonesia	107	21	−80
Thailand	83	42	−50
South Korea	464	281	−39
Malaysia	97	64	−34
Philippines	55	39	−30
The rest of Asia Pacific	102	74	−28
Singapore	85	82	−3
Taiwan	146	152	4
Hong Kong	90	99	11
Australia	399	3,990	15
New Zealand	45	54	18
China	634	806	27
India	153	200	31
Total	2,400	2,305	−4

Source: Computerworld, June 1998.

c. Singapore PC shipments by vendor

Vendor	1Q 1997		1Q 1998	
	Units	Share (%)	Units	Share (%)
HP	10,559	12.4	18,726	22.7
Compaq	11,692	13.7	13,720	16.6
Acer	11,510	13.5	8,650	10.5
IBM	6,690	7.9	6,245	7.6
Dell	2,758	3.2	5,957	7.2
Toshiba	6,800	8.0	3,560	4.3
Others	35,081	41.2	25,634	31.1
Total	85,098	100	82,492	100

Source: Computerworld, July 1998.

for Intel or Microsoft, since these two firms often earned most of the value added in the industry. As products became increasingly uniform and prices declined rapidly, PC manufacturers increasingly focused their research efforts on manufacturing, assembly, and logistics improvements, as these directly affected speed and cost of bringing products to the market.

The rapid changes in the industry and the differing skills required for different parts of the PC industry encouraged firms to focus on particular activities within the industry and further encouraged specialization within the industry.[1] Outsourcing of products or of product assembly and distribution functions was common among PC manufacturers, who focused on key value-added activities such as designing of the product or final assembly. Efforts to reduce costs drove some PC firms to outsource the manufacturing process to specialist contract manufacturers. Others resorted to what became a major trend in the U.S. market in the 1990s, mail-order sales. Direct sellers such as Dell and Gateway enjoyed significant cost and flexibility advantages from bypassing retailers and other middlemen to deal directly with customers. Direct contact with consumers also allowed these firms to better understand and predict consumer needs, an important advantage in a rapidly changing industry. To minimize costs, the few firms that established retail outlets or that attempted to integrate vertically quickly abandoned these efforts.

In general, the highly competitive nature of the industry, short product cycles, the lack of brand loyalty, and the difficulty of product differentiation led many firms to converge on a model of efficient manufacture of well-designed, made-to-order PCs based on the latest components, which were delivered directly to consumers. Other factors important for success appeared to be efficient logistics, a high-quality, efficient, and flexible manufacturing process, minimizing fixed investments in product specific assets and inventories, and the ability to react rapidly to change in markets, products, consumer needs, and technologies.

---

[1] The competencies required for developing PC application software and PC hardware differed significantly, and few firms achieved significant success in both sets of activities. Similarly, the manufacture of components such as hard disk drives or memory chips required very different skills, and only a handful of large firms manufactured many components. Firms had generally moved from being vertically integrated to focusing on narrow and defined segments of the industry. This trend was often referred to as the deconstruction of the computer industry.

IPC CORPORATION

History

IPC Corporation was started by brothers Patrick and Benjamin Ngiam in 1976 under the name Essex Electric. Instead of carrying on the family business of seafood sales, the two brothers with engineering degrees chose the uncertain path of the computer manufacturing industry. With financial help from the Local Enterprise Finance Scheme of the Singapore government's Economic Development Board, Essex Electric got off the ground.

In 1981, still as Essex Electric, the Ngiam brothers began to manufacture printed circuit boards for multinational corporations. Realizing that their deal with the multinationals could not be permanent or secure, the Ngiam brothers decided that their company needed to manufacture, distribute, and market its personal computers under its own brand name.

This led to the incorporation of Essex Electric Pte Ltd in 1985 with $50,000 in paid-up capital, to purchase machines and equipment for the manufacture of PCs. However, the newly-named company did not immediately attack the domestic computer market or even other regional markets of Southeast Asia. Instead, Essex Electric introduced its first personal computer, an IBM PC/XT clone, into the European markets. As Chairman and CEO Patrick Ngiam explained, "Not everyone can go abroad. In our case, our market was elsewhere and not in Singapore, so we started with overseas markets." Sweden and the Netherlands were among its first targets with distributors being appointed in 1986. Despite being new to the industry, Patrick Ngiam chose to participate in a leading industry trade show, CEBIT, in Germany in 1987. IPC's products attracted the attention of a small French electronics distributor, Systec. Being new to the PC business, Systec decided to sell IPC's products by mail order, a novel approach for France. The lower delivery costs and Systec's reliability allowed sales to increase rapidly, inadvertently establishing IPC as an early success in the mail-order business.

GROWTH

Using the brand name IPC, an acronym for "Integrated Processors and Communication," Essex Electric's first PC product caught on quickly in Europe. It achieved particular success in France where Systec spearheaded a marketing push that saw the company's market share surge from zero to 2.9% over the next six years. IPC achieved consistently high ratings in France and, in 1993, had briefly the largest sales of any PC manufacturer in the country, ahead even of leading brands such as Dell and HP.[2] By 1993, IPC France accounted for just over a quarter of IPC sales worldwide, counting among its customers giant French companies like Thomson and Matra, and a thriving countrywide mail-order delivery network. IPC's German subsidiary, IPC Europa, was set up in 1990 and achieved a fair degree of success, establishing IPC as a strong niche brand. Competitive pricing combined with excellent after-sales service from Systec inspired high levels of customer satisfaction. This was the key to IPC's immediate success in the face of such storied rivals as IBM, Compaq, Bull, and Olivetti. It was a strategy that was to stand the company in good stead all over Europe, including Spain, Germany, the Netherlands, and the U.K., all of which saw rapid establishment of IPC's presence in the late 1980s and early 1990s.

By 1991, the Ngiam brothers' venture into the computer world started to lengthen its stride. On the wings of a five-year tax-free holiday granted by the Singapore government, by virtue of its "pioneer" status, IPC took to the expansion trail. First, they capitalized on the recognition that the IPC brand name had won them by renaming the company IPC Corporation (Pte) Ltd. They then made capacity expansion a priority by constructing a handsome $12 million IPC building to house their production and headquarters. Importantly, the company also invested in the construction of an R&D department to house their innovative talent. Next, the company also expanded into network hardware manufacturing for the first time, producing in late 1991, a line of RISC multiprocessor server computers, large office systems that connected other nearby terminals and allowed multiple uses simultaneously. Another product, the IPC point-of-sale (POS) terminal, a computer terminal used at a cash register in a retail store or supermarket, caught on rapidly in Europe. Finally, to ensure full control over its successful European efforts, Patrick Ngiam expanded his control over the distribution of IPC products by taking over its distributors and establishing a series of retail outlets. In France, for example, IPC purchased Systec and renamed it IPC France. Consistent with its retail distribution strategy, IPC de-emphasized its mail-order business.

By end-1991, such international giants as IBM had signed contracts with IPC for the manufacturing of personal computers, a clear testament to the quality and efficiency with which IPC was producing PCs. IPC also became a moderately successful brand at home, occupying a niche as a relatively high-end local brand in Singapore. Recognition for IPC's achievements was widespread, with major awards including the Singapore KPMG High-tech

---

[2] 01 Informatique, October 9, 1989.

Entrepreneur Award for Patrick Ngiam in 1990, the 1991 Enterprise Award in Singapore, which recognized "innovation, financial performance, productivity, management, and contribution to the community" and, most significantly, the Singapore Businessman of the Year for Patrick Ngiam in 1993.

RAPID EXPANSION

IPC's expansion continued at full steam in 1992, only this time the trail led to Australia, the U.S., and East Asia and to investments in overseas production.[3] IPC used its German subsidiary IPC Europa to expand its market share in Western Europe. Plans were also under way to undertake a joint venture with Mexican firm Plus Sistemas to manufacture for the North American market, which was about to be liberalized by the North American Free Trade Agreement (NAFTA). The rationale for these expansions was that proximity to the given market would increase profit margins. As Ngiam noted, "The time to market is very important ... the first to get the product on the market makes the money."

The practice of penetration into foreign PC markets by acquiring or incorporating a subsidiary in the country started in 1993, as IPC acquired Texas-based Austin Computer Systems for about $2 million (while taking on a debt of $15 million and paying other fees of $5 million) to enter the U.S. market. Benjamin Ngiam explained the acquisition:

> In order to be a key player in the international marketplace, where I believe IPC belongs, we have to continue to embark on our aggressive marketing strategy. Austin has a good name, and it is a direct sales, mail-order company. We bought the company solely for the name with the purpose of establishing ourselves in the U.S., and also to use it as a media to place our products on the U.S. market and using this office to generate global advertising and promotional strategies. American PC magazines are read all over the world and the name will spin off from there.[4]

Austin was a small mail-order computer firm (1992 sales: $85 million) with its own manufacturing plant and product line. Despite some visibility in the competitive U.S. market, Austin was not profitable and was struggling against

---

[3] IPC's timing was somewhat fortuitous. In 1993, the Singapore government launched a major new initiative to regionalize the economy. This involved the encouragement and the provision of support for Singapore firms to expand abroad.

[4] *Global Computer Express*, October 1993.

larger and more successful PC firms. One of the major aims IPC established was to have Austin spearhead its efforts in the multimedia segment, with the target of becoming the "No. 3 in the U.S. within the next 12 months."[5]

IPC also established subsidiaries in Australia and Korea, to access these important Asian markets. Further proposed acquisitions in China and India made it imperative that the company raised more capital. Thus in April of 1993 IPC offered 250 million shares for public subscription, representing 25% of the company's stock, in an initial flotation that raised $148 million for the company. Over the next year, IPC became a heavily traded stock and was added to the main index of the Singapore Stock Exchange, and to the prominent Morgan Stanley Capital Index.

The rapidly growing PC market had attracted thousands of entrants from around the world and competition was severe. In order to differentiate itself from the rest and gain a market niche, the company began to emphasize its brand name, target new customers, expand its retail channel, broaden its product range, and build up its R&D capabilities. IPC placed particular emphasis in Asia on the small business segment. By the end of 1994, within three years of opening its first store, IPC had 120 retail outlets in Southeast Asia and Europe, and owned all but a handful of them. The firm planned to have 300 outlets in existing and new markets by 1997. With the exception of IPC France and its Austin subsidiary, IPC sold its products through its own distribution channels and retail outlets. Patrick Ngiam explained that the expansion into retail outlets was an essential element of IPC's strategy:

> IPC's not only just thinking about technology or production, but also has equal emphasis on channel and distribution management. This has differentiated us tremendously. We're a company that has a totally integrated business model, rather than just emphasizing one area and not investing in the others.[6]

To deal with the competitiveness of the electronic and computer sectors, IPC placed high priority on research and development:

> To complement its product development policy, IPC introduced a proactive five-year R&D program to maintain its long-term competitiveness and product vibrancy. The company commits over $3 million to R&D in each fiscal year and harnesses a ready pool of international talent through its

---

[5] *The Business Times*, November 22, 1999.

[6] *Electronics Business Asia*, July 1995.

network of direct R&D centers in China, Singapore, Taiwan, the U.K., and the U.S.[7]

IPC entered into three R&D contracts in 1994. The first of these was with AT&T to develop sound and telephony products (such as answering machines) for PCs. The second was with Information Technology Institute for the development of a series of multimedia products, including video and CD-ROM storage. The third was with Singapore Digital Media Consortium, a forum for local companies to collaborate on R&D ideas.

In addition to a stream of PC products, IPC was successful in introducing additional related products, such as its POS terminals[8] and a line of RISC multiprocessor server computers, which the company chose to market under the IPC name. Its initial success in the POS markets in Europe and Korea encouraged it to aggressively target this market, setting the objective of becoming the world's leading vendor of these systems within three years.[9]

Elsewhere on the globe, the company turned its attention to finding a joint-venture partner for its entry into manufacturing in China. IPC acquired a 51% stake in a consumer electronics manufacturer, Zhuhai Torita Group in May 1994. While the new acquisition was initially expected to act as a cheap manufacturing center for low-end components, the long-term objective was to use Torita as a beachhead into the potentially vast and lucrative Chinese market. IPC also acquired and operated 24 wholesale and distribution hubs as part of this deal. These stores would form the base for a rapid expansion of IPC's electronics and electrical outlets, of which 100 would be set up throughout China by 1997. The drive into China was further reinforced in 1995 with a $6 million joint venture that would provide value-added data processing services such as credit/debit card transactions, electronic data interchange, and database and network communications in China.

By the mid-1990s, IPC products were available in at least 66 countries in North and South America, Western and Central Europe, the Middle East and Asia Pacific. It had core businesses in four main areas: IT products, IT services, consumer electronics, and distribution, as described in Table 19–2.

While IPC was quickly expanding geographically, its R&D investment allowed it to tap into new markets in terms of product innovation too. In 1995,

---

[7] *1996 Annual Report.*

[8] With typical ambition, IPC announced in September 1995 that it aimed to become the world's leading POS vendor within the next three years.

[9] *The Straits Times*, September 7, 1995.

Table 19–2   IPC's product and service range (mid-1990s)

IT products

- *General purpose computers (GPC)*
  Entry-level desktop PCs to servers created for the home and corporations.
- *Consumer computing products (CCP)*
  Mobile computing products such as notebooks, sub-notebooks, and personal interactive organizers.
- *Application specific products (ASP)*
  Point-of-sale terminals to cater to all major segments of the retail automation industry.
- *Multimedia products*
  A range of audio and video boards, simultaneous communication add-on peripheral boards, and complete multimedia upgrade kits for PC multimedia applications.
- *Peripherals*
  Computer-related peripherals such as PCMCIA cards and motherboards.

IT services

- *Interactive media services*
  IT-based services such as video-on-demand, karaoke-on-demand and home shopping.
- *Commercial value-added network (VAN) operators*
  Operation of value-added networks such as electronic funds transfer authorization, electronic data interchange, and Internet in China.

Consumer electronics

- Consumer electronics (under IPC's subsidiary Torita in Zhuhai, China) comprises television sets, tape recorders, video cameras, fax machines, cordless phones, pagers, video CDs, and karaoke players.

Distribution

- Distribution of computer parts and peripherals to OEMs and system assemblers in Asia Pacific (via the Corex Group).

it established a new vision: to be a "total IT solutions provider." This meant furnishing all of the client's computer needs, from basic PC manufacturing to video-on-demand service to value-added network services like electronic mail. Patrick Ngiam described the new direction as follows: "Our overall strategy is to be seen as an IT conglomerate—a hardware, peripherals, and service provider." As Ngiam noted, "The only way to create a bigger market share is through new products."[10] To further these interests, IPC took the substantive steps of acquiring shares in two Israeli firms, Optibase ($3.33 million for a 10% stake) and VCON ($1.8 million for a 26% stake). These firms supplied it with the necessary digital compression and videoconferencing technology to introduce videoconferencing products. This technology also allowed IPC to introduce Singapore's first video and karaoke-on-demand systems in a condominium. IPC also achieved some success in other areas. IPC Interactive, its U.S. subsidiary, developed what was billed as the world's first global hotel television network to offer premium services to guests throughout the world via in-room television sets. IPC Interactive also developed an interactive in-room credit card authorization system, an in-room TV gaming lottery system for the cruise line industry, and interactive in-room shopping for a hotel. The company also built a big commerce network system in China and ventured into the manufacture of flat panel displays and batteries for its line of notebook PCs.

IPC's acquisition of the two Israeli companies encouraged it to pursue four joint ventures worth $28 million with Groupe Bull. As part of these ventures, IPC acquired a 3.7% stake in the government-linked French technology giant, with whom it hoped to develop smart card technology. When Groupe Bull fell into serious difficulties, IPC emerged as the leading potential buyer of its much larger partner (1994 sales exceeded US$5 billion). However, the marriage was short lived. In May 1996, after Bull sold its Zenith computer division to IPC's rival Packard Bell, the Singapore firm opted to liquidate its stake at a substantial profit.

As IPC celebrated the tenth anniversary of its incorporation, it looked to be in a healthy position. IPC was touted as a Singapore success story and was a leader in several markets in Asia. It was the second largest PC supplier in Singapore, and the third largest in the corporate PC market. It had a 23% market share of the Korean POS market. Its products were available around the world. It was expanding aggressively into a wide variety of IT areas, and appeared to be well on its way to becoming a total IT solutions provider. Overall revenue grew by 135%, and those from the Asia-Pacific region, by 140%. IPC appeared to be poised for growth and success.

CRISIS

By 1995, IPC had grown into a mid-sized firm with sales of $1.5 billion (see Tables 19–3 and 19–4 for a summary of IPC's financial performance). Yet this was not enough for the ambitious firm. It established sales targets of $2.5

---

[10] *The Business Times*, March 20, 1995.

Table 19–3 IPC's financial highlights

($ million)	1988	1989	1990	1991	1992	1993	1994	1995	1996	1997
Turnover	30.2	54.9	67.7	183.6	274.5	579.5	1,359.4	1,542.4	801.9	410.4
Operating profit	0.3	0.9	6.4	14.4	42.6	52.5	81.8	54.3	13.7	3.7
Tax	(0.7)	(0.6)	(0.02)	(0.11)	(1.04)	(0.9)	(3.6)	(0.8)	(0.3)	(0.17)
Extraordinary items	—	—	—	(0.9)	—	2.0	—	—	(37.4)	(113.3)
Profit after tax, extraordinary & other items	0.2	0.9	6.4	13.0	41.5	53.6	72.3	52.7	(23.9)	(109.4)
Fixed assets	0.2	0.9	1.2	3.5	11.1	18.9	147.5	193.3	49.6	46.5
Current assets	6.6	9.6	15.7	25.6	99.9	268.7	485.3	625.9	426.7	269.7
Current liabilities	6.5	9.1	9.1	13.9	53.1	117.8	359.9	504.7	238.9	246.2
Long-term liabilities	0.1	0.2	0.2	0.2	0.1	0.2	97.8	105.4	118.7	84.1
Net tangible assets	0.3	1.2	8.0	27.5	49.4	—	—	—	—	—
Gross dividends	—	—	—	(0.5)	(20)	(10)	(12)	(8)	(5.2)	—

Table 19–4 Sales by region

Region	1992	1993	1994	1995	1996	1997
America	8.79	145.82	408.69	443.70	59.64	42.18
Europe	121.88	213.83	386.27	329.99	127.51	102.93
Asia Pacific	136.15	202.58	491.28	720.60	608.81	260.10
Others*	7.69	17.22	73.16	48.08	5.94	5.21
Total	274.51	579.45	1,359.40	1,542.35	801.90	410.43

* Others include the Middle East and Africa.

billion for 1998 and $5 billion for 2005.[11] The announcement of these targets marked what proved to be IPC's high point for several years.

IPC's problems with Austin, its 1993 acquisition, heralded a change in its fortunes. IPC promised that Austin's retail operations would turn around within months of the acquisition. In fact, Austin did well in 1994, returning a profit of $2.9 million against a loss of about $8 million in the year before IPC's acquisition. Unexpectedly, however, IPC aborted its retail operations in the U.S. in 1996 at the cost of US$100 million in lost annual revenues. Patrick Ngiam explained the decision with typical bluntness:

> It's a question of whether we continue to carry the dead baby or let it go ... Why continue with an effort that may not eventually lead us to the top tier of players? We want to concentrate in Asia Pacific, and that itself will require a lot of cash.[12]

IPC's Australian operations also suffered a severe blow in 1996. Though it had previously been selling its products through other distributors, IPC decided to establish its own distribution network. IPC had aggressively expanded its retail outlet chain in Australia in 1994, establishing 54 within a 13-month period.[13] However, many of these stores were not profitable and 28 stores were closed in July 1995. Even the remaining stores proved to be costly and unprofitable, so that IPC sold its remaining 25 stores in January 1996 for $15 million. This was done to reduce costs and to increase access through retailers and mass merchandisers, which IPC indicated it would no longer view as competitors. However, the sudden closure of the stores resulted in some consumers not receiving warranted technical assistance, which harmed IPC's reputation in the country.

These closures and limited returns from its diversification into multimedia and value-added network services were reflected in poor 1996 results. First-half profits in 1996 fell an astounding 85%, killing any further plans to finance diversification ventures. Poor second-half sales caused the annual sales tally to be 48% lower than the year before, when IPC sales had crossed the $1 billion mark.

---

[11] *The Straits Times*, February 13, 1995.

[12] *The Business Times*, February 8, 1996.

[13] IPC had expanded its retail outlets rapidly by arranging an unusual reward structure with its Australian CEO: his compensation would increase greatly with the number of retail stores opened.

Worse news arrived shortly thereafter. In January 1997, IPC Corporation (Korea) Ltd. defaulted on $923,400 worth of promissory notes. After its Korean CEO absconded, investigations revealed massive mismanagement and fraud. This ultimately resulted in total losses of $45.5 million, causing IPC to suffer a net loss for 1996.[14] IPC subsequently closed down its operations in Korea, one of Asia's most promising PC markets. To raise additional capital, IPC disposed of the Hong Kong and Netherland operations, and reduced its holdings in Corex Technology from 100% to 18.87%, and in Essex Electric from 100% to 19%.

It also became clear in 1997 that IPC's major product launch of the last few years, a highly integrated computer for the home, had failed. Launched with an expensive advertising campaign, the MY.G.E.N.I.E computer was intended to drive IPC's entire home PC product line for several years. This PC served multiple functions, receiving television and radio broadcasts, and serving as a telephone answering machine and a games machine in addition to performing standard PC tasks. Though sales were expected to reach between 200,000 and 300,000 units a year in Singapore alone, actual sales probably did not exceed 25% of targets. Observers pointed to a poor concept, poor product quality, and unresponsive service as the reasons for the failure of this line.

These difficulties, increasing competition, and rapid technological change in the PC industry encouraged IPC to search for more stable industries where it could more effectively exploit its investments in technology. As a result, IPC chose to expand into telecommunications, entering the mobile telecommunications industry in 1996 by acquiring a 37% stake in German firm Hagenuk Telecom (1996 sales $400 million). This venture introduced a new GSM (Global System for Mobile Communications) handphone and other products such as DECT (Digital Enhanced Cordless Telephone) and ISDN (Integrated Digital Services Network). Already significant in 1996, the mobile telecommunications industry was rapidly growing into one of the largest industries in the world. Competition was severe, and the industry was fragmented (see Table 19–5). IPC, however, felt it had selected the right partner. Describing Hagenuk as a leading telecommunications giant and a

---

[14] Considerable doubt arose among analysts when this loss was first announced, as $13.7 million of the loss was not accounted for. In addition, IPC also announced that sales for the second half of the year had fallen to less than 10% of the sales for the first half. When executives were queried on these figures, IPC was not able to provide any explanation because Patrick Ngiam was away in Germany (*The Straits Times*, March 11, 1997).

Table 19–5 Mobile phone market shares (1997)[16]

	Worldwide (%)	Europe (%)
Motorola	24.5	21.3
Nokia	19.9	23.1
Ericsson	15.5	21.4
Matsushita	7.3	5.0
NEC	5.0	2.3
Siemens	3.6	8.0
Samsung	3.0	0
Mitsubishi	3.0	1.7
Sony	2.6	0.8
Alcatel	2.5	5.5
Philips-Lucent*	2.0	4.5
Northern Telecom	0.6	1.6
Others	10.5	4.8

* In 1998 Philips-Lucent abandoned their less than two-year-old joint venture because of their inability to capture market share and heavy losses. Write-offs for the firm exceeded $500 million.

thoroughbred, IPC indicated that telecommunications and computers would now represent its two core businesses.[15] Patrick Ngiam indicated that IPC's future would largely be in telecommunications, which would account for between 60% and 80% of profits:

> We have decided to be a niche player in the computer world, and we are putting major efforts in telecommunications ... With its strong core technology in GSM, DECT, and ISDN, we strongly believe Hagenuk will be a major telecom player, with 10% to 20% global market share, in the next two to three years.[17]

Despite the range of products and technologies it had ventured into, Ngiam dismissed suggestions that IPC had diversified too broadly and indicated that IPC had a new vision:

---

[15] *1996 Annual Report.*

[16] Data from Dataquest, cited in *The Asian Wall Street Journal*, October 21, 1998.

[17] *The Business Times*, March 18, 1997.

It's only a matter of transformation of the company as dictated by the changes in competition, the environment, and so forth.[18] It is not a question of diversification, but a question of participation in the digital business area because it will become a digital world.[19] We want to provide a total market solution integrating computers, communications, and services on demand.[20]

During the first half of 1997, the new enterprise seemed to be successful, and Hagenuk raked in a profit of $9.2 million. Encouraged, IPC took a 49% stake in a US$10 million venture with state-owned Guangzhou Post & Telecommunication Equipment in China to produce 800,000 handphones a year for the China market. As part of the joint venture, Guangzhou Post signed a deal to buy US$50 million worth of handphones from IPC over 12 months.

However, in August 1997, just as IPC planned to double its stake in Hagenuk, problems arose. Unexpectedly, Hagenuk filed for court protection against its creditors. Much to IPC's surprise, Hagenuk was discovered to be in severe financial difficulties. The poor reputation of Hagenuk's management prevented it from obtaining crucial debt clearances from German banks, forcing the beleaguered firm to file for bankruptcy protection. Hagenuk's actions would eventually cost IPC a $79.6 million charge against its 1998 profits.

In August 1997, IPC was hit with lawsuits for $32 million in Korea and the U.S. These were in addition to an ongoing case in Australia and three others in Singapore. Most of these suits were for "breached component orders," the failure to supply promised computer parts. Though such cases were not uncommon in the PC industry, the large number of suits against IPC caused some concern among analysts and customers.

THE POSITION IN MID-1998

In the aftermath of these events, IPC took several steps, including selling its loss-making American subsidiary, IPC Interactive, in exchange for a 2% interest in SeaChange International, a Nasdaq listed television technology company. IPC also forged an alliance with Boundless Technologies, a U.S.-

---

[18] *The Business Times*, March 18, 1997.

[19] *The Straits Times*, February 13, 1995.

[20] *Asia Computer Weekly*, March 27–April 2, 1995.

based computer vendor catering to thin-base clientele.[21] Under this agreement Boundless would market IPC's computers in Asia, Australasia, India, and the Middle East. The marketing drive would spearhead IPC's newly unveiled, low-cost network computers or thin clients, built to target large institutions who would save significantly by switching from conventional PCs. For its own line of PCs, IPC introduced another bold change: from the fully integrated MY.G.E.N.I.E. machines, IPC would now concentrate on bare bones machines which would only contain minimal components, allowing retailers to tailor machines to users' specifications. IPC hoped that this flexibility would boost demand significantly. Another major change to its strategy saw IPC entering the real estate market in China in 1998 through a swap of its ownership in the Torita Group, which gave it a land bank in Zhuhai worth $113 million.

Inevitably, however, IPC's most pressing problem was how to turn its performance around to recover its former position in the IT sector. This task was made more complicated by the renewed interest in the Asia-Pacific markets shown by computing giants IBM, Hewlett Packard, and Compaq, and mail-order firms Dell and Gateway. Though the PC market in Asia Pacific approached ten million units in 1997, IPC did not figure among the top ten brands and had much less than 1% of the market. Competition was expected to increase greatly, lower prices, encourage further migration to the major PC brands, and place even greater pressure on small indigenous manufacturers in the region. To top it all, the major economic crisis that struck Southeast and East Asia in mid-1997 devastated PC sales, causing demand to fall drastically.

In mid-1998, IPC was undertaking a major re-evaluation of its strategy. The titles of its 1996 and 1997 annual reports indicated the importance and direction of this effort: "Change & Challenge" and "The Fundamental Approach." The question commonly asked was, "What could IPC do to reposition itself, to replicate the heady growth it enjoyed in its earlier days?"

---

[21] Thin clients or network computers were essentially PCs which had certain components removed or reduced in capabilities, to reduce costs. These PCs were intended to be networked, with more processing being undertaken at the central server level. Despite the support of IBM, Sun, and other leading industry firms, the market for thin clients remained small in 1998.